International Family Change

International Family Change

Ideational Perspectives

Edited by
Rukmalie Jayakody
Arland Thornton
William Axinn

Lawrence Erlbaum Associates
Taylor & Francis Group

New York   London

Lawrence Erlbaum Associates
Taylor & Francis Group
270 Madison Avenue
New York, NY 10016

Lawrence Erlbaum Associates
Taylor & Francis Group
2 Park Square
Milton Park, Abingdon
Oxon OX14 4RN

© 2008 by Taylor & Francis Group, LLC
Lawrence Erlbaum Associates is an imprint of Taylor & Francis Group, an Informa business

Printed in the United States of America on acid-free paper
10 9 8 7 6 5 4 3 2 1

International Standard Book Number-13: 978-0-8058-6070-2 (Softcover) 978-0-8058-6069-6 (Hardcover)

Library of Congress Cataloging-in-Publication Data

International family change : ideational perspectives / [edited by] Rukmalie Jayakody, Arland Thornton, and William Axinn.
    p. cm.
    Includes bibliographical references and index.
    ISBN 978-0-8058-6069-6 (alk. paper)
    1. Family--Research. 2. Social change--Research. I. Jayakody, Rukmalie. II. Thornton, Arland. III. Axinn, William G.

HQ728.I563 2008
306.85--dc22   2007010611

Visit the Taylor & Francis Web site at
http://www.taylorandfrancis.com

Contents

Preface

This book is designed to summarize, integrate, and stimulate research concerning ideational perspectives on international family change. It brings together the work of a respected group of international scholars in the broad area of family change, consolidating current knowledge and theories, evaluating available theoretical approaches and data, and identifying productive new research avenues. The book considers historical trends in family attitudes, beliefs, and relationships, with an emphasis on theoretical models for explaining this family change. Particularly central to this book are the ideational and motivational underpinnings of family life and the ways that attitudinal and value changes have influenced family behavior and relationships. The book also considers the adequacy of the theoretical and empirical bases for our understanding of family change and the forces producing it—in particular, exploring how theoretical orientations, research methods, and empirical data can be improved.

This book has several compelling rationales. First, many dimensions of family life have changed tremendously over the past century, and especially in the past several decades. Age at marriage has risen dramatically in many of the world's populations, arranged marriage has declined, children's involvement in mate selection has increased, parental authority has declined, premarital sex has increased, extended families have declined, relationships between women and men have changed, contraceptive usage has become widespread, and fertility has declined. And, although they have been less thoroughly documented empirically than behavioral changes, attitudes and values concerning family life have changed concomitantly. In many ways these transformations have been ubiquitous enough to think in terms of global trends and their causes, whereas it remains important to recognize both regional distinctions and also significant continuities in family life.

Second, most explanations of family change have focused primarily on structural influences, such as shifts from an agricultural to an industrial to a service economy, the movement of populations from rural to urban areas, the expansion of education, the increase in income, changes in technology, increases in knowledge, and declines in disease and mortality. Although in many ways these explanations of family change have been hegemonic in the social sciences for decades—and, in fact, they continue to dominate—a growing number of researchers recognize that structural forces alone are insufficient for explaining the family changes experienced around the globe. The academic community is turning increasingly to alternative explanations, including a focus on international politics, networks and interpersonal relationships, and motivational and ideational factors.

Of particular relevance to this book are broad ideational and normative forces, such as the increasing emphasis on freedom, equality, and individual prerogative, that continue to spread around the world. These forces are related to new ideas about the place and role of individuals relative to the family and larger community, and to changing norms concerning marriage, the relationships between women and men, the connections across generations, and the place of children in families. Also, because historically the family has been the primary social means by which individuals influence and are influenced by virtually every other dimension of life, changing beliefs concerning institutional factors such as religion, education, and the economy have direct relevance for understanding family changes. For these reasons, integrating ideas and norms concerning the family with those related to the larger system plays an important part in the book.

The scope of the book is international—encompassing discussions on family change in each of the world's major regions, including the Middle East, Europe, Africa, North America, South America, and several parts of Asia. This international breadth provides the authors of the book the opportunity to challenge several widely held misconceptions about the nature of family change. Among these are that current family life in the Western world is the inevitable product of social and economic trends in the West, that family change outside the West is destined to follow the same trajectory of the West, and that governments and ideational forces have little influence on the nature of family change. Instead, the book persuasively demonstrates that family trends have varied dramatically across societies, influenced by differential shifts in beliefs and norms, and by evolving government ideologies and policies.

Indeed, the book makes the case that, rather than following a Western model, family changes in some parts of the world have resulted from an explicit rejection of the Western family model. For example, the chapter focusing on Iran discusses how the abnegation of Western ideas played an important role in the Islamic Revolution and the family changes that followed. Similarly, the chapter on Vietnam discusses the tension between wanting to adopt Western economic models while eschewing Western family ideas or behavior. Chapters focusing on Nepal and Africa illustrate how the introduction of new ideas—via mass media in Nepal and Christianity in Africa—have reshaped family beliefs and ideals. Other chapters on Japan and Argentina demonstrate how the unique cultural and historical circumstances in each country produce important variations in family change.

With its broad treatment of many aspects of international family change, the book has relevance for a large readership, including sociologists, demographers, anthropologists, economists, historians, human development and family studies scholars, and social psychologists. Given that it substantially expands knowledge in the area of family change and its variation across societies, the book has importance both as a unique contribution to the scientific literature and as a resource for teachers and students. Interest in understanding global conditions and families outside the United States continues to grow, and faculty in various disciplines that focus on the family are increasingly looking to add an international perspective to their courses. This book fills a specific gap through its coverage of both theory and methods and in its international scope. Classes on the American family, comparative family studies, social change, population problems, family history, and family development in departments of sociology, history, family studies, developmental economics and sociology, and psychology will find this book useful.

About the Editors

The editors of the book are Rukmalie Jayakody, Arland Thornton, and William G. Axinn.

Axinn is a professor of sociology at the University of Michigan, where he is also a research professor at the University's Population Studies Center and Survey Research Center. He is currently serving as associate director of the Population Studies Center. He studies the interrelationships among social change and family structure and processes in the United States and Nepal, the interrelationships between population and the environment, and new techniques for the collection of social science data. He has directed the Population and Ecology Research Laboratory in Nepal for 13 years.

Jayakody is a sociologist with an interest in family change and public policy in the United States and Vietnam. She has collaborated with colleagues at the Institute of Sociology in Vietnam on the first large-scale data collection designed to study family change in that country. She is currently working with the Vietnam Museum of Ethnology to study the impact of television on family change. Jayakody is at Pennsylvania State University, where she is a member of the Department of Human Development and Family Studies and the Population Research Institute.

Thornton is a professor of sociology at the University of Michigan, where he is also affiliated with the University's Survey Research Center and Population Studies Center—currently serving as director of the Population Studies Center. He has studied various aspects of family life for more than a quarter century, with particular interest in family change. In addition to his work in the United States, he has studied family change in Argentina, Nepal, and Taiwan. His 1994 book *Social Change and the Family in Taiwan*, coauthored with Hui-Sheng Lin, won two major book awards from the American Sociological Association. More recently (2005), he has published a book emphasizing ideational influences on family change around the world—*Reading History Sideways: The Fallacy and Enduring Impact of the Developmental Paradigm on Family Life*.

Acknowledgments

We are indebted to many individuals and groups for their many valuable contributions to this book. Of particular importance are the ideas and encouragement that we received from Carolyn Makinson, formerly of the Mellon Foundation, and Chris Bachrach, of the National Institutes of Health, to hold a workshop and publish a book concerning ideational factors in international family change. Their input provided the spark that led to this volume, without which it is unlikely that we would have proceeded far along the path to publication.

We also acknowledge the critical importance of the grant from the Mellon Foundation that provided resources for our workshop concerning ideational factors in international family change. The grant from the Mellon Foundation also provided support for the production of the present volume. Additional financial support for the conference and the production of this volume was provided by the following units within the University of Michigan: the Population Studies Center; the Survey Research Center; the Department of Sociology; the Advanced Study Center of the International Institute; and the Office of the Vice President for Research. We appreciate the interest and financial support of the Mellon Foundation and the various units within the University of Michigan.

The workshop that led to this volume was held at the University of Michigan in June 2004. In addition to the editors of the book and the authors of the chapters included in this volume, the workshop included numerous other colleagues who participated in discussions and provided formal feedback as discussants. These included Toni Antonucci, Ria Baker, Sarah Brauner, Cameron Campbell, Joe Chamie, Albert Hermalin, Martha Hill, Rosalind King, James Lee, Mansoor Moaddel, Nadine Naber, Brienna Perelli, Pete Richardson, Pamela Smock, Rachel Snow, Etienne van de Walle, Nathalie Williams, Kathryn Yount, Li-Shou Yang, and Yu Xie. Their input was important for the success of both the workshop and this volume.

The activities of the workshop and the production of this volume have been greatly facilitated by the contributions of the members of the Family and Demography Program, sponsored jointly within the Population Studies Center and the Survey Research Center at the Institute for Social Research of the University of Michigan. Judy Baughn has provided overall administrative support for the project, while Jana Bruce, Julie de Jong, Paul Schulz, Linda Young-DeMarco, and Shirley Roe also gave assistance. Julie de Jong also provided valuable assistance in the preparation and management of the book.

We are also indebted to the administrative, information, and computing cores of the University of Michigan's Population Studies Center—and to the infrastructure grant from the National Institute of Child Health and Human Development supporting these cores (2 R24 HD041028). Michael McIntyre provided computer and web support for the administration of the workshop and for the distribution of papers and information. N. E. Barr provided editorial assistance in the preparation of the book.

The computing, administrative, and information cores of the Population Research Institute at the Pennsylvania State University and the infrastructure grant from the National Institute of Child Health and Human Development (R24 HD041025) that provides support for core services provided further assistance. Sheila Bickle in the Department of Human Development and Family Studies at Penn State worked tirelessly on the reference lists for the book chapters, and we are grateful for her dedication.

The preparation of this book has benefited from the comments, suggestions, and contributions of several people associated with Lawrence Erlbaum Associates, including Rebecca Larsen, whose attention to details at the later stages was invaluable. We are most grateful to Lisa Pearce from the University of North Carolina and Mick Cunningham from Western Washington University for their helpful suggestions and review of this book.

Finally, and most importantly, we give special thanks to our spouses and children: Rukmalie to her husband Greg; Arland to his wife Shirley and children Richard, Blake, Rebecca, and Amy; and Bill to his wife Jennifer and children Elena and Noah. The loving support of each of these family members has been a substantial contribution to our scholarly careers and the production of this book.

Perspectives on International Family Change

Rukmalie Jayakody
Population Research Institute
Department of Human Development and Family Studies
Pennsylvania State University

Arland Thornton
The Population Studies Center
Department of Sociology
University of Michigan

William G. Axinn
The Population Studies Center
Department of Sociology
University of Michigan

This book is about family change around the world. It considers historical trends in family behavior, attitudes, beliefs, and relationships, with an emphasis on theoretical models for explaining this family change. Particularly central to this book are the ideational and motivational underpinnings of family life and the ways that attitudinal and value changes have influenced family behavior and relationships. The book takes a global perspective on family change—and ideational influences on that family change—including case studies from virtually every region of the world, including Africa, the Middle East, Europe, both North and South America, and East, South, and Southeast Asia.

Many dimensions of family life have changed tremendously over the past century, and especially in the past several decades. These changes have been extensive not only in their geographic scope, covering most of the populations of the world, but also in the breadth of family dimensions affected. For example, in many parts of the world, age at marriage has risen dramatically, children's involvement in mate selection has increased, parental authority has declined, premarital sex has increased, extended families have declined, relationships between men and women have changed, contraceptive use has become widespread, and fertility has declined. Although less thoroughly documented than behavioral changes, attitudes and beliefs affecting family life have also shifted over this period.

These transformations in family life have been so ubiquitous that they are often thought of in terms of global trends and causes. Globalization and internationalization are increasingly used to describe worldwide changes beyond economics and trade. Those who subscribe to the globalization of families, and in particular the emergence of a global youth culture (Arnett, 2002; Larson, 2002), argue that social changes driven primarily by media and new technologies are producing substantial similarities in family patterns and attitudes around the world. Discussions on the globalization of families, however, often mask substantial regional distinctions and significant continuities in family life, and ignore the active efforts made to resist change and globalizing influences.

Theories of family change have focused primarily on structural influences, such as the shifts from an agricultural to an industrial to a service economy, the movement of populations from rural to urban areas, the expansion of education, the increase in income, changes in technology, increases in knowledge, and declines in disease and mortality. The fundamental argument of these theories is that changes in social and economic circumstances and constraints—for example, industrialization and the expansion of education—have ramifications throughout a society. These large social and economic changes modify the ways in which individuals relate to family members, with implications for husband–wife relationships, the influence of parents over children, relationships among siblings, and the role of children in the care of the elderly.

Although structural explanations still dominate in theories of family change, there is growing recognition that structural forces alone are insufficient for explaining family changes across the globe. Scholars are increasingly recognizing that the empirical connections between many of these structural changes and trends in family life are less clear than previously assumed. For example, many family patterns and relationships have persisted in the face of substantial structural changes, while other family behaviors have undergone rather substantial changes without structural changes sufficient to explain them.

The growing evidence of the inadequacy of structural explanations for family change is leading many researchers to look at alternative explanations. Important among these explanations are broad ideational and normative forces—such as the growing emphasis on personal freedom, social equality, and individual prerogative—which continue to spread around the world. These forces are related to new ideas about the place and role of individuals relative to family and larger community, and to changing norms concerning marriage, the relationships between men and women, the connections across generations, and the place of children in families. Especially relevant are ideas about marriage and the ways it connects and affects women and men and influences relationships across the generations, and ideas about the place of children in families, including their number and spacing, the way they are raised, and their responsibilities to siblings and parents as members of the family grow older. Also, because historically the family has been the primary social means by which individuals influence and are influenced by virtually every other dimension of life, changing beliefs concerning institutional factors such as religion, education, and the economy have direct relevance for understanding family changes.

The scientific community has accumulated extensive evidence that beliefs and values are important in influencing family behavior. Religious beliefs and commitments, ideas about freedom and equality, and values and beliefs concerning family life have been shown to correlate with family change at the macro level, although establishing causal connections can be difficult (Cherlin, 1992; Lesthaeghe, 1983; Lesthaeghe & Neels, 2002; Thornton, 1985; Thornton & Young-DeMarco, 2001). Sophisticated panel studies have shown that individual values and beliefs have substantial effect on family behavior at the micro level (Axinn & Thornton, 1993; Barber, 2001; Lesthaeghe, 2002; Thornton, Axinn, & Xie, in press). These studies underscore the need for research concerning the role of ideation in multiple settings around the world.

Of course, our distinction between structural and ideational forces is both simplistic and arbitrary, as structure and ideology are themselves interrelated in complex and multifaceted ways. The social and economic systems of any human population have an empirical reality that must be taken into account in any ideational models or frameworks that specify approaches for experiencing and living with that reality. Similarly, ideational models provide a framework for constructing and modifying social and economic systems. Also, social and economic systems—and changes in them—can be important in facilitating or limiting the spread of beliefs, values, and motivations across geographical and social boundaries. Furthermore, it is often the intersection of ideational and structural forces that combines to influence family change. Thus, although this book emphasizes the importance of ideational forces in affecting family change around the world, we believe that any comprehensive explanation of family change must consider both ideational and structural forces and the ways they interrelate to influence family change.

Therefore we begin with a discussion of some of the major structural explanations of family change before turning to ideational perspectives and their role in family change. As we discuss structural and ideational forces in various contexts, we emphasize the influence of mediational factors that transcend international boundaries. In fact, we believe that it is impossible to understand changes in any country or population without taking into account the forces of globalization that may transcend regional or local influences.

STRUCTURAL EXPLANATIONS OF FAMILY CHANGE

Social scientists have offered a wide range of explanations for family changes in both Western and non-Western parts of the world. For the most part, these explanations have emphasized changes in the social, economic, and political structures of society, chiefly through the growth of industrialization, urbanization, education, income and consumption, communications, transportation, and various forms of new technology.

Changing Modes of Organization

The first and perhaps foremost explanation of family change centered on the changing modes of economic production (Lehmann, 1960/1979; Meek, 1976; Thornton, 2005). This perspective emphasizes the importance of the shift in modes of subsistence from hunting or herding, to agriculture, to manufacturing for the transformation of other elements in society. Particularly important in this argument for recent periods is the process of industrialization, which transferred many aspects of economic production from family enterprises to bureaucratic organizations and relied mostly on wage labor. Industrialization shifted economic production and consumption from being organized primarily within the family, and largely directed by the father, to occurring primarily outside the family unit and outside of the father's control. When fathers no longer controlled the means of production and family members no longer relied on family enterprises for their livelihoods, fathers experienced diminished control over the activities and well-being of wives and children.

Building on the explanation for family change that relies on the changing modes of economic production is a framework that looks at the changing modes of organizing and participating in social activities. The "modes of social organization" framework includes a wider range of human activities and interactions than economic models. It focuses on (a) the degree to which individuals are involved in family-organized activities versus activities managed outside the family, such as in schools, factories, nonfamilial places of employment, and government bureaucracies; and (b) the level of information and skills obtained through kin versus non-kin sources, such as the mass media, the state, and schools (Thornton & Lin, 1994). A shift from societies organized primarily around families to societies in which fundamental activities occur outside the family has been experienced throughout much of the world in the past two centuries, and has been increasingly important outside the West during the past few decades.

Educational Expansion

The expansion of formal education in schools is an important element in the transformation of the social organization of society. In fact, in many ways education has come to be seen as the primary engine transforming society and improving economic and social well-being (Macaulay, 1974). The expansion of education opportunities is one of the most remarkable phenomena of the past century, as very large percentages of the world's children now attend elementary school, and substantial fractions go on to high school, and in some cases, even college. Although education levels still vary greatly by country and sex, educational attainment has expanded in all regions of the world and among both males and females. These increases, along with subsequent delayed entrance into employment, were believed to modify gender relations, decrease the authority of elders, and postpone marriage, among other things.

Growth in the number and types of schools and in school attendance can profoundly change relationships with family and community members (Cleland, 2001; Jejeebhoy, 1995; Thornton, Fricke, Yang, & Chang, 1994). With increased school attendance, children spend much of the day at school being socialized and supervised by teachers rather than by parents, which creates alternative authority structures. Also, the resulting generation gap in education level may reduce the prestige of the older, less educated generation in children's eyes. Skills increase with education level, opening up more job opportunities. School attendance is also a time-consuming activity that can lead to the postponement of marriage, childbearing, and entry into work.

Urbanization and Migration

Industrialization is frequently accompanied by urbanization, involving both the expansion of old cities and the establishment of new ones, which is often associated with the migration of residents from rural agricultural areas to urban industrial ones. Although entire families sometimes move, it is often younger people who migrate to the cities and take advantage of the new urban employment opportunities. This migration is frequently associated with new living arrangements (Diamond, 1979; Hareven, 1982; Kung,1983; Modell & Hareven, 1973; Tilly & Scott, 1978; Thornton & Lin, 1994). In addition, the density of the population in urban areas often changes interactions and communication patterns, with relationships being much more specialized and unfamiliar (Hawley, 1971; Wirth, 1938).

Income and Consumption Growth

A key feature of social change in most but not all societies of the world has been a growth of income among at least some groups of people, which permits the expansion of consumption. A growth in consumption frequently expands the types of goods available and can shift the distribution of items consumed. Increased income can also allow the purchase of independent living and the possibility of terminating family relationships (Kobrin, 1976; Ruggles, 1994, 2001; Smith,1981). Particularly important here are increases in consumption aspirations that may outpace the growth of income itself (Easterlin, 1980), leading to a restriction of time and money spent on family activities in order to satisfy these new consumption aspirations. Similarly, it has been argued that as income and consumption growth fills certain basic human needs, other needs emerge as more important (Inglehart, 1997).

Faster Communication and Transportation Networks

In most societies of the past, the access of individuals to information about the world was largely determined by people in the local environment, particularly family members and neighbors. This has changed dramatically in recent decades as individuals around the world have become enmeshed in impressive national and international systems of transportation and communication (Thornton, 2005). Goods and services—as well as people—now move relatively easily within and across international boundaries. In addition, news and media programs produced in one country are disseminated widely around the world, frequently to villages and towns that until recently had little access to the international media. As we discuss later, these new transportation and communication facilities have greatly changed people's access to new products and ideas, including those about family life.

Other New Technologies

Additional new technologies have also changed the nature of the world, with implications for family change. Among these are the new medical and public health measures that have substantially reduced mortality and increased life expectancy. These changes have nearly eliminated childhood mortality in many parts of the world—an important factor in the decline of fertility. These changes have also produced longer adulthoods, which, along with declining fertility, have lengthened the number of years adults live without children in their households. These changes in mortality and fertility have substantially modified the constraints and opportunities for different kinds of family and living arrangements (Ruggles, 1987, 1994; Watkins, Menken, & Bongaarts 1987). However, more recently, new diseases, especially the HIV/AIDS epidemic, have increased illness and mortality in some settings, again with dramatic implications for family structures and relationships (Clark, 2005; Knodel, 2001, 2004; Wachter, Knodel, & VanLandingham, 2002).

Also of high relevance here is the contraceptive revolution and the international family planning movement that has assisted in the nearly worldwide dissemination of contraceptive use. The introduction of the oral pill, Depo-Provera, implants, and the IUD (intrauterine device) has helped make possible the dramatic declines in childbearing that have occurred in many countries around the world (Westoff & Ryder, 1977). Some scholars have also suggested that these birth control methods and the confidence they provide in the separation of sex and childbearing have encouraged nonmarital sex, delayed marriage, increased nonmarital cohabitation, and brought increases in female employment (Bailey, 2004; Goldin & Katz, 2000).

IDEATIONAL CONSTRUCTS

As Clifford Geertz and others have argued, ideational frameworks or schema provide models for experiencing reality and for living with that reality (D'Andrade, 1984; Fricke, 1997a, 1997b; Geertz, 1973; Thornton et al., 2001). As models *of* reality, ideational frameworks provide perspectives for viewing and understanding the world. They provide classification systems for describing the world, models for interpreting both variation and change in human behavior and relationships, and definitions of the significance of various elements of social, economic, and familial life for the human condition. In this way they define the relevant actors in a system and the significance of specific behaviors and institutions for defining and shaping social structures and relationships. As models *for* reality, ideational systems provide frameworks for dealing with and reacting to the world, defining for actors a framework for identifying what is important and good in life and what appropriate methods are available for achieving desired goals. In this way, these models specify a framework detailing what is acceptable and moral, and they help to establish motivations for actors within a common context—prescribing both appropriate end goals and mechanisms for reaching those ends. These ideational systems often go beyond identifying appropriate goals and methods to specify inappropriate goals, behavior, and means. In this way they form a moral system of rules and judgments for evaluating ends and means.

As Thornton and colleagues (2001) discuss, there are many different elements in ideational systems for dealing with the world. They include beliefs about the nature of the world and how it works. These beliefs can vary both in their centrality to individuals and in their stability across time. Ideational systems also include values, prescribing what means and ends are good or desirable. Values thus provide a hierarchy for deciding among various ends and means and become the basis of preferences, or the ranking of various possible goals, activities, and behaviors. As such, values and preferences are essential elements underlying motivations for behavior and relationships. They can even be important in defining the things that are or are not specified as needs. Values and beliefs are also associated with attitudes, which are dispositions to respond or act toward certain people or things in a specified way.

In addition, beliefs, values, and attitudes are frequently shared within communities, countries, and increasingly, with globalization, around the world. As these values, beliefs, and attitudes are shared across individuals, they become social norms or societal standards. These social norms also frequently prescribe or proscribe certain goals and means, assuming a moral character as they define right and wrong, acceptable and unacceptable. In addition, sanctions—both rewards and punishments—are often connected to following or violating social norms. Many elements of family beliefs, values, and norms are frequently incorporated into religious belief and normative systems, where they become part of a larger cosmological system of beliefs, sanctions, and rewards.

Although it is important to recognize that ideational frameworks— especially the elements of norms—have communal components that are shared across individuals, ideational systems do not necessarily produce uniformity of behavior and thought, but often permit substantial variability in what is acceptable (Hannerz, 1992; Marini, 1984), in the extent to which behaviors are viewed as voluntary or prescribed (Taylor, 1985), in the firmness with which values and beliefs are held, and, generally, in the latitude permitted for freedom of behavioral choice. Finally, cultural values and norms can be so diverse and differentially held in a society that they become the focus of extensive contestations that escalate into full-blown cultural confrontations (Hunter, 1991).

Particularly important for our purposes is the element of changeability in ideational systems. Values, beliefs, norms, attitudes, preferences, and motivations are not static, either in individuals or in societies. Instead, these ideational factors can be changed through a range of mechanisms. In fact, we argue throughout this book that ideational frameworks around the world have changed dramatically and that these changes have had dramatic implications for family life itself.

Ideational Explanations of Family Change

Although structural explanations have predominated as explanations of family change, recent critiques have emphasized the failure of such structural models to explain trends in a range of family behaviors and have called for the inclusion of ideational factors (Caldwell, 1982; Chesnais, 1992; Cleland & Wilson, 1987; Mason, 1997; Thornton, 2001, 2005). Lesthaeghe and his colleagues have argued that changes in religiosity and secularism are essential components for explanations of changing family behavior in Western Europe (Lesthaeghe, 1983; Lesthaeghe & Neels, 2002; Lesthaeghe & Wilson, 1986). In this volume (chap. 4), Lesthaeghe and Surkyn extend this line of thinking and argue that the substantial changes in marriage, cohabitation, sexual freedom, divorce, and nonmarital childbearing that they label the second demographic transition has extended beyond Western Europe to Eastern Europe. They also hypothesize that these dramatic changes are poised to spread to other parts of the world as well.

Caldwell (1982), Freedman (1979, 1987), and van de Kaa (1996) have posited that Western family ideas and values, which have been disseminated around the world, have been influential in changing family values and behavior in many places outside the West. In chapter 3 of this volume, Locoh and Mouvagha-Sow argue that Western ideas and values have penetrated into Africa sufficiently to establish a Western model of family life that seriously undermines the indigenous family systems in Africa (also see Locoh, 1988, and Watkins, 2000). Similar arguments have been made for the creation and influence of alternative Western family models in the Middle East, India, and Nepal (Abu-Lughod, 1998a, 1998b; Ahearn, 2001; Caldwell, Hanumantha, & Caldwell, 1988; Cuno, 2003; Moaddel, 1992; Pigg, 1992; Thornton, 2005).

Thornton (2001, 2005) argues that the Western model of family life has been important outside the West at least partially because it is intricately related with the ideas of development that have permeated Western thought for thousands of years and, in recent centuries, have been disseminated in many non-Western places. The developmental model suggests that Western social, economic, and family life is at the pinnacle of progress and development; that these aspects of Western life serve as ideals to societies outside the West; that Western family life is connected as both cause and effect to economic success and well-being; and that freedom and equality are fundamental human rights. Thornton argues that the worldwide dissemination of these ideas has been crucial in changing family systems around the world. In chapter 2 of this volume, Thornton, Binstock, and Ghimire discuss the power of this developmental model and demonstrate that it is widely understood and used among people in everyday life in Argentina and Nepal.

Many mechanisms have disseminated the developmental model and the accompanying beliefs that Western family forms are superior and help bring about development, and that freedom and equality are fundamental human rights. For centuries Western scholars have taught and disseminated these ideas, with their treatises being widely distributed in Europe and elsewhere. The chapter by Axinn, Ghimire, and Barber focusing on Nepal illustrates the importance of the introduction and expansion of mass education and mass media in the spread of new ideas about development and Western family forms. The flow of ideas, both within countries and across borders, has also been facilitated by industrialization and the urbanization of the population.

The ideas of development and Western family superiority have also been spread actively through social movements and organizations devoted to them. The chapter on Africa by Locoh and Mouvagha-Sow emphasizes the role of Christianity in the spread of new ideas. The messages spread by Christian churches throughout Africa, the Americas, and parts of Asia included not only an idealization of Western family forms, but the rejection of certain indigenous familial customs and practices as backward (Thornton, 2001, 2005; Yount, 2004). European exploration, conquest, and colonization affected much of the world from the 1500s through the 1900s and provided impetus for the spread of various ideas about development and Western superiority. The movement for political democracy that has influenced the world for at least a quarter century was an important force for the spread of the ideals of freedom and equality. Marxism and socialism have also been important factors in the spread of a specific theory of development and the goal of creating a new world characterized by new family and societal forms (Nisbet, 1980). Also important have been the United Nations and other international government and nongovernmental organizations that have helped to create and spread a world culture explicitly endorsing the propositions of individual and social development, freedom, equality, and Western family forms (Meyer, Boli, Thomas, & Ramirez, 1997; United Nations Development Program, 2001, 2002; United Nations, 1948, 1962, 1979).

Additional social movements have adopted and actively disseminated specific dimensions of development, freedom, and equality. Among the most noteworthy ones is the movement for ethnic and racial equality that had its roots in the Enlightenment and actively promulgated the principles of freedom and equality. Similarly, women's movements in many countries advocated for women's rights and the principles of freedom and equality for women and men in public and private domains. And, finally, the international family planning movement has been especially powerful in the past half century in mobilizing groups and agencies to spread various aspects of the Western family, especially family planning and low fertility.

Of course, Western ideals of development, family forms, and individual freedom and equality have not met with universal and easy acceptance around the world. Although they have sometimes been adopted readily in some form, more frequently they have been ignored or resisted vigorously. Even when adopted, the developmental model has been usually modified or hybridized to fit the circumstances and conditions of the society. Acceptance and adoption of these Western ideals have been contingent on the people's religious and cultural heritage, their social and economic organization, their historical experiences, the specifics of their interactions with the West, and their economic and military power to resist. These considerations make the spread of Western family ideals both contingent and path dependent.

Indeed, although this book makes the case that the Western family form is frequently modeled, its explicit rejection is also the impetus for family change in some parts of the world. For example, Abbasi-Shavazi and McDonald discuss in chapter 7 how the abnegation of Western ideas in Iran played an important role in the Islamic Revolution and the family changes that followed. Similarly, Jayakody and Huy (chap. 8) discuss the tension felt in Vietnam between wanting to adopt Western economic models while eschewing certain aspects of Western family ideas or behavior. Other chapters on Japan (Atoh) and on Argentina (Binstock) demonstrate how the unique cultural and historical circumstances in each country have produced important variations in family change.

ORGANIZATION OF THE BOOK

We devote the remaining chapters of this book to investigating family change in a range of countries around the world, with emphasis on the importance of ideational forces in those changes. In chapter 2, Arland Thornton, Georgina Binstock, and Dirgha Ghimire focus on a set of conceptual explanations for family change referred to as *developmental idealism*, which has been substantially influential in changing family behavior, beliefs, and values throughout the world. The authors evaluate their propositions empirically in Argentina and Nepal, where the data provide evidence that most people in these two countries have considerable knowledge about the world, an understanding of the development model, and a belief in the causal connection between economic development and family structures and relationships. The authors posit that these ideas are also widespread and influential of family life in other settings.

In chapter 3, Thérèse Locoh and Myriam Mouvagha-Sow show that historically, African family ideals have centered on the solidarity of the extended family, the power and respect commanded by elders, and the importance of having children. However, rapid social changes following independence after World War II and recurring economic crises are exerting profound influences on family lifestyles, especially union formation, fertility, and living arrangements. This chapter examines changes experienced by the African family and explores its uncertain future by highlighting the influence of transitions to market economies, migration, the media, and the introduction of new models from outside Africa (e.g., education, religions, and democracy).

In chapter 4, Ron Lesthaeghe and Johan Surkyn focus on what they call the second demographic transition (SDT) in Western societies, arguing that the decline in mortality and fertility of the 19th and 20th centuries was followed by many additional family changes at the end of the 20th century, including alterations in nonfamily living arrangements and a disconnection between marriage and procreation. The authors identify and evaluate characteristic signs of the SDT, including rising divorce rates, falling fertility, increasing age at marriage, increasing numbers of single individuals, and rising rates of cohabitation. They also discuss the extent of the SDT in Europe, the likelihood that it will spread to other parts of Europe and to other continents and societies, and the role of cultural factors in the spread of the SDT.

In chapter 5, William Axinn, Amie Emens, and Colter Mitchell summarize some of the major family changes experienced in the United States, with an emphasis on the 20th century, and discuss structural and ideational models for understanding these changes. They highlight the significance of ideational perspectives for understanding recent transformations in the American family.

In chapter 6, Georgina Binstock describes Argentina's dramatic family transformations over the past few decades, including increases in age at marriage, marital dissolution, nonmarital childbearing, and cohabitation. Binstock synthesizes what is known about these changes and places them within the context of broader social trends. She includes a discussion on the effects of colonization, race, and religion.

In chapter 7, Mohammad Jalal Abbasi-Shavazi and Peter McDonald focus on changes in the Iranian family during the 20th century, and discuss both social structural and ideational explanations for these changes. The two crucial periods for changes in family attitudes and behaviors were the periods before and after the 1979 Islamic Revolution, and the resulting complex mosaic of individual and family change and persistence is described. Particular attention is given to the role of religion, revolution, and the state in family dynamics and change, with a strong role noted for each.

Chapter 8, by Rukmalie Jayakody and Vu Tuan Huy, explores the dramatic changes characterizing Vietnam during the past century, including prolonged periods of war, socialist collectivization, political reunification, a shift from a centrally planned to a market-based economy, and an extensive opening to the outside world. Additionally, the Vietnamese government has adopted major policy initiatives designed to affect basic aspects of family life—including mate selection and marriage, gender relations, and family size. This chapter explores how the combination of wartime and revolutionary experiences, socialist ideology, market reforms, and the exposure to Western ideas and media has affected the Vietnamese family. In chapter 9, Makoto Atoh examines family changes in postwar Japan and the role of ideational factors in explaining these changes. Particular attention is given to the decreases in household size, the nuclearization of families, changes in demographic behavior (especially below-replacement fertility), increases in premarital sexual activity, the post-ponement of marriage and childbearing, and rising divorce rates.

William Axinn, Dirgha Ghimire, and Jennifer Barber document in chapter 10 how Nepal, a subsistence agricultural society until the early 1970s, experienced dramatic changes in some rural areas between 1975 and 1995 with the spread of wage labor employment, schools, markets, transportation, government services, and the mass media. This chapter examines the impact of these changes on the timing and arrangement of marriage, family size and fertility preferences, birth timing, and con-traceptive use. This chapter provides strong empirical evidence that ideational mechanisms of social change are linked to long-term changes in marital and childbearing behavior.

In the final chapter, William Axinn, Rukmalie Jayakody, and Arland Thornton summarize knowledge of ideational influences on family change and highlight some of the major findings from the previous chapters. They also present an agenda for future studies on family change, addressing both theoretical and data issues.

CONCLUSION

Families worldwide have experienced similar structural changes. In par-ticular, dramatic reductions in mortality, educational expansion, increasing urbanization and migration, and faster transportation and communication networks are nearly universal. However, these similar changes have not resulted in a single global family. The chapters that follow reveal significant continuity in family life in some parts of the world, as well as substantial regional variations. Each of the chapters examines family change in a particular country or region of the world. Ideational factors are cited as crucial forces for family change in virtu-ally every country or region that we examine here. At the same time, the changes that have occurred and the forces influencing them have varied dramatically across societies and have been influenced by dif-ferential shifts in beliefs and norms and by evolving government ideologies and policies.

REFERENCES

Abu-Lughod, L. (1988b). The marriage of feminism and Islamism in Egypt: Selective repudiation as a dynamic of postcolonial cultural policies. In L. Abu-Lughod (Ed.), *Remaking women: Feminism and modernity in the Middle East* (pp. 243–269). Princeton, NJ: Princeton University Press.

Abu-Lughod, L. (1998a). Feminist longings and postcolonial conditions. In L. Abu-Lughod. (Ed.), *Remaking women: Feminism and modernity in the Middle East* (pp. 3–32). Princeton, NJ: Princeton University Press.

Ahearn, L. M. (2004). Invitations to love: Literacy, love letters, and social change in Nepal. Ann Arbor: University of Michigan Press.

Arnett, J. J. (2002). The psychology of globalization. *American Psychologist, 57*(10), 774–783.

Axinn, W. G., & Yabiku, S. T. (2001). Social change, the social organization of families, and fertility limitation. *American Journal of Sociology, 106*(5), 1219–1261.

Bailey, M. J. (2004). *More power to the pill: The impact of contraceptive freedom on women's lifecycle labor-force participation.* Working paper (No. 04-WG01). Vanderbilt University.

Barber, J. S. (2001). Ideational influences on the transition to parenthood: Attitudes towards childbearing and competing alternatives. *Social Psychology Quarterly, 64*(2), 101–127.

Caldwell, J. (1982). *Theory of fertility decline.* London: Academic Press.

Caldwell, J. C., Hanumantha, R., & Caldwell, P. (1988). *The causes of demographic change: Experimental research in South India.* Madison: University of Wisconsin Press.

Cherlin, A. (1992). *Marriage, divorce, remarriage.* Cambridge, MA: Harvard University Press.

Chesnais, J.-C. (1992). *The demographic transition: Stages, patterns, and economic implications.* Oxford, UK: Oxford University Press.

Clark, S. J. (2005). *Demographic impacts of the HIV epidemic and consequences of population-wide treatment of HIV for the elderly: Results from microsimulation.* Washington, DC: National Academy of Sciences.

Cleland, J. (2001a). The effects of improved survival on fertility transition: An iconoclastic view. *Population Studies, 41*(1), 5–30.

Cleland, J. (2001b). The effects of improved survival on fertility: A reassessment. In J. B. Casterline & R. Bulatao (Eds.), *Global fertility transition* (pp. 60–92). Supplement to Vol. 27, *Population and Development Review.*

Cuno, K. M. (2003). Ambiguous modernization: The transition to monogamy in the Khedibal House of Egypt. In B. Doumani (Ed.), *Family history in the Middle East* (pp. 247–70). Albany: State University of New York Press.

D'Andrade, R. G. (1984). Cultural meaning systems. In R. A. Shweder & R. A. LeVine (Eds.), *Culture theory: Essays on mind, self, and emotion* (pp. 88–119). Cambridge, NY: Cambridge University Press.

Diamond, N. (1979). Women and industry in Taiwan. *Modern China, 5*(3), 317–340.

Easterlin, R. (1980). *Birth and fortune: The impact of numbers of personal welfare*. Chicago: University of Chicago Press.

Freedman, R. (1979). Theories of fertility decline: A reappraisal. *Social Forces, 58*(1), 1–17.

Freedman, R. (1987). The contribution of social science research to population policy and family planning program effectiveness. *Studies in Family Planning, 18*(2), 57–82.

Fricke, T. (1977a). Culture theory and population process: Toward a thicker demography. In D. I. Kertzer & T. Fricke (Eds.), *Anthropological demography: Toward a new synthesis* (pp. 248–277). Chicago: University of Chicago.

Fricke, T. (1997b). Marraige change as moral change: Culture, virtue, and demographic transition. In G. W. Jones, R. M. Douglas, J. C. Caldwell, & R. M. D'Souza (Eds.), *The continuing demographic transition* (pp. 183–212). Oxford, UK: Oxford University Press.

Geertz, C. (1973). *The interpretation of cultures*. New York: Basic Books.

Goldin, C., & Katz, L. F. (2000). Career and marriage in the age of the pill. *American Economic Review, 90*(2), 461–465.

Hannerz, U. (1992). *Cultural complexity*. New York: Columbia University Press.

Hareven, T. K. (1982). *Family time and industrial time*. New York: Cambridge University Press.

Hawley, A. H. (Ed.). (1971). *Urban society*. New York: Ronald Press.

Hunter, J. D. (1991). *Culture wars: The struggle to define America*. New York: Basic Books.

Inglehart, R. (1997). *Moderization and postmodernization: Cultural, economic and political change in 43 societies*. Princeton, NJ: Princeton University Press.

Jejeebhoy, S. J. (1995). *Women's education, autonomy, and reproductive behavior: Experience from developing countries*. Oxford, UK: Clarendon Press.

Knodel, J. (2001). Older people and AIDS: Quantitative evidence of the impact in Thailand. *Social Science and Medicine, 52*(9), 1313–1327.

Knodel, J. (2004). The economic consequences for parents of losing an adult child to AIDS: Evidence from Thailand. *Social Science and Medicine, 59*(5), 987–1001.

Korbin, F. E. (1976). The fall of household size and rise of the primary individual in the United States. *Demography, 13*, 127–138.

Kung, L. (1983). *Factory women in Taiwan*. Ann Arbor, MI: UMI Research Press.

Larson, R. (2002). Globalization, social change, and new technologies: What they mean for the future of adolescence. *Journal of Research on Adolescence, 12*(1), 1–30.

Lehmann, W. C. (1979–1960). *John Millar of Glasgow: 1735–1801*. New York: Arno Press.

Lesthaeghe, R. (1983). A century of demographic and cultural change in Western Europe: An exploration of underlying dimensions. *Population and Development Review, 9*(3), 411–435.

Lesthaeghe, R. (Ed.). (2002). *Meaning and choice: Value orientations and life course decisions*. The Hague: Netherlands Interdisciplinary Demographic Institute.

Lesthaeghe, R., & Wilson, C. (1986). Modes of production, secularization and the pace of fertility decline in Western Europe, 1870–1930. In A. Cole & S. C. Watkins (Eds.), *The decline of fertility in Europe* (pp. 261–292). Princeton, NJ: Princeton University Press.

Locoh, T. (1988). Evolution of the family in Africa. In E. van der Walle, P. O. Ohadike, & M. D. Sala-Diakanda (Eds.), *The state of African demography* (pp. 47–65). Liege, Belgium: International Union for the Scientific Study of Population.

Macaulay, C. (1974). *Letters on education.* New York: Garland.

Marini, M. M. (1984). Age and sequencing norms in the transition to adulthood. *Social Forces, 63*(1), 229–234.

Mason, K. O. (1997). Explaining fertility transitions. *Demography, 34*(4), 443–454.

Meek, R. I. (1976). *Social science and the ignorable savage.* Cambridge, UK: Cambridge University Press.

Meyer, J. W., Boli, J., Thomas, G. M., & Ramirez, F. O. (1997). World society and the nation-state. *American Journal of Sociology, 103*(1), 144–181.

Moaddel, M. (1992). *Class, politics and ideology in the Iranian revolution.* New York: Columbia University Press.

Modell, J., & Hareven, T. K. (1973). Urbanization and the malleable household: An examiniation of boarding and lodging in American Families. *Journal of Marriage and the Family, 35*(3), 467–479.

Nisbet, R. A. (Ed.). (1980). *History of the idea of progress.* New York: Basic Books.

Pigg, S. L. (1992). Inventing social categories through place: Social representations and development in Nepal. *Comparative Studies in Society and History, 34*(3), 491–513.

Ruggles, S. (1987). *Prolonged connections: The rise of the exended family in nineteenth century England and America.* Madison: University of Wisconsin Press.

Ruggles, S. (1994). The transformation of American family structure. *American Historical Review, 99*(1), 103–128.

Ruggles, S. (2001). Living arrangements and well-being of older persons in the past. In A. Palloni (Ed.), *Population bulletin of the United Nations: Living arrangements of older persons: Critical issues and policy responses* (pp. 111–161). New York: United Nations.

Smith, R. M. (1981). Fertility, economy, and household formation in England over three centuries. *Population and Development Review, 7*(4), 595–622.

Taylor, C. (1985). *Philosophy and the human sciences.* Cambridge, NY: Cambridge University Press.

Thornton, A. (1985). Reciprocal influences of family and religion in a changing world. *Journal of Marriage and the Family, 47*(2), 381–394.

Thornton, A. (2001). The developmental paradigm, reading history sideways, and family change. *Demography, 38*(4), 449–465.

Thornton, A. (2005). *Reading history sideways: The fallacy and enduring impact of the developmental paradigm on family life.* Chicago: University of Chicago Press.

Thornton, A., Axinn, W. G., Fricke, T., & Alwin, D. F. (2001). Values and beliefs in the lives of children and families. In A. Thornton (Ed.), *The well-being of children and families* (pp. 215–143). Ann Arbor: University of Michigan Press.

Thornton, A., Axinn, W. G., & Xie, Y. (in press). *Marriage and cohabitation.* Chicago: University of Chicago Press.

Thornton, A., Fricke, T., Yang, L. S., & Chang, J. S. (1994). Theoretical mechanisms of family change. In A. Thornton & H.-S. Lin (Eds.), *Social change and the family in Taiwan* (pp. 88–115). Chicago: University of Chicago Press.

Thornton, A., & Lin, H.-S. (1994). *Social change and the family in Taiwan.* Chicago: University of Chicago Press.

Thornton, A., & Young-DeMarco, L. (2001). Four decades of trends in attitudes toward family issues in the United States: The 1960s through the 1990s. *Journal of Marriage and the Family, 63*(4), 1009–1037.

Tilly, L. A., & Scott, J. W. (1978). *Women, work, and family.* New York: Holt, Rinehart, and Winston.

United Nations. (1948). *Universal declaration of human rights*: General Assembly Resolution, 217 A (III).

United Nations. (1962). *Convention on consent to marriage, minimum age for marriage and registration of marriages*: General Assembly Resolution 1763 A (XVII).

United Nations. (1979). *Convention on the elimination of all forms of discrimination against women*: General Assembly Resolution 34,180.

United Nations Development Program. (2001). *Human development report 2001: Making technology work for human development.* New York: Oxford Press.

United Nations Development Program. (2002). *Human development report 2002: Deepening democracy in a fragmented world.* New York: Oxford Press.

van de Kaa, D. J. (1996). Anchored narratives: The story and findings of a half century of research into the determinants of fertility. *Population Studies, 50*(3), 389–432.

Wachter, K. W., Knodel, J. E., & VanLandingham, M. (2002). AIDS and the elderly of Thailand: Projecting familial impacts. *Demography, 39*(1), 25–41.

Watkins, S. C. (2000). Local and foreign models of reproduction in Nyanza Province, Kenya. *Population and Development Review, 26*(4), 725–759.

Watkins, S. C., Menken, J. A., & Bongaarts, J. (1987). Demographic foundations of family change. *American Sociological Review, 52*(3), 346–358.

Westoff, C. F., & Ryder, N. B. (1977). *The contraceptive revolution.* Princeton, NJ: Princeton University Press.

Wirth, L. (1938). Perspectives on Urbanism as a way of life. *American Journal of Sociology, 44*(1), 1–24.

Yount, K. M. (2004). Symbolic gender politics, religious group identity, and the decline in female genital cutting in Minya, Egypt. *Social Forces, 82*(3), 1063–1090.

2

International Dissemination of Ideas about Development and Family Change

Arland Thornton
The Population Studies Center
Department of Sociology
University of Michigan

Georgina Binstock
Centro de Estudios de Población
Buenos Aires, Argentina

Dirgha Ghimire
The Population Studies Center
University of Michigan

This chapter looks at family change, and in particular at family behavior and family attitudes, values, and beliefs. The perspective is large in that we consider family change around the world and over the last two centuries, with an emphasis on the last several decades. We focus on one particular ideational factor in family change—developmental idealism—that we consider especially influential in producing family change around the world. To buttress our ideas about the importance of developmental ideology on family change, we present initial findings from recent studies in Argentina and Nepal.

This chapter is motivated by the observation that family change—both behavioral and ideational—has been substantial and consequential in both Western and non-Western countries. Almost every aspect of family life has been modified in the West during the past two centuries, especially in the past several decades (see Thornton, 2005, for a summary). The role of marriage as a fundamental organizer of family life has declined substantially. This is evident in the dramatic weakening of the norms against and increased incidence of premarital sex, unmarried cohabitation, and childbearing and childrearing outside of marriage. In addition, the norms against divorce have been weakened, divorce laws have been liberalized, and the incidence of divorce has increased. Independent living has also increased dramatically among both the young and the elderly. The roles of women and men have also changed dramatically with the increased participation of women in school, the labor force, and politics. Similarly, attitudes toward gender roles have become much more egalitarian. Sexuality and childbearing have been transformed with the widespread availability and use of contraception, sterilization, and abortion. Fertility levels have declined dramatically, and the norms against voluntary childlessness among married couples have weakened substantially. Independent thinking among young people is also increasingly valued, whereas strict obedience now receives less endorsement. Relatedly, although morality and personal and family behavior were previously regulated and controlled legally, the new focus on individual rights has been accompanied by a decline in the public regulation of private lives and behavior (Schneider, 1985). In fact, in many aspects of life a norm of tolerance has emerged that dictates against interference in the lives of others (Caplow, Bahr, & Chadwick, 1983; Roof & McKinney, 1987).

Changes in non-Western countries have been equally dramatic, although of a somewhat different nature because of long-standing cross-cultural differences (see Thornton, 2005, for a summary). These include shifts from extended to nuclear households, from familism to individualism, and from parental control to youthful independence. They also include changes from arranged marriages to love matches, from young to older ages at marriage, and from universal marriage to the potential for extensive celibacy. Also relevant is the dramatic movement from natural fertility to the control of childbearing and from large numbers of births to small families. Also important is the rise of feminism, with its emphasis on gender egalitarianism and the rights of women both in families and the public arena. Although data from non-Western settings concerning family attitudes and values are generally less available than data on family behavior, the data we do have generally suggest that ideational and behavioral changes have been in the same general direction.

As discussed in chapter 1 of this volume, social scientists have offered a wide range of explanations for these family changes. Among them are changes in the economic, social, and political structure of society, including the dramatic restructuring of societies through industrialization, urbanization, increases in education and knowledge, and increased consumption and social mobility. Also cited as factors are changes in science and technology, in particular more rapid transportation and communication networks, the expansion of the mass media, more effective contraceptives, and medical and public health innovations that have decreased morbidity and mortality. Ideational forces have also been suggested as important sources of family change. For example, Lesthaeghe and his colleagues have argued persuasively that changes in religiosity and secularism are essential in explaining changing family behavior in Europe (Lesthaeghe, 1983; Lesthaeghe & Wilson, 1986). Similarly, Caldwell (1982), Freedman (1979, 1987), and van de Kaa (1996) have emphasized the importance of the spread of Western ideas and beliefs for changes in family behavior and ideals in non-Western populations.

Our purpose here is not to choose between structural and ideational explanations of family change. In fact, we believe that both are important and that the larger and more appropriate task is to demonstrate how the two fit together in mutually reinforcing ways. Our agenda in this chapter, however, is much more humble: to demonstrate how one ideational factor, developmental idealism, has been a particularly powerful influence in changing both ideas and social structure. We consider its influence in the world generally and then discuss how it has been widely disseminated in two countries, Argentina and Nepal.

DEVELOPMENTAL IDEALISM

Thornton (2001, 2005) has described the elements of developmental idealism and the ways it has influenced a broad array of family and demographic behaviors across time and around the world. Here we only highlight the basic arguments concerning developmental idealism and its impact on family change.

Developmental idealism grows out of the developmental paradigm—a model of natural, universal, necessary, and directional change that has dominated much of Western thinking from the Enlightenment of the 1600s and 1700s onward. This paradigm suggests that all societies progress through the same stages of development, but at different rates, so that at any single time point all societies can be viewed as occupying different stages along a single developmental continuum. Scholars using this paradigm believed that the most advanced societies were in northwestern Europe and among the northwestern European diaspora, whereas other societies were at less advanced positions on the pathway of development. They used this cross-sectional variation to infer the nature of developmental trajectories across time. That is, they read history sideways by assuming that the most developed nations had been like their less-developed contemporaries in the historical past, and that, with continued progress, the least developed nations would become more like their more advanced neighbors in the future.

These scholars observed that the family systems of northwestern Europe were very different from those in many other parts of the world. They found societies outside northwestern Europe that were generally family-organized, had considerable family solidarity, and were frequently extended. Marriage was frequently universal and often contracted at a young age. These societies also placed considerable authority in the hands of parents and the elders, had arranged marriages and provided little opportunity for affection before marriage, and maintained gender relationships that were interpreted as reflecting the low status of women. By contrast, scholars found northwestern European societies to be less family organized and more individualistic; to have less parental authority and weaker intergenerational support systems; to have more nuclear households, less universal marriage, older marriage, and more affection and couple autonomy in the mate-selection process. They also perceived women's status as higher in northwestern European societies. Given the developmental paradigm and reading history sideways methodology, it was easy for these 18th- and 19th-century scholars to conclude that the process of development had transformed family systems from the traditional patterns observed outside of northwestern Europe to the contemporary patterns observed within northwestern Europe.

These scholars also observed differences in the social and economic systems of northwestern Europe and those in many other parts of the world. They noted that northwestern Europe was more industrial, urban, and educated than many other parts of the world; it also had higher levels of knowledge, consumption, geographic mobility, secularism, democracy, and religious pluralism. They also knew that many of these dimensions of northwestern European social and economic life had increased over the years. They made the inference that the unique northwestern European family system was causally connected to the northwestern European social and economic system—as both a cause and an effect.[1]

Developmental idealism emerged from the developmental paradigm, reading history sideways, and the conclusions of generations of social

---

[1]These ideas permeated the scholarly literature from the 1700s through the middle 1900s. However, in the second half of the 1900s a number of studies that used the

scientists about family change, forming a strong model to guide and motivate subsequent social change. Within developmental idealism was a set of propositions that have had an enormous effect on family and demographic change during the past two centuries. This package of developmental idealism included a set of ideas specifying new goals to be achieved, new methods for achieving goals, a means for evaluating various forms of human organization, an explanatory framework identifying social relationships (including the family) as both cause and effect of socioeconomic achievement, and statements about the fundamental rights of individual human beings.

Developmental idealism relies on four main propositions. The first is that modern society is good and attainable. By *modern society* we mean the dimensions of social and economic structures identified by generations of scholars as developed—including, for example, being industrialized, urbanized, highly educated, highly knowledgeable, and wealthy. The second proposition of developmental idealism is that the modern family is good and attainable. By modern family we mean the aspects of family identified by generations of earlier scholars as modern, including the existence of many nonfamily institutions, individualism, nuclear households, intergenerational independence and autonomy, marriages arranged by mature couples, courtship preceding marriage, and a high valuation of women. The third proposition is that a modern family is both a cause and an effect of a modern society. The fourth proposition of developmental idealism is that individuals have the right to be free and equal and have their social relationships based on consent. Our argument is that these four propositions comprise a system of beliefs that can influence a broad array of family and demographic behaviors and, in fact, have been especially powerful in changing family and demographic structures and relationships around the world.

It is important to note that we do not offer the propositions of developmental idealism as factual statements representing truths about the world, but as beliefs and ideas that people may or may not endorse or use

---

north-western European historical record to read history from the past to the present rather than from cross-sectional variation revealed that there was no such historical transformation in northwestern Europe. This new wave of scholarship revealed that the modern family system of northwestern Europe during the 1700s and 1800s had been in place for centuries, rather than being the product of recent development. This discovery discredited the idea that societies progressed over time from the traditional family systems outside of northwestern Europe to the modern family system of northwestern Europe. It also cast doubt on the idea that modern family systems were the products of modern socioeconomic systems, while strengthening the belief that modern family systems were causal forces producing socioeconomic development.

as guides in their lives. In addition, we do not take a position concerning whether the effects of these propositions are negative or positive, although we recognize this as an important issue.

As discussed by Thornton (2001, 2005) and in the first chapter of this volume, there have been many mechanisms for the worldwide dissemination of the developmental paradigm, the conclusions of social scientists, and the propositions of developmental idealism. These include the distribution of the treatises of the scholars of the 1700s and 1800s, mass education, the mass media, and industrialization and urbanization. The ideas of development and developmental idealism have also been spread actively through social movements and organizations, including Christian churches, the movement for political democracy, and Marxism and socialism. Additional social movements have adopted and disseminated specific dimensions of developmental idealism, including the civil rights movement, the women's movement, and the international family planning movement. Developmental principles and conclusions also became embedded in American foreign policy and in the doctrines and programs of the United Nations and other international organizations, including both governmental and nongovernmental organizations (Latham, 2000; Meyer, Boli, Thomas, & Ramirez, 1997; United Nations [UN], 1948, 1962, 1979).

We claim that through these many mechanisms the ideas of the developmental paradigm, reading history sideways, the conclusions of social scientists, and the propositions of developmental idealism have been widely disseminated in both European populations and in many other parts of the world.[2] As they have been disseminated and accepted by government agencies, nongovernment organizations, community leaders, families, and individuals, they have become powerful forces for changing cultural understandings and family ideologies and behaviors for centuries.

Of course, the spread of developmental idealism has not been without substantial opposition in many parts of the world. Western forms pronounced as modern in developmental idealism are sometimes viewed as foreign and strange, especially to those outside the West, and at times this resistance has been sufficiently strong that it could only be overcome with strong coercion or even physical force (Comaroff & Comaroff,

---

[2]For further documentation and discussion, see Ahearn, 2001; Amin, 1989; Blaut, 1993; Comaroff & Comaroff, 1997; Dahl & Rabo, 1992; Dussel, 1995; Escobar, 1988; Kahn, 2001; Kulick, 1992; Latham, 2000; Lee, 1994; Lerner, 1958; LiPuma, 2000; Myrdal, 1968; Nisbet, 1980; Pigg, 1992; Robertson, 1992; Samoff, 1999; Sanderson, 1990; Wallerstein, 1979/1997, 1991; Welch, 1999.

1991; Hetherington, 2001). Thus, the ideas of developmental idealism have been ignored, resisted, modified, or hybridized as circumstances and conditions have permitted and required.

Thornton (2001, 2005) has presented a wide array of evidence to support the thesis that developmental idealism has spread widely around the world and has had substantial influence on family change.[3] Much of this evidence comes from the writings of government, political, and community leaders who have elaborated the arguments and approaches of the developmental paradigm and developmental idealism. For example, Thornton has documented extensive reliance on developmental thinking and arguments among European travelers, colonial administrators, Christian missionaries, and family planning advocates. In addition, the role of developmental models has been demonstrated in the documents of the United Nations, numerous governments, including those of China and the United States, and international nongovernmental organizations. This kind of evidence suggests that developmental thinking has been widely disseminated and influential in the thinking and policies of important decision makers around the world.

Data from ordinary people around the world are also consistent with the idea that developmental thinking is both widespread and influential (Thornton, 2005). For example, observers in such disparate locations as Africa, India, Nepal, and New Guinea report examples of ordinary people using the developmental idealism framework in evaluating various attributes and behavior.[4] In addition, social science analyses of surveys reveal that attitudes and behavior consistent with developmental idealism are associated with access to and contact with the main avenues for the dissemination of developmental idealism.[5] For example, urban living, education, and contact with the mass media have been shown to be strongly related to the timing of marriage, the arrangement of marriage, the number of children born, living arrangements, and commitment to the ancestors. In addition, trends in urban living, education, and mass media contact can account for much of the trends in

---

[3]For examples of this evidence, see Ahearn, 2001; Amin, 1989; Blaut, 1993; Comaroff & Comaroff, 1997; Kahn, 2001; Lee, 1994; Nisbet, 1980; Pigg, 1992; Robertson, 1992; Sanderson, 1990.

[4]For examples, see Abu-Lughod, 1998a, 1998b; Ahearn, 2001; Caldwell et al., 1988; Comaroff & Comaroff, 1997; LiPuma, 2000; Locoh, 1988; Pigg, 1992; Watkins, 2000.

[5]For examples of this literature, see Axinn & Yabiku, 2001; Barber, 2004; Barber & Axinn, 2004; Caldwell & Caldwell, 1997; Cleland & Wilson, 1987; Ghimire, Axinn, Yabiku, & Thornton, 2006; Hornik & McAnany, 2001; Kottak, 1990; Thornton, 2005; Thornton & Lin, 1994.

these family behaviors in various parts of the world. Furthermore, the power of factors such as education and mass media contact in explaining family ideas and behavior is much stronger than the explanatory power of factors such as urbanization and industrialization (see Thornton, 2005). It is likely that this differential is the result of education and the mass media being explicitly designed to transmit ideas and information, whereas cities and factories are designed with different purposes.

DEVELOPMENTAL THINKING AND BELIEFS IN ARGENTINA AND NEPAL

We now turn to a discussion of developmental thinking and beliefs in two widely disparate countries, Argentina and Nepal. Our goal is to document the extent to which ordinary people in these countries believe and accept the propositions of developmental idealism and related aspects of developmental thinking. We keep our discussion brief, as each country is discussed extensively elsewhere in this volume (Argentina in chap. 6 and Nepal in chap. 10). Additional information about the data we have collected in these two countries can be found in Binstock and Thornton (2006) and Thornton, Ghimire, and Mitchell (2005).

Argentina is a sparsely populated South American country of about 37 million people, with almost 90% living in urban areas. It was a Spanish colony for more than two centuries before it declared its independence in 1816. The country is largely populated by European immigrants (mainly from Italy and Spain) and their descendants, with only a limited indigenous population. The Catholic Church has had a strong, although weakening, influence in the country. With its strong European heritage, Argentina has for the most part followed Western family patterns. Recent decades have seen significant changes in matters of family formation, family dynamics, and union dissolution that mirror those observed in Western societies.

Nepal is an Asian country located between the two great countries of China and India. It has never been colonized and has its unique independent history that dates back as far as the ninth century before the Christian Era (Rana, 1998). Nepal is primarily a Hindu country, although with a strong Buddhist minority and people from other religions as well. Nepal had very little contact with the outside world until the 1950s, when the country slowly and cautiously established bilateral relations with other countries in Asia, Europe, and America. The difficult terrain, the historical isolation, exploitation by the ruling elite, and the Hinduization of the non-Hindu population have had an enduring influence on many aspects of Nepali life. Nepal currently ranks as one of the poorest countries in the world. Over 85% of the population still lives in rural areas, and more than half of the population is still illiterate. In addition, several long-maintained attributes of family life in Nepal are viewed as "traditional" in developmental idealism terms. These include extended households, young-age marriages, arranged marriages, parental control over children, and low status of women.

Our data collection project in Argentina was conducted in 2003–2004 with high school teenagers (see Binstock & Thornton, 2006) drawn from seven public high schools in two areas of the country—five schools in rural Santa Fe state and two schools in Buenos Aires City. Within each setting, we collected data from a broad group of students attending the last 3 years of high school using both focus groups and surveys. A self-administered questionnaire with both demographic items and questions about various aspects of developmental idealism was used to collect data from 456 students in both areas. In addition, we conducted eight focus groups in rural Santa Fe and eight focus groups in the city of Buenos Aires, with each group ranging from 6 to 10 students. The focus groups discussed a range of topics centered on the meanings of modernity and traditionality and the ways they were connected with social structure, families, and change.

Our data collection in Nepal, conducted in 2003–2004, also combined focus groups and survey interviews, with primary emphasis on the survey (see Thornton et al., 2005). We conducted 10 focus group interviews first, and used insights gained from them in designing the survey questionnaire. The survey was conducted using face-to-face interviews with 537 people aged 17 and older living in the Western Chitwan Valley. Participants were chosen using a stratified sample based on distance from the valley's urban center. This sampling procedure resulted in slightly more than 100 individuals from each of five strata being selected.

In discussing our findings, we address several specific questions: How much knowledge do the people of Argentina and Nepal have about the larger world? How informed are they about the concept of development? How well are the people of Argentina and Nepal able to apply the concept of development to the international community? What aspects of family life do they associate with development? And, do they believe that modern family life and socioeconomic development are causally connected? Most of this discussion centers on the survey data we collected, although the focus group information and survey data are broadly consistent in both settings.

Comparing Nepal and the United States

We turn first to Nepal and a set of questions asking Nepali respondents to compare basic elements of social, economic, and family life in Nepal and the United States. More specifically, we asked the respondents to tell us if a particular attribute was more or less common in one setting than another. The responses to these questions reveal that Nepalis are very knowledgeable about basic facts concerning the world (data not shown in tables). The vast majority can properly evaluate the differences between the socioeconomic and family circumstances in Nepal and the United States. More specifically, between 86 and 95% correctly report that cities, education, high incomes, and paid employment are higher in the United States, while child mortality and farm employment are higher in Nepal (see Thornton et al., 2005). In addition, 88% or more correctly report that polygamous families, activities organized around the family, marriages arranged by parents, and large families with many children are more common in Nepal than in the United States. Somewhat smaller percentages, but still between 74 and 84%, report that married sons living with their parents and child marriage are more common in Nepal, whereas between 69 and 80% believe that personal freedom, women who never marry, and women having a high degree of respect are more common in the United States. These findings suggest that most Nepalis are knowledgeable about the United States and realize that it varies dramatically from Nepal in terms of wealth, education, health, wage employment, and family systems.

Respondents were also asked to compare Nepal and the United States on their overall quality of life—a purely subjective comparison with no objective metric for evaluation. Despite the potential pressures of ethnocentrism, 87% of Nepali respondents rated a good quality of life as more common in the United States than in Nepal (see Thornton et al., 2005).

Comparing Rich/Poor, Developed/Traditional, and Educated/Uneducated Places

In a similar way, we asked Nepali respondents to make comparisons between poor and rich places, between traditional and developed countries, and between less-educated and more-educated places. The univariate distributions for these three comparisons are contained in the six columns of Table 2.1. The answers that are consistent with centuries of developmental thinking are noted in bold.

These data confirm that the vast majority of Nepalis explicitly understand the correlation between family matters and various indicators of

TABLE 2.1

Nepali Perceptions of Whether Certain Family Attributes Are More Common in Poor or Rich Places, in Traditional or Developed Places, and in Educated or Uneducated Places (Percent Giving Answers)[a]

	More common in[b]					
	Poor	Rich	Traditional	Developed	Uneducated	Educated
People marrying at older ages	24.5	**74.0**	19.1	**80.7**	18.6	**80.8**
Women getting treated with respect	17.0	**80.2**	19.2	**79.9**	8.4	**90.6**
Young people choosing their own spouse	26.7	**66.8**			8.5	**90.4**
(Married couples) using contraception[c]	15.1	**82.3**	7.5	**92.0**	6.4	**92.9**
Couples getting divorced	43.0	**52.2**	33.4	**64.4**	55.3	**42.0**
Same father's children living away from their older parents			32.5	**64.8**		
Parents controlling who their children marry			**67.7**	31.1		

[a]Respondents could chose among the categories of "more common" in one of the places or "about the same." The percentage of people answering "about the same" is the difference between 100% and the sum of the two reported percentages.
[b]The response that we believe to most closely match that provided by developmental thinking is in bold.
[c]The words "married couples" were included in the traditional–developed comparisons but not in the uneducated–educated and poor–rich comparisons.

socioeconomic position, including wealth, development, and education. Between 64 and 93% of Nepalis report that people marrying at older ages, women getting treated with respect, married couples using contraception, and children living away from their older parents are more common in rich, developed, and educated places than in poor, traditional, and uneducated places. The 90% plus reporting a positive correlation between education and women's status, spouse choice, and the use of contraception is quite remarkable.

Note, however, that the respondents are more split on the correlation for divorce. Approximately half of them believe that the correlation with wealth or education is positive. We do not have a straightforward explanation of this split on the relative prevalence of divorce.

Table 2.2 reports similar information from the teenagers in Argentina, but with slightly different questions and a different methodology. The self-administered questionnaire used in Argentina included an "about the same" option not offered to the Nepali respondents in the face-to-face interview (but was recorded if they volunteered it). In addition, the brevity of the Argentina questionnaire permitted us to only make one set of comparisons—that between developed and less developed places.

One of the first things to observe in Table 2.2 is that many more Argentineans than Nepalis chose the "about the same" answer in making their comparisons, probably an artifact of the different methodology. As we discuss later, little evidence indicates that the Nepalis are generally better informed about the ideas of development than are the teenagers from Argentina.

Between 73 and 61% of the respondents from Argentina reported a positive correlation between development and women's status and the use of contraception. In addition, between 52 and 55% reported a positive correlation between development and age at marriage, and couples getting divorced or separated. And nearly 50% reported a positive correlation between development and men and women doing the same work, valuing one's family less, and women never marrying. This suggests a strong understanding of the relationship between development and several dimensions of family behavior—a correlation that is consistent with the developmental model and developmental idealism.

Rating Countries on Education and Development

We now turn to Table 2.3, where we summarize data for two different sets of questions for both Nepal and Argentina. The first set of items presented respondents with a scale of education from 0 to 10, with 0

TABLE 2.2

Argentina Perceptions of Whether Certain Family Attributes Are More Common in Developed or Less Developed Places (Percent Giving Answers)[a]

	More common in[b]		
	Less Developed	Developed	About Same
People marrying at older ages	22.4	**52.5**	25.1
Women getting treated with more equality	19.3	**60.8**	20.0
Married couples using contraception	11.5	**73.3**	15.2
Parents controlling who their children marry	**38.5**	36.6	24.9
Women and men doing same work	30.0	**48.5**	21.6
Couples getting divorced/separated	15.0	**54.6**	30.4
People deciding not to get married or living with a partner	21.4	**44.6**	34.0
People valuing family life more	**46.9**	24.9	28.2

[a]Respondents could chose among three response categories: more common in less developed places; more common in developed places; and about the same.
[b]The response that we believe to most closely match that provided by developmental thinking is in bold.

TABLE 2.3
Mean Country Scores on Education and Development as Reported by the United Nations, Nepali Respondents, and Argentinean Respondents

Countries rated	Education			Development		
	United Nations Education Index (x 10)[a]	Nepal respondents[c] mean	Argentina respondents[c] mean	United Nations Human Development Index (x 10)[b]	Nepal respondents[c] mean	Argentina respondents[c] mean
England	9.9	7.3	8.1	9.3	7.5	8.4
United States	9.7	8.4	8.1	9.4	8.4	9.1
Japan	9.4	7.3	8.3	9.3	7.5	9.0
Brazil	9	6.5	6.3	7.8	6.4	6.3
China	7.9	6.9	7.1	7.2	7.3	7.8
India	5.7	6.0	4.5	5.9	5.9	4.5
Nepal	5	4.8		5.0	3.8	
Bolivia	8.5		5.1	6.7		4.8
Nigeria	5.9		4.5	4.6		4.5
Argentina	9.4		6.3	8.5		6.0
Somalia[d]	1.6	5.6		2.9	5.8	
Correlation between UN and Nepal/Argentina respondents' scores		0.80	0.82		0.77	0.86
Correlation between UN and Nepal respondents' scores without Somalia		0.88			0.90	

[a]2003 Human Development Report, Education Index. The Education Index is composed of the literacy rate and school enrollment percentages of the country (www.undp.org/hrd2003).

[b]2003 Human Development Report, Human Development Index. The Human Development Index is composed of GNP per Capita, life expectancy and the Education Index (www.undp.org/hdr2003).

[c]The total number of respondents in Nepal is 537. The total number of respondents in Argentina is 456.

[d]United Nations scores were imputed.

being the least educated place in the world, 10 being the most educated place in the world, and 5 indicating moderate education. The respondents were then asked to rate several countries on this scale of education, with the countries varying between Argentina and Nepal. The respondents were asked to rate the same set of countries on a similar scale of development. The data in Table 2.3 indicate the mean education and development scores for each of the countries rated. Also listed in Table 2.3 are the scores assigned by the United Nations, an organization expending considerable resources to assess the education and development of the world's countries.

Perusal of Table 2.3 reveals that the average scores for Nepalis and Argentineans are remarkably similar to each other and to the United Nations scores. As a summary measure of this correspondence, we calculated Pearsonian correlation coefficients between the United Nations scores and the mean scores for the respondents in the two countries, which range from .77 to .86.[6]

A separate set of correlations was estimated for Nepali respondents, with Somalia excluded because a significant number of Nepalis indicated their unfamiliarity with this African country, causing us to worry about the measurement unreliability introduced by including this country. Indeed, with Somalia excluded from the analysis, the correlations for Nepal reach .90, indicating in the aggregate a remarkable amount of agreement with our colleagues at the United Nations.

Just as Pearsonian correlation coefficients can be computed between the aggregate scores of respondents and the United Nations, correlations can be computed between the scores of an individual and the scores of the United Nations. That is, for Nepal one can calculate 537 correlations for education and 537 correlations for development between each individual's scores and the United Nations scores. Similarly, 456 education correlations and 456 development correlations can be calculated for the Argentina respondents.

These calculations revealed that 25% of the Nepali respondents gave country scores on education that correlated at .12 or lower with the education scores of the UN, indicating a relatively low level of agreement of some individuals with the UN. This low individual-level correlation on education is consistent with the fact that a significant number of Nepalis (15%) gave Nepal a score of 10 on the education scale, which virtually guaranteed a low overall correlation with the UN. It is not clear

---

[6]These correlations are estimated from only a small number of countries rated observations (less than 10 in each case), but are still remarkable in their magnitude.

whether these respondents misunderstood the question or were using a different criterion of education than the UN.[7]

Many Nepalis, however, displayed a relatively high correlation with UN scores on education. Over half had a correlation greater than .56, and 25% had correlations of .8 or greater.

The correlations between UN scores and individual Nepali scores on development were generally higher than those for education. There are substantially fewer very low correlations and more high correlations on development than on education. This suggests the possibility that the concept of development—and the distribution of countries on this scale—may be more salient in Nepal than is the concept of education.

Turning now to Argentina, we find that the magnitudes of individual-level correlations for both education and development are substantially higher than in Nepal. Most noteworthy here is that very few respondents in Argentina had extremely low correlations with the UN scales. That is, 75% had correlations on education at .42 or above and 75% had correlations at .55 or above on development. Furthermore, the median correlation on education in Argentina was nearly .66 and on development it was .75.

Also note that, as in Nepal, the respondents in Argentina are able to replicate the UN development index more closely than the UN education index. As we speculated earlier, this may indicate a higher level of salience for development and its distribution than for education.

Our purpose in presenting the country scores for education and development is not to suggest that we can put our colleagues at the UN out of business by asking a group of Nepali adults or Argentinean teenagers to rate the countries of the world on these aspects. Instead, we use these results to demonstrate the widespread understanding of development and education and their distribution across countries.

The ability of most respondents in Argentina and Nepal to perform so well on this evaluation task suggests that they were able to reliably use our crude measurement devices; that they have a fairly sophisticated understanding and conception of development and education; that their conceptions of development and education are similar to those of the UN; and that they have knowledge of some of the major countries of the world and are able to evaluate their levels of education and development. The simultaneous existence of all of these characteristics is necessary to obtain such high correlations among so many of the respondents.

---

[7]Twelve percent gave Nepal a score of 10 on development.

We are especially impressed with the knowledge and sophistication of the people in Nepal, a country closed to the Western world until approximately 50 years ago. Also, it is impressive that even higher levels of knowledge and sophistication are shown among the teenagers of Argentina, suggesting that these ideas and abilities are acquired at a relatively young age. Of course, as we also noted earlier, Argentina is a country with a European heritage, which has probably made developmental ideas widespread there for centuries.

Causal Connections between Socioeconomic and Family Change

As shown in Tables 1 and 2, we documented in both Nepal and Argentina a general understanding of the correlations between a country's family structures and its socioeconomic position. We also evaluated respondents' causal theories for those correlations through a series of questions in both Nepal and Argentina about the family consequences of socioeconomic change and the socioeconomic consequences of family change.

In Nepal we asked three series of questions about the possible family consequences of Nepal becoming more developed, more educated, or richer. All questions took the following form: "Now let us talk about whether the following things would be more common or less common if Nepal became more developed. People marrying at older ages? If Nepal were more developed, would people marrying at older ages be more common or less common?" That is, we asked respondents how an increase in each of the socioeconomic factors—development, education, or wealth—would change the prevalence of various family characteristics, as shown in Table 2.4. (Respondents could also volunteer that prevalence would remain about the same.) The percentages listed in Table 2.4 indicate the proportion of Nepalis who thought that greater national development, education, or wealth would make the family characteristics more or less common; the percentages appearing in bold are consistent with developmental thinking and conclusions.

It is notable that the aggregate responses concerning the effects of development, education, and wealth are nearly identical, which is likely because Nepalis perceive them as highly correlated, perhaps both conceptually and empirically. Given the similarity of responses and the greater number of family items examined in the development series, we focus the rest of our discussion on the perceived development consequences.

TABLE 2.4

Nepali Respondents' Evaluation of the Proposition That More Development, Education, or Wealth Would Change Family Life (Percent Giving Answers)[a]

	If Nepal were to become ...[b]					
	More developed		More educated		Richer	
	More Common	*Less Common*	*More Common*	*Less Common*	*More Common*	*Less Common*
People marrying at older ages	**73.4**	26.6	**80.8**	19.2	**75.5**	24.5
Women getting treated with respect	**89.2**	10.2	**88.5**	11.3	**90.6**	9.2
Young people choosing their own spouse	**80.0**	19.4	**83.5**	16.3	**82.6**	16.6
Married couples using contraception	**80.7**	19.3	**85.4**	14.6	**81.5**	17.9
Children living away from their older parents	50.9	48.5				
Women and men doing the same work	**78.7**	20.9				
Parents controlling who their children marry	47.4	**51.9**				
Couples getting divorced	**29.4**	70.3	**26.3**	73.4	**31.9**	67.4
People working away from their family for pay	**54.5**	45.5				
Adult children having more control over their earnings	**72.1**	27.5				
Men marrying multiple wives	28.6	**70.3**				
Families having a lot of children	27.0	**72.4**				
People valuing their families less	**82.5**	17.1				
People deciding not to get married	**35.3**	63.6				
Families having fewer children	**60.2**	39.2				
More men having only one wife	**56.2**	43.6				

[a]The questions eliciting these responses about development were as follows, including the introduction. "Now let us talk about whether the following things would be more common or less common if Nepal became more developed. People marrying at older ages? If Nepal were more developed, would people marrying at older ages be more common or less common?" Respondents could also volunteer that age at marriage would remain about the same. Similar questions were asked about development in Nepal and the other dimensions of family life. In a similar fashion, respondents were asked about the family consequences of Nepal becoming more educated and richer. The percentage of people answering "about the same" is the difference between 100% and the sum of the two reported percentages.

The data in Table 2.4 provide evidence that many Nepalis believe that family characteristics would change as a result of greater national development, education, and wealth. For development in particular, Nepalis predict that virtually all of the 16 dimensions of Nepali family life would be affected and, in most cases, these predictions are in the same direction as the assumptions of developmental idealism. A full 60 to 89% of those surveyed predicted that socioeconomic development would be associated with trends toward a later age at marriage, higher status of women, more use of contraception, more equality of gender roles, less polygamy, lower fertility, and valuing families less.

In some other cases, the results are mixed or unclear. For example, a substantial majority (80%) believed that development would increase the prevalence of young people choosing their own spouse, but only about one-half said that development would decrease parental control over whom their children married. Nepalis were also mixed in their expectations about the impact of development on children living away from their older parents and people working away from their families. In addition, the majority of Nepalis expected that development would decrease both divorce and the number of people who decided not to marry, both contrary to the usual theories of development. More investigation is required to understand the reasoning behind these expectations.

We also asked respondents in Nepal to shift the evaluation from the impact of development, education, and wealth on family life to the influence of changes in family life on wealth, being better or worse off, and education. The data about the impact of family changes on life in Nepal were collected using the following format: "Some people talk about making Nepal richer. For each of the following things, please tell me whether you think it would help make Nepal richer or help make Nepal poorer. If more people married at an older age? Would that help make Nepal richer or help make Nepal poorer?" Similar questions were asked about the consequences of changes in other aspects of family life. In addition, a similar but smaller set of questions was asked about the consequences of family change on general quality of life and education.

We found several striking similarities between the data on the predicted influences of changes in family life on socioeconomic position (not shown in tables) and the data about the predicted influences of socioeconomic changes on family life. As before, the proportions expecting consequences of changes in family life are frequently very substantial and usually in the direction predicted by most theories and ideologies of development. More specifically, substantial fractions of Nepalis predict that Nepal would become richer if people married later, women were treated with more respect, more couples used contraception, more women and men did the same work, and families had fewer children. Also, just as there were mixed or unclear reactions about whether or not socioeconomic change would affect parental control over marriage, there were mixed reactions about the influence of changes in parental control on socioeconomic factors. And, just as most Nepalis thought that improvements in socioeconomic position would decrease divorce, most believed that increased divorce would make Nepal poorer.

Although much of the story about the perceptions of the influence of family change on socioeconomic circumstances is similar to the story about the perceptions of the influence of socioeconomic change on family life, there are some notable exceptions. First is the fact that Nepalis overwhelmingly see development leading to people valuing their families less—as suggested in most developmental theories—but at the same time, they see any trend toward devaluing families as leading to poorer socioeconomic circumstances. Clearly, this is an area where many Nepalis must be conflicted about the interrelationships they see between socioeconomic change and family change.

Second, although most Nepalis perceive a strong reciprocal causal relationship between socioeconomic and family change, in many, but not all, instances more Nepalis perceive an effect of family change on socioeconomic position than see an effect of socioeconomic change on family life. This tends to be true for the following aspects of family life: age at marriage, the use of contraception, women and men doing the same work, people working away from their families for pay, polygamy, and fertility. In any event, most Nepalis see many, but not all, family changes in the modern direction as leading to improved socioeconomic circumstances.

We now switch our attention from Nepal to Argentina, where we asked teenagers a similar series of questions about the causal interconnections between socioeconomic and family change. In Argentina, we limited our focus of socioeconomic change to development and asked about 6 rather than 16 dimensions of family life.

All items in the self-administered questionnaire took the following format: "Now we would like you to think that Argentina became more developed than it is nowadays. . . . If Argentina were more developed, would people marrying late be more common or less common?" The response categories included "about the same," as well as "more common" and "less common." The questions about other aspects of family life were asked in a similar way. The distribution of responses is shown in Table 2.5.

TABLE 2.5

Evaluation of Respondents in Argentina of the Effects of Development in Argentina on Family Life (Percent Giving Answers)[a]

	If Argentina became more developed…[b]		
	More common	*Less common*	*About same*
People marrying late	**43.6**	19.7	36.7
Women getting treated with equality	**74.4**	11.9	13.7
Married couples using contraception	**75.8**	9.7	14.5
Couples getting divorced/separated	**31.2**	33.8	34.9
People putting their individual needs above their family needs	**34.9**	33.6	31.6
People deciding not to get married or live with a partner	**26.5**	30.2	43.3

[a]The questions eliciting these responses about development were as follows, including the introduction. "Now we would like you to think that Argentina became more developed than it is nowadays. We would like to know your opinion if each of the following situations would be more common or less common if Argentina were to become a more developed country. People marrying late? If Argentina were more developed, would people marrying late be more common or less common?" Respondents could also volunteer that age at marriage would remain about the same.
[b]The response that we believe most closely matches that provided by developmental thinking is in bold.

The data in Table 2.5 suggest that the causal theories held by most teenagers in Argentina predict consequences of development on only two aspects of family life (that we asked about) in Argentina: women's status and the use of contraception. In both cases, about three-fourths of Argentina teenagers perceived that these two dimensions of family life would increase with development. Furthermore, more than two-fifths believed that development would lead to older ages at marriage. These answers are consistent with the prevailing theories of the impact of development on family life.

These teenagers, however, had more conflicting ideas about the influence of development on divorce, individualism versus familism, and never marrying. For each of these aspects of family life, a substantial fraction of the respondents expected that development would have no influence, while among those who expected it would, approximately equal proportions thought the effect would be positive as did negative.

Our evaluation of the effects of changes in family life in Argentina used self-administered questions that took the following form: "Some people talk about making Argentina more developed. For each of the following things, please mark whether you think it would help make Argentina more developed, it would help make Argentina less developed, or it would be about the same. If more people married later? Would that help make Argentina more developed or help make Argentina less developed?" "About the same" was included as a response category. Similar questions were asked of other dimensions of family life.

These data (not shown in tables) indicate that teens predicted a clear causal effect for only one dimension of family life on Argentina's development: a higher status for women (with 83% reporting this expectation). This expectation is consistent with prevailing theories of family change and development. Interestingly, however, only a minority of respondents believed that an increase in the age at marriage, the use of contraception, or people deciding not to get married would lead to greater development—expectations contrary to prevailing theories. Although Argentineans and Nepalis share substantially similar views about the causal interconnections between socioeconomic change and family change, they also have important differences, as we outlined earlier. These could be due to many influences, including the following: the different ages of the respondents; the different knowledge and belief systems in the two settings; and the different methodologies used. In addition, Nepalis were asked to evaluate change in Nepal while Argentinians were asked to evaluate change in Argentina. Because the country to be evaluated is very different, this could also lead to different responses, even though the respondents may have similar causal ideas. It is not possible here to evaluate the extent to which these various differences might have affected the responses in the two countries.

CONCLUSIONS

As we noted in the beginning of the chapter, many places in the world have experienced changes in family life, for which social scientists have accumulated a wide array of structural and ideational explanations. Here we focused on one particular ideational force for changing family life—that of developmental idealism. We contend that it has been disseminated widely around the world, where it has had enormous influence on family behavior, beliefs, and values.

Our contentions are supported by new evidence from Nepal and Argentina, where we found that most ordinary people have considerable knowledge of the ideas of development, substantial knowledge about the major countries of the world, can rate countries on their levels of education and development, believe that there is an association between socioeconomic development and family structure, and believe that economic development and family structures and relationships are causally connected, with economic development causing family change and family change causing economic development.

REFERENCES

Abu-Lughod, L. (1998a). Feminist longings and postcolonial conditions. In L. Abu-Lughod (Ed.), *Remaking women: Feminism and modernity in the Middle East* (pp. 3–32). Princeton, NJ: Princeton University Press.

Abu-Lughod, L. (1998b). The marriage of feminism and Islamism in Egypt: Selective repudiation as a dynamic of postcolonial cultural policies. In L. Abu-Lughod (Ed.), *Remaking women: Feminism and modernity in the Middle East* (pp. 243–69). Princeton, NJ: Princeton University Press.

Ahearn, L. M. (2001). *Invitations to love: Literacy, love letters, and social change in Nepal.* Ann Arbor: University of Michigan Press.

Amin, S. (1989). *Eurocentrism.* New York: Monthly Review Press.

Axinn, W. G., & Yabiku, S. T. (2001). Social change, the social organization of families, and fertility limitation. *American Journal of Sociology, 106*(5), 1219–1261.

Barber, J. S. (2004). Community social context and individualistic attitudes toward marriage. *Social Psychology Quarterly, 67*, 236–56.

Barber, J. S., & Axinn, W. G. (2004). New ideas and fertility limitation: The role of mass media. *Journal of Marriage and Family, 66*, 1180–1200.

Binstock, G., & Thornton, A. (2006). *Knowledge and use of developmental thinking about societies and families among teenagers in Argentina.* (PSC Research Report No. 06-587). Ann Arbor, MI.

Blaut, J. M. (1993). *The colonizer's model of the world: Geographical diffusionism and Eurocentric history.* New York: Guilford Press.

Caldwell, J. C. (1982). *Theory of fertility decline.* London: Academic Press.

Caldwell, J. C., & Caldwell, P. (1997). What do we know about fertility transition. In G. W. Jones, R. M. Douglas, J. C. Caldwell, & Rennie M. D'Souza (Eds.), *The continuing demographic transition* (pp. 15–25). Oxford: Oxford University Press.

Caldwell, J. C., Reddy, P. H., & Caldwell, P. (1988). *The causes of demographic change: Experimental research in South India.* Madison: University of Wisconsin Press.

Caplow, T., Bahr, H. M., & Chadwick, B. A. (1983). *All faithful people.* Minneapolis: University of Minnesota Press.

Cleland, J., & Wilson, C. (1987). Demand theories of the fertility transition: An iconoclastic view. *Population Studies, 41*(1), 5–30.

Comaroff, J., & Comaroff, J. L. (1991). *Of revelation and revolution: Christianity, colonialism, and consciousness in South Africa.* Chicago: University of Chicago Press.

Comaroff, J., & Comaroff, J. L. (1997). *Of revelation and revolution: The dialectics of modernity on a South African frontier.* Chicago: University of Chicago Press.

Dahl, G., & Rabo, A. (Eds.). (1992). *Kam-Ap or take-off: Local notions of development.* Stockholm: Stockholm Studies in Social Anthropology.

Dussel, E. (1995). *The invention of the Americas.* New York: Continuum.

Escobar, A. (1988). Power and visibility: Development and the invention and management of the Third World. *Cultural Anthropology, 3*(4), 428–443.

Freedman, R. (1979). Theories of fertility decline: A reappraisal. *Social Forces, 58*(1), 1–17.

Freedman, R. (1987). The contribution of social science research to population policy and family planning program effectiveness. *Studies in Family Planning, 18*(2), 57–82.

Ghimire, D. J., Axinn, W. G., Yabiku, S. G., & Thornton, A. (2006). Social change, premarital non-family experience, and spouse choice in an arranged marriage society. *American Journal of Sociology, 111*(4).

Hetherington, P. (2001). Generational changes in marriage patterns in the central province of Kenya, 1930–1990. *Journal of Asian and African Studies, 36*(2), 157–180.

Hornik, R., & McAnany, E. (2001). Mass media and fertility change. In J. B. Casterline (Ed.), *Diffusion processes and fertility transition* (pp. 208–239). Washington, DC: National Academy Press.

Kahn, J. S. (2001). Anthropology and modernity. *Current Anthropology, 42*(5), 651–680.

Kottak, C. P. (1990). *Prime-time society.* Belmont, CA: Wadsworth.

Kulick, D. (1992). Coming up in Gapun: Conceptions of development and their effect on language in a Papua New Guinean village. In G. Dahl & A. Rabo (Eds.), *Kam-Ap or take-off: Local notions of development* (pp. 10–34). Stockholm: Stockholm Series in Social Anthropology.

Latham, M. E. (2000). *Modernization as ideology*. Chapel Hill: University of North Carolina Press.

Lee, R. L. M. (1994). Modernization, postmodernism and the Third World. *Journal of the International Sociological Association, 42*(2), 1–66.

Lerner, D. (1958). *The passing of traditional society: Modernizing the Middle East*. Glencoe, IL: Free Press.

Lesthaeghe, R. (1983). A century of demographic and cultural change in Western Europe: An exploration of underlying dimensions. *Population and Development Review, 9*(3), 411–435.

Lesthaeghe, R., & Wilson, C. (1986). Modes of production, secularization, and the pace of fertility decline in Western Europe, 1870–1930. In A. J. Coale & S. C. Watkins (Eds.), *The decline of fertility in Europe* (pp. 261–292). Princeton, NJ: Princeton University Press.

LiPuma, E. (2000). *Encompassing others: The magic of modernity in Melanesia*. Ann Arbor: University of Michigan Press.

Locoh, T. (1988). Evolution of the family in Africa. In E. V. D. Walle, P. O. Ohadike, & M. D. Sala-Diakanda (Eds.), *The state of African demography* (pp. 47–65). International Union for the Scientific Study of Population.

Meyer, J. W., Boli, J., Thomas, G. M., & Ramirez, F. O. (1997). World society and the nation-state. *American Journal of Sociology, 103*(1), 144–81.

Myrdal, G. (1968). *Asian drama: An inquiry into the poverty of nations* (Vol. 2). New York: The Twentieth Century Fund.

Nisbet, R. A. (1980). *History of the idea of progress*. New York: Basic Books.

Pigg, S. L. (1992). Inventing social categories through place: Social representations and development in Nepal. *Comparative Studies in Society and History, 34*(3), 491–513.

Rana, P. S. (1998). The history of Nepal. In P. S. J. B. Rana & D. N. Dhungel (Eds.), *Contemporary Nepal*. New Delhi, India: Vikas.

Robertson, R. (1992). *Globalization: Social theory and global culture*. London: Sage.

Roof, W. C., & McKinney, W. (1987). *American mainline religion*. New Brunswick, NJ: Rutgers University Press.

Samoff, J. (1999). Institutionalizing international influence. In R. F. Arnove & C. A. Torres (Eds.), *Comparative education: The dialectic of the global and the local* (pp. 51–89). Lanham, MD: Rowman and Littlefield.

Sanderson, S. K. (1990). *Social evolutionism. A critical history*. Oxford: Basil Blackwell.

Schneider, C. E. (1985). Moral discourse and the transformation of American family law. *Michigan Law Review, 83*(8), 1803–1879.

Thornton, A. (2001). The developmental paradigm, reading history sideways, and family change. *Demography, 38*(4), 449–65.

Thornton, A. (2005). *Reading history sideways: The fallacy and enduring impact of the developmental paradigm on family life*. Chicago: University of Chicago Press.

Thornton, A., Ghimire, D., & Mitchell, C. (2005, April). *The measurement and prevalence of developmental thinking about the family: Evidence from*

Nepal. Paper presented at the Population Association of America annual meeting, Philadelphia, PA.

Thornton, A., & Lin, H. (1994). *Social change and the family in Taiwan.* Chicago: University of Chicago Press.

United Nations. (1948). *Universal declaration of human rights.* General assembly resolution 217 A (III).

United Nations. (1962). *Convention on consent to marriage, minimum age for marriage and registration of marriages.* General assembly resolution 1763 A (XVII).

United Nations. (1979*). Convention on the elimination of all forms of discrimination against women.* General assembly resolution 34/180.

Van de Kaa, D. J. (1996). Anchored narratives: The story and findings of half a century of research into the determinants of fertility. *Population Studies, 50*(3), 389–432.

Wallerstein, I. (1991). *Unthinking social science: The limits of nineteenth-century paradigms.* Cambridge, UK: Polity Press.

Wallerstein, I. (1997). *The capitalist world-economy: Essays by Immanuel Wallerstein.* Cambridge, UK: Cambridge University Press. (Original work published 1979)

Watkins, S. C. (2000). Local and foreign models of reproduction in Nyanza province, Kenya. *Population and Development Review, 26*(4), 725–59.

Welch, A. (1999). The triumph of technocracy or the collapse of certainty; Modernity, postmodernity, and postcolonialism in comparative education. In R. F. Arnove & C. A. Torres (Eds.), *Comparative education: The dialectic of the global and the local* (pp. 25–49). Lanham, MD: Rowman and Littlefield.

3

An Uncertain Future for African Families

Thérèse Locoh
Insitut National Etudes Démographiques, Paris

Myriam Mouvagha-Sow
CERPOS, Université Paris X-Nanterre

African societies are notable for the preeminence of ideals concerning the family: the solidarity maintained among members of extended family groups, the power of and respect engendered by family elders, and the importance placed on having many children. These values have structured African societies in the past and continue to do so, perhaps all the more so since the young independent states are encountering many problems in fostering new constitutive values for their nations.

The cohesion of large family groups around shared values has so far constituted a survival strategy in societies where the balance between population and resources was difficult to achieve. When production is largely accomplished through manual labor, with low-performance technologies, and in uncertain climatic conditions, it is necessary to mobilize everyone's energy. The pyramidal family organization that places power in the hands of the elders is one means of ensuring such mobilization. However, the situation in Africa is rapidly changing. The beneficial effects of social changes since independence and the recurrent economic crises are undoubtedly exerting profound influences on family lifestyles, seen especially in union formation, fertility behavior, and the living arrangements of families.

In this chapter we first identify aspects of African families that have remained stable for a very long time. These include elder control over the young, male dominance, and intergenerational solidarity. We then provide a statistical analysis of the evolution of families in Western and Central Africa, focusing on marriage, the management of reproduction, and rules of residence. We conclude by examining what African families may be like in the future and identify the main sources of change that may be influential on family systems.

We have limited this analysis of family changes in Africa to Western and Central African societies, which share a body of characteristics concerning nuptiality, fertility, and domestic organization. The statistical data of the Demographic and Health Surveys,[1] from nationally representative household surveys whose coverage includes household characteristics, reproductive behavior and intentions, and the status of women, which provide us with repeated observations, are particularly appropriate for describing the main outlines of the changes that have occurred in Africa since the mid-1980s. But we also rely on a series of sociological surveys and field observations to identify new trends.

A HERITAGE FROM THE PAST

The changes in family structures in sub-Saharan Africa have been dramatic in recent years. Age at first marriage has increased, arranged marriages have declined, and premarital sex and premarital births have both increased. Fertility has started to decline in several countries, especially in towns, largely because of an increase in contraceptive use, but also because of an increase in induced abortions. These transformations call into question family ideals that have been privileged until now in these societies (Goody,1976; Caldwell, 1976; Lesthaeghe, 1989a; Diop, 1985; Hertrich, 1996).

To take stock of these changes we must briefly recall some of the structuring principles inherited from the past, because—although challenged by life in modern cities—they are still largely respected among the majority of rural populations.

The Elders Have Control over the Young

In African societies the elders tend to have the power to make decisions for the younger members of the family/lineage. From childhood people learn to respect older persons and to submit to their decisions. This power is exercised in two highly significant areas: selecting brides and granting access to land. Choosing one's spouse is a privilege only

---

[1]The following Western and Central African countries will have more than one Demographic and Health Survey: Benin, Burkina Faso, Cameroon, Côte d'Ivoire, Ghana, Guinea, Mali, Niger, Senegal, Nigeria, and Togo.

afforded to a minority of young adults; for most, the parents still decide. To satisfy the principle of exchanging gifts and countergifts with other lineages, elders decide which unions to approve, thus controlling reproduction (Bledsoe & Pison, 1994). Similarly, the distribution of farming land to young adults still depends on the decisions of the elders, who thereby control the production and distribution of wealth as well.

This authority of the elders, although still influential, is not as strong in cities, where the choice of brides is less socially controlled and where part of the production is ensured within the framework of a market economy.

Male Domination Is the Governing Principle in All Social Relations

Generally speaking, African women are considered social "minors" who remain for their entire lives dependent on the men of their lineage and, after marriage, on their husbands and the men of their family of "alliance" (Meillassoux, 1976; Lesthaeghe, Kaufman, & Meekers, 1989). Their indisputable power to give birth, which they exercise for the benefit of their family of origin (matrilineal societies) or, more frequently, for the benefit of their family of "alliance" (patrilineal societies), is strictly controlled. Furthermore, their capacity to produce wealth is also controlled and appropriated by those who have the power to make decisions. Their tenure of the land conceded to them for farming is precarious, and their husbands maintain control over their production (Adjamagbo, 2000). All they are allowed to keep is the possible income from small trade activities or from a plot of land to garden, although this potential revenue is almost always used to feed their children.

Recently, the status of women has improved somewhat in areas of Africa. In cities some women acquire true autonomy, especially if they have been to school. The gradual adoption of contraception in African cities also bears witness to the new decision-making powers of women. Yet generally African women are not affected in any substantial way by these new prospects and still have very little freedom.

The Key Role of Intergenerational Solidarity

In these societies, where the balance between resources and population has always been threatened by a variety of scourges (droughts, cricket invasions, epidemics, epizootic diseases, etc.), the firmly established hierarchy of decision-making powers made it possible to mobilize the production of all the members of a lineage for the survival of the group. The distribution of the goods produced ensured care was provided for the dependents (essentially the elderly, the sick, orphans, and young children).

Deeply rooted in the education of children, in the behaviors of adults, and in religious and magic beliefs, family solidarity remains important in these societies today. It is still very rare to witness the neglect of these customs. This is certainly one of the great strengths of African families, most of which have to cope with extremely precarious conditions.

FUNDAMENTAL SHIFTS IN FAMILY STRUCTURES

Changes in three areas—nuptiality, reproduction, and rules of residence—bear witness to what is happening implicitly or explicitly in the social construction of ideals and standards governing aspirations, roles, and behaviors within families. Although the patriarchal organization of family life and, more widely, of societies is still officially recognized and traditional cultural references persist, they are confronted with new models.

Several factors have combined to bring about this evolution: the progress of a market economy; migrations to cities, which have furthered contacts among different cultures and ethnic groups; education; and the emergence of media in the daily lives of populations, even those living in the most remote areas (via radio). The latter two have introduced new ideas and models from very different societies. The states have also facilitated new modes of organization for communities through the introduction of modern law and, in certain rare cases, through the first attempts at democracy. These changes indirectly challenge certain essential values in the organization of families, such as the primacy of seniority and of ties with the family of origin, over ties with individuals who are not relatives, and, to a lesser degree, the control over women, with their fertility as well as their economic capacity.

Gradually the modern sector of economies and substantive law are promoting the principle of the private appropriation of property and its direct transmission from one of the parents to his or her son or daughter instead of transmission according to lineage rules. Meanwhile, Christian religions, modern literature, and television and other media expose Africans to situations in which marriages are established by individuals and not according to family strategies. Finally, the isolation of urban migrants increased economic problems and the focus on strategies of promotion within a "smaller" family, especially among these city migrants, call into question the traditional duties owed to the elders.

Nuptiality, the First Sign of Change

A Significant Increase in Age at First Union among City Dwellers.   In Western and Central African societies, women tend to get married young to men who are older and sometimes who are even married because of polygynous unions. Marriage, which is more an alliance between two families than the free union of two individuals, constitutes the basis of new family units. It is a long-term process with successive stages in which exchanges are made between the two family groups forming the alliance. Such an alliance is often marked by reciprocity[2] and the giving of a bride-wealth by the husband's family. Unions are generally soon followed by a birth, which actually seals the union. Although this model of marriage has not changed in any statistically significant way, it is beginning to shift in a manner that suggests greater changes are underway. According to the most recent surveys, the proportion of young women already married at 18 has declined in all the countries for which we are able to compare two periods, except for Burkina Faso. Concerning men, the changes are subtler (Hertrich, 2001). The proportion of men already married at 25 is declining in certain countries (Niger, Senegal, and especially Cameroon) but is remaining almost stable in others (Côte d'Ivoire and Mali) and is increasing in Ghana (Table 3.1).

Increases in school enrollment for young men and women mean that new stages intervene in family formation. Age at first marriage, and thus age at first birth, is increasing for young women. For young men the change is not homogeneous (Hertrich & Locoh, 1999; Thiriat, 1998). In certain towns age at first union of young men is actually declining, but this is not the case among all categories and in all countries, particularly those in which economic crisis has made it difficult for young men to enter the labor market or start a family (Antoine et al., 2001). Even in urban settings, the tradition of bride-wealth is still widely practiced and acts as a restraint on formal unions. In

---

[2]It is the exchange of women between lineages over a long period which regulates, at a given moment, the union of two individuals more than their personal choice (Levi-Strauss, 1956).

TABLE 3.1

Proportions of Women Married before 18 (Among Women Aged 20–24); Proportions of Men Married before 25 (Among Men Aged 30–34)

Country	Years of Observation	% Married before 18, per 100 Women Aged 20–24		% Married before 25, per 100 Men Aged 30–34	
		Before 1996	After 1996	Before 1996	After 1996
Burkina Faso	1992/1993 and 1998/1999	62	62		
Cameroon	1991 and 1998	58	43	66	49
Côte d'Ivoire	1994 and 1998/1999	44	33	41	40
Ghana	1988 and 1998	41	36	44	51
Guinea	1992 and 1999	67	65		
Mali	1995 and 2001	70	65	46	47
Niger	1992 and 1998	84	77	78	65
Nigeria	1990 and 1999	52	40		
Senegal	1992/1993 and 1997	48	36	28	24
Togo	1988 and 1998	44	31		

Note. Source: Demographic and Health Survey (DHS), 1988–2001.

cities, many more young women currently benefit from a period of adolescence and celibacy before marriage, since they marry later. Over a period of 7 to 8 years during the 1990s, the mean age at first union of women aged 25–29 substantially increased in Senegal, Mali, Burkina Faso, Cameroon and Côte d'Ivoire. The change is less marked in Niger and Nigeria (Figure 3.1 and Table 3.2).

In rural areas, although the changes are more moderate, they constitute an upward trend in age at first union (except for in Mali, Niger, and Togo). Figure 3.1 illustrates the recent changes in median age at first union in rural and urban areas in this region of sub-Saharan Africa.[3] In any case, women's age at first union tends to be lower in villages than in cities, which is attributable to educational and social status differentials for women in urban populations.

---

[3]For a complete analysis of nuptiality trends in Africa, see Hertrich (2001).

TABLE 3.2
Married Women Aged 25–29, Median Age at First Union (Urban and Rural Areas)

		Urban Area		Rural Area	
Country	*Years of Observation*	*Before 1994*	*After 1994*	*Before 1994*	*After 1994*
Burkina Faso	1992/1993 and 1998/1999	18	20	17	18
Côte d'Ivoire	1994 and 1998/1999	19	22	18	19
Ghana	1988 and 1998	20	21	18	19
Mali	1987 and 2001	16	19	16	16
Niger	1992 and 1998	16	17	15	15
Nigeria	1990 and 1999	20	21	16	18
Senegal	1992/1993 and 1997	20	23	16	17
Togo	1988 and 1998	20	20	18	18
Cameroon	1991 and 1998	18	20	16	17

Note. Source: DHS, 1987–2001.

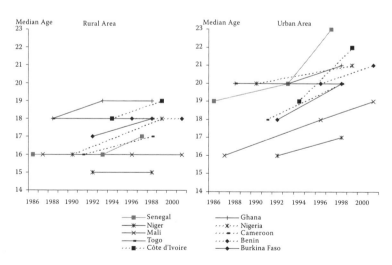

FIGURE 3.1   Median age at first marriage for women (1986–2001).

Older age at first union is only one sign of current changes. Until recently, very few adults in sub-Saharan Africa did not marry, but this is changing in certain cities (Antoine & Nanitelamio, 1990). Informal unions, which often give rise to separations and to the creation of female-centered households, are already quite widespread. Economic crisis has contributed to the emergence and spread of precarious consensual unions—partners may not want to make formal financial commitments to each other or they may find the conventional marriage process, and especially the bride-wealth, too costly.

In Central and Western African cities, where premarital relations are widely tolerated, marriage is quite often preceded by the birth of a child, with each of the future spouses still living with their respective families (Mouvagha-Sow, 2001b, 2002a). These "unions," which are seldom if at all acknowledged by family and community members, are both more easily granted and more fragile. In rural as in urban areas many observers talk of the increasing precariousness of unions (Mouvagha-Sow, 2002a; Thiriat, 1998).

This shift away from traditional and young-age marriages has been accompanied by an upswing in union dissolution through separation or divorce. More pronounced in cities than in rural locales, union dissolution has been affected by increasing independence among women, because they generally take the initiative in the dissolution of the union (Hertrich & Locoh, 1999; Locoh & Thiriat, 1996; Mouvagha-Sow, 2002a). Separations caused by migrations and the greater fragility of "informal" unions are also reasons for the increasing number of dissolutions.

An Initial Decline in Polygyny. Because the increase in age at first union among women is accompanied to a lesser extent by an increase in age at first union among men, Africa has seen a reduction in the gender differential in age at first union (Table 3.3). The marriage age gap is an essential aspect of polygyny. By modifying the numbers of the marriageable population, the reduction in the age difference at marriage will eventually render the practice of polygyny more difficult. The first signs of a decline, which are still very modest, are already being observed. Unsurprisingly, people living in cities are more often in monogamous unions than those in rural areas. The economic crisis, combined with rising expectations among city dwellers for children's education and health care, has made it more difficult for men to support two (or more) families in cities (Hertrich, 2003; Locoh, 2002). A new form of living arrangement is also developing in African cities, that

TABLE 3.3
Age Difference between Men and Women at First Union
(1975–1982 and 1994–1999)

Country	Years of Observation	1975–1982	1993–1999
Burkina Faso	1975[b] and 1999[a]	10.3	7.2
Cameroon	1978[a] and 1998[a]	8.8	6.8
Côte d'Ivoire	1979[c] and 1994[a]	9.3	7.4
Gabon	1993[b]		5.7
Ghana	1979[a] and 1998[a]	6.9	5.7
Mali	1976[b] and 1996[a]	9.7	7.7
Niger	1977[b] and 1999[a]	—	5.5
Nigeria	1981–82[a] and 1999[a]	—	7.6
Senegal	1976[b] and 1997[a]	10.3	9.5
Togo	1981[b] and 1998[a]	7.1	5.3

Note. Source: Hertrich, 2001.
[a]World fertility surveys (before 1985), then Demographic and Health Surveys.
[b]Censuses.
[c]National panel surveys.

of polygyny without co-residence, with each wife having a separate dwelling[4] (Wa Karanja, 1987).

Demographic and Health Surveys (DHS) show, for nine West African countries, the evolution in the proportion of wives in polygynous unions before 1997 (around 1990) and from 1997 forward (Table 3.4). Although the decline is most evident in Ghana, Cameroon, Nigeria, and Togo, still 1 in 3 women in Nigeria and 2 in 5 women in Togo are married to polygynous husbands. And in Guinea, Burkina Faso, and Niger—where fertility has not yet started to decline—we see a slight increase in the proportions of women in polygynous unions.

In fact, polygyny started to decline in Western Africa during the 1980–1990 decade in the countries of the Gulf of Guinea, but it remained stable in the countries of the Sahel region (Hertrich, 2003). These trends have been observed in urban as well as in rural areas.

---

[4]This is reflected in the rather high proportion of female heads of households (see Table 8).

TABLE 3.4

Percent of Married Women in Polygynous Unions: Western and Central Africa

Country	Years of Observation	Percent women in Polygynous Union	
		Before 1997	1997 and After
Benin	1996 and 2001	50	45
Burkina Faso	1993 and 2003	51	48
Cameroon	1991 and 1998	38	33
Côte d'Ivoire	1994 and 1999	38	35
Ghana	1988 and 2003	28	23
Guinea	1992 and 1999	50	54
Mali	1987 and 1998	45	44
Niger	1992 and 1998	36	38
Nigeria	1990 and 1999	41	36
Senegal	1992 and 1997	48	46
Togo	1988 and 1998	52	43

Note. Sources: Demographic and Health Surveys (DHS).

Before the economic crisis, the countries in the Gulf of Guinea had reached a socioeconomic level of development (primarily measured in school attendance of girls) that was higher than the countries of the Sahel region. This resulted in social challenges to the institution of polygyny. This opens a new perspective in the field of matrimonial relations to the benefit of monogamy, even if this recent decline is yet to be confirmed.

Fertility Is Declining, But with Substantial Differentials

During the period from 1960 to 1985, Africa's apparently stable or even increasing fertility rates constantly fueled a debate among specialists: Was African fertility an "exception" that would remain high contrary to the significant declines observed in other developing countries from 1975? It was only in the mid-1980s that the first survey findings showed fertility declines underway in several African countries, although not in Western and Central Africa, where only cities had begun to show a decline.

By conducting comparable surveys over time, DHS provided evidence of fertility declines in most African countries by the end of the 1980s. In Côte d'Ivoire, for example, the total fertility rate (TFR) fell from 7.4 children per woman in 1980–1981 to 5.7 in 1994. In Senegal, the TFR fell from 7.1 children per woman in 1978 and 6.6 in 1986 to 6.0 children per woman in 1992 and 5.7 in 1997. In Ghana, the stability of the 1978–1988 period at around 6.5 children per woman dropped to 4.5 between 1988 and 1998, but between 1998 and 2003 the fertility level remained stable at 4.4 children per woman (see Table 3.5). However, fertility remains relatively low in the countries of the Sahel, such as Mali (6.8 in 2001), Guinea, Burkina Faso, and Niger. And surprisingly, in the 2003 survey in Nigeria, a slight increase in fertility was observed.

However, fertility is still precocious. Fully half of all women give birth to a child before their 18th birthday in Guinea, Niger, and Mali. This is also true of 1 in 3 women in Burkina Faso, Cameroon, and Côte d'Ivoire; of 1 in 4 women in Senegal; and of 1 in 5 women in Ghana and Togo. The proportion of women who have children before the age of 18 has remained stable or has slightly increased in 2 of the 10 countries where there have been at least two surveys since 1987 (Burkina Faso and Mali). However, it has declined in Niger, Nigeria, Senegal, Togo, and Cameroon. Older age at first union is often accompanied by an increase in prenuptial conceptions or births (for Togo, see Thiriat, 1998; for Senegal, see Delaunay, 1994), and other evidence indicates that prenuptial sexuality is becoming more widespread (Mouvagha-Sow, 2002a).

Since the early 1980s, it has been evident that factors contributing to fertility decline are affecting an increasing proportion of Africa's population (Locoh & Hertrich, 1994). Increasing school enrollment of women now entering their mothering age range, improved survival rates among children, rapid urbanization, and improved family planning programs[5] and campaigns to promote them have all had effects on fertility rates (see Table 3.5). Added to these influences, the deep economic crisis leads an increasing number of Africans to realize that big families are a thing of the past.

However, although fertility rates have declined in cities, they have remained rather stable in the countryside (Figure 3.2). In the 12 African surveys (DHS) after 1995, fertility in rural areas never fell below 5 children

---

[5]But also their inefficiency or absence, which results in more frequent illegal abortions (Guillaume, 2003).

TABLE 3.5
Evolution of the Total Fertility Rate (TFR) in Western and Central African Countries Where at Least Two Surveys Have Been Conducted

Country	WFS 1977–1983 Year	TFR	DHS 1987–1990 Year	TFR	DHS 1991–1996 Year	TFR	DHS 1995–2003 Year	Total	TFR Capitals	
Benin	1981–1982	7.1	—	—	1996–	6.3	2001	5.6	Cotonou	3.4
Burkina Faso	—	—	—	—	1993	6.9	2003	5.9	Ouagadougou	3.1
Cameroon	1978	6.3	—	—	1991	5.8	1998	4.8	Douala, Yaoundé	3.1
Côte d'Ivoire	1980–1981	7.4	—	—	1994	5.3	1998	5.2	Abidjan	3.4
Ghana	1979–1980	6.5	1988	6.4	1993	5.5	2003	4.4	District Accra	2.9
Guinea	—	—	—	—	1992	5.7	1999	5.5	Conakry	4.0
Mali	—	—	1987	6.9	—	—	2001	6.8	Bamako	4.7
Niger	—	—	—	—	1992	7.4	1998	7.2	Niamey	5.2
Nigeria	1981–1982	5.9	1990	6.0	1999	4.7	2003	5.7	Lagos	
Senegal	1978	7.1	1986	6.6	1992–1993	6.0	1997	5.7	Dakar	3.5
Togo	—	—	1988	6.4	—	—	1998	5.4	Lomé	2.9

Note. TFR is calculated for the period of 1 to 59 months preceding the survey.
Source: World Fertility Survey (WFS) and Demographic and Health Surveys (DHS).

56

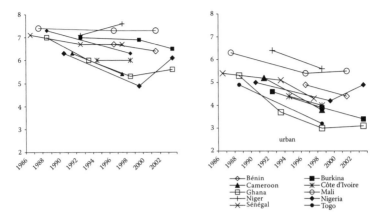

FIGURE 3.2   Evolution of the total fertility rate (TFR) in Western and Central African countries (where at least two surveys have been conducted).

per woman. The latest DHS data show that rural fertility is more than 7 children per woman in 2 countries and between 6 and 7 in 6 countries.

All major cities in the 12 countries studied are currently experiencing fertility decline, with urban fertility rates above 5 children per woman only in 3 of the 12 countries studied. This urban–rural differential reflects the progress in education, the decline in child mortality, and new family ideals found in cities. It also translates the problems families have, due to their higher expectations for their children, which leads to them revising their traditional ideals in favor of high fertility. In cities, people have greater access to family planning services and other facilities, such as schools and health centers, that encourage new behaviors. In cities, adults are also better educated on average, women are more independent, and the media more broadly disseminates information and ideas.

In the capital cities of Accra and Lomé, for example, the average fertility is less than 3 children per woman; in Douala and Yaoundé it is about 3 children; and in Abidjan, Cotonou, and Dakar it seems to be approaching this rate as well (Table 3.5). In the space of one generation the capitals of countries in the coastal region have largely begun their fertility transition, whereas the capital cities of the Sahel region are only at the beginning of the process. African cities are very diverse in terms of assigned population categories. It is therefore highly likely that fertility rates among urban areas will evolve differently according to social category and level of schooling.

From Birth Spacing to Birth Limitation? Given family pressure to reproduce, women's minority status, and a general lack of contraception services, many African women have few means to limit their fertility. Their room for maneuver was and still is, for many of them, limited to a postpartum period during which they are able to refuse to resume sexual relations too soon (Page & Lesthaeghe, 1981).

However, although the early manifestations of fertility control were essentially attempts to increase spacing between births, current fertility surveys started to reveal the desire to limit number of births, a new and still marginal aspiration in African societies. The proportion of women with three living children who reported their preference to stop at that number passed from 14% in 1988 to 36% in 1998 in Ghana and almost doubled in Togo during the same period, whereas it remained stable and even declined in the countries of the Sahel and in Cameroon (Table 3.6). Although the desire to have many children is not as widespread as 20 or 30 years ago, the preferred number remains at four or more in many areas. Today, increasing the time between births, either through traditional means or the use of contraception or even abortion (Desgrées du Lou, Msellati, Viho, & Welffens-Ekra, 1999; Guillaume, 2003), remains the primary means of regulating fertility.

**Modes of Residence, the Expression
of Daily Family Life**

In Africa today, many large families cohabit in compounds, or courtyards, under the authority of the older family members, but this is no longer the only model. Cities propose different residential models: dwellings that are not spacious enough to house large households and even smaller "bed-sits" for poor households, for migrants who do not yet have a family, or for elderly people whose children have left home. DHS data include a number of indicators on household living arrangements. Households usually comprise a family unit, but they may also include distant relatives or unrelated individuals who share with cohabitants the kind of solidarity generally found within a family unit (Table 3.1).

Persistence of "Extended" Households. Table 3.1 indicates the rather large average size of African households, and the rural–urban

TABLE 3.6
Women with Three Living Children Who Do Not Want to Have More

Country	Years	Want No More Children		TFR Around 1998
		Around 1990	Around 1998	
Benin	1996 and 2001	14.0	14.6	6.0
B-Faso	1993 and 2003	12.0	14.0	6.8
Cameroon	1991 and 1998	7.5	9.8	5.2
Ghana	1988 and 2003	13.7	34.1	4.5
Guinea	1992 and 1999	10.8	12.8	5.5
Mali	1987 and 1996	14.6	10.6	6.7
Niger	1992 and 1999	5.8	4.8	7.5
Nigeria	1990 and 1999	8.8	11.0	5.2
Senegal	1992 and 1997	9.0	9.1	5.7
Togo	1988 and 1998	13.6	22.0	5.4

Note. Sources: Demographic and Health Surveys (DHS).

size differentials. Although Senegal (with 9.5 people per household in rural areas and 8.2 in urban areas) and Ghana (with 3.8 and 3.3, respectively) have the pole positions on the household size scale, most countries have averages between 4.5 and 6.0 persons per household. Single householders are no longer a rarity, except in rural areas of the Sahel (2.9% in Burkina Faso, 1.7% in Senegal, 4.1% in Niger), and one encounters them more often in town than in the country. Here again Ghana distinguishes itself, with almost a third of urban households and a quarter of rural households with one person only.

Toward a Nuclear Family? A concern of studies on African families in the years following independence was changing household and family structures. Specifically, researchers wondered when a nuclear family model—that is, a couple and their children living together (without others) under one roof—would emerge. Many posited that the Westernizing of attitudes and habits would progress rapidly in African societies, leading to the spread of nuclear-unit households, at least in

---

[6]For a detailed assessment about the "nuclearization theory" of the African families, see Cordell and Pichè (1997).

TABLE 3.7
Typology of Households in Togo (%), According to Place of Residence, 2000

Composition of Household	Type of Household	Place of Residence		Sex of Head of Household (HH)		Total
		Rural	Urban	Men	Women	
HH* + children	(1) Single-parent household	7.7	7.8	2.2	26.4	7.7
HH + children + others	(2) Extended single-parent household	10.8	17.8	2.4	50.2	13.5
HH + wife(wives) + children	(3) Monogamous household	25.3	20.3	30.4	0.2	23.4
	(4) Polygynous household	8.7	2.4	8.2	0	6.2
HH + wife(wives) + children + others	(5) Extended monogamous household	27.2	36.8	39.8	1.2	30.9
	(6) Extended polygynous household	11.5	5.6	12.0	0	9.3
	(7) Nonfamily (collective) household	6.5	7.2	3.0	19.2	6.8
	(8) Single householder	2.3	2.1	2.0	2.8	2.2
		100	100	100	100	100
	Number of households	1709	1064	2133	640	2773

Note. Source: URD, DGSCN (2002).
HH, head of household.

cities (Goode, 1963).[6] The statistics available for the last 40 years have demonstrated that this has not been the case; living arrangements still vary greatly. There are "nuclear households" in Africa, but they represent a minority. As a general rule, families have continued to prefer the living arrangement of the extended family, or a family nucleus housing a variable number of dependents, young or elderly. Although it is true that rural compounds with several dozen persons are no longer the most widespread living arrangement, courtyard dwellings where several family nuclei live and share the same facilities still exist even in bigger cities such as Bamako, Lomé, or Cotonou.

A recent survey conducted in Togo illustrates the distribution of household types. Nuclear households, in the strictest sense of the term (i.e., a monogamous couple with children but without other dependents), represent about a quarter of all households (line 3 in Table 3.7), but if one includes the households that do include other dependents (line 5 in Table 3.7), the proportion jumps to more than half. Households in which the head is polygynous make up 15% (line 4 plus line 6), and 20% of households among those headed by a man.

TABLE 3.8

**Proportion (%) of Women among Heads of Households
According to Place of Residence, Around 1999**

Country	Year of Observation	Rural	Urban
Benin	2001	19.3	23.5
Burkina Faso	2003	7.5	16.5
Cameroon	1998	20.7	19.9
Côte d'Ivoire	1998/99	13.3	16.1
Gabon	2000	25.4	26.2
Ghana	1998	35.4	34.9
Ghana	2003	28.9	39.7
Guinea	1999	10.8	17.8
Mali	2001	10.7	13.2
Niger	1998	12.9	15.5
Nigeria	1999	16.2	18.0
Senegal	1997	13.1	19.7
Togo	1998	22.1	29.9

Note. Source: DHS surveys.

Households headed by a single person (lines 1 and 2) are widespread at about 20% of all households, and are overwhelmingly female headed. Gabon's proportion of extended monogamous households—or nuclear family households that include other dependents such as brothers and sisters, nephews and nieces, or even the grandchildren of the head of the household or of his spouse (Mouvagha-Sow, 2003)—is similar at 29%. A detailed analysis of the 1987 Cameroonian census led to similar findings (Wakam, 1997).

TABLE 3.9
Proportion (%) of Children Aged under 15 Fostered in Rural and Urban Areas

Country	Year	Urban	Rural
Benin	1996	31.2	23.4
Burkina Faso	1992	26.8	19.7
Cameroon	1998	23.7	21.8
Côte d'Ivoire	1994	25.7	26.4
Ghana	1998	14.9	16.1
Guinea	1999	35.5	26.5
Mali	1996	20.2	13.5
Niger	1998	22.2	23.2
Senegal	1993	28.1	35.0
Togo	1998	26.9	23.1

Note. Source: DHS surveys.

Female Heads of Households.   In this region of Africa a substantial percentage of women report that they are "heads of households" (HOH) in surveys and censuses (Table 3.8). This status is strongly linked to marital status—many of the HOH women are separated, widowed, or divorced—and is most common in the large cities of the coastal countries. This status is also partly explained by the new forms of polygyny in which each co-spouse lives separately.

But the female HOH model also exists in rural areas. In Ghana, for instance, in 1998, it was as widespread in the country as it is in town (one-third of households are headed by women, Table 3.8), but in 2003, again a differential occurs between rural and urban settings. Here again migration plays a part, in this case the migration of the men who leave a spouse and children behind, often to keep the right to use a piece of land. The remarkable capacity shown by increasing numbers of these women without a husband and their economic independence suggest that women-headed households will become more widespread, and that children will be increasingly in the care of their mothers, whether or not these women are assisted by their husbands or partners.

Management of the Dependents, a Family Issue. Until recently, caring for children was rarely considered the exclusive responsibility of the biological parents. Grandparents, uncles and aunts, older siblings, and other members of the lineage have traditionally taken a role in looking after children through the system of fosterage. Fostering children within the kinship group has always been an important means of coping with health crises and of protecting children whose parents have died, and it has become especially crucial with the AIDS epidemic. The grandparents, but also the uncles and aunts and older brothers and sisters, are the first to take in the orphans. However, the circulation of the children among related households is not limited to the exigency of parental sickness or death (Vandermeersch, 2002). Rather, it is a common practice for incorporating children within their larger lineage family (Table 3.9). For example, in Senegal, in 1993, among children under the age of 15, 28% in urban areas and 35% in rural areas were put into the care of a household other than that of their biological parents (Vandermeersch, 2000). This practice makes it possible to distribute the demographic weight of the descendants of a lineage, but it attenuates the personalization of the relations between biological parents and their children as it diminishes the responsibility of parents. This circulation of children has always been favored as an apprenticeship to living within a large family group. For some children it is an apprenticeship to work and to the indifference of adults. For others it is an opportunity to receive, in town, better schooling than if they stay with their rural family. Fostering of children is widely practiced to improve children's access to education, but also, it should be noted, it is sometimes practiced to provide unpaid labor to members of a kinship group. More and more now, people are speaking up against this practice, which is often simply a way of exploiting child labor.

African families take in young adults as well as children. A survey conducted in 1999 in Libreville (Gabon), for example, found that two-thirds of young people aged 20 to 35 were living as "dependents," with half of this group living in households headed by adults other than their biological parents. This practice of placing young adults in the care of other households occurred more frequently in middle-class neighborhoods than in poor and rich areas (Mouvagha-Sow, 2003). At the other end of the life course, this framework of family solidarity often ensures care for elderly persons. These elders may receive support because they are still in control as the heads of households, or simply because they have become dependent and must rely on their family in the near absence of any institutional care or state pension.[7] Although some elderly people live alone,[8] it is much more common that they have one or more of their children, grandchildren, or other relatives with them to provide subsistence. In these societies, where elders are respected and social conventions highly favor family-based old-age support, the elderly may almost always count on their families to provide for them at the end of their lives. This solidarity has so far been easily provided thanks to the age structure of populations, in which only 5 to 8% of people are over the age of 60. Even if fertility is declining, as one may predict, population aging remains a distant prospect in these areas of Africa, and the demographic dependency ratios between adults and elderly people will remain favorable for a few more decades to come (Locoh & Makdessi, 2002).

THE FUTURE OF AFRICAN FAMILIES

During the first 20 postcolonial years in sub-Saharan Africa, expected changes in family structures were largely unrealized. No obvious preference was shown for the "nuclear" family or for limiting fertility, in spite of increased school enrollment and access to employment in the modern sector and increased access to modern means of information. The change was there, in the making, but imperceptible as far as family behaviors were concerned. It took the combined effects of this real social improvement and the economic crisis in Africa for new behaviors to emerge (Coussy & Vallin, 1996).

Multiple Causes for the Weakening of Old Models

For most African societies, essentially rural societies, the pace of social change accelerated during the 20th century and especially since their

---

[8]Ghana is an exception. The proportion of persons aged over 65 living alone increased from 10 to 23% between 1988 and 1998 (Locoh & Makdessi, 2002).

independence, with some obvious effects on unions and fertility. We now explore factors that have contributed to these changes and how Western and Central African societies may evolve in the coming decades.

Mortality Decline and the AIDS Challenge.   At first, real progress was made in improving population health and a greater number of children survived into adulthood, modifying the pace of population growth. Reducing child mortality is an important factor in the evolution of desired fertility and therefore in family size. As parents increasingly realize that their children have improved chances of survival, their preference for many children declines.

Unfortunately the AIDS epidemic came along, fundamentally changing union formation decisions (Pisani, 1998; Desgrées du Lou, 2000) and relations between spouses, and ravaging many families—thus jeopardizing the new balances that were emerging. Young people are obliged to take AIDS into account in their sexual and family relations. Given the problems encountered by young people in openly talking about sex with their parents or with their partners, much is left unsaid concerning AIDS, and this weighs heavily on the establishment of partner relationships where the patriarchal hangovers of male domination are far from vanishing (Hassoun, 1997). Relations between men and women, individually and collectively, are durably affected by the existence of the epidemic.

New Modes of Production, Migration, and Urbanization.   The development of the market economy and the establishment of central administrations for the new states have considerably favored urban growth. Urban elites have emerged and started to adopt new lifestyles. Market economy production modes have given a very small minority of workers access to regular income independent from their "elders," contrary to when they cultivated the land of their lineage. Cities have attracted rural populations, notably young educated people in search of employment, who have been exposed to new models of family structures and who have found themselves less directly "controlled" by the elders in their families. For them, solidarities concerning the parents and alliances have become less constraining even though they remain the norm to be respected. For women, in particular, even when they are illiterate, the city provides alternative models of family structures, and what was an "absolute" is now seen in "relative" terms.

Although urban development leads to an increasing diversification in family structures and in the behaviors that condition them, these changes do not necessarily constitute a break with rural societies from which most city dwellers originate. Families in cities still inherit family models from a past life in rural communities confronted with high mortality and the need to manage production means for family survival. However, these urban families also adopt the many innovations required by new urban living conditions and the political, social, and economic changes that have occurred over the last 40 years and have greatly changed African societies.

Education, an Undeniable Motor for Change. School attendance, which has constantly increased since independence, has produced new generations of literate adults who are better equipped to participate in the new market economies and who also harbor new aspirations and demands for themselves and their children (Table 3.10).

The majority of people in cities can now read and write—fewer women than men, but this gap is narrowing. In Ghana, UNESCO (2003) estimated that 91% of young people aged 15 to 24 could read and write in 2000. Central African countries (Cameroon and Congo) are in practically the same situation. The countries of the Sahel region are the ones that are lagging behind with the most glaring gender inequalities. In Niger in 2000, only 32% of men and 14% of women aged 15 to 24 could read and write. From 1990 to 2000, although literacy rates vary greatly among countries, all show progress reflecting increased efforts in education, in spite of the economic crisis during this decade. Much remains to be done to improve the quality of teaching and to reduce inequalities between boys and girls, but the progress is there and has been fueled by the decisions of often uneducated parents to send their children to school. Education, even if it is of poor quality, offers new prospects for children. It introduces them to different models of marriage and family structures and changes their aspirations for themselves and their children. In particular, education may increase their understanding and use of birth control, including contraception (Lloyd et al., 2000).

Imported Models. Imported models of family structures are found in the media. The radio is an especially important source of information and, although television is not yet common in rural areas, it is widely watched in cities. Many serials, films, and plays are shown on television, not to mention the information on family planning that is broadcast by an increasing number of national broadcasters. According to

---

[9]Translated as, "The image of romantic love widely disseminated by cinema and television has contributed to profoundly modified representations of love."

TABLE 3.10

Proportion of Young People Aged 15 to 24 Able to Read and Write, Western and Central Africa

Country	Percent Boys 1990	Percent Boys 2000	Percent Girls 1990	Percent Girls 2000	Total 1990	Total 2000
Benin	56.6	70.5	24.7	36.0	40.4	53.1
Burkina Faso	35.7	45.8	14.0	24.9	34.6	
Cameroon	86.0	92.0	75.9	88.0	81.1	90.0
Congo	95	98	90	97	93	97
Côte d'Ivoire	65	71	40	52	53	62
Ghana	88	94	75	89	82	91
Liberia	75	85	39	53	57	69
Mali	38	47	17	25	28	36
Niger	25	32	9	14	17	23
Nigeria	81	87	67	84	74	87
RCA	66	76	39	59	52	67
Senegal	50	60	30	42	40	51
Togo	79	87	48	64	64	76

Note. Source: UNESCO (2003).

Anne Attané (2003, p. 188), *"l'image de l'amour romantique largement diffusée au cinéma et à la télévision a contribué à modifier en profondeur les représentations du sentiment amoureux"[9]* in Mossi society in Burkina Faso, a remark that could be applied to other societies in the subregion. Television viewing has a particularly strong impact on city dwellers, many of whom are young people who aspire to greater social and sexual freedoms. In rural areas, the dissemination of new models is slower in coming but has been helped along by recent migrations that create close contacts between neo-urbanites and people in rural areas.

At the time of independence, many states expressed their modernity by promulgating family laws inspired by the former colonial powers. Registration of marriages and births was rendered mandatory, although the implementation was somewhat disorganized. Marriage law (and its effects on spouses and children) was defined, including in most countries the polygynous option. But the structuring effect of modern family law remains rather weak because it only applies to a small part of the population and the majority remains ignorant of it. Customary law cohabits with modern law in this region of Africa, and village procedures still take precedence in most cases.

Providing opportunities for social exchange, religious, humanitarian, and neighborhood associations may be crucial in the elaboration of new concepts concerning family roles and the sharing of rights and duties (Mbow, 1997). Some women's associations are starting to play a significant role in changing marriage practices in favor of freedom of choice for women, the sharing of family decisions, greater economic independence, and respect between spouses (Adjamagbo-Johnson, 1999).

The Influence of Religions. For some time now in sub-Saharan Africa, traditional religions have coexisted with the imported religions of Christianity and Islam. Traditional religious beliefs are based on the worship of ancestors, who are also revered as the intercessors to the gods or the Supreme Being (Mawu in the Benin Gulf). Ancestor worship still holds pride of place. It supports the notion of respect due to the elders and of standards of solidarity for individuals toward their family group. Imported models have gradually been added without any antinomy regarding underlying beliefs. Islam, the religion imported earliest on, does not contradict ancestor worship. Regarding inheritance, Islam represents a theoretical improvement in gender inequality because under the Islamic system women are allowed to inherit up to half what men inherit, whereas in African lineage societies they do not have the right to inherit at all. However, regarding marriage, Islam reinforces inequalities in relations between men and women because it allows, as in traditional societies, the practice of polygyny and encourages the segregation of women in the home.

The Catholic and Protestant churches promote the model of the family based on a lasting marriage and spouses remaining faithful to each other. Among elite groups in cities in the coastal region, who long ago converted to Christianity, this model had, and still has, some influence, but men find it difficult to renounce the prerogatives offered by polygyny (Clignet, 1987; Donadjè, 1992). Very recently, polygyny has shown signs of weakening, and it is likely that this change in polygyny owes more to economic constraint than to an ideological or religious "conversion." Thus, the ideals transmitted by imported religions have direct consequences on family life.

In recent years, established Christian churches and, to a lesser degree, Islam have been challenged by the rapidly growing sectarian and fundamentalist movements in many countries. The evangelical churches of Anglo-American inspiration, in particular the Pentecostal movements, have been spreading since the 1980s in most African cities. They claim to provide possible solutions through the practices of healing and exorcism to the growing problems encountered by city-dwellers. They offer their followers the possibility of finding "a new family" in the church, and set out strict precepts concerning marriage (e.g., marriage by mutual consent, monogamy, fidelity, indissolubility of marriage, condemnation of conjugal violence) and leisure activities (e.g., no consumption of alcohol or tobacco, no going to the cinema or night clubs) (Laurent, 2003). These churches also promote self-fulfillment and material success (Dubresson & Raison, 2003). However, the freedom to choose a spouse is relative among the young "brothers and sisters in prayer" of the evangelical churches, because the pastors serve as intermediaries and may oppose certain "candidatures" (Laurent, 2003).

Some young women in rural areas of Burkina Faso, wanting to escape their arranged marriages, have sought refuge with the Catholic mission or with the pastor of an evangelical church (Attané, 2003). It is probable that an increasing number of people will seek refuge in these churches, especially women disappointed by an unhappy union and hoping to find a more ideal partner there. However, given the demanding nature of the ideals and precepts advocated by these new religions, one may assume that the number of converts will remain a minority.

As for African Islam, it has shown real evidence of tolerance so far. But since the 1980s, in places where Islam was already well established, Islam is being influenced by fundamentalism imported from Saudi Arabia, Iran, and Libya, who finance the construction of mosques and the sale of audio and video cassettes (Schmitz, 2000). At the political level, this increased influence is visible. For example, in Nigeria since January 2000, 11 of 36 states have adopted the Sharia—the Islamic law that draws no distinction between religious and secular life.[10] In other countries, part of the population—often young and a minority so far—display their Muslim identity and demand the strict application of the Koran. This is the case in Senegal with the *Ibadou Rahmane,* who claim to belong to Wahhabism, a fundamentalist Islamic movement imported from Saudi Arabia, and who impose the wearing of the veil and strict sexual control on women.

In the structural crisis of African economies and even more so where political unrest and civil wars upset daily life, significant numbers of

---

[10]For example, two women have recently been threatened with stoning for adultery.

people have sought refuge in religion. The need for some kind of hope gives rise to a variety of offerings, where charlatans and confidence tricksters as well as genuine devotees are to be found. Family ideals are among the things that are called into question by new religious movements.

The Effects of Impoverishment. During the first two decades of independence (1960–1980), African societies benefited from real progress, primarily in health and education improvements made by the young states. But since then, structural adjustment programs and the economic crisis[11] have compromised prospects for further progress and have dashed the hopes of implementing wide-ranging welfare policies. Increasingly, families are obliged to cover the costs of schooling, health care, and even job creation themselves via mutual assistance within the family. The drastic reduction in the standard of living of families has undermined the optimism inspired by independence.

Today's young people, and especially girls, are more educated than their parents. However, they are also entering adult life during a particularly difficult period from a macroeconomic standpoint, and must confront unemployment and job instability, affordable housing shortages, and poor access to health care. Some are neo-urbanites, having swapped the minimum food security offered by a rural environment for the insecurity of "informal jobs." Evidence indicates that boys and girls are beginning to delay marriage, by choice or out of constraint, but not always childbirth, which has resulted in an increase in prenuptial births with the accompanying uncertainties. The combination of development factors (education, urbanization, and access to information) and the constraints of poverty have called into question traditional family models. Marriage practices and fertility are inevitably affected (Lesthaeghe, 1989b). Individuals, caught in the crisis, are sometimes obliged to obey new rules, with much less support than before from their families.

Which Family Models for the 21st Century?

During the 45 years since the independences, family structures have changed significantly in these African nations, but not always in ways anticipated by outside observers. Union formation remains largely under the control, at least symbolically, of the head of the family, polygyny resisted for a long time, and although fertility is starting to decline in certain settings, it still allows large families to predominate (see

---

[11]Not to mention the devaluation of the CFA Franc in French-speaking African countries in 1994.

earlier discussion). As far as daily life within the family is concerned, the nuclear family is not yet a reality. Instead of the expected adoption of models from the North, there was a diversification of family models, recompositions borrowed from different ideological systems. They are sometimes expressed in the new attitudes of the young, but more often in daily family behaviors: entry into unions, attitudes concerning fertility, and living arrangements. The patriarchal and lineage model of the traditional family is gradually being replaced by less rigid family living arrangements that provide more room for individual aspirations, which has had the strongest effect on young people and women. Family solidarities are preserved but essentially for the benefit of the closest relatives. Unions are marked by greater fragility. Stronger partner relationships are emerging, but they are still a small minority.

Erosion of Intergenerational Solidarities. In self-subsistence rural societies, family solidarities operate within the framework of the co-residence of generations and the indispensable participation of all age groups in production. When people depart from this production system, which often occurs in big cities, family solidarity continues[12] more under a mode of "voluntary" constraint (backed up by psychological and magic–religious coercion) than through a hierarchical organization of the distribution of goods and products. For a long time, family solidarity and sometimes community support made up for the absence of a generalized welfare system. During the past 15 years, however, with the economic crisis and the impoverishment of populations, the limits of this solidarity became apparent in certain contexts.

Although families still tend to give great respect and old-age support to their senior members, several factors may contribute in coming years to a change in this system of family support for elderly persons, either because the economic crisis will dramatically reduce their children's means, or because the migration of adults will have depopulated disinherited regions. Moreover, the AIDS epidemic has required many elderly people to give care to their children and their grandchildren.

Part of the population cannot count on family support (e.g., single householder women with children, young school dropouts or the "qualified unemployed," street kids, young women forced into prostitution). Thus increasing numbers of people, especially in urban areas, try to survive by developing all sorts of activities, generally informal, and establishing new networks disconnected from their family or community. This is evidence of

---

[12]The economy of affection referred to by Francois-Regis Mahieu (1997).

the start of a process leading to greater independence from the extended family, often under the constraint of necessity. New "fraternities" have emerged within evangelical churches, Islamic associations, and Freemasons (Marie, 1997, 2002), but also in the form of gangs of abandoned street children, which was, until recently, a rare occurrence in African cities.

However, even if the system of intergenerational support does not apply to everyone, the tenets of family solidarity are rarely explicitly called into question. It is likely that family solidarity will persist in Africa, but perhaps it will focus increasingly on the immediate family or adopt different forms. For example, in relatively affluent urban areas of Gabon, many people prefer to send money to their families in lieu of fostering children (Mouvagha-Sow, 2003). And when resources are scarce, assistance for education is often concentrated on those children showing the most promise, to the detriment of the others (and often of the girls) (Bledsoe, 1994).

Increasing Independence of the Young. Changes in intergenerational dependence and erosion of traditional control over marriage have been accelerated by migration to cities. In rural areas this control continues to weigh heavily, but in town, even in multigenerational households, young people are exhibiting signs of independence. Young women are entering into unions later, and an adolescent phase is emerging. This time allows young people, and especially young women, to build a self-identity by experiencing a period between childhood and adulthood conducive to consolidating their independence. The greater their independence, the more likely it is that they will want to participate in decisions concerning them, such as marriage and contraceptive use in marriage. For young men, access to nonfamily jobs could contribute to individualization in the face of traditional family imperatives.

The reduction in the age gap between spouses at first marriage could well be a sign of changes in couple relations. The age gap has contributed to ensuring male preeminence, by reinforcing it with seniority, and a declining gap may signal greater parity and closeness between spouses. Also, the decline in family control over union formation may favor love matches. Although parents are still consulted by their children, their advice or injunctions concerning unions are not as binding. In Togo, for example, in 1988, 75% of women said they chose their spouse by themselves, of which 62% indicate that they also asked for parents' agreement (Thiriat, 1998). In Mauritania, approximately 50% of

---

[13]Source: ONS Mauritanie and ORC Macro (2001).

women declared to have made a personal choice of their spouse,[13] and 90% of Gabonese women said they chose their spouse independently (Mouvagha-Sow, 2001a, 2002a). In Mali, qualitative studies about marriage procedures show that family control is also becoming more flexible, even in a context of remote villages (Bwa area) very marginally affected by cultural and economic change (Hertrich, 1996).

This increase in the number of marriages by mutual consent has also been observed in qualitative surveys in Burkina Faso (Attané, 2003; Laurent, 2003), including rural areas where *"le désir d'émancipation du pouvoir des aînés et l'aspiration à une plus grande autonomie se focalisent d'abord autour du libre choix du conjoint"*[14] (Laurent, 2003, p. 96).

The Hesitant Emergence of Cohesive Couples. Even if more unions are chosen freely, sociocultural standards persist that define the pool of potential spouses. Ethnic endogamy, although decreasing, continues in Gabon (Mouvagha-Sow, 2001a, 2002a), and remains very high in Togo (Thiriat, 1998) and in Cameroon (Kuépié, 2002). Family endogamy also exists in certain countries, such as Mauritania, where 68% of unions are interfamily marriages (ONS Mauritanie & ORC Macro, 2001). With the increase in marriages motivated by love, however, some forms of homogamy are developing.

Evidence suggests that young couples are increasingly seeking emotional fulfillment in marriage and lifestyle, and have higher aspirations for their children. Generally, these couples are among educated young city-dwellers representing what might be termed an emerging middle class. They adopt precise objectives for their children concerning health care, education, and career prospects, and these aspirations, occurring in a context of economic uncertainty, motivate them to limit the number of children they have. It is among this group of educated young urbanites that the highest rates of convergence of opinions and behaviors are found concerning fertility. They feel the need for modern contraception, have better access to it, and tend to use it judiciously to limit fertility. Fertility levels attained in Western and Central African capitals (2.9 children per woman in Lomé, 3.1 in Yaoundé and Doula, 3.4 in Abidjan, and 2.7 in the district of Accra) reflect changes mainly due to this section of the population. As revealed in the last DHS survey in Ghana (Andro & Hertrich, 2001), Ghanaian couples are increasingly in agreement about limiting fertility and in their aspirations for their children. This evolution

---

[14]"The desire to be freed from the control of the elders and the aspiration toward greater independence is focused first on the choosing of a spouse."

differs with the countries of the Sahel region, however, where there is very little agreement between spouses and where only the males play a determining role in whether or not couples use contraception. The more cohesive African couples are often found among groups converted to Christianity, which value this type of family model. Because the number that subscribe to this new family model is small, and because the model is very different from that governing previous generations and much of the current rural population, it is too early to speculate on how widely the model will be adopted. But the changing aspirations of the young for themselves and their children, as well as economic problems, may foster the emergence of this new family model. A third factor, the promotion of greater equality in gender relations, may play an ambiguous role. When women's search for equality is accepted by their partners it may lead to greater cohesion between them. When challenged it will probably produce the opposite effect and may lead to union disruptions.

New Gender Roles and More Fragile Unions. The issue of the freedom of individual choices concerns relations not only between elder and younger family members but also between men and women. The evolution of certain male and female roles is fed by social and economic challenges to traditional values as well as by models imported from other societies and disseminated by the media (Locoh, 1993, 1996). Men see their traditional dominant role challenged by the economic problems that may deprive them of gainful activity, and thereby destabilize their social and family positions (Silberschmidt, 1991).

The dynamics of gender relations have direct consequences at every level on the social organization of production and reproduction (Kritz, Makinwa-Adebusoye, & Gurak, 2000). Gender systems play a role at the individual level concerning reproductive strategies, and at the societal level in the reproductive models promoted or sanctioned. Negotiation between spouses about the number of children wanted is closely dependent on family structure and gender relations and will be decisive in this period of transition and change in family aspirations (Bankole, 1995; Andro, 2000; Andro & Hertrich, 2001). The incipient fertility decline suggests, in spite of strong resistance on the part of the patriarchal culture, that women will win new marital decision-making powers. Women have already improved their position in the area of production, which has enabled many of them to gain freedom of movement, and even to set up separate residences, a situation that differs greatly from other developing countries. Women are dominated within the framework of patriarchal African societies and at the same time extremely resourceful in ensuring the survival of their families, very often without the help of their spouses. The tradition of polygyny has taught women not to count on their spouses and to provide for their children if necessary.

The redefining of gender roles also has an impact on the care of the children. With a decline in the control of more distant relatives, the education of children is increasingly becoming the prerogative of the biological parents. There is reason to believe that a decline in the preference for large families will be accompanied by an increased individualization in child–parent relations. However, increases in separations between couples, in single-parent households, and in family recompositions contribute to a new parent–child distance, in most cases with the father, because women find themselves increasingly obliged to shoulder parental responsibility alone. In a study in Gabon in 1999, it was observed that fewer than half the children lived with both parents, and usually they lived with solely their mother. Men want more children than women do, but seem ill-prepared to shoulder their paternal responsibilities in the case of a dissolution. This situation is aggravated by increasing difficulties in entering the labor market in urban areas (Mouvagha-Sow, 2002b).

Declining numbers of unions established and controlled by families; older ages at first marriage, especially for women; and more direct participation of young people in spousal choice all favor both greater personal commitment in union formation and greater potential for union dissolution. Because of economic problems, an increasing number of young people form consensual unions that are dissolved as quickly as they are formed. The families, less involved in the marriage process, apply less pressure in supporting the continuation of the relationship in the case of a conflict. It is often the women and the children born into these relationships who suffer from this weakening of partnerships.

CONCLUSION

African families have an uncertain future before them. They find themselves at the crossroads, influenced by both strongly rooted traditions concerning marriage, fertility, polygyny, the caring for dependents, and by exposure to new models of independent living, smaller families, and greater egalitarianism between genders and generations, all introducing the first attempts at individualization. What assets will enable young adults to build families able to provide greater stability for their children and more independence for women while still providing security for the elderly? Will they be more at a loss than their predecessors or will they be freer in their initiatives to shake off the weight of the obligations and taboos imposed by tradition? They face their future with the heavy handicap inherited from the international economic disorder that has exploited their societies and the AIDS epidemic that has destabilized their societies. They will also benefit, to a much greater degree than their predecessors, from the increased education, albeit insufficient, for some of their population.

But they will also need the support of public policies implemented by states more keenly aware of their responsibilities. Indeed, in African families, with strong family solidarity and support for dependents and control over their members, standards often respected until now governing solidarity and assistance to dependents have greatly contributed to preserving the social fabric in often disastrous macroeconomic and political situations. It is only in extreme cases (wars and migrations of refugees) that these standards have been swept away. But however effective these traditional family systems may be, they are not able to make up for irresponsible states suffering from recurrent bankruptcy. The collapse of African economies leads to governments abandoning whole areas of responsibilities (public health and education), with individuals and families left to pay for schooling, health care, and often job creation. In the absence of efficient economic and social policies, there is a risk that these family solidarities may collapse under the weight of their burdens (Locoh, 1995). In order to sustain them during these very difficult periods, ambitious and well-informed policies are needed.

Urbanization and improved health care and education have initiated new relations between elder and younger family members, and between husbands and wives. New types of partner relations, and sometimes female heads of households, have led to new preferences for fertility and new aspirations for children. Moreover, increased economic constraints and shortages have developed awareness of the need for improved birth control. The progress brought by growth between 1960 and 1975 and the negative effects of the economic crisis that has worsened since that period have converged to inspire new family models in Africa.

REFERENCES

Adjamagbo-Johnson, K. (1999). Les lois, une expression officielle des rapports de genre. In T. Locoh & N. Koffi (Eds.), *Genre, population et développement en Afrique de l'Ouest*. Abidjan: Fnuap, Ensea, coopération française.

Adjamagbo, A. (2000). Rapports de production et relation de genre dans les sociétés rurales des pays en développement. In T. Locoh & M. Bozon (Eds.),

Rapports de genre et questions de population dans les pays du Sud (pp. 35–51). Paris: INED.

Andro, A. (2000). La maîtrise de la reproduction, un enjeu majeur des rapports de genre. In T. Locoh (Ed.), *Rapports de genre et questions de population dans les pays du Sud* (pp. 95–104). Paris: INED.

Andro, A., & Hertrich, V. (2001). La demande contraceptive au Sahel: Les attentes des hommes se rapprochent-elles de celles de leurs épouses? *Population, 5,* 721–771.

Antoine, P., & Nanitelamio, J. (1990). *La montée du célibat féminin dans les villes africaines, trois cas: Pikine, Abidjan et Brazzaville.* Paris: CEPED.

Antoine, P., Razafindrakoto, M., & Roubaud, F. (2001). Contraints de rester jeunes? Évolution de l'insertion dans trois capitales africaines: Dakar, Yaoundé, Antananarivo. *Autrepart, 18,* 17–36.

Attané, A. (2003). *Cérémonies familiales et mutations des rapports sociaux de sexe, d'âge et de génération. Ouahigouya et sa région, Burkina Faso.* Unpublished doctoral thesis in social Anthropology and ethnology, Marseille, EHESS.

Bankole, A. (1995). Desired fertility and fertility behaviour among the Yoruba of Nigeria: A study of couple preferences and subsequent fertility. *Population Studies, 49*(2), 317–328.

Bledsoe, C. (1994). The social construction of reproductive outcomes: social marginalization in Sub-Saharan Africa. In T. Locoh & V. Hertrich (Eds.), *The onset of fertility transition in Sub-Saharan Africa* (pp. 221–234). Liège: International Union for the Scientific Study of Population.

Bledsoe, C., & Pison, G. (1994). *Nuptiality in Sub-Saharan Africa. Contemporary anthropological and demographic perspectives.* Oxford: Clarendon Press.

Bongaarts, J. (1978). A framework for analysing the proximate determinants of fertility. *Population and Development Review, 3,* 63–102.

Caldwell. (1976). Towards a restatement of fertility transition theory. *Population and Development Review, 2,* 3–4.

Clignet, R. (1987). On dit que la polygamie est morte: Vive la polygamie. In D. Parkin & D. Nyamwaya (Eds.), *Transformations of African marriage* (pp. 199–209). London: International African Seminars.

Cordell, D., & Pichè, V. (1997). Pour une histoire de la famille en Afrique. In M. Pilon, T. Locoh, V. K. Vignikin, & P. Vimard (Eds.), *Ménages et familles en Afrique: Approches des dynamiques contemporaines* (pp. 55–74). Paris: CEPED.

Coussy, J., & Vallin, J. (1996). *Crise et population en Afrique. Crises économiques, programmes d'ajustement et dynamiques démographiques.* Paris: CEPED.

Delaunay, V. (1994). *L'entrée en vie féconde. Expression démographique des mutations socio-économiques d'un milieu rural sénégalais.* Paris: CEPED.

Desgrées Du Lou, A. (2000). Le sida, un révélateur des disparités de genre: en Afrique les femmes affrontées à une multiplicité de risques. In T. Locoh & M. Bozon (Eds.), *Rapports de genre et questions de population II. Genre, population et développement* (pp. 105–116). Paris: INED.

Desgrées du Lou, A., Msellati, P., Viho, I., & Welffens-Ekra, C. (1999). Le recours à l'avortement provoqué à Abidjan: Une cause de la baisse de la fécondité. *Population*, 427–446.

Diop, A.-B. (1985). *La famille wolof: Tradition et changement*. Paris: Karthala.

Donadjè, F. (1992). *Nuptialité et fécondité des hommes au sud-Bénin: Pour une approche des stratégies de reproduction au Bénin*. Louvain-la-Neuve: Academia.

Dubresson, A., & Raison, J.-P. (2003). *L'Afrique subsaharienne. Une géographie du changement*. Paris: Armand Colin.

Goode, W. (1963). *World revolution and family patterns*. New York: Free Press.

Goody, J. (1976). *Production and reproduction: A comparative study of the domestic domain*. New York: Cambridge University Press.

Guillaume, A. (2003). The role of abortion in the fertility transition in Abidjan (Côte d'Ivoire) during the 1990s. *Population, 58,* 657–686.

Hassoun, J. (1997). *Femmes d'Abidjan face au sida*. Paris: Karthala.

Hertrich, V. (1996). *Permanences et changements de l'Afrique rurale. Dynamiques familiales chez les Bwa du Mali*. Paris: CEPED.

Hertrich, V. (2001). *Nuptialité et rapports de genre en Afrique. Un premier bilan des tendances de l'entrée en union au cours des 40 dernières années. Communication présentée au colloque "Genre, population et développement en Afrique."* Abidjan: ENSEA, INED, IFORD, UEPA.

Hertrich, V. (2003). *Polygamie et pauvreté. Tendances en Afrique de l'Ouest. Communication présentée à la Quatrième Conférence africaine sur la population Population et pauvreté en Afrique*. Tunis: UEPA.

Hertrich, V., & Locoh, T. (1999). *Rapports de genre, formation et dissolution de la famille dans les pays en développement*. Liège: UIESP.

Kritz, M., Makinwa-Adebusoye, P., & Gurak, D. T. (2000). The role of gender context in shaping reproductive behaviour in Nigeria. In H. B. Presser & G. Sen (Eds.), *Women's empowerment and demographic processes: Moving beyond Cairo* (pp. 239–260). Oxford: Oxford University Press.

Kuépié, M. (2002). *L'accès à la responsabilité familiale à Yaoundé: Évolution intergénérationnelle et facteurs explicatifs*. Unpublished doctoral thesis in demography, Paris.

Laurent, P.-J. (2003). *Les pentecôtistes du Burkina Faso. Mariage, pouvoir et guérison*. Paris: IRD-Khartala.

Lesthaeghe, R. (1989a). *Reproduction and social organization in Sub-Saharan Africa*. Berkeley: University of California Press.

Lesthaeghe, R. (1989b). Social organisation, economic crises and the future of fertility control. In R. Lesthaeghe (Ed.), *Reproduction and social organization in Sub-Saharan Africa* (pp. 475–497). Berkeley: University of California Press.

Lesthaeghe, R., Kaufmann, G., & Meekers, D. (1989). The nuptiality regimes in Sub-Saharan Africa. In R. Lesthaeghe (Ed.), *Reproduction and social organization in Sub-Saharan Africa* (pp. 238–337). Berkeley: University of California Press.

Levi-Strauss, C. (1958). *Anthropologie structurale*. Paris: Plon.

Lloyd, C., Kaufmann, C. E., & Hewett, P. (2000). The spread of primary schooling in Sub-Saharan Africa. *Population and Development Review, 26,* 483–515.

Locoh, T. (1994). Social change and marriage arrangements: New types of union in Lomé. In C. Bledsoe & G. Pison (Eds.), *Nuptiality in Sub-Saharan Africa. Contemporary anthropological and demographic perspectives* (pp. 215–231). Oxford: Clarendon Press.

Locoh, T. (1995). *Familles africaines, population et qualité de la vie.* Paris: CEPED.

Locoh, T. (1996). Changements des rôles masculins et féminins dans la crise: La révolution silencieuse. In J. Coussy & J. Vallin (Eds.), *Crise et population en Afrique. Crises économiques, politiques d'ajustement et dynamiques démographiques* (pp. 215–230). Paris: CEPED.

Locoh, T. (2002). *Structures familiales et évolutions de la fécondité dans les pays à fécondité intermédiaire d'Afrique de l'Ouest* (No. ESA/P/WP 172). New York: United Nations.

Locoh, T., & Hertrich, V. (1994). *The onset of fertility transition in Sub-Saharan Africa.* Liège: Derouaux-Ordina.

Locoh, T., & Makdessi, Y. (1996). *Population policies and fertility decline in Sub-Saharan Africa.* Paris: CEPED.

Locoh, T., & Makdessi, Y. (2002). Transition démographique et statut des personnes âgées en Afrique, Quelles perspectives? In AIDELF (Ed.), *Vivre plus longtemps, avoir moins d'enfants, quelles implications?* (pp. 615–626). Paris: PUF.

Locoh, T., & Thiriat, M.-P. (1996). Multinuptiality and gender relations in Sub-Saharan Africa: The case of Togo. In P. Makinwa-Adebusoye & A.-M. Jensen (Eds.), *Women's position and demographic change in Sub-Saharan Africa* (pp. 39–72). Liège: IUSSP.

Mahieu, F.-R. (1997). Face à la pauvreté: Stratégies universelles et recompositions africaines. In M. Pilon, T. Locoh, K. Virgnikin, & P. Vimard (Eds.), *Ménages et familles en Afrique: Approches des dynamiques contemporaines* (pp. 327–345). Paris: CEPED.

Marie, A. (1997). Du sujet communautaire au sujet individuel. Une lecture anthropologique de la réalité africaine contemporaine. In A. Marie (Ed.), *L'Afrique des individus* (pp. 53–110). Paris: Khartala.

Marie, A. (2002). Une anthropo-logique communautaire à l'épreuve de la mondialisation. De la relation de la dette à la lutte sociale (l'exemple ivoirien). *Cahier d'Études Africaines, 166,* 207–255.

Mbow, P. (1997). Les femmes, l'Islam et les associations religieuses au Sénégal. In E. Rosander (Ed.), *Transforming female identities* (pp. 148–169). Uppsala: Nordiska Africa Institutet.

Meillassoux, C. (1975). *Femmes, greniers, capitaux.* Paris: Maspero.

Mouvagha-Sow, M. (2001a). Le choix du conjoint à Libreville (Gabon). In A. Andro et al. (Eds.), *Genre et développement. Huit communications présentées à la chaire Quetelet 2000* (pp. 27–46). Paris: INED.

Mouvagha-Sow, M. (2001b). *Changements matrimoniaux et rapports de genre au Gabon.* Abidjan: ENSEA, INED, IFORD, UEPA.

Mouvagha-Sow, M. (2002a). *Processus matrimoniaux et procréation à Libreville (Gabon).* Doctoral thesis, Université Paris X-Nanterre, Paris.

Mouvagha-Sow, M. (2002b). *L'implication des pères dans l'éducation des enfants au Gabon*. Paper presented at the international AIDELF colloquium Enfants d'aujourd'hui, diversité des contextes, pluralité des parcours, Dakar.

Mouvagha-Sow, M. (2003). *Transformations familiales et pauvreté au Gabon*. Paper presented at the 4th African population conference Population et pauvreté en Afrique, relever les défis du XXIè siecle, Tunis, UAPS-UEPA.

Okojie, F. (1988). Aging in Sub-Saharan Africa: Toward a redefinition of needs research and policy directions. *Journal of Cross-Cultural Gerontology, 3*(1), 3–19.

ONS, Mauritania, & ORC, Macro. (2001). *Enquête démographique et de Santé Mauritanie 2000–2001*. Calverton, MD, DHS.

Page, H., & Lesthaeghe, R. (1981). *Child spacing in tropical Africa*. London: Academic Press.

Pisani, E. (1998). *Data and decision-making: Demography's contribution to understanding AIDS in Africa*. Liège: IUSSP Policy and Research Papers.

Schmitz, J. (2000). L'Islam en Afrique de l'Ouest: Les méridiens et les parallèles. *Autrepart, 16*, 117–137.

Silberschmidt, M. (1991). *Rethinking men and gender relations. An investigation of men, their changing roles within the household, and the implications for gender relations in Kisii District, Kenya*. Copenhagen: Center for Development Research.

Thiriat, M.-P. (1998). *Faire et défaire les liens du mariage, évolution des pratiques matrimoniales au Togo*. Paris: CEPED.

UNESCO. (2003). *Genre et éducation pour tous, le pari de l'égalité*. Paris : Unesco.

United Nations. (1995). *Women's education and fertility behaviour: Recent evidence from the DHS*. New York: United Nations, Department of Economic and Social Information and Policy Analysis.

URD, DGSCN. (2002). *Famille, migrations et urbanisation au Togo. Fascicule 3, Structures familiales et conditions de vie des ménages au Togo*. Lomé: Unité de recherche démographique.

Vandermeersch, C. (2000). *Les enfants confiés au Sénégal*. Doctoral thesis, Institut d'études politiques, Paris.

Vandermeersch, C. (2002). Child fostering under six in Senegal in 1992–1993. *Population-E, 57*(4–5), 659–688.

Wa Karamja, W. (1994). The phenomenon of "outside wives": Some reflections on its possible influence on fertility. In C. Bledsoe & G. Pison (Eds.), *Nuptiality in Sub-Saharan Africa: Contemporary anthropological and demographic perspectives* (pp. 257–278). Oxford: Clarendon Press.

Wakam, J. (1997). Différenciation socio-économique et structures familiales au Cameroun. In M. Pilon, T. Locoh, K. Vignikin, & P. Vimard (Eds.), *Ménages et familles en Afrique: Approches des dynamiques contemporaines* (pp. 194–215). Paris: CEPED.

4

When History Moves On: The Foundations and Diffusion of a Second Demographic Transition

Ron Lesthaeghe
Johan Surkyn
Interface Demography, Vrije Universtiteit, Brussels

The *first demographic transition* refers to the original declines in fertility and mortality, as witnessed in Western countries already from the 18th and 19th centuries onward, and during the second half of the 20th century in the rest of the world. At present, there is hardly any country left without a beginning of a fertility decline brought by the manifest use of contraception. Moreover, this first demographic transition (FDT) was equally accompanied by an overhaul of family formation systems. In the West, the control of fertility within wedlock occurred in tandem with a reduction in final celibacy and a lowering of ages at marriage, signaling a major departure from its old Malthusian nuptiality system. In the rest of the world, early marriage for women—often the result of arrangements between families or lineages—gave way to much later marriage, partly because of more individual partner choice and partly as a response to economic factors. But on the whole, William Goode's prediction of 1963 forecasting a rise in non-Western ages at marriage has largely been borne out by the record of the last 40 years. This increase in ages at marriage has furthermore been a major component in the overall fertility decline in many such countries.

One cannot be but impressed by the speed of the fertility and nuptiality changes associated with the FDT. In the 1960s, nobody dared forecast that several subSaharan African populations would begin adopting contraception already in the 1980s, and that almost all of them would do so prior to 2000. With the exception of rapidly industrializing countries of the Far East, such as Japan after World War II, and then Taiwan and South Korea, fertility transitions were rare prior to 1970. Demographic giants such as India, Bangladesh, Pakistan, and Indonesia still seemed far away from their FDT in fertility. It was believed that cultural and economic factors jointly formed a formidable obstacle to it. Now, some 30 years later, nobody believes in "formidable obstacles" anymore. In this very short period of time, world history has taken a decisive turn. Evidently, the feature of the demographic growth momentum, linked to the young age distribution of the world population, will still produce substantial population growth over the next forty years, but the foundations for the end of global population expansion were definitely laid in the 1970–2000 period.

Even before the FDT started spreading from the West and Japan to other countries, Western populations were initiating a move that would take them way beyond what classic "demographic transition theory" had forecasted. The fertility decline did not stop in the close vicinity of two children on average, and Western marriage would not stay early or attract the vast majority of men and women. The end product does not seem to be a balanced stationary population with zero population growth and little or no need for immigrants. The "second demographic transition" (SDT) brings sustained sub-replacement fertility, a multitude of living arrangements other than marriage, the disconnection between marriage and procreation, and no stationary population (Lesthaeghe & van de Kaa, 1986; van de Kaa, 1987, 1994; Lesthaeghe & Willems, 1999). Instead, Western populations face declining sizes, and if it were not for immigration, that decline would have started already in many European countries. In addition, extra gains in longevity at older ages in tandem with sustained sub-replacement fertility will produce a major aging effect as well.

The first signs of the SDT emerged already in the 1950s: Divorce rates were rising, especially in the United States and Scandinavia, and the departure from a lifelong commitment was justified by the logic that a "good divorce is better than a bad marriage." Later on and from the second half of the 1960s onward, fertility also started falling from its "baby boom" high after World War II. Moreover, the trend with respect to ages at first marriage was reversed again, and proportions of single people started rising. Soon thereafter it became evident that premarital cohabitation was on the rise and that divorce and widowhood were followed less by remarriage and more by postmarital cohabitation. By the 1980s even procreation within cohabiting unions had spread from Scandinavia to the rest of Western Europe. Both France and the United Kingdom now have more than 40% of all births occurring out of wedlock. In 1960 both had 6%.

The notion of a second demographic transition has been criticized from different angles. For instance, it would merely be the continuation of the one and only transition (e.g., Cliquet, 1992). Or, according to David Coleman (2003), it would not be a "second transition" but merely a "secondary feature." The SDT would, still according to Coleman, not even be demographic in nature, but only a "partial analysis of life style preferences." Others have pointed to the regional variations, which are indeed quite substantial, or have argued that it is an archetypical Western European (+ Canadian, Australian, U.S.) feature that would not spread to Southern or to Central and Eastern Europe. Instead, the demographic changes in the latter parts of Europe could be accounted for by the economic crisis associated with the transition from Communist to market economies, without involving the operation of a cultural shift at all. And finally, Coleman poses the question of the SDT spreading further to Asia or other continents. His answer is obviously that it will not: "It is solely a parochial Western European idiosyncrasy."

With these considerations in mind, we can set the task for the present chapter by posing the following questions:

* Is the SDT indeed merely the continuation of the FDT, and only a secondary "nondemographic" feature?
* Is the SDT spreading to the rest of Europe, and to the Mediterranean and Eastern European countries in particular?
* Is the role of the cultural factor negligible in Central or Eastern Europe, and are their demographic changes purely a response to the economic crisis following the transition to market economies?
* Can the SDT spread to other continents and societies? And if so, why?

IS THE SDT MERELY THE CONTINUATION OF THE FDT?

The idea of the *distinctness* of the SDT stems directly from Philippe Ariès's analysis of the history of childhood (1962) and particularly from his Bad Homburg paper (1980) on the two successive and distinct motivations for parenthood. During the FDT, the decline in fertility was "unleashed by an enormous sentimental and financial investment in the child" (i.e., the "king child era" to use Ariès's term), whereas the motivation during the SDT is adult self-realization within the role or lifestyle as a parent or more complete and fulfilled adult. This major shift is also propped up by the innovation of hormonal and other forms of highly efficient contraception. During the FDT the issue was to adopt contraception in order to avoid pregnancies; during the SDT the basic decision is to stop contraception in order to start a pregnancy.

The other "root" of the SDT theory was connected to a reaction of van de Kaa and myself toward the cyclical fertility theory, as formulated by Richard Easterlin (1973). In this theory, small cohorts would have better employment opportunities and hence earlier marriage and higher fertility, whereas large cohorts would have the opposite life chances and inverse demographic responses. The theory accounts very nicely for the marriage and baby boom of the 1960s, and also for the subsequent "baby bust" of the 1970s. But the theory equally predicts further cycles produced by the earlier ones, and hence expects a return of fertility to above-replacement levels when smaller cohorts reach the reproductive span. By the middle of the 1980s we had become convinced that sub-replacement fertility was not only going to last much longer, but could even become an "intrinsic" feature of a new demographic regime. Exit the model of an ultimate stationary population with a long-term population equilibrium, and exit the improved version of it with cyclical fertility swings around replacement fertility.

Having pointed out the intellectual origins of the SDT, we now turn to a more systematic treatment of the contrasts between the FDT and the SDT. Table 4.1 gives a summary of the points to be discussed.

Opposite Nuptiality Regimes

As already indicated, a first major contrast between the FDT and SDT is the opposite trend in nuptiality. In Western Europe the Malthusian late marriage pattern weakens, mainly as the result of the growth of wage earning labor, and this basic trend toward earlier and more universal marriage continues all the way till the middle of the 1960s. Hence, the lowest mean ages at first marriage since the Renaissance were reached in the middle of the 20th century. Furthermore, the pockets in Western Europe where cohabitation and out of wedlock fertility had remained high during the 19th century were under siege during the first half of the 20th century. Such behavior was not in line with both the religious and secular views on what constituted a proper family. Extramarital fertility rates all decline in Europe after 1900.

By contrast, after 1965, ages at marriage rose again and cohort proportions ever-married started declining (Council of Europe, 2004). This resulted not only from the insertion of an interim period of premarital cohabitation, but also from later home leaving and more and longer single living. The very rapid prolongation of education for both sexes since the 1950s and the ensuing change in educational composition of Western populations contributed to this process. But the unfolding of

TABLE 4.1

Overview of Demographic and Societal Characteristics Respectively Related to the FDT and SDT in Western Europe

FDT	*SDT*
A. Marriage	
• Rise in proportions marrying, declining age at first marriage	• Fall in proportions married, rise in age at first marriage
• Low or reduced cohabitation	• Rise in cohabitation (pre- and post-marital)
• Low divorce	• Rise in divorce, earlier divorce
• High remarriage	• Decline of remarriage following both divorce and widowhood
B. Fertility	
• Decline in marital fertility via reductions at older ages, lowering mean ages at first parenthood	• Further decline in fertility via postponement, increasing mean age at first parenthood, structural subreplacement fertility
• Deficient contraception, parity failures	• Efficient contraception (exceptions in specific social groups)
• Declining illegitimate fertility	• Rising extramarital fertility, parenthood within cohabitation
• Low definitive childlessness among married couples	• Rising definitive childlessness in unions
C. Societal background	
• Preoccupations with basic material needs: income, work conditions, housing, health, schooling, social security. Solidarity prime value.	• Rise of "higher order" needs: individual autonomy, self-actualization, expressive work and socialization values, grass-roots democracy, recognition. Tolerance prime value.
• Rising memberships of political-, civic-, and community-oriented networks. Strengthening of social cohesion.	• Disengagement from civic and community-oriented networks, social capital shifts to expressive and affective types. Weakening of social cohesion.
• Strong normative regulation by State and Churches. First secularization wave, political and social "pillarization."	• Retreat of the State, second secularization wave, sexual revolution, refusal of authority, political "depillarization."
• Segregated gender roles, familistic policies, "embourgeoisement," promotion of breadwinner family model.	• Rising symmetry in gender roles, female economic autonomy.
• Ordered life course transitions, prudent marriage, and dominance of one single family model.	• Flexible life course organization, multiple lifestyles, open future.

the nuptiality features of the SDT did not solely stop at a rise in ages at marriage and at a mere insertion of an interim "student" period. Postmarital cohabitation too was on the rise, and so was procreation outside wedlock. And in many instances the latter trend is to some extent a "revenge of history": Cohabitation and procreation by non-married couples are now often highest where the custom prevailed longest during the 19th and early 20th centuries.

The next contrast between FDT and SDT pertains to divorce and remarriage. The FDT is preoccupied with strengthening marriage and the family, and divorce legislation remains strict. The State offers little opposition to religious doctrine in this respect. Divorce on the basis of mutual consent is rare, but mostly based on proven adultery. The SDT witnesses the end of a long period of low divorce rates, and the principle of a unique, lifelong legal partnership is questioned. This takes the form of a rational "utility" evaluation of a marriage in terms of the welfare of each of the adult partners first and children second. This is accompanied by attacking the hypocrisy of the earlier restrictive divorce legislation that fostered concubinage instead. The outcome in Western Europe, the United States, Canada, Australia, and New Zealand was a succession of legal liberalizations in the wake of a singularly rising demographic trend. And, as pointed out in the introduction, the onset of the rise in divorce was probably the very first manifestation of the accentuation of individual autonomy in opposing the moral order prescribed by Church and State. It should be noted, however, that resistance to divorce was stronger in countries or regions with a Catholic background than in those with a Protestant one. This is not so surprising because divorce versus the indissolubility of marriage was one of the key issues that led to the Reformation in the first place.

And last, but not least, FDT and SDT have also opposite patterns of remarriage. During the former, remarriages were essentially involving widows and widowers, whereas remarriage for divorced persons meant a new beginning and the start of a new family: "new children for a new lifelong commitment." In other words, even if divorce occurred, the institution of marriage was not under serious threat, and remarriage propped up fertility as well. Nothing of this is left in the SDT: Remarriages among widowed or divorced persons decline in favor of cohabitation or other looser arrangements such as living-apart-together relationships or close and intimate friendships. This may not only have tax advantages or protect the inheritance rights of one's own children, but it also essentially leaves all further options open and safeguards individual autonomy.

Fertility Contrasts

The SDT is not merely focusing on changing nuptiality and family patterns, but equally concerned with fertility. During the FDT fertility becomes increasingly confined to marriage, contraception affects mostly fertility at older ages and higher marriage durations, mean ages at first parenthood decline, and among married couples childlessness is low. There are examples of below-replacement fertility during the FDT, but these correspond to exceptional periods of deep economic crises or war only. Sub-replacement fertility is not an intrinsic characteristic of the FDT. Under better conditions, as for instance after World War II, fertility levels are well above replacement level. The "baby boom" and the "marriage" boom of the late 1950s and early 1960s are the last typical features of the FDT (whereas rising divorce in that period signals the start of the SDT). Another salient characteristic of the FDT fertility regime was its reliance on imperfect contraception. Until the 1960s, *coitus interruptus* was largely the method used by the working classes and "rhythm" by the more highly educated or more religious couples. Both methods led to contraceptive failures and unintended pregnancies, and these also kept fertility above replacement level. Particularly such parity failures at higher ages became increasingly undesirable and fueled the demand for more efficient contraception.

The SDT starts with a multifaceted revolution, and all aspects of it impact on fertility. First, there was a *contraceptive revolution* with the invention of the pill and the reinvention of IUDs. All of these were perfected very rapidly, and particularly hormonal contraception was suited for postponing and spacing purposes. A. J. Coale's 1974 "learning curve" of contraception (Coale & Trusselt, 1974), which was monotonically increasing with age and which fitted the FDT experience so well, was no longer applicable in the West. After an interim period with increased incidence of "shotgun marriages" (often 1965–1975), the use of highly efficient and reliable contraception starts at young ages and permits postponement of childbearing as a goal in its own right. Second, there was also a *sexual revolution*, and it was a forceful reaction to the notions that sex is confined to marriage and mainly for procreation only. The younger generations sought the value of sex for its own sake and accused the generation of their parents of hypocrisy. Ages at first sexual intercourse decline during the SDT. Third, there was the *gender revolution*. Women were no longer going to be subservient to men and husbands, but would seize the right to regulate fertility themselves. They no longer underwent the "fatalities of nature," and this pressing wish for "biological autonomy" was articulated by subsequent quests for the liberalization of induced abortion. Finally, these "three revolutions" fit within the framework of an overall rejection of authority and of a complete overhaul of the normative structure. Parents, educators, churches, army, and much of the entire State apparatus end up being questioned and challenged. This entire ideational reorientation, if not revolution, occurs during the peak years of economic growth, and shapes all aspects of the SDT.

The overall outcome with respect to the SDT fertility pattern is its marked degree of postponement. Mean ages at first parenthood for women in sexual unions rise quite rapidly and to unprecedented levels in several Western European populations. The net outcome is sub-replacement fertility: Without the ethnic component (such as Hispanics and Blacks in the United States or Maoris in New Zealand) all Organization for Economic Cooperation and Development (OECD) countries have sub-replacement fertility. Admittedly, period measures such as the TFR are extra depressed as a result of continued postponing, but even the end of such postponement is not likely to bring period fertility back to 2.05 children. Most cohorts of the world's White (+ Japanese) national populations born after 1960 will not make it to that level (cf. Frejka & Calot, 2001; Lesthaeghe, 2001; Council of Europe, 2004). However, the degree of heterogeneity is substantial and by no means solely the outcome of ethnic composition factors. In the West, Scandinavian, British, and French cohorts born in 1960 still come close to replacement fertility, whereas these cohort levels fall below 1.70 in Austria, the whole of Germany, and Italy. In Central and Eastern Europe, the cohort of 1960 will still get to two children on average, but not in the Russian Federation, Slovenia, and the three Baltic countries (Council of Europe, 2004). Moreover, in Western and Southern European countries with current total period fertility rates below 1.5, the catching up of fertility at the later childbearing ages, that is, after age 30, has simply remained too weak to offset the postponement effect. The result of sustained sub-replacement fertility is that another, but originally unanticipated, trait of the SDT may be in the making: continued reliance on international migration to partially offset the population decline that would otherwise emerge within a few years.

Evidently, we are very far from the ideal FDT outcome of a new stationary population corresponding to high life expectancies, replacement fertility, and little need for immigration. And we are getting further and further removed from the FDT prop of that demographic model, that is, the dominance of a single form of living arrangement for couples and children (namely, marriage). Finally, the linchpin of the

FDT system has totally eroded: Collective behavior is no longer kept on track by a strong normative structure based on a familistic ideology supported by both Church and State. Instead, the new regime is governed by the primacy of individual freedom of choice. Or as van de Kaa (2004) has put it, fertility is now merely a "derivative," meaning that it is the outcome of a prolonged "process of self-reflection and self-confrontation on the part of prospective parents.... Then the pair will weigh a great many issues, direct and opportunity costs included, but their guiding light is self-confrontation: would a conception and having a child be self-fulfilling?"

Underlying Societal Contrasts

So far, we have mainly discussed the differences between the FDT and SDT in terms of their demographic contrasts. But both demographic transitions have, of course, their roots in two distinct historical periods. Table 4.1 again contains a summary.

With the exception of the very early fertility decline in France and a few other smaller areas in Europe, much of the FDT is an integral part of a phase in which economic growth fosters material aspirations and improvements in material living conditions. The preoccupations of the 1860–1960 period were mainly concerned with increasing household real income, improving working and housing conditions, raising standards of health and life expectancy, improving human capital by investing in education, and providing a safety net for all via the gradual construction of a social security system. In Europe, these social goals were shared and promoted by all ideological, religious, or political factions (also known as "pillars" because each of them integrates a political party, a cluster of labor unions, news media, and social services into a closely tied organizational network). And in this endeavor solidarity was a central concept. All pillars also had their views on the desirable evolution of the family. For the religious pillars (Catholic, Protestant, and later on Christian-Democrat) these views were based on the holiness of matrimony in the first place, but their defense of a closely knit conjugal family also stemmed from fears that the industrial society would lead to immorality, social pathology, and atheism. The secular pillars (i.e., Liberal and Socialist) equally saw the family as a first line of defense against the social ills of the 19th century, and as the foundation for their building of a new social order based on humanistic principles. Hence, although for partially different reasons, all pillars considered the family as the cornerstone of society. Both material and moral uplifting would be served best by a sharp gender-based division of labor within the family: Husbands assume their responsibilities as devoted bread-winners, and wives become the caretakers of all quality-related matters. For this to be realized, male incomes needed to be high enough so that women could assume the role of housewives. In other words, all pillars, including the Socialist and even Communist ones, contributed to the *embourgeoisement* of the working class through this propagation of the breadwinner–housewife model.

In short, for all social classes there should be a single family model and it should be served by highly ordered life-course transitions: no marriage without solid financial basis or prospects, and procreation strictly within wedlock. The Malthusian preconditions of a "prudent" marriage were readapted to the social aspirations of the new industrial society.

The SDT, on the other hand, is founded on the rise of the "higher order needs," as, for instance, defined by Maslow (1954). Once the basic material preoccupations, and particularly that of long-term financial security, are satisfied via welfare state provisions, more existential and expressive needs become articulated. These are centered on *self-actualization* in formulating goals, *individual autonomy* in choosing means, and *recognition* for their realization. These features emerge in a variety of domains, and this is why the SDT can be linked to such a wide variety of empirical indicators of ideational change.

In the political sphere such higher order or "postmaterialist" (Inglehart, 1970) needs deal, inter alia, with the quest for more direct grass-roots democracy, openness of government, rejection of political patronage, decline of lifelong loyalty to political or religious pillars (= "depillarization"), and the rise of ecological and other quality- rather than quantity-oriented issues on the political agenda. The downturn of it all is rising distrust in politics and institutions and growing political anomy that can fuel right-wing extremism. The state is no longer viewed in terms of a benign provider, but again more as an Orwellian "big brother." A corollary thereof is the disengagement from civic, professional, and community-oriented networks (e.g., Putnam, 2000). It is likely, however, that these were partially substituted by more expressive (fitness clubs, meditation gatherings, etc.) or more affective (friendships) types of social capital. Work values and socialization values equally display a profound shift in favor of the expressive traits, and above all, away from respect for authority. In the former sphere, one is no longer satisfied with good material conditions (pay, job security, vacations), but more and more expressive traits are being valued (e.g., interesting work, contact with others, work that meets one's abilities, challenging and innovative work, variation in tasks, flexible time use, etc.). Obviously this orientation is initially the result of rising education and the growth of white-collar employment (e.g., Kohn, 1977), but it has now spread to all social classes and types of employment. A strong parallel can be found in the domain of socialization as well (e.g., Alwin, 1989): All elements typical of conformity (obedience, order and neatness, thrift and hard work, traditional gender roles, religious faith) and those linked to social orientations (loyalty, solidarity, consideration for others) have gradually given way to expressive traits that stress personality (being interested in how and why, capability of thinking for oneself, self-presentation, independence and autonomy). Needless to say, the quest for more symmetrical gender relations fits within this overall framework of articulation of higher order needs and expressive social roles.

One or Two Transitions

Evidently the higher order needs can only be articulated if the lower order ones are sufficiently met. Similarly, the SDT squarely stands on the shoulders of its predecessor, the FDT. But to consider the SDT features as "secondary" as suggested by David Coleman, or as part and parcel of one sole transition, is another matter. Our problem with these views is that they fail to realize both the amplitude of the contrast and the importance of the societal implications for the future.

More specifically, the "one transition only" view fails to recognize that the FDT and SDT are sufficiently differentiated and even antagonistic in terms of most family formation variables (including fertility motivations!). The "unitarian" view furthermore misses the point that FDT and SDT each correspond to two distinct historical phases, have a distinct "*logique sociale*," and are buttressed by distinct patterns of political organization as well. In short, the "one transition view" simply blurs history.

Last but not least, the demographic implications of the SDT for the future are fundamentally different from the equilibrium implication of the FDT. The SDT expects much rougher seas ahead: (a) more pronounced aging as a result of sub-replacement fertility, and hence more pressure on the welfare state foundations, (b) more reliance on immigration and consequently a further expansion of multiethnicity and multicultural traits in societies, (c) less stress on social cohesion (e.g., Surkyn, 2003), and (d) a greater incidence of family instability and concomitant social problems (e.g., poverty among singles or in one-parent households).

So far, we have explained why it makes sense to make distinctions and to number the successive historical moves from one system to the next. In the following section we address the issue of the geographical diffusion of the SDT to other parts of Europe.

IS THE SDT ONLY A NORTHERN AND WESTERN EUROPEAN IDIOSYNCRASY?

Toward the end of the 1980s, several features of the SDT seemed to stop at the northern slopes of the Alps and Pyrenees: The incidence of cohabitation remained very low, and also the rise in extramarital fertility was either absent or very modest. Instead, younger adults predominantly remained in or stayed attached to their parental homes. Also until 1990, earlier patterns of both marriage and fertility had been maintained in Central and Eastern Europe. Fifteen years ago, one could still argue that the SDT would remain a "parochial" idiosyncrasy, limited to Western and Northern Europe. Admittedly, the SDT features had emerged in European populations across the oceans (Canada, Australia, New Zealand and the United States), but they failed to cross two other geopolitical divides on the old continent.

Central and Eastern Europe

For Central and Eastern Europe, this picture changed completely after the collapse of the Communist regimes in 1989. All SDT features emerged simultaneously: Ages at first marriage, which had remained quite young during the preceding era, started increasing, premarital cohabitation rose, and so did the proportions of extramarital births. In tandem with later union formation there was also a dramatic postponement of fertility at all ages and parities, leading to a precipitous drop of period indicators. In Central and Eastern Europe, total fertility rates (TFRs) fell below 1.5 children and even below 1.3. A new term was coined: "*lowest low fertility*" (Kohler et al., 2002). Evidently, period measures can be dramatically depressed when such systematic postponement occurs. However, the degree to which there could be catching up in cohort fertility is still uncertain, and so is the amount of recovery in prospective period TFR levels. But the outcome seems to be that fertility will stay well below replacement at any rate. In 2002, all former Communist countries still had TFRs below 1.35, and as low as 1.10 (Ukraine). The sole exceptions were Albania, with a TFR probably around 2.0, and Macedonia together with Serbia-Montenegro, with levels around 1.75.

Initially, few observers in the former Communist countries thought that this could be the start of an SDT. Especially the older generation of demographers was highly skeptical about the concept to start with, and remained convinced that these marked marriage and massive fertility postponements were exclusively the consequence of the economic crisis (cf. Rychtarikova, 2000). Also the UN Economic Commission for

Europe initially held this view (2000). And the transition to capitalism was indeed a very painful one: There was the end of guaranteed lifelong employment, a reduction in activity rates for women, a steep drop in the standard of living, a decline in state support for families, a privatization of the housing sector, and in several countries also a highly visible rise in poverty. But there was also a countercurrent of younger demographers, mainly in Russia (Zakharov & Ivanova, 1996; Zakharov, 1997) and especially the Czech Republic (Stloukal, 1998; Zeman, Sobotka, & Kanatarova, 2001; Rabusic, 2001; Sobotka, Zeman, & Kantorova, 2003), who thought that not only the crisis was to be held responsible, but that an SDT could be in the making as well. In fact, after 1997 the economy of several of the former Communist countries was recovering and so were per capita incomes. But there was no return to earlier patterns of marriage, nor an end to fertility postponement. Also the steady rise in extramarital fertility, which, incidentally, often started before 1989, continued and even accelerated (see Figure 4.1). Of 18 such countries, only 5 still had proportions of extramarital births below 20% in 2002. At the upper tail of the distribution, 4 had already reached Northern European levels of above 40% (Council of Europe, 2004). Fifteen years earlier, these countries had percentages between 3 and 15 only, and solely the former German Democratic Republic stood out with 34% extramarital births in 1985. These rapid increases are admittedly also the result of the rise in proportions of first births in the declining total, but they undeniably reflect that procreation outside marriage and in cohabiting unions is rapidly spreading in Central and Eastern Europe as well.

The verdict seems to be that the economic crisis had indeed destabilized the earlier demographic regime, but also that the SDT had been in the making before 1990, and that it is developing further, that is, also during economic recoveries. In other words, the SDT is emerging in Central and Eastern Europe as a feature that is there to stay, just as in the West. Once more it is emerging as a salient characteristic of capitalist economies and of cultures that recognize the primacy of *individual autonomy* and that develop the higher order needs.

Southern Europe

As indicated earlier, also the demographic patterns of Southern Europe, from Portugal to Greece, have been considered as an exception to the theory of two successive transitions. In fact, in one crucial respect these countries were not an exception at all, because their marriage and fertility postponements were even more pronounced than in Western and Northern Europe. The postponement started later than in

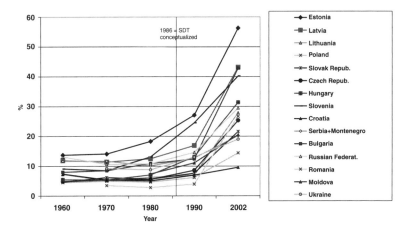

FIGURE 4.1   Extramarital births as percent of all births:
Baltic, Central, and Eastern Europe.

the West, but the intensity was equally striking. Moreover, as was also
true for a few Western countries like Austria and to some degree also of
Germany (former FRG), cohort fertility patterns in Southern Europe
hardly exhibit signs of fertility recuperation after age 30 (Lesthaeghe,
2001; Calot & Frejka, 2001). This means that not only is progression to
the second or third child rarer than in Northern and Western Europe,
but also that in the younger cohorts a larger proportion—typically in
excess of 20%—will not make it to parenthood at all. All of that together
is of course a recipe for prolonged "lowest low" fertility, and not for a
temporary dip and swift return to replacement level. Hence, seen from
the fertility angle, Southern Europe did follow the overall postponement trends in nuptiality and fertility, and these countries are by no
means exceptions to these core SDT-features.

    What made the Southern European starting pattern of the SFT so
special and so exceptional when compared to the northern neighbors
was the absence of home leaving in favor of independent single living or
in favor of premarital cohabitation. Furthermore, marriage still remained
the predominant precondition for procreation. In other words, a part of
the SDT package was missing. Cohesive explanations for this syndrome
have been offered by R. Palomba (1995), G. Micheli (1996, 2000), and G.
Dalla Zuanna (2002). The latter author also directly refers to D. Reher's
(1998) distinction between the historically "strong family system" of

Southern Europe and the traditionally "weak" one of Western and Northern Europe.

In the "weak system," children can leave the parental household before marriage, and then they fend for themselves in an interim period of celibacy prior to marriage. Historically, they became servants, apprentices, landless and/or seasonal laborers, industrial workers, soldiers, seamen, or clergymen. In contemporary Northern and Western Europe, welfare provisions still stress this earlier independence via sufficient student housing, scholarships, student transportation subsidies, youth unemployment benefits and employment programs, and even guaranteed minimum incomes for single persons older than 18 and no longer living at home. The result is still earlier home leaving for independent living, sharing, or cohabiting. Moreover, young adults learn to take on responsibilities and coping strategies, which are all needed later on in life. Even men learn to stand on their own feet also when typical household tasks are involved. Greater gender symmetry also fosters higher female employment rates, and vice versa. The household standard of living is based on dual incomes, but women can take off spells of time for family reasons (e.g., maternity leave, optional leaves for childrearing or caring for sick partner or parent, etc.). Either or both partners can also opt for part-time employment, and labor market flexibility enhances these options. Furthermore, this system is perfectly compatible with the shift toward expressive values and roles, and it creates less tension between self-fulfillment and parenthood.

In the "strong family" type, familial ties and solidarity—even allegiance to alliances of families as in Southern Italy—are more persistent throughout life. Men and women only leave the parental family to marry, and sons can even bring their wife into the parental home. Men are looked after by their mother and then immediately thereafter by their wife. The old gender roles persist and men stay away from housework. Furthermore, the family bonds continue to function throughout life, both between siblings (e.g., in business) and between generations. Older people are still taken in by their children. Mediterranean societies furthermore developed their welfare provisions on the assumption that such strong familial solidarity would continue to hold, and they have very few provisions that allow young adults to become economically more independent. On top of that, housing falls largely within the private sector, and most couples want to become homeowners. The resulting relatively high housing costs tend to retard the departure. The overall outcome has been that home leaving is much later than in Western and Northern Europe, and that there is little cohabitation or fertility among unmarried couples. Instead, young adults continue to live in their "gilded nests" provided by caring parents. And for women, motherhood also means dropping out of the labor force, not only because this is to be expected from a "good mother," but also because child care facilities are scarce and the returning to an earlier job more difficult. Opportunity costs are hence increased as a consequence of the persistence of old role patterns and inflexible labor markets. The ultimate outcome is what Dalla Zuanna calls "a pyrrhic victory of the strong family system," because, quite paradoxically, it will disappear for lack of adaptive capacity and lack of children.

But does history stop here? Will the Mediterranean demographic system maintain this hitherto characteristic lack of alternative household types occupied by younger adults? The presence of such households is not routinely flagged by European registration systems, and hence we have to wait for special surveys (or an occasional census) to monitor changes in household forms. Given that the European Fertility and Family Surveys (FFS) of the early 1990s are outdated by now, and really give the history of the 1970s and 1980s at any rate, we are short of indicators. The major exception is that most European countries still make the distinction between births occurring within marriage and those occurring out of wedlock. From this information we cannot infer the respective shares of extramarital births contributed by single mothers and by cohabiting couples. But, as the record has shown for most continental Western and Northern European countries, the lion's share has gone to the latter. Hence, extramarital fertility provides an imperfect but still very useful early indicator of SDT progression to one of the later phases, that of procreation within cohabitation.

Figure 4.2 gives the percentage of extramarital births for the Southern European countries. This figure is directly comparable to the one provided for Central and Eastern Europe. The outcome is quite revealing. Portugal—which historically had a tradition of cohabitation and out-of-wedlock fertility (cf. Livi-Bacci, 1971) in its southern provinces—has had steadily increasing proportions of extramarital births since the 1970s. And if the Portuguese figures are compared to those for Western European countries, displayed in Figure 4.3, then the Portuguese rise precedes that of the corresponding increase in the Netherlands, Belgium, Germany (FRG), and Switzerland. Moreover, Spain started at a lower level, but the Spanish curve runs parallel to Portugal's, and in 2002, Spain's extramarital births share was larger than Switzerland's. Apparently, the Pyrenees were not that formidable an obstacle to the diffusion of the SDT, and the "strong family system" of Iberia proved to be more adaptive than the Italian authors had estimated for their own country.

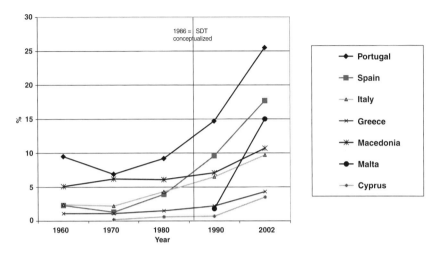

FIGURE 4.2   Extramarital births as percent of all births: Southern Europe.

Figure 4.2 has a few more surprises. First, there is a very steep and continuing increase in out of wedlock fertility in Malta during the last decade. Second, there has been a steady increase in Italian extramarital fertility as well. It started from very low levels in the 1960s, but the indicator is now reaching 10%. Judging from this record, the strong family system in Italy may be just that bit stronger than in Portugal, Spain, or Malta, but it is clearly not completely impermeable to the SDT. In fact, Italy is now catching up with the most "conservative" case in the Western European set, Switzerland, which has already quite a widespread occurrence of cohabitation, but equally matched to a low level of extramarital fertility limited to 10% of all births. This is further corroborated by results of the latest Italian census: In the 1980s unmarried cohabitation was restricted to the German-speaking district of Alto Adige (also known as South Tirol), but in 2000 cohabitation was widespread in many more northern areas, both rural (e.g., in Aosta, Emilia-Romagna) and urban (e.g. Rome, Milan). Third, the percentage of nonmarital births also reached the 10% level in 2000 in the FYR of Macedonia. And finally, in the last part of the Mediterranean "strong family belt," Greece and Cyprus also have an upward acceleration of the trend, but the levels of extramarital fertility are still too low to justify any firmer conclusion. But if Central and Eastern Europe follow suit, and now also the Iberian countries and Malta, one can imagine that there is also a take-off of nontraditional household forms in Italy or even

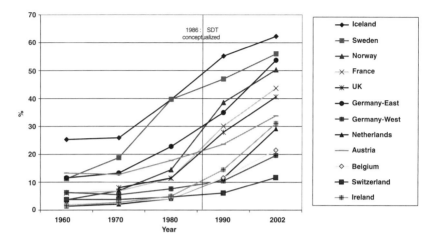

FIGURE 4.3   Extramarital births as percent all births:
Northern and Western Europe.

Macedonia. The Eastern Mediterranean then constitutes the last area to
be affected. Compared to 10 years ago, history has moved on in the
predicted direction in Southern Europe as well.

Western and Northern Europe

To end this section on the European diffusion of the SDT, we would also
like to point out that the process is not yet complete in Western and
Northern Europe either. As the extramarital fertility indicator shows,
the proportions of births out of wedlock are still increasing in all countries considered on Figure 4.3, and this includes the ones with the highest incidence of all, namely Iceland, Sweden, Eastern Germany (former
GDR), Norway, and France. Apparently the figure of 60% of all births
being born outside marriage is a possibility for these vanguard countries. Yet it should also be pointed out that there is a distinctly more
conservative version of the Western European SDT in which single living, sharing, or cohabitation has become common, but where a marriage is still connected to the transition to parenthood. Then the
parenthood decision often comes first, and the marriage decision follows suit. In such situations extramarital fertility is also rising, but more
slowly and at lower levels. Good examples of this variant are Switzerland,
Western Germany (former GFR), Belgium (mainly Flanders), and to some

extent also the Netherlands. Ireland, by contrast, now seems to make the jump from the latter, more conservative category to the former, more advanced SDT category of countries. In fact, Ireland has already crossed the 30% level, whereas in 1980 it barely had 5% of births out of wedlock. History has moved on at the Western frontiers of the continent too—and at quite a pace!

VALUE ORIENTATIONS AND HOUSEHOLD CHOICES: THE FOOTPRINTS AT THE MICRO LEVEL

The initial article on the SDT (Lesthaeghe & van de Kaa, 1986) posited that the new living arrangements and cohabitation in particular were the expressions of secular and anti-authoritarian sentiments of better educated younger cohorts with a more egalitarian world view, and who also put greater emphasis on the "higher order needs." At the same time, the correlates of Inglehart's "postmaterialist" orientation were high on the research agenda of the political scientists, and both the Eurobarometer surveys in the European Union (EU) and the first round of European Values Studies (EVS) of 1981 provided data for more detailed empirical research on attitude and value profiles for various social groups, including those based on living arrangements. Also in the United States, statistical associations between living arrangements and specific value orientations drew attention. Not only was it realized that cohorts were steadily progressing to higher levels of "postmaterialism" (Inglehart, 1980) and other higher order needs (e.g., van Rysselt, 1989), but also that there was a recursive relationship between demographic choices and values orientation. As Thornton and colleagues in Michigan illustrated (Thornton, 1985; Thornton, Axinn, & Hill, 1992), higher secularism fostered choices in favor of premarital sex and nontraditional household formation patterns, but the latter also reinforced further secularization. In other words, there was a *selection* into various types of behavior based on existing values to start with, and then an *affirmation* or strengthening of these values based on the behavioral choice. Clearly, the statistical associations between value orientations and the various types of households are merely the "*footprints*" of this ongoing life course process of selection followed by affirmation or negation of values. On the basis of successive cross-sections we cannot disentangle the two directions of causation involved. American social scientists took the lead in organizing panel surveys, and it is mainly on the basis of these that the recursive model of selection/adaptation could be checked (e.g., Goldscheider and Waite, 1987; Clarkberg, Stolzenberg, &

Waite, 1995; Barber, Axinn, & Thornton, 2002). More recently, also a few European panels measured various value orientations at successive waves, and they too now lend themselves to disentangling the causal components of the recursive relationship (e.g., Moors, 2002; Jansen & Kalmijn, 2000, 2002).

The Cross-Sectional "Footprints" of the Recursive Selection and Adaptation Model

On the whole, there are now many documented effects of values as they influence choices with respect to family formation (*selection effect*), and of the ways in which the life-course choices feed back onto value orientations, either to reinforce or to alter them (*adaptation effect*) (see Lesthaeghe, 2002; Lesthaeghe & Surkyn, 2002). The overall picture of the process is given in Figure 4.4. First, on the vertical axis we have placed two poles: One brings together the nonconformist and more libertarian values (e.g., stress on individual autonomy, less respect for authority, expressive values of self-actualization, secularism, tolerance for alternative behavior and minorities, world-citizenship, etc.), and the other the more conventional value orientations (e.g., respect for tradition, ethical and religious values, trust in institutions, solidarity and social cohesion). Second, we have put the transitions into the various household states on the horizontal axis, typifying "life-course progression." Upward arrows indicate that a particular transition in household position is associated with a move in the nonconformist values direction, and downward-pointing arrows indicate transitions associated with value adaptations in the conformist sense. This leads to the positioning of the various living arrangements along this vertical axis of value orientations. This is also what we refer to as the cross-sectional "*footprints*" of the recursive selection/adaptation model.

The starting point on Figure 4.4 is the individual's residence in the parental household (*Respar*). At that point, the formative years and late adolescence are approaching completion, and individuals have been subject to the "triple P" influences (parents, peers, professors). Peer influences have gained importance over time, and also increased parental divorce pushes the value orientations of such young adults in the nonconformist direction. During the next steps in the life course unfolding, it is expected that home leaving in favor of independent single living (*Single*) is predicated on the dominance of nonconformist values, whereas leaving home and directly getting married (*Mar0*) reflects a choice based on conventional value orientations. At the same

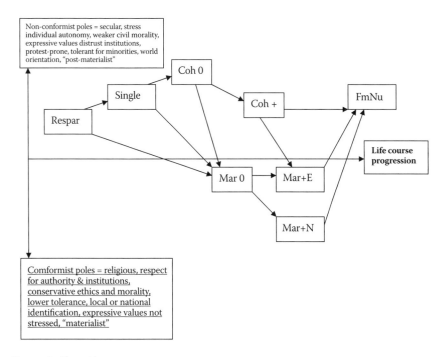

Non-conformist poles = secular, stress individual autonomy, weaker civil morality, expressive values distrust institutions, protest-prone, tolerant for minorities, world orientation, "post-materialist"

Coh 0

Single

Coh +

FmNu

Respar

Life course progression

Mar 0   Mar+E

Mar+N

Comformist poles = religious, respect for authority & institutions, conservative ethics and morality, lower tolerance, local or national identification, expressive values not stressed, "materialist"

Respar = Resident with parents.
Single = Living alone or sharing, never married and not in union
Coh 0 = Cohabiting, no children
Coh + = Cohabiting with children
Mar 0 = Married, no children
Mar + E = Married, children, never cohabited
Mar + N = Married, children, ever cohabited
FmNu = Formerly married or in union, not in new union.

FIGURE 4.4   Flow chart of life course transitions and hypothesized changes in values orientation stemming from selection–adaptation mechanism.

time, these two choices both reinforce the original values sets in their respective directions.

Singles face the option of moving into cohabitation (*Coh0*) or of marrying (*Mar0*). The former transition strengthens nonconformism even further, also because the cohabiting partner is also likely to be selected on the basis of nonconformist convictions. The mutually reinforcing attitudes of both partners may then enhance the consistency of various values sets, so that childless cohabitants (*Coh0*) can be expected to score highest on all nonconformist subdimensions associated with pole 1 on Figure 4.4. By contrast, singles who move immediately into marriage may do so because of a greater respect for traditional institutions or for their parents' opinions, or because they choose a partner with a more conservative outlook. Once the institution of marriage is accepted, a move to more conformism is also expected, not least because married couples tend to drop the old singles network in favor of new ones with other more like-minded settled couples as well. A similar process of readjustment would also apply to cohabitants who move into marriage prior to parenthood. For them, the value adjustment associated with marriage would be more substantial, given that they come from a strongly nonconformist position. However, it may also be that they never adjust to the same level of conformity as the directly married, and therefore exhibit a *lifelong nonconformist imprint* dating back to their earlier cohabitation period. Whenever possible, we therefore make a distinction between married couples who *ever* (*E*) and who *never* (*N*) cohabited.

The adjustment effects of parenthood are expected to be even stronger than those of marriage. In fact, values already shift in the conformist direction in anticipation of parenthood, and the transition from cohabitation into marriage is often made as such a form of anticipation. Parenthood corresponds to a firm commitment of both partners and closes open futures. And most importantly, it redirects attention to the well-being of the next generation. Moral, civil, and ethical values are reaffirmed, and again other social networks—of those with children—are being activated. Tolerance for deviance diminishes, authority gains greater prominence, and more attention is being paid to solidarity and social cohesion. In Figure 4.4, all positions with children (indicated by a + *sign*) are therefore located further down toward the conformist pole. However, the position of ever-cohabiting married parents (*Mar* + *E*) remains above that of the never-cohabiting married parents (*Mar* + *N*).

Finally, a separation or divorce that has not yet been followed by a new partnership (*FmNu* = formerly married, not in union) causes a complete overhaul of the value system. New doubts emerge with respect to religion, morality, authority, trust in institutions, and so on. The individuals are more likely to become self-focused, and therefore pay again greater attention to expressive values and self-actualization. We therefore place the *FmNu* group further toward the nonconformist pole of Figure 4.4.

The household positions used in Figure 4.4 are incomplete, and so are the types of transitions. However, they capture the dominant streams of household formation and dissolution through the life course. The main reason for the incompleteness of positions is that surveys do not capture the more complex trajectories. They typically only record the current status and do not pose questions about earlier states (i.e., the "ever" questions). In fact, only at the third round in 1999–2000 did we manage to insert the "ever-cohabited" question in the European Values Survey (EVS). In the two earlier rounds, there are large samples of married respondents, but no information whatsoever about their different household formation experiences.

The overall outcome of this section is that there should be an ordering of individual household positions along the vertical axis of Figure 4.4. In this ordering, cohabitants without children (*Coh0*) should score highest on all nonconformist value orientations, followed by singles and formerly married (*FmNu*). Residents in parental households should come next. More toward the opposite pole are married persons without children, cohabiting parents, and married parents who ever cohabited. Married parents who never cohabited should constitute the most conservative group.

The "footprints" scheme is important for the SDT theory for several reasons. First, it connects demographic choices explicitly to a dynamic model of cultural change. In doing so, it goes much further than the neo-classic economic "adjustment for tastes" which merely recognizes static "addictions" (Becker, 1996). Second, empirically the "footprints" can be checked in cross sections and for a wide variety of items. And third, we can use the "footprints" to follow the SDT geographic diffusion throughout Europe, and further to other, non-European settings. The latter has become possible mainly thanks to the European and World Values Surveys. We now turn our attention to these empirical findings for a set of European countries.

Do We Find the Footprints of Selection and Adaptation in the New SDT Countries?

In this empirical section we make use of 80 attitude or value items that were used in the 1999–2000 round of the European Values Studies. In this chapter, EVS data are used for all respondents in the age bracket 18 to 45. The items are listed in Table 4.2, and they are all dichotomized with the score of unity given to the nonconventional or nonconformist end of the scale. Such a uniform recoding facilitates the subsequent inspection of value profiles according to household situation.

The list of Table 4.2 contains 9 major subjects. The largest number of items (15) pertains to attitudes related to marriage as an institution, to the qualities needed for the success of marriage, to the meaning of parenthood and parent–child duties, and to the degree of permissiveness with respect to sexual freedom, divorce, and abortion. Secularism is covered by 9 items. They indicate the rejection of traditional beliefs (heaven, hell, etc.), a low level of individual religious sentiments, and a low level of participation and trust in religious institutions and practices. The civil

TABLE 4.2

Overview of 80 Items Used in the Current Analysis, EVS 1999–2000

Topics and Corresponding Items	Item Description
Marriage and family: A1–A15	Marriage outdated institution (A1); children not necessary life fulfillment (A2); parents must not sacrifice for children (A3); justified: casual sex (A4), adultery (A5), divorce (A6), abortion (A7); important for marriage: tolerance and understanding (A8), sharing chores (A9), talking (A10), time together (A11), happy sexual relations (A12); not very important for success marriage: faithfulness (A13), children (A14); single motherhood acceptable (A15).
Religion: A16–A24	Not believing in: god (A16), sin (A17), hell (A18), heaven (A19); no comfort from religion (A20), no moments of prayer or meditation (A21); god not at all important in life (A22); distrust church (A23); religious faith not mentioned as socialization trait (A24).
Civil morality: A25–A36	Justified: soft drugs (A25), homosexuality (A26), joyriding (A27), suicide (A28), euthanasia (A29), speeding (A30), drunk driving (A31), accepting bribe (A32), tax cheating (A33), lying (A34), tax evasion by paying cash (A35), claiming unentitled state benefits (A36).
Politics: B1–B11	Distrust in institutions: education system (B1), army (B2), police (B3), justice system (B4), civil service (B5); participated or willing to participate in: unofficial strikes (B6), attending unlawful demonstrations (B7), joining boycotts (B8), occupying buildings (B9); not more respect for authority (B10); postmaterialist (B11).
Identification: B12–B17	Identification with "Europe and World" (B12), not with "own village or town" (B13), not very or quite proud with own nationality (B14); no priority for national workers (B15); no trust in EU (B16) or UN (B17).
Retreat: B18–B21	Not member of any voluntary organization (B18); no voluntary work (B19); people cannot be trusted (B20); never discuss politics (B21).
Socialization: C1–C7	Not mentioned as desirable trait in educating children: hard work (C1), obedience (C2), good manners (C3), unselfishness (C4), tolerance and respect (C5); stressed as desirable: independence (C6), imagination (C7).
Work qualities: C8–C15	Not mentioned as desirable job aspect: good hours (C8), promotion (C9); stressed as desirable: respected job (C10), responsible job (C11), meeting people (C12), useful for society (C13), interesting work (C14), enabling initiative (C15).
Social distance: C16–C23	Not wanted as neighbors: large families (C16), right-wing people (C17); no objection to have as neighbours: AIDS patients (C18), unstable people (C19), criminal record (C20), drug addicts (C21), homosexuals (C22), immigrants (Western countries) or gypsies (central European countries) (C23).

Note. All items have been coded in the "nonconformist" direction.

morality set, with 12 items, captures permissiveness toward various forms of deviance, but also ethical acceptance of interference in life and death (abortion, suicide). The political set of 11 items deals with distrust in institutions, protest proneness, "postmaterialism," and the rejection of authority more generally. The social distance and tolerance set is made up of 8 items, which indicate the acceptability as neighbors of various types of persons belonging to ethnic or sexual minorities. The expressive values contain both the work and the socialization batteries. The former group of 8 items indicates the preference for intrinsic work qualities over material rewards and status. The socialization items (7) show the preference for independence and imagination rather than for conformity and respect. The identification items (6) distinguish between more global and transnational interests versus national or local ones. However, a global or Third World orientation is not only negatively correlated with national pride, but also with trust in international organizations. The last set of 4 items indicates a retreat from social and political life, absence of memberships or voluntary activities, a distrust in people more generally, and a lack of interest in politics. In all analyses, these 80 items will be used without prior data reduction, such as factor analysis. Hence, no particular structure or simplification is imposed prior to further statistical analysis.

At this point the value profiles can be established according to the various household positions used in the "footprints" diagram. The profiles that are being displayed here are "net" ones; that is, they are those of the 8 household positions remaining after controls for age and age squared (continuous), gender (2 categories), education (4), profession and occupation (9 categories, including separate ones for "students," "unemployed," and "housewives"), and urbanization (2). The controls themselves were performed through multiple classification analysis (MCA), and the outcomes take the form of net household types deviations from the overall mean (here: overall percentage with the given attitude). Such net "household profiles" of deviations are computed for all 80 items. Subsequently a first simple tally of the number of net *positive* deviations, that is, in the nonconformist direction, can be produced for each household position. Such a tally is already highly revealing of the overall nonconformism profile and of the "footprints" of the selection/adaptation process.

The outcomes are displayed in Figures 4.5, 4.6, and 4.7. Figure 4.5 gives the number of net positive deviations in the nonconformist direction for the 80 items and the 8 household positions for major groups of countries. Scandinavia-2 is made up of Sweden and Denmark, West-3 consists of Belgium, France, and Germany, South-2 contains Spain and

Portugal (not yet enough cohabitants in 1999 in the sample of other Mediterranean countries), Central-7 comprises Croatia, Slovenia, Slovak Republic, Czech Republic, Hungary, Poland, and Lithuania, and East-5, finally, is composed of Belarus, Ukraine, Russian Federation, Romania, and Bulgaria.

Figure 4.5 immediately shows that the "footprints" are found in all these major regions of Europe, including the "old SDT" countries like Sweden and Denmark as well as in the "SDT-newcomers" of Southern, Central, and Eastern Europe. The five profiles are also remarkably similar:

- Cohabitants without children (*Coh0*) indeed tend to exhibit the most nonconformist values profile of all.
- Marriage and parenthood are associated with major readjustments in the conventional and conformist direction.
- Married parents who never cohabited (*Mar + N*) display by far the most conservative attitudes on all dimensions involved.
- The earlier cohabitation experience indeed appears to leave a more permanent imprint in the nonconformist direction, even after marriage and parenthood have been achieved (compare *Mar + E* to *Mar + N*).
- Also, divorce (*FmNu*) produces a move away from the stability of conventional opinions held by married parents.

The main surprise of the exercise was that respondents who were still living in the parental home displayed a high degree of heterogeneity according to the country grouping used here. One could expect that in the early SDT countries late home leavers are more rare and more clearly a "residual group" is left behind as a result of more conservative values. This holds very clearly in the Scandinavian group, with the smallest number of net positive deviations for the *Respar* category. But it does not hold as well for the Western group, and particularly not for France, where home stayers have much more libertarian and nonconformist attitudes. Evidently, there are more intricate mechanisms at work here that we cannot capture with the simple and small surveys of the EVS-type.

Figures 4.6 and 4.7 provide a finer breakdown to illustrate that the "footprints" pattern still holds remarkably well for smaller geographical units (single countries or pairs of countries) and that it emerges for the various subsets of attitude items as well. As indicated in Table 4.2, the items in the "A" set deal with secularism, ethics, and morality including these pertaining to the family, the "B" items with the political and societal orientations, and the "C" items mainly with the expressive values.

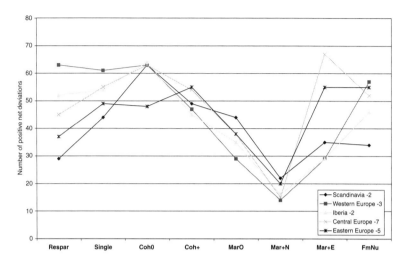

FIGURE 4.5   Number of positive net deviations in nonconfirmist direction for 80 value items according to household position.

Note. 1999 EVS results for 5 groups of European countries (controlling for gender, age, age squared, education, profession, and urbanicity—maximum overall nonconformist score = 80)

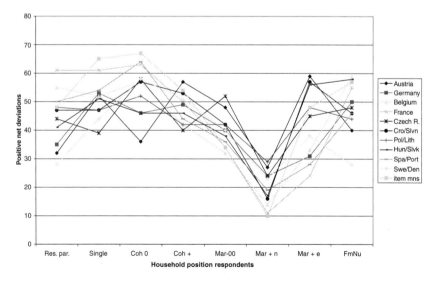

FIGURE 4.6   Number of positive (= unconventional) net deviations, 80 items EVS 1999.

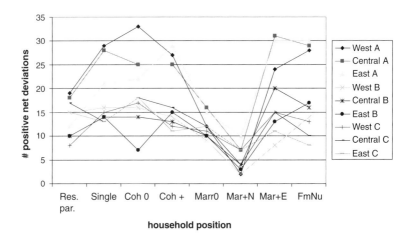

FIGURE 4.7   Number of positive (= nonconformist)
net deviations for groups of tems and countries, EVS 1999.

Figure 4.7 then illustrates that the typical footprints profiles according
to the household positions are showing up for all three sets of attitudes
and in all major country groups.

The bottom line is that the Central and Eastern European countries
and the two Iberian ones are not in any way exceptional with respect to
the dynamics that link values to choices and choices to values as
hypothesized in the selection/adaptation framework. Also, earlier values and choices retain a more lasting imprint, even after the completion
of other transitions later on in life. Finally, these strikingly similar profiles illustrate that the dynamics of the SDT are equally operating in the
former Communist and Iberian countries as in the Western and
Northern parts of Europe. These parts of Europe are squarely no longer
exceptional. And the emerging of the new SDT living arrangements in
the Eastern Mediterranean will not come as a surprise either.

CONCLUSION

At present everyone has come to terms with the fact that the FDT is a
worldwide phenomenon. Furthermore, everyone equally agrees with
the observation that the FDT can take off at just about any level of economic development, and in strictly rural as well as urban societies. But
will the SDT be equally universal? Or indeed, as David Coleman expects,
will it remain a regional idiosyncrasy? Obviously, we can only speculate

about the probabilities of such a more global diffusion, in the same way that one could only speculate in the 1950s and 1960s about the eventuality of pervasive fertility control emerging in the then developing countries. Hence, what are the chances of the SDT spreading beyond European populations in the coming decades?

We propose to answer this question for two demographic components separately. First, will sub-replacement fertility spread far beyond Europe and become an intrinsic part of non-European reproductive systems too? And second, will the nuptiality system diversify and accommodate new forms of partner choice and living arrangements as well?

There is already a sound factual basis for a positive answer to the first question, as illustrated by the most recent total fertility rates (TFRs) published in the 2000 United Nations (UN) Demographic Yearbook (UN, 2002). Not only Japan (latest TFR = 1.34), but also South Korea (1.41) and all Chinese populations [Mainland (1.80), Hong Kong (0.97), Macao (0.91), Taiwan (1.76), Singapore (1.58)] currently have sub-replacement fertility or have had it for more than a decade. At present, Thailand (TFR = 2.00) is about to join that group as well. Hence, much of the Far East is already a part of the sub-replacement group. But sub-replacement fertility also emerged in other countries with less accommodating religions and/or with much lower standards of living than the industrialized West or Far East. Striking examples of largely Muslim populations with sub-replacement fertility are those of Kazakhstan (TFR = 1.75) and several Persian speaking provinces of Iran. But also Caribbean populations have joined the sub-replacement group: Barbados (TFR = 1.50), Cuba (1.60), Trinidad and Tobago (1.72), Martinique (1.80), and Puerto Rico (1.87). And last but not least, sub-replacement fertility is also reported by the Demographic and Health surveys held in Indian states in 1998–1999 (International Institute for Population Sciences, 2000). More specifically, sub-replacement fertility is found in Goa (1.77) and Kerala (1.96), and furthermore in the urban parts of the states of Karnataka (1.89), Himachal Pradesh (1.74), Punjab (1.79), Jammu and Kashmir (1.66), West Bengal (1.69), and Assam (1.50). It comes therefore as no surprise that the United Nations Population Division now envisages the possibility of sustained sub-replacement fertility spreading to much larger parts of the world, and that the latest set of UN World Population projections (2004, in press) provides a new "sub-replacement scenario."

In the domains of nuptiality and household formation, very significant increases in mean ages at first marriage for both men and women have occurred in the last four decades, and this was witnessed in all types of societies, including Muslim and Sub-Saharan populations. But the most rapid rises in ages at marriage are in major Asian countries such as Japan, Taiwan, Korea, Singapore, and especially China (Jones, 2006). Probably this is not yet a sign that cohabitation is on the rise there too, but at least in Japan there is very recent evidence from two large surveys that 10 to 20% of marriages for women born respectively in the 1950s and 1970s were preceded by spells of cohabitation (Raymo & Iwasawa, 2006).

William J. Goode's 1963 prediction, formulated some 40 years ago, that these transformations were going to happen as a part of an overall demographic revolution was visionary in this respect. Equally impressive in Goode's *World Revolution and Family Patterns* is that he connects these increases in ages at marriage not only to the classic structural features such as industrialization and urbanization, but equally to shifts in the ideational system, and more particularly to the rise in individual autonomy, gender egalitarianism (he calls it "equalitarianism"; 1963, p. 54), free partner choice, and a weakening of older normative and institutional influences. In other words, families all over the world would converge to both more nuclear households and more conjugal relations, and would move away from extended and "patriarchal" types. And families would not solely do so because of structural changes or economic constraints but also because of the growing importance attached to individual freedom of choice and right to self-determination (which Goode unambiguously applauds in his last paragraphs; p. 380). Yet in Goode's reasoning, this individualistic outlook is not so much a goal in its own right but mainly an outcome, as the last sentence in *World Revolution* shows:

> For me, then, the major and sufficing justification for the newly emerging family patterns is that they offer people at least the potentialities of greater fulfillment, even if most do not seek it or achieve it. (1963, p. 380)

In the sense of the SDT, self-fulfillment and articulations of autonomy are *primary* ideational goals *in their own right*, sought by a majority of people and on a global level, and these, frequently in conjunction with structural factors, set the direction of change in household formation and composition. And if rising ages at marriage connected to longer male schooling, rising costs of living and economic hardship relative to material expectations, and occurring within the framework of arranged unions, are still part and parcel of the FDT, further rises in ages at marriage for women connected to expanding female education and empowerment, diminishing age gaps between spouses, free partner choice, premarital sex, and eventually a rise in cohabitation or in other unconventional types of union are sure signs of the onset of the SDT. However, because the classic statistical data collection apparatus is still oriented to the traditional household types, we may be slow in discovering the emergence of nontraditional and more transient living arrangements. In short, we will only discover such new patterns if sufficiently fine tuned demographic surveys are consciously and purposefully making the effort of probing into these matters.

The answer to the question whether or not the SDT can spread well beyond the Western societies and cultures is probably positive. Admittedly, it will remain difficult to make a neat separation between the effects of structural factors and ideational ones respectively on marriage postponement and low fertility. But that has never been easy, not even in the case of the FDT, in the first instance because these sets of factors are often causally interconnected. Furthermore, one should also realize that mass media are producing a "world culture" in which individual autonomy and self-actualization have a very prominent, if not dominant, place, and that these provide both motivations and justifications for the onset of the SDT. Political, religious, and ideological backlashes are of course always possible (e.g., both Christian and Muslim fundamentalist reactions), but at least until now the experience has been that such reactions have not been strong enough to cause decisive trend reversals.

Our bet is that David Coleman's conjecture that the SDT will only remain a local European or Western "parochial" phenomenon will turn out to be wrong as well, and that more and more evidence pointing in the direction of the SDT will emerge in the next two decades in many non-Western populations.

CONCLUSIONS

Before formulating an answer to the four questions addressed in this chapter, we would like to make a major preliminary point. We do so to avoid subsequent misunderstanding about the role of culture in the SDT. And this point is that the SDT theory fully recognizes the effects of macro-level structural changes and of micro-level economic calculus. However, it does not consider these explanations as "sufficient," but merely as "necessary" or "nonredundant." By the same token, cultural explanations are nonredundant, but equally insufficient. More specifically, the SDT theory does not consider cultural change as endogenous to any economic model, but as a necessary additional force with its own exogenous effects on demographic outcomes. Also, culture is not treated as some form of "addiction," nor as a fixed script, but as a dynamic set of value orientations. As such, these orientations can change at the individual level and they can be linked recursively to the unfolding of the life course. And they can also change at the collective level during particular periods of time, or shift to new configurations with the succession of cohorts. Moreover, these ideational shifts can occur at very different household income levels, at a wide variety of durations of education, and at highly varied levels of economic development.

With these remarks in mind, we now turn to the four questions formulated in the introduction.

Question 1: Is the SDT Merely a Continuation of the FDT and Only a Description of a "Secondary" Set of Phenomena?

The SDT differs significantly from the FDT both in terms of demographic predictions and in terms of the underlying motivations. Because the SDT predicts generalized sub-replacement fertility (in tandem with a greater plurality of living arrangements and household structures), it also points at the growing importance of international and global migration. Furthermore, the SDT predictions are departing from the benign equilibrium outcomes of the FDT (such as a stationary population, not much need for migration, and the predominance of the stable conjugal family). By contrast, the SDT sees much rougher seas ahead. First, sustained sub-replacement fertility will cause extra aging and shake all welfare systems. Second, such low fertility will stimulate replacement migration, not so much as an antidote to aging but as a means of countering labor force shortages. And third, some of the new living arrangements may be more unstable than the traditional arrangements, or even less adequate as a setting for procreation and especially socialization. Union dissolution will continue to be a major cause of low fertility as well. Would such outcomes be no more than "secondary" phenomena?

Question 2: Is the SDT Spreading to the Rest of Europe?

Here, the answer is definitely positive. The SDT did not stop at the Pyrenees or the Alps, and it crossed into Central and Eastern Europe as well. In all these areas we witnessed a rise in the share of extramarital births, which clearly points in the direction of new contexts of procreation (cohabitation, single parenthood). Equally striking is the finding that the individual value profiles according to living arrangement turned out to be so similar in all parts of Europe. Admittedly, the indicators used here are not perfect, but they are not exactly meaningless either. However, for a finer resolution and a much needed update of the picture, a new round of demographic surveys is required.

Question 3: Were the Demographic Changes Since 1990 in Central and Eastern Europe Mainly the Outcome of the Crisis Associated with the Transition to a Market Economy?

The crisis of the 1990s in Eastern and Central Europe was definitely propitious for the postponement of marriages and births, and hence for the precipitous dip to very low levels of fertility. But a purely crisis-based explanation is untenable. First, much of the crisis is over in countries such as Slovenia, the Czech Republic, and Hungary, where gross domestic product (GDP) per capita has risen to levels higher than in the 1980s, and there has been no return to earlier marriage or higher fertility. Instead, cohabitation is spreading and so is procreation outside marriage. Hence, something else must have happened in addition to the initial crisis response. Second, the SDT seems to advance faster in the countries with the more successful economic and political performance, which is again indicative of the importance of factors other than those associated with the economic crisis. Among these other factors that produce the sustained trend in the direction of the SDT there are again major structural and cultural ones. On the structural side, for instance, the post-Communist era has been characterized by expanding female education in several of these countries, and this has definitely contributed to the postponement of marriages and births (e.g., Kantarova, 2004). Similarly, the rise of individual autonomy and freedom of choice has legitimized the adoption of nontraditional living arrangements in a very short time. These features will not be reversed that easily, and hence the SDT will continue on its course as in the former Western part of Europe.

Question 4: Can the SDT Spread to Other Continents and Non-European Societies?

At present this is obviously a major new question for demographers and other social scientists to ponder. The SDT prediction may ultimately prove to be wrong and end up on the scrap heap together with other erroneous forecasts, but its expectations are nonetheless very clear:

1. The normative and institutional props of traditional union formation and household structures will systematically weaken in all societies that move in the direction of egalitarian and democratic systems governed by the respect for individual choice. This implies that other forms of union formation will expand in the

wake of such ideational developments. The political evolution of countries is then at least as crucial for the onset of the SDT as their economic futures.

2. Alongside individual autonomy, self-realization will also become a major goal in its own right. This will simultaneously produce a rising demand for higher education, especially among women, stimulate other tastes and lifestyles, and result in sub-replacement fertility.

3. Communication technology and mass media are spreading knowledge about all new forms of behavior to the remotest corners of the world. Moreover, as the Thornton, Binstock, and Ghimire chapter (this volume) shows, new forms of behavior are associated by the public itself with being "more advanced" and "more developed." Just as the FDT in many developing countries benefited from this communication revolution, so also will the diffusion of the SDT be enhanced by global communication. Fundamentalist reactions are likely to occur in response to these global ideational shifts, but so far their success has been too limited to stem the overall shift toward "postmaterialist" and expressive value orientations.

ACKNOWLEDGMENTS

The authors thank the Consortium of the European Values Surveys for the insertion of the questions on earlier cohabitation and divorce/separation in the 1999 questionnaire, which permitted the necessary fine tuning of household positions used in this paper. Without these two new but simple "ever cohabited "or "ever divorced" questions we would not have been able to inspect the "footprints" model. We also thank the Consortium for the use of the national EVS data sets. Finally, David Coleman provided the slides of his EAPS-Conference presentation in Warsaw in 2003, so that we had a more precise notion of his criticisms.

REFERENCES

Alwin, D. (1989). Changes in qualities valued in children, 1964–1984. *Social Science Research*, *44*(2), 1–42.
Ariès, P. (1962). *Centuries of childhood: A social history of family life*. New York: Random House.
Ariès, P. (1980). Two successive motivations for the declining birth rates in the West. *Population and Development Review*, *6*(4), 645–650.

Barber, J. S., Axinn, W., & Thornton, A. (2002). The influence of attitudes on family formation processes. In R. Lesthaeghe (Ed.), *Meaning and choice: Value orientations and life course decisions* (pp. 45–93). The Hague: Netherland Interdisciplinary Demographic Institute.

Becker, G. S. (1996). *Accounting for tastes.* Cambridge, MA: Harvard University Press.

Calot, G., & Frejka, T. (2001). Cohort reproductive patterns in low-fertility countries. *Population and Development Review, 27*(1), 103–132.

Clarkberg, M. (2002). Family formation experiences and changing values: The effects of cohabitation and marriage on the important things in life. In R. Leshtaeghe (Ed.), *Meaning and choice: Value orientations and life course decisions* (pp. 183–250). The Hague: Netherland Interdisciplinary Demography Institute.

Clarkberg, M., Stolzenberg, R. M. & Waite, L. (1995). Attitudes, values and entrance into cohabitational versus marital unions. *Social Forces, 74,* 609–634.

Cliquet, R. (1992). *The second demographic transition: Fact or fiction?* Strasbourg, France: Council of Europe Population Studies.

Coale, A. J., & Trussell, T. J. (1974). Model fertility schedules: Variations in the age structure of childbearing in human populations. *Population Index 40*(2), 185–258.

Coleman, D. (2003). *Why we don't have to believe without doubting in the Second Demographic Transition: Some agnostic comments.* Paper presented at the Conference of the European Association for Population Studies, Warsaw, Poland.

Council of Europe. (2004). *Recent demographic developments in Europe, 2003* (pp. 66–68). Strasbourg, France: Council of Europe Publishing.

Dalla Zuanna, G. (2002). The Banquet of Aeolus: A familistic interpretation of Italy's lowest-low fertility. *Demographic Research 4*(5), 133–161.

Easterlin, R. (1973). Relative economic status and the American fertility swing. In E. Sheldon (Ed.), *Family economic behavior* (pp. 170–223). Philadelphia, PA: Lippincott.

Goldscheider, F., & Waite, L. (1987). Nest-leaving patterns and the transition to marriage for young men and women. *Journal of Marriage and the Family, 49,* 507–516.

Goode, W. J. (1963). *World revolution and family patterns.* New York: Free Press.

Inglehart, R. (1970). *The silent revolution.* Princeton, NJ: Princeton University Press.

Inglehart, R. (1980). Aggregate stability and individual flux: The level of analysis paradox. *American Political Science Review, 79,* 97–116.

International Institute for Population Sciences. (2002). *India National Family Health Survey 1998–99* (pp. 87–89). Calverton, MD: ORC-MACRO.

Jansen, M., & Kalmijn, M. (2000). Emancipatiewaarden en de levensloop van jong-volwassen vrouwen: Een panelanalyse van wederzijdse invloeden. *Sociologische Gids, 47,* 293–314.

Jansen, M., & Kalmijn, M. (2002). Investment in family life: The impact of value orientations on patterns of consumption, production and reproduction in married and cohabiting couples. In R. Lesthaeghe (Ed.), *Meaning and choice: Value orientations and life course decisions* (pp. 129–159). The Hague: Netherland Interdisciplinary Demographic Institute.

Jones, G.W. (2006). *Delayed marriage in Pacific Asia, gender relations and the fertility crisis.* National University of Singapore, Asia Research Institute Working Papers 61.

Kantorova, V. (2004). Education and entry into motherhood: The Czech Republic during state socialism and the transition period, 1970–1997. *Demographic Review, S3*(10).

Kohler, H-P., Billari, F., & Ortega, J. A. (2002). The emergence of lowest-low fertility in Europe during the 1990s. *Population and Development Review, 28*(4), 641–680.

Kohn, M. L. (1977). *Class and conformity: A study in values.* Chicago: University of Chicago Press.

Lesthaeghe, R. (2001, March). *Postponement and recuperation: Recent fertility trends and forecasts in six Western European countries.* Paper presented at the IUSSP Seminar on Below Replacement Fertility, Tokyo.

Lesthaeghe, R. (2002). *Meaning and choice: Value orientations and life course decisions.* (NIDI-CBGS Monograph 37). The Hague: Netherlands Interdisciplinary Demographic Institute.

Lesthaeghe, R., & Surkyn J. R. (2002). New forms of household formation in Central and Eastern Europe: Are they related to newly emerging value orientations? *Economic Survey of Europe, 1*(6), 197–216. Geneva: United Nations Commission for Europe.

Lesthaeghe, R., & van de Kaa, D. J. (1986). Twee demografische transities? In R. Lesthaeghe & van de Kaa, D. J. (Eds.), *Bevolking: Groei en krimp, mens en maatschappij book supplement* (pp. 9–24). Deventer: Van Loghum-Slaterus.

Lesthaeghe, R., & Willems, P. (1999). Is low fertility a temporary phenomenon in the EU? *Population and Development Review, 25*(1), 211–228.

Livi-Bacci, M. (1971). *A century of Portuguese fertility.* Princeton, NJ: Princeton University Press.

Maslow, A. (1954). *Motivation and personality.* New York: Harper and Row.

Micheli, G. (1996). New patterns of family formation in Italy. Which tools for which interpretation? *Genus, 52*(1–2), 15–52.

Micheli, G. (2000). Kinship, family and social network: The anthropological embedment of fertility change in Southern Europe. *Demographic Research, 3*(13).

Moors, G. (2002). Reciprocal relations between gender role values and family formation. In R. Lesthaeghe (Ed.), *Meaning and choice: Value orientations and life course decisions* (pp. 217–250). The Hague: Netherland Interdisciplinary Demography Institute.

Palomba, R. (1995). Italy: The invisible change. In R. Palomba & H. Moors (Eds.), *Population, family and welfare* (pp. 158–176). Oxford: Clarendon Press.

Putnam, R. (2000). *Bowling alone.* New York: Simon and Schuster.

Rabusic, L. (2001). Value change and demographic behaviour in the Czech Republic. *Czech Sociological Review 9*(1), 99–122.

Raymo, J., & Iwasawa, M. (2006, March). *Unmarried cohabitation and family formation in Japan.* Paper presented at the Annual Meetings of the Population Association of America, Los Angeles.

Reher, D. S. (1998). Family ties in Western Europe: Persistent contrasts. *Population and Development Review 24*(2), 203–234.

Rychtarikova, J. (2000). Demographic transition or demographic shock in recent population development in the Czech Republic? *Acta Universitas Carolinae Geographica, 1,* 89–102.

Sobotka, T., Zeman, K., & Kantorova, V. (2003). Demographic shifts in the Czech Republic after 1989: A second demographic transition view. *European Journal of Population, 19*(1), 1–29.

Stloukal, L. (1998). *Declining nuptiality in the Czech Republic, 1989–1996.* Paper presented at the Annual Conference of the British Society for Population Studies, Cambridge, UK.

Surkyn, J. (2003, August). *Changing attitudes and values across Europe: Social cohesion and the family.* Paper presented at the Conference of the European Association for Population Studies(EAPS), session Q1, Warsaw.

Thornton, A. (1985). Reciprocal influences of family and religion in a changing world. *Journal of Marriage and the Family, 47,* 381–394.

Thornton, A., Axinn, W., & Hill, D. (1992). Reciprocal effects of religiosity, cohabitation and marriage. *American Journal of Sociology, 98,* 628–651.

Thornton, A., Binstock, G., & Ghimire, D. (2004, June). *International networks, ideas and family change.* Paper presented at the Conference on Ideational Factors in International Family Change, University of Michigan, Ann Arbor.

United Nations. (2002). *Demographic yearbook 2000,* (ST/ESA/STAT/SER.R/31, pp. 125–142). New York: UN Publishing Division.

van de Kaa, D. J. (1987). Europe's second demographic transition. *Population Bulletin, 42*(1), 1–59.

van de Kaa, D. J. (1994). The second demographic transition revisited: Theories and expectations. In G. Beets et al. (Eds.), *Population and family in the low countries 1993* (pp. 91–126). NIDI-CBGS Monograph 30. Lisse, the Netherlands: Zwets & Zeitlinger.

van de Kaa, D. J. (2004). The true communality: In reflexive societies fertility is a derivative. *Population Studies 58*(1), 77–92.

van Rysselt, R. (1989, June). *Developments in attitudes and values orientations: A comparison between birth cohorts in the Netherlands over the period 1970–1985.* Symposium on Life Histories and Generations at the meeting of the Netherlands Institute for Advanced Studies, Wassenaar.

Zakharov, S., & Ivanova, E. (1996). Fertility decline and recent changes in Russia: On the threshold of the second demographic transition. In J. Davanzo (Ed.), *Russia's Demographic Crisis* (pp. 36–82). Santa Monica CA: Rand Corporation.

Zakharov, S. (1997, November). *Fertility trends in Russia and the European new independent states: Crisis or turning point?* Expert Group Meeting on Below-Replacement Fertility, (ESA/P/WP.140). New York: United Nations Population Division.

Zeman, K., Sobotka, T., & Kantarova, V. (2001, June). Halfway between socialist greenhouse and postmodern plurality: Life course transitions of young Czech women. Paper presented at the Euresco Conference on the Second Demographic Transition, Bad Herrenalb, session 2B.

Ideational Influences on Family Change in the United States

Amie Emens
Population Studies Center

Colter Mitchell
University of Michigan

William G. Axinn
Department of Sociology

In this chapter we summarize the literature about ideational influences on family formation behaviors in the United States. The U.S. population has been characterized by substantial changes in marriage, divorce, childbearing, cohabitation, and gender roles over the past half century. We begin by describing these changes briefly as background for our summary of research on ideational influences on those changes. Then we review the key streams of social theory motivating research into the influence of ideational factors on changes in family formation processes in the United States. Next we review the powerful measurement resources that have fueled unparalleled research on this topic in the United States, again very briefly. Finally we turn to a topic-by-topic review of the literature on ideational influences on cohabiting, marital, divorce, and childbearing behavior. Because the empirical literature on ideational influences on family change in the United States is large, it is not possible to provide a comprehensive review of that literature here. Nevertheless, the summary we provide points toward key insights into ideational influences on family change.

FAMILY CHANGE IN THE UNITED STATES

The past several centuries have been characterized by both continuity and change in family formation behaviors in the United States

(Thornton, Axinn, & Xie, in press). In the summary provided here we focus on changes between the early 1900s and the beginning of the 21st century. We focus on changes in marriage, divorce, nonmarital cohabitation, and childbearing. Our review begins by summarizing behavioral changes and then moves on to describe changes in attitudes about those same behaviors. Although our primary agenda is descriptions of changes in family formation, we briefly comment on other closely related changes including labor force participation, education, religion, and gender role attitudes.

Changing Family Formation and Related Behaviors

Behavioral changes in family formation in the United States during the 1900s follow a well-known pattern documented in many previous historical studies (Cherlin, 1992; Fitch & Ruggles, 2000; Teachman, Tedrow, & Crowder, 2001). In general, rates of marriage and childbearing declined slowly and steadily during the first half of the 1900s, had a sharp rise between 1950 and 1960 directly following World War II, and then returned to decline after 1960. Rates of divorce followed the opposite trend, rising slowly through the first half of the century, bumping up during World War II, dipping after World War II, and then rising again after 1960. Premarital cohabitation was extremely rare until the late 1960s, rising steadily after 1970 and compensating for much of the post-1970 decline in marriage rates. In the paragraphs that follow we describe these well-documented trends in greater detail.

Marriage. Although changes in the age structure of the U.S. population can account for some changes in crude rates of marriage, the U.S. population has also been characterized by important changes in age specific rates of marriage. Changes in age specific rates of marriage reflect both changes in the fraction of the population who never marry and changes in the timing of marriage. However, changes in the fraction who never marry account for relatively little of the long-term decline in age specific rates of marriage in the United States.

Between 1860 and 1920 the percentage of White men and women age 45–54 years who had never married increased steadily (from 5.7 to 12.8 for men and 7.3 to 11.0 for women). From 1920 to 1980 there was a fairly steady decline in the percent who never married, to 5.6 and 4.2 for men and women, respectively. Between 1980 and 2000 there was a slight increase for both men and women, with both around 8% near the end of the millennium (Fitch & Ruggles, 2000). This trend was slightly different for Blacks, who began with percentages comparable to those of Whites

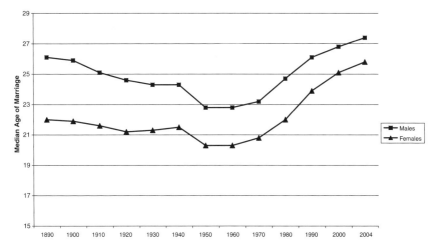

FIGURE 5.1   Estimated median age at first marriage
for U.S. males and females 1890–2004.

Source: U.S. Census Bureau, Current Population Survey: March and Annual Social
and Economic Supplements, 2004 and earlier. Internet Release, 2005, Table MS-2.

in the late 1800s, but increased steadily to about 12% never marrying
for both men and women by the end of the millennium (Fitch & Ruggles,
2000). Thus the vast majority of Americans will probably eventually
marry, and this has only changed slightly over the last 140 years.

Although there have been only moderate changes in the fraction of
people who never marry, there has been a much larger change in the
timing of marriage. This change is reflected in the median age of marriage (the age when half of the never married population has married
once), as shown in Figure 5.1 (U.S. Census, 2005a). Between 1890 and
1940, women's median age of first marriage remained relatively steady,
fluctuating between 21.2 and 22 years, whereas men's median age at
first marriage for the same time period declined, from 26.1 years, to 24.3
years. Median age at first marriage declined sharply in the decade after
1940 for both sexes, with women falling to age 20.3, and men to 22.8 by
1950. This postwar decline in median age at first marriage leveled off in
the 1950s, and by the early 1960s, median age at first marriage began to
slowly increase. Beginning in the early 1970s, the median age at marriage climbed significantly for both sexes for two decades, reaching 26.1
years for men and 23.9 years for women by 1990. Median age at first
marriage has continued to increase from 1990 to the present, though at
a slightly slower rate, reaching 27.4 years for men and 25.8 years for

women by 2004. This dramatic rise in median age at marriage corresponds to an equally dramatic rise in enrollments in college (discussed later), and the two changes are probably linked (Marini, 1978; Thornton, Axinn, & Teachman, 1995).

Cohabitation. Nonmarital cohabitation was rare in the United States of the 1950s and rapidly grew more common beginning in the 1960s (Thornton et al., in press). Bumpass and Sweet (1989, p. 619) found that "the proportion of persons who cohabited before first marriage quadrupled from 11% for marriages in 1965–1974 to 44% for marriage in 1980–1984." The growth of cohabitation slowed, but continued to increase to 56% for marriages in 1990–1994 (Bumpass & Lu, 2000). If union formation is defined as both marriage and cohabitation, the rate of union formation for ages 20–25 has remained fairly constant since 1970 (Cherlin, 1992; Raley, 2000), with the decline in marriage offset by the rise in cohabitation. Contrary to early speculation, enrollment in college reduces rates of premarital cohabitation and once out of school those with more education are less likely to cohabit than those with less education (Thornton et al., 1995).

Divorce. Contrary to popular opinion, the increase in divorce in the United States is not a recent phenomenon, but rather a long-term trend that began at least as early as the Civil War. From 1860 until 1915, the crude divorce rate[1] (the number of divorces per 1,000 population) steadily increased from about 0.3 to 1. After 1915 this trend continued, but the fluctuations in the crude divorce rate became more dramatic (NCHS, 1973). As shown in Figure 5.2, three major peaks in this trend occurred between 1900 and 2004 (NCHS, 1973, 2004; U.S. Census, 2005b). The first major change occurred near the beginning of World War I, when rates increased by over 50% in only a few years. However, by 1920 the divorce rate began to decline again, returning to levels that were relatively consistent with the earlier trend. Through the early 1940s the increase in the divorce rate was roughly offset by a long-term decline in the rate of marital dissolution by widowhood, so that the total rate of dissolving marriages through either divorce or widowhood remained relatively stable. The divorce rate suddenly increased again during World War II, up to 3.7 per thousand in 1946, an increase of nearly 75%

---

[1]The crude divorce rate can be affected by changes in population age distribution and marriage timing. Nevertheless, the general pattern seen in the crude divorce rate was very similar to more precise estimates of divorce.

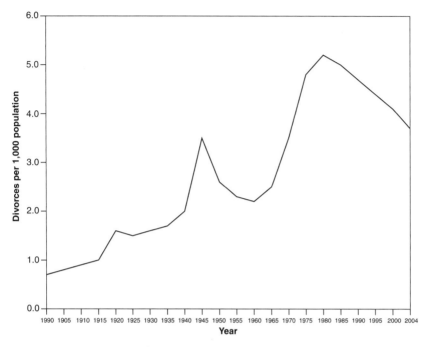

FIGURE 5.2   Crude divorce rate 1990–2004.
Source: 1900–1950, 100 years of marriage and Divorce Statistics 1867–1967. Series 21(24), Table 1: 1950–2002, 2004–2005, U.S. Statistical Abstract: 2002–2004, Natbialvital statistics, Report, Vol. 53(21)

over 5 years. Just as quickly as it increased, the crude divorce rate dropped again, reaching a low of about 2.1 in 1958. This decline in the crude divorce rate was so large that through most of the 1950s the crude divorce rate was much lower than predicted by the initial trend set almost 80 years before. It was during the late 1960s and 1970s, however, that the crude divorce rate had its largest increase, reaching its highest point in the early 1980s at 5.3. Since the mid-1980s there has been a decline the crude divorce rate, so that by early in the 21st century these rates returned to the level of the long-term trend beginning many decades earlier (Cherlin, 1992; Goldstein, 1999). In 2004, the crude divorce rate was at its lowest since the mid-1970s, at 3.7. Based on these rates some scholars have estimated that of those marriages begun over the last several decades, about half will end in divorce (Cherlin, 1992; Teachman et al., 2001).

Childbearing.   The overall trend in childbearing since the beginning of the 20th century has been downward, but as shown in Figure 5.3, there has been substantial variation in that trend (NCHS, 1977; U.S. Census, 2005b). From 1917 to 1940 there was an overall decline in fertility, from a total fertility rate[2] (TFR) of 3.3 to 2.2. Following World War II there was a large increase in childbearing, often called the Baby Boom, which peaked in the late 1950s at a TFR of about 3.7, and was then followed by a quick decline in fertility until the early 1980s (TFR of about 1.8). Childbearing increased slightly after that and has remained a TFR between 2 and 2.1 until the end of the century (Anderton, Barrett, & Bogue, 1997). Although total fertility has declined, marital fertility has declined faster than nonmarital fertility (Teachmanet al., 2001). As a result, the proportion of all births that occur outside of marriage has grown substantially over time in the United States. In 1950, only 2% of White women who gave birth experienced a nonmarital birth, but by 2000 this percent had steadily increased to 26%. Black women experienced a similar increase in nonmarital fertility, with 26% of births being nonmarital in 1963, and 62% in 2000 (Pagnini & Rindfuss, 1993; Bachu & O'Connell, 2001). Nonmarital births are most commonly found at younger ages and at lower levels of education (Bachu & O'Connell, 2001).

Education.   These long-term changes in family formation processes have taken place in a context of equally important changes in individual activities outside of the family (Ogburn & Tibbets, 1933; Thornton & Fricke, 1987). One of these changes in nonfamily activities is a long-term increase in participation in formal schooling, and an increase in levels of educational attainment among those who go to school. Prior to the 1960s few people in the United States attended college; however, in the last four decades attendance has increased substantially for both men and women. In 1960, 9.7% of men and 5.8% of women were college graduates or higher, and by 2000 these percentages had increased to 27.8 for men and 23.6 for women. In fact, at the time this chapter was completed, more women were enrolled in college and graduate school than men (U.S. Census, 2005c).

---

[2]The total fertility rate (or TFR) is a synthetic cohort-based period rate that controls for the age structure of a population and estimates the average number of children each woman would have over her lifetime if exposed to the age-specific fertility rates of that period.

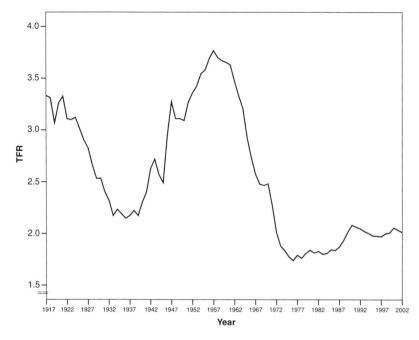

FIGURE 5.3   Total fertility rate, 1917–2002.

Source: 1917–1970, 1977 NCHS Treads in Fertility in the United States, Series 21, Number 28, Table 13: 1970–2002, 2004–2005 Statistical Abstract of the United States. Table Figure 7.5.

Labor Force Participation.   The past two centuries have been characterized by a parallel increase of women participating in the paid labor force. Since the 1960s female labor force participation (for people ages 16–64) has increased, particularly among married women. In 1960 the single female labor force participation rate was around 58%; this was substantially higher than the married female rate of 32%. By the end of the century both groups of women had increased labor force participation and married females had closed the gap, with 68% of single women and 62% of married women in the labor force. By comparison, married men's labor force participation rates actually declined, but still remained higher than those for women. Although single men increased slightly over the last four decades, from 70% to 73%, married men declined substantially, from 89% to 78% (Teachman et al., 2001; U.S. Census Bureau, 2002). Thus these dramatic changes in nonfamily social activities, particularly for women, have paralleled the dramatic changes in family behaviors in the United States.

Religiosity. Religion has a particularly strong connection to ideational change over time. Over this same century of dramatic change in both family formation and nonfamily activities, religiosity in the United States was characterized by both continuity and change. By the late 1990s over 60% of Americans claimed membership in some religious organization, with approximately 45% reporting at least monthly attendance (Sherkat & Ellison, 1999). These levels have remained fairly constant over the last several decades (Hout & Greeley, 1987; Sherkat & Ellison, 1999), but women are more likely than men to both be affiliated with any religion and to attend regularly (Miller & Hoffmann, 1995; Sherkat, 1998). Despite this consistency in attendance, perceptions of religious authority over everyday life, the importance of religion in everyday life, and the frequency of prayer have all declined since the 1960s (Glenn, 1987).

Changing Ideas about the Family

These same decades that have been characterized by dramatic macro-level changes in family and nonfamily behaviors have also been characterized by dramatic macro-level ideational changes. These ideational changes feature reduced conformity to a set of behavioral standards, an increased emphasis on individual freedom and personal autonomy, and the emergence of a norm of tolerance (Thornton, 1989). These U.S. changes occurred at the same time as a parallel set of changes in Europe, where a variety of studies have documented the spread of individualistic ideas in general, and more individualistic attitudes toward family behaviors in particular (Lesthaeghe, 2002; Lesthaeghe & Surkyn, 1988). In the United States these macro shifts can be seen in many different domains of life, including the legal system, sexuality, childrearing, and politics. For the legal system, Schneider (1985) documents a trend toward reduced amounts of moral discourse in family law, as well as a transfer of moral responsibility from the society (and courts) to the individual. In part he suggests that this change is a product of U.S. society's increased focus on individualism and freedom. Alwin documents a corresponding trend in childrearing values. From 1924 until the mid-1990s, U.S. society experienced a decreasing parental desire for obedience in children and an increasing preference for children to be tolerant and autonomous (Alwin, 1988, 1996). Similar to Alwin's finding, Bahr, Mitchell, Li, Walker, and Sucher (2004) find that since 1924, children have increased in their desire to have to have a parent who respects their opinions. This suggests increased desires for children's autonomy from both the parent and the child (Bahr et al., 2004). The sexual revolution of the 1960s is another example of this increased emphasis on personal freedom. In politics, key social movements such as the Women's Movement and the Civil Rights Movement echoed similar themes.

These macro-level general ideational shifts had strong parallels in macro-level changes in family formation attitudes and beliefs. Unfortunately, systematic documentation of attitudes toward family matters in the general population does not extend as far back in time as our documentation of family behaviors. Most of our empirical evidence about attitude begins in the late 1950s and becomes more detailed by the 1970s. Nevertheless, this evidence does reflect important trends in family formation attitudes, trends that closely parallel the behavioral trends documented earlier in this chapter.

Marriage. First we consider trends over time in views of marrying versus remaining single. Although most measures of these attitudes begin in the late 1970s, one earlier study documents a significant decline in negative attitudes toward remaining single between 1957 and 1976 (Veroff, Douvan, & Kulka 1976). Veroff and colleagues show that 53% of adults were negative toward a person who did not marry in 1957, but that by 1976 only 34% of adults were negative toward those who remained single. Their analyses of closely related attitudes demonstrate a similar trend toward less imperative to marry and more tolerance of remaining single over the period 1957 to 1976 (Veroff et al., 1976).

Beginning in the 1970s, however, we find a great deal of stability in attitudes toward marriage. For example, respondents to the Monitoring the Future[3] studies were asked whether they agree or disagree with the statement that "Married people are happier than those who go through life without getting married." The data for women indicate that women's attitudes toward marriage, as measured by this specific item, have remained quite stable from the mid-1970s to the mid-1990s. In the 1990s, 58.5% of women reported agreeing that married people are happier, and in the mid-1970s, 59.5% felt the same way. Men's attitudes toward marriage remained quite stable from the mid-1970s through the mid-1980s, but there was a slight increase from the 1980s to the 1990s in the percentage who agreed that married people are happier. As we discuss later, this increase in the view that married people may be happier cannot be confirmed from other data sources (Thornton & Young-DeMarco, 2001, Table 2).

_____

[3]Monitoring the Future (MTF) has been conducted by the Survey Research Center of the University of Michigan every year since 1976, using a nationally representative sample of high school seniors in the United States (Thornton & Young-DeMarco, 2001).

We also examine responses to a similar statement from the son/daughter sample in the Intergenerational Panel Study.[4] The percentage of women who agreed that married people are happier has remained relatively stable from the mid-1980s to the mid-1990s in this survey as well, but the level of men's agreement with the statement has actually declined slightly. That is, sons in the Intergenerational Panel Study have become a little less positive toward marriage during the same time interval when young men in Monitoring the Future have become a little more positive toward marriage.[5] Both these differences are statistically significant, although neither difference is substantively large. Overall, we fail to find strong or consistent evidence of specific directional trends in young people's attitudes toward marriage between the mid-1970s and the mid-1990s (Thornton and Young-DeMarco, 2001, Table 2).

An exploration of attitudes toward marriage as reflected in other specific measures demonstrates a similar pattern. The percentage of respondents who agree that "there are few good marriages these days" has remained stable in Monitoring the Future data from the mid-1970s to the mid-1990s among both men and women (Thornton & Young-DeMarco, 2001, Table 2). Likewise, the fraction of young men and women participating in the Monitoring the Future study who said that having a good marriage is extremely important and definitely prefer to have a mate remained high (around 82% for women and 72% for men in 1998) and quite stable from the 1980s into the 1990s (Thornton & Young-DeMarco, 2001, Table 2). Thus, there is little evidence of dramatic shifts in attitudes toward marriage between the mid-1970s and the mid-1990s (also see Glenn, 1996).

Cohabitation.   Values, attitudes, and beliefs about heterosexual nonmarital cohabitation have become substantially more accepting in recent decades. The percentage of Monitoring the Future respondents who agree that living together is a good idea increased dramatically throughout the period from the mid-1970s to the mid-1990s for both men and

---

[4]The Intergenerational Panel Study of Parents and Children (IPS) is a survey of White mothers who gave birth in 1961 in the Detroit Metropolitan area and their children. The mothers were interviewed by the Survey Research Center of the University of Michigan twice in 1962 and then again in 1963, 1966, 1977, 1980, 1985, and 1993. The children born in 1961 were interviewed in 1980, when they were aged 18, and then again in 1985 and 1993 (Axinn & Thornton, 2000).

[5]Of course, panel data from the Intergenerational Panel Study confound age effects and period effects, whereas the repeated cross-sectional data from the Monitoring the Future studies do not.

women (an increase from 47 to 62% for men, and from 33 to 51% for women). In fact, there are statistically significant increases in this fraction both from the mid-1970s to the mid-1980s and then again from the mid-1980s to the mid-1990s (Thornton & Young-DeMarco, 2001, Table 5; also, see Schulenberg et al., 1995). Other studies demonstrate the same increase in acceptance of nonmarital cohabitation between the mid-1980s and the mid-1990s. In both the National Survey of Families and Households[6] and the son/daughter sample of the Intergenerational Panel Study we see a significant increase in the fraction of women who believe cohabitation is all right and a more modest increase in the fraction of men who believe cohabitation is all right.

Although marriage was once the only social relationship Americans found acceptable for heterosexual co-residence in an intimate relationship, this is changing. Marriage continues to involve sharing of residence for the vast majority of couples. However, today marriage is not the only acceptable route to co-residence for many American couples. This is one dimension in which the meaning of marriage continues to change in the United States.

Divorce. Like attitudes toward marriage, for attitudes toward divorce we also find dramatic shifts across the 1960s and early 1970s, followed by relative stability since the 1970s. Over the 15 years from 1962 to 1977 it appears there was a dramatic increase in tolerance of divorce. Only 51% of the mothers sampled in the Intergenerational Panel Study disagreed with the statement that "parents should stay together for the sake of the children, even if they do not get along" in 1962, but by 1977 fully 80% disagreed with the same statement (Thornton, 1989). By contrast, the same study shows stability in the fraction of mothers disagreeing with same statement from the mid-1970s to the mid-1990s (Thornton & Young-DeMarco, 2001). Similarly, in the Monitoring the Future studies there are no significant changes over time for either men or women in the percentage of respondents who say that once married, it is very likely they will stay married. Likewise, we find in the NSFH that, for both men and women, the percentage who agree that "marriage is for a lifetime" is almost the same in the mid-1990s as it was in the mid-1980s

---

[6]The National Survey of Families and Households (NSFH) is a nationally representative survey of the noninstitutionalized population aged 18 and over directed by the University of Wisconsin and conduced by the Institute of Survey Research at Temple University. It was first conducted in 1987–1988 with a follow-up approximately 5 years later.

(about 72% for women and 78% for men). Thus, we find stability in attitudes toward divorce from the mid-1970s through the mid-1990s in all three of these studies (Thornton & Young-DeMarco, 2001, Table 3).

Childbearing. We examine two ways to think about attitudes and values regarding the intersections between marriage and childbearing in the United States. One is the extent to which people believe that in order to have a child couples should be married. A second is the degree to which people believe that married couples should have children.

Monitoring the Future data indicate that there have been significant declines in the fraction of women who believe "unmarried childbearing is destructive to society" between the mid-1970s (23%) and the mid-1990s (15%). The fraction of men who share this belief also declined over the same period, although this decline was not statistically significant (Thornton & Young-DeMarco, 2001, Table 8). Thus the negative stigma individuals attribute to having a child outside of marriage appears to be declining across recent decades (Schulenberg et al., 1995).

These results are very consistent with the findings of Ku et al. (1998) from the National Survey of Young Men and the National Survey of Adolescent Men. In these studies, adolescent males were asked their views about the best resolution to a pregnancy for an unmarried girl. Between 1979 and 1995, the percentages recommending marriage, abortion, and adoption all declined substantially, whereas the percentage suggesting that the mother have the baby and the father help to support it increased dramatically from 19 to 59%. Increased support for unmarried childbearing has also been reported by Pagnini and Rindfuss (1993).

The extent to which parenthood within marriage is viewed as mandatory also changed since the 1960s. In the mother sample from the Intergenerational Panel Study, the fraction of women who agreed that "all married couples who can have children should have children" fell from 85% in 1962 to 43% in 1980 (Thornton, 1989). It also appears this imperative to have children has continued to decline between the mid-1980s and the mid-1990s, with the son/daughter sample from the Intergenerational Panel Study demonstrating significant declines in agreement with the same item over this later period (Thornton & Young-DeMarco, 2001, Table 8). This indicates that the view that married couples should also be parents is also weakening.

Overall, then, the extent to which marriage and childbearing are viewed as closely linked behaviors has been changing in at least two ways. Americans are becoming less inclined to believe that marriage is the only appropriate social relationship for childbearing, and they are also becoming less inclined to believe that childrearing should be a necessary dimension of the marital relationship. Both of these changes constitute important transformations in the meaning of marriage. The meaning of marriage is continuing to evolve, so that the activities of childbearing and childrearing are less often seen as fundamentally tied to marriage.

Other Family Attitudes. Since the early 1960s sex role attitudes have become more egalitarian, plateauing in the late 1990s at very high levels of support for egalitarian relationships and societies (Thornton, Alwin, & Camburn, 1983; Thornton & Young-DeMarco, 2001). Attitudes toward premarital sex are also characterized by a dramatic increase in tolerance during 1960s and 1970s (Thornton, 1989). Tolerance toward extramarital sex increased in the 1960s and 1970s but has since declined in the last two decades, with 92.9% of women and 89.2% of men saying they view it as always wrong or almost always wrong (Thornton & Young-DeMarco, 2001).

Overall, these findings point toward two general conclusions. First, family remains a highly valued institution in the United States. Second, tolerance for a diversity of family types and transitions has increased. Thus, the United States is characterized by a high fraction of people who plan on getting married and plan on staying married for life. These represent stable family values and beliefs in the United States over recent decades. On the other hand, the United States is also characterized by dramatic changes in other attitudes over recent decades, including egalitarian gender role attitudes, tolerance of premarital sex and nonmarital cohabitation, and tolerance of childbearing outside of marriage.

Perhaps most striking about these macro-level ideational trends is their close similarity to the macro-level behavioral trends. Of course, it is a tremendously difficult task to link these macro-level ideational and behavioral trends together to determine the extent to which one set of trends may be causing the other. Instead, a series of studies in the United States has investigated the micro-level relationships between family formation ideas and behaviors with the aim of learning more about the plausible connections between ideational changes and behavioral changes. We quickly review the theoretical and empirical foundations of these studies, then turn to a review of their findings.

THEORETICAL FOUNDATIONS OF U.S. RESEARCH ON IDEATIONAL INFLUENCES ON FAMILY CHANGE

Four central theoretical models are at the foundation of U.S. micro-level research on ideational influences of family change. They focus on (a) the link between attitudes and behavior; (b) the reciprocal effects of experiences and attitudes; (c) role conflict as an influence on family-formation decision-making; and (d) the intergenerational transmission of family-formation behavior (Thornton et al., in press).

Attitude–Behavior Links

The most widely used frameworks for linking attitudes and behavior at the micro level are Fishbein and Ajzen's theories of reasoned action and planned behavior. Attitudes, defined as "disposition[s] to respond favorably or unfavorably to an object, person, institution, or event" (Ajzen, 1988, p. 4), along with social pressures, predict intentions, which predict behavior. Thus, positive attitudes toward a particular behavior make that behavior more likely (Barber & Axinn, 2005; Fishbein & Ajzen, 1975). For example, individuals with positive attitudes toward children and childbearing are likely to enter parenthood earlier and have more children than their peers who have more negative attitudes toward children and childbearing (Barber & Axinn, 2005).

Following this theoretical model, the spread of more tolerant attitudes toward premarital sex, cohabitation, out-of-wedlock childbearing, and divorce would each be expected to increase rates of premarital sex, cohabitation, out-of-wedlock childbearing, and divorce at the micro level (Barber, 2001a). Likewise, the spread of less positive attitudes toward marriage or childbearing would be expected to reduce marriage rates and birth rates at the micro level (Barber, 2001a). Thus this model provides a key reason why micro-level evidence of associations between attitudes and subsequent behaviors may help to understand the origins of the macro-level trends.

Reciprocal Effects of Experiences and Attitudes

Although the theory just described focuses on the potential of attitudes to predict behavior at the micro level, there are also strong theoretical reasons to expect links in the opposite direction, with behavior also affecting attitudes (Ajzen, 1988). A key way behaviors influence attitudes is through cognitive consistency (Festinger, 1957). From this perspective, individuals are driven to interpret their past experiences and behaviors in a favorable way. When one's behavior is inconsistent with one's attitudes, the individual is faced with discomfort. Because past behaviors cannot be changed, attitudes toward those behaviors are likely to become more favorable (Festinger, 1957). This hypothesis is consistent with a main proposition of the life course perspective, namely, that individuals' preferences, expectations, and choices are influenced by prior experiences (Bronfenbrenner, 1979; Elder, 1977, 1978).

This theoretical perspective on micro-level relationships between ideas and behaviors points toward the potential importance of macro-level behavioral trends in shaping macro-level ideational trends. For example, even those who are initially unaccepting of divorce tend to develop more positive attitudes toward divorce after they themselves experience a divorce (Thornton, 1985). At the macro level this may mean that the spread of divorce behavior may have reshaped ideas about divorce.

Role Conflict

Because individuals' time and resources are limited, at the micro level attitudes toward a wide variety of behaviors are likely to affect family formation. As young people make the transition to adulthood, they must choose among a variety of possible roles. Choosing one role may make the fulfillment of other roles quite difficult (Rindfuss, 1991; Rindfuss, Swicegood, & Rosenfeld, 1987), or it might later ease the transition to some roles (Barber & Axinn, 2005). Role conflict theory asserts that individuals will avoid making the transition into roles perceived as conflict- or tension-inducing (Burr, Leigh, Day, & Constantine, 1979; Crimmins, Easterlin, & Saito, 1991; Goode, 1960). For example, the role of parenthood calls for spending time with children, whereas the roles of student and worker usually involve spending large amounts of time away from home. Thus, holding positive attitudes toward one of these roles may cause the individual to delay or forgo the other, conflicting, role (Barber & Axinn, 2005). Barber (2001a) explains how role conflict may make attitudes toward various nonfamily activities an important influence on family formation behaviors at the micro level. As a result, positive attitudes toward nonfamily activities that may conflict with family formation, such as education or labor-force participation, may reduce subsequent rates of marriage or childbearing (Barber. 2001a).

This theoretical model points toward another way that micro-level associations may inform our understanding of the connections among macro-level trends. The macro-level increases in educational attainment and labor force participation may be closely related to the spread of positive attitudes toward these nonfamily activities. When such activities conflict with family formation, these positive attitudes toward education and work may reduce rates of marriage or childbearing and may increase rates of divorce. They may also reduce rates of cohabitation less than they reduce rates of marriage if people perceive less role conflict with cohabitation than with marriage (Thornton et al., 1995).

Intergenerational Transmission

Social theory outlines two ways in which parents influence their children's behavior: socialization and social control (Campbell, 1969; Chodorow, 1978; Coleman, 1990; Gecas & Seff, 1990). Socialization is the process through which parents affect how their children want to behave. This is achieved in two ways: First, parents' own preferences for their child shape their child's preferences, attitudes, and intentions; and second, children's attitudes and preferences become similar to their parents' because they share similar social positions, backgrounds, and experiences with their parents (Barber, 2000; Bengtson, 1975). "Overall, children are socialized to evaluate behaviors similarly to their parents; thus, by behaving in accordance with their own attitudes and preferences, children may be conforming to their parents' wishes as well" (Barber, 2000).

In contrast to socialization, social control is a mechanism through which parents influence their children's behavior, regardless of the child's own attitudes. Parents rely on various punishments or rewards in order to make their children behave according to their wishes. These rewards include parental approval, so that children may act in accordance with their parents' wishes to avoid causing parents embarrassment or pain. These social control methods change a child's behavior independent of the child's own attitudes (Barber, 2000; Smith, 1988).

These micro-level mechanisms linking parents to children may have a macro-level consequence linking the family behaviors or attitudes of one generation to the family behaviors and attitudes of the next generation. These cross-generation links may help to propel trends across time, fueling attitudinal and behavioral changes for many years at a time.

Together these four theoretical mechanisms—attitudinal influences, reciprocal effects of experiences on attitudes, role conflict, and intergenerational influences—represent the main theoretical foundation for micro-level research on the relationships between family attitudes and behaviors in the United States. These theories have shaped the key research designs, measurements, and analyses of ideational influences on family behaviors at the micro level in the United States. As we discuss later, although relatively simple, together they have generated complex and comprehensive studies that provide some of the most thorough documentation of micro-level family attitude–behavior relationships anywhere in the world.

LONGITUDINAL DATA RESOURCES FOR STUDYING ATTITUDE–BEHAVIOR LINKS

At the micro level it is difficult to use cross-sectional studies that measure attitudes and behavior at the same point in time to advance our understanding of the relationships between family attitudes and family behaviors. This is because at the same time attitude may affect subsequent behavior, it is also likely that behaviors help to shape subsequent attitudes. As a result, the observation of an empirical correlation between family attitudes and behavior in cross-sectional data is just as likely to reflect the influence of behavior on attitudes as it is to reflect the influence of attitudes on behavior. This problem is exacerbated when cross-sectional measures of behavior actually ask about behaviors that must have occurred *before* the day of the measurement, such as experiences with cohabitation, marriage, divorce, childbearing, or childrearing. Measures of attitudes from such studies reflect respondents' attitudes on the day of the study, and study participants' past experiences are more likely to be causes of those attitudes than consequences of those attitudes.

More convincing evidence of attitudinal or ideational influences on behavior is made possible by longitudinal measurement that features measures of attitudes at one point in time and a *subsequent* record of behavior. Such longitudinal studies of family attitudes and family behaviors are relatively rare worldwide. One reason the United States has been fertile ground for the study of the relationship between family attitudes and family behaviors is that this country has multiple longitudinal studies documenting family attitudes and family behaviors from the same individuals over time. Together these studies constitute an important resource for the investigation of attitude–behavior links. Among the many examples, the National Study of Families and Households, the Intergenerational Panel Study of Mothers and Children, the National Study of Children, the Monitoring the Future studies, and the National Longitudinal Surveys of Youth each appear frequently in the research literature on these topics.

Many of these longitudinal studies include multiple measures of the same attitudes over time from the same individuals, making them particularly useful for documenting the effects of family behaviors on changes in family attitudes over time. For example, they show that marriage behavior affects attitudes toward marriage (Axinn & Thornton, 1992; Clarkberg, 2002; Marchena & Waite, 2002), divorce behavior affects attitudes toward divorce (Thornton, 1985), and cohabitation behavior affects attitudes toward cohabitation (Axinn & Thornton, 1993; Clarkberg, 2002). Even more interesting, behaviors in one family domain affect attitudes in other family domains. So, childbearing behavior affects gender role attitudes and attitudes toward marriage (Marchena & Waite, 2002; Morgan & Waite, 1987; Thomson, 2002), cohabiting behavior affects attitudes toward marriage, divorce, childbearing, money, and external social ties (Axinn & Barber, 1997; Axinn & Thornton, 1992; Clarkberg, 2002; Marchena & Waite, 2002), and living alone or with unrelated house-mates affects attitudes toward sex roles, marriage, and childbearing (Axinn & Barber, 1997; Cunningham, Beutel, Barber, & Thornton, 2005; Waite, Goldscheider, & Witsberger, 1986).

Thus these U.S. longitudinal studies provide a great deal of evidence that family behaviors shape changes in family attitudes over time—evidence that strengthens our conviction that cross-sectional measures of attitudes and behaviors can teach us relatively little about the effects of attitudes on subsequent family behaviors. In the pages that remain, therefore, we restrict our summary of findings from U.S. research to longitudinal studies that use measures of attitudes at one point in time to predict subsequent measures of family behavior.

MICRO-LEVEL FINDINGS

Marriage

Various attitudes held prior to marriage influence individuals' marriage behavior, and some of the first attitudes studied concerned education and work. Bayer (1969) conducted one of the first longitudinal studies of ideational effects on family by using a nationally representative sample of 39,000 high school seniors interviewed in 1960 and 1965. Bayer found that the educational and marital expectations of high school students predict later marriage behavior, even after controlling for parent socioeconomic status (SES) and school aptitude. Another study utilized the National Longitudinal Survey of Work Experience of Young Women, a nationally representative survey of women ages 14–24 in 1968, who were reinterviewed nearly every year until 1975. When asked "What kind of work would you like to be doing when you are 35 years old?" those previously unmarried women who answered "housewife" (or something similar) were significantly more likely to marry over the following 2-year interval (Cherlin, 1980). Although this effect is fairly constant for Whites between the ages of 18 and 23, it only appears to operate for slightly older Blacks—ages 22–23 (see also Waite & Spitze, 1981, for similar results).

In addition to educational and occupational ideals, family attitudes affect marital outcomes. Using the 1980 and 1985 waves of the IPS, one study finds that sons who report more agreement with the statement "divorce is usually the best solution when a couple can't seem to work out their problems" in 1980 (sons age 18) have much lower rates of marriage between 1980 and 1985 (Axinn & Thornton, 1992). The authors also find that even after controlling for their mothers' attitudes, children who report that they would be more bothered if they did not get married have significantly higher rates of marriage over the 5-year period. Using the same data, other studies focus on the link between attitudes about the division of household labor and marriage timing. One study finds that attitudes supporting egalitarian roles for women and men in families are related to delayed entry into marriage (Cunningham et al., 2005). Another study focuses on the contingent nature of this relationship—young women who expect only to complete high school and agree that "wives should remain in the home" have higher marriage rates (Barber & Axinn, 1998a), but young women who expect to complete 4 years of college and agree that "wives should remain in the home" have lower marriage rates (Barber & Axinn, 1998a).

Along with individual's own attitudes, the attitudes of people around them also have an effect on their later marital behavior. For example, Marini (1978) uses a 15-year follow-up of students in 10 Illinois high schools originally surveyed in 1957 to examine the effect of friends on marital behavior. Along with finding that students who plan to attend college marry at later ages than those who do not plan to attend college, she also found that people with *friends* who plan to attend college marry at later ages than those whose friends do not plan on attending college. The effect of friends' school plans remains even after controlling for the person's own desires to attend school. Interestingly, this effect is much larger for women than for men.

Along with friends, parents have a particularly strong influence on young adults' marital behavior. Due to its unique design, the IPS has provided a significant amount of data on effects of parental values and attitudes on children's later family formation patterns. Using the 1980 attitudes of the mothers and children to predict the child's marriage behavior until 1985 (when all the children were 23) allows for a powerful test of the effect of both parents' and children's attitudes on behavior. Studies using the IPS data have shown that young people's mothers' attitudes and values affect their marriage patterns, even after controlling for their own attitudes. For example, the children of mothers with more favorable attitudes toward cohabitation (e.g., those mothers who agreed that "its all right for a couple to live together without planning to get married") had lower marriage rates over the subsequent 5 years—an effect even stronger than the child's own attitudes toward cohabitation (Axinn & Thornton, 1993). In addition, the older the mother's ideal age of marriage for her child, the longer the child delays marriage—especially for mothers with higher financial resources; however, as the child ages, this effect of mothers' ideal age weakens (Axinn & Thornton, 1992a).

Not surprisingly, not all parental effects are so uniform. For example, mothers who report agreeing with the statement "married people are usually happier than those who go through life without getting married" have sons, but not daughters, with higher rates of marriage (Axinn & Thornton, 1992b). Another study finds that the higher a mother's fertility preferences are for her son (i.e., the number children the son should have), the more likely he is to form any union (marriage or cohabitation) (Barber & Axinn, 1998b). On the other hand, the higher the mother's fertility preferences are for her daughter, the more likely the daughter is to marry (compared to cohabiting) (Barber & Axinn, 1998b). It is also interesting to note that for both of these findings the mother's fertility preferences for her children exert a stronger effect than the child's own fertility preferences (Barber & Axinn, 1998b).

Cohabitation

Cohabitation, although often studied in comparison to marriage, has its own small body of research concerning ideational effects. One study, using the 1986 wave of the National Longitudinal Study of the High School Class of 1972, reports that high school seniors who place higher importance in "finding the right person to marry and having a happy family life" have lower rates of cohabitation (Clarkberg, Stolzenberg, & Waite, 1995). Similarly, they find high school seniors with more favorable attitudes toward "living close to parents and relatives" have lower rates of first union and cohabitation.[7] More specifically for men, placing more importance on "being able find steady work" and "having leisure time to enjoy my own interests" decreases the rate of cohabitation after high school. Also, female high school seniors who report higher importance of "being successful in my line of work" and "being able to find

---

[7]In a study using the High School and Beyond data, a similar question was asked and those young people who reported that it was not important to live close to family were more likely to live away from home (not including getting married or going to school). A similar result was found for people with more egalitarian gender role attitudes (Goldscheider & Goldscheider, 1993).

steady work" have lower rates of first union during the first few years after high school, whereas finding more importance in "having lots of money" in high school leads to higher rates of cohabitation. Finally, for both males and females, more egalitarian sex role attitudes in high school increase the rate of cohabitation for several years after high school (Clarkberg et al., 1995; Cunningham et al., 2005).

Returning to the IPS data, mothers who agree that "married people are usually happier than those who go through life without getting married" and who report they would be more bothered if "your child did not get married" have daughters with significantly lower chances of cohabiting, even after controlling for the daughters' own attitudes (Axinn & Thornton, 1992b). On the other hand, daughters who agree that "divorce is usually the best solution when a couple can't seem to work out their problems" have significantly higher risk of cohabiting over the same 5-year interval, even after controlling for their mother's attitude toward divorce (Axinn & Thornton, 1992b). In a different paper the same authors report that more tolerant attitudes toward cohabitation (e.g., disagreeing that "a young couple should not live together unless they are married") are associated with higher rates of cohabitation (Axinn & Thornton, 1993). It is also interesting to note that although mothers' attitudes do not have an effect on sons' cohabitation rates, the cohabitation rates of daughters are much higher for mothers with positive attitudes toward cohabitation (Axinn & Thornton, 1993). Another study finds that net of early adulthood experiences with education, work, cohabitation, marriage, and childbearing, young adults who expect "that work will be a source of life satisfaction" have higher rates of cohabitation (Barber, Axinn, & Thornton, 2002). Rates are also higher for young adults who have more tolerant attitudes toward premarital sex and those who have mothers with more tolerant attitudes toward premarital sex (Barber et al., 2002).

Divorce

Although all studies of ideational effects on family formation are difficult and require extensive longitudinal data, the study of divorce is particularly difficult. Although the vast majority of people will marry, of those who do marry about half will divorce (Cherlin, 1992). Also, unlike the other family formation processes, divorce occurs over a much longer period of time, requiring a much longer longitudinal study. Despite the difficulties of divorce studies, some findings have emerged. For example, using the IPS data, Thornton et al. (1983) report that women's 1962 sex role attitudes (measured using four questions) do not appear to have an effect on the probability of divorce over the subsequent 18 years. Thornton (1985) also uses the IPS data to find that holding more tolerant attitudes toward divorce in 1962 (i.e., disagreeing with "When there are children in the family, parents should stay together even if they don't get along" and agreeing with "divorce is usually the best solution when a couple can't seem to work out their marriage problems") appears to have little effect on the later chance of divorce over the next 15 years. Bumpass (2002) finds that individuals with conservative family attitudes—measured by an index combining attitudes toward unmarried teens having sex, cohabitation, premarital childbearing, the acceptability of divorce, and marital independence—have marital separation rates that are only about 50% the rates of those with with least conservative attitudes. The same study finds that those with fundamentalist religious affiliations and those who attend church weekly have lower marital disruption rates, and that couples who perceive their relationship to be of high quality have lower marital disruption rates as well (Bumpass, 2002). Considering these results and the current state of data on divorce, future studies will be needed to provide evidence of ideational effects on divorce behavior comparable to the other family events discussed in this section.

Childbearing

Empirical evidence has repeatedly provided support for attitude–behavior links in the area of childbearing. These relationships between attitudes and behavior come in many forms, including childbearing attitudes affecting childbearing behavior, attitudes toward other behaviors affecting childbearing behavior, one's own attitudes affecting subsequent behavior, and others' attitudes affecting one's behavior. We begin with attitudes related to childbearing influencing childbearing behavior.

    Not surprisingly, women's family size preferences are strongly related to their subsequent number of births. Using the Intergenerational Panel Study (IPS), Coombs (1974) tests her fertility preference "I-scale" as a predictor of subsequent fertility. Respondents were asked to report the number of children they would have "if you could start life over again, knowing that things would turn out just they way they have for you and your husband." They were then asked to report second- and third-best numbers of children. The resulting choices were mapped onto a scale of fertility preferences. Coombs found a consistent, positive relationship between location on the fertility preference scale and number of subsequent births, which was not fully explained by fertility *expectations* (Coombs, 1974).

In an analysis of the effect of fertility *intentions* on fertility behavior, Schoen, Astone, Nathanson, Kim, and Murray (1999) also found strong effects of attitudes on childbearing. Using panel data on a sample of non-Hispanic White women from the NSFH (1987–1988 and 1992–1994), Schoen and colleagues model respondents' intentions to have a(nother) child, as well as the strength of those intentions, and the relative strength of spouses' intentions on the subsequent birth of a child. They found a strong association between childbearing intentions and the strength of those intentions, and the probability of having a birth. The most certain fertility intentions ("very sure, yes" and "very sure, no") had the strongest effects on subsequent childbearing. Measures of spouses' fertility intentions also had consistent positive effects on the probability of a birth (Schoen et al., 1999).

In previous analyses, Thompson and colleagues also demonstrate the importance of spouses' fertility desires and intentions for subsequent fertility. Using the Princeton Fertility Survey, a three-wave panel study of couple fertility in major metropolitan areas, Thompson and colleagues (Thompson, McDonald, & Bumpass, 1990) examined the effects of spouses' desires for a third child on the rate of third births. They found that, relative to couples who both wanted to stop childbearing at two children, couples in which either spouse desired a third child were more likely to have a third birth. Furthermore, when *both* spouses desired a third birth, the birth rate was double that of couples who disagreed about the desire for a third birth. Wives' and husbands' family size desires showed equal effects on subsequent birth rates (Thompson et al., 1990). In a later study using the NSFH, Thompson (1997) conducted a similar analysis on spouses' childbearing desires, but also considered measures of each spouse's childbearing *intentions.* Thompson found that, as in the earlier analysis, couples where both spouses want no more children have substantially lower probabilities of a birth than couples where both spouses want another child. Birth probabilities of couples whose fertility desires are in disagreement fall in between these two groups, but are more similar to couples who want no more children. Results were similar for childbearing intentions—couples where both spouses strongly intended to have another child had the highest rates of subsequent births, followed by couples with less certain intentions toward another birth. Couples who disagreed (one partner intended, one did not intend) were much less likely to experience a birth, but more likely than couples who both did not intend another birth (Thompson, 1997).

Other related attitudes are also important predictors of childbearing behavior. Using the IPS, Barber (2001b) finds that for married women, enjoyment of activities with children (caring for, playing with, and talking to little children), preference for larger families, and the belief that children do *not* cause worry and strain all lead to earlier first birth timing.

In addition to attitudes toward children and childbearing, attitudes toward many other areas of life have significant influence on childbearing behavior. Using IPS data, Thornton and colleagues find that women's less egalitarian sex-role attitudes, measured by eight questions on the roles of men and women in the family and work force, subsequently led to less participation in the work force, less educational accumulation, earlier entry into parenthood, and increased family size (Thornton et al., 1983; Cunningham et al., 2005). Using the National Survey of Families and Households (NSFH), Thomson finds that women's attitudes toward conjugal familism (an index combining multiple attitudes toward childbearing, marriage, and divorce) and men's attitudes toward extended familism (an index combining attitudes toward parents' and children's obligations to one another) lead to earlier entry into parenthood. Using the National Longitudinal Survey of Youth (NLSY), Plotnick (1992) found that more egalitarian sex-role attitudes led to higher adolescent premarital pregnancy rates. In contrast, positive attitudes and expectations for education, and favorable attitudes toward school are linked to lower premarital pregnancy rates (Barber, 2001a; Plotnick, 1992). Similarly, positive attitudes toward consumption of luxury goods lead to lower premarital first birth rates, and delay marital childbearing (Barber, 2001a; Crimmins et al., 1991).

Parents' attitudes toward childbearing and competing behaviors also have significant effects on their children's childbearing behavior. Using IPS data, Axinn, Clarkberg, and Thornton (1994) find that mothers' preferences for their children's completed family size have strong positive effects on their children's family size preferences. Additionally, using the same data, Barber (2000) finds that both sons and daughters whose mothers prefer lower levels of education, early marriage, large families, and stay-at-home motherhood become parents earlier than their peers. In both studies, mothers' preferences for their children's childbearing have stronger effects on that behavior than the children's own preferences for themselves (Axinn et al., 1994; Barber, 2000).

CONCLUSION

So, what does this long list of micro-level results mean? Using individual-level longitudinal panel data that maintains appropriate temporal ordering between measures of ideas and measures of behavior, researchers in the United States have accumulated a large volume of evidence that variations in ideas are closely associated with subsequent variations in marital, cohabiting, divorce, and childbearing behavior. These include ideas about marriage, cohabitation, divorce, and childbearing along with ideas about premarital sex, appropriate gender roles, education, work, and consumption. They include individuals' own ideas about behavior, and the ideas of important others, such as their parents. There is also evidence that behavior shapes subsequent ideas, but even considering the important reciprocal relationship, there is still a great deal of evidence that ideas are associated with variation in these family formation behaviors.

Of course, even with longitudinal measurement, because of the observational nature of research on ideational influences on family behavior, empirically there is ample room to doubt that these associations represent causal effects of ideas on family behaviors (Moffitt, 2005). But social psychological theory, role conflict theory, and intergenerational theory each provide strong reasons to expect that at least part of the observed association represents a causal influence of variations in ideas on family behaviors. This reasoning is consistent with the repeated large, robust associations found in the empirical literature, even in well-specified multivariate models that include the most likely potential prior factors. Attitudinal variation is often found to have quite large effects of family formation behaviors—as large as 100 to 200% differences across the observed range of attitudinal variations. In general, U.S. research demonstrates that these ideational effects are independent of factors such as education, work experience, or income that are often believed to explain variations in behavior. There is no proof here, but the evidence is certainly mounting.

What does this mean in the context of the macro-level behavioral shifts and accompanying macro-level attitudinal trends outlined at the beginning of this chapter? Longitudinal studies from the United States demonstrate important micro-level consequences of behaviors for ideational changes over time. Some of the relationships among these trends likely reflect the influence of changing behaviors on changes in beliefs. However, the micro-level evidence of important effects of ideas on subsequent behavior is also consistent with the conclusion that some of the association among these trends is the product of ideational influences on family change.

Ideational shifts in the United States are best documented beginning in the early 1960s. That decade saw the spread of family ideas favoring individual freedoms and a norm of tolerance, a change that may have stabilized, but has not reversed. Not only did that change probably fuel changes in family behaviors, it may also have strengthened the association between ideas and family behaviors. As societal-level values become more varied and a broader range of family behaviors is considered acceptable, individuals are likely to be increasingly free to act on their own attitudes and preferences in making behavioral decisions (Barber, Pearce et al., 2002; Bellah et al., 1985; Bumpass, 1990; Lesthaeghe & Surkyn, 1988; Preston, 1987; Thornton, 1989; Veroff, Douvan, & Kulka, 1981). This change increases the likelihood ideas will act as an important force in shaping family behavior. The evidence reviewed earlier shows that attitudes and values have strong intergenerational consequences, affecting the behavior of both individuals and their children. As a result, recent changes over time in attitudes and values documented here are likely to continue to shape family behaviors for some time to come. Thus we leave this summary of U.S. research on the ideational influences on family behaviors with the strong conviction that consequences of ideational change and variation deserve to be one of the very highest priorities in research on the family, both in the United States and elsewhere around the world.

AUTHOR NOTE

Authorship of this chapter is given in alphabetical order.

REFERENCES

Ajzen, I. (1988). *Attitudes, personality, and behavior*. Chicago: Dorsey.

Alwin, D. F. (1996). From childbearing to childrearing: The link between declines in fertility and changes in the socialization of children. *Population and Development Review, 22*, 176–196.

Alwin, D. F. (1988). From obedience to autonomy: Changes in traits desired in children, 1924–1978. *Public Opinion Quarterly, 52*(1), 33–52.

Anderton, D. L., Barrett, R. E., & Bogue, D. J. (1997). *The population of the United States*. New York: Free Press.

Axinn, W. G., & Barber, J. S. (1997). Non-family living and family formation values in early adulthood. *Journal of Marriage and the Family, 59*(3), 595–611.

Axinn, W. G., Clarkberg, M. E., & Thornton, A. (1994). Family influences on family size preferences. *Demography, 31*(1), 65–79.

Axinn, W. G., & Thornton, A. (1992a). The influence of parental resources on the timing of the transition to marriage. *Social Science Research, 21*, 261–285.

Axinn, W. G., & Thornton, A. (1992b). The relationship between cohabitation and divorce: Selectivity or causal influence? *Demography, 29*(3), 357–374.

Axinn, W. G., & Thornton, A. (2000). The Transformation in the meaning of marriage. In L. Waite, C. Bachrach, M. Hinden, E. Thompson, & A. Thornton (Eds.),

Ties that bind: Perspectives on marriage and cohabitation (pp. 147–165). Hawthorne, NY: Aldine de Gruyter.

Axinn, W. G., & Thornton, A. (1993). Mothers, children, and cohabitation: The intergenerational effects of attitudes and behavior. *American Sociological Review, 58*(2), 233–246.

Bachu, A., & O'Connell, M. (2001). Fertility of American women: June 2000. *Current population reports, P20-543RV*. Washington, DC: U.S. Census Bureau.

Bahr, H. M., Mitchell, C., Li, X., Walker, A., & Sucher, K. (2004). Trends in family space/time, conflict, and solidarity: Middletown 1924–1999. *City and Community, 3*(3), 263–291.

Barber, J. S., (2000). Intergenerational influences on the entry into parenthood: Mothers' preferences for family and nonfamily behavior. *Social Forces, 79* (1), 319–348.

Barber, J. S., (2001a). Ideational influences on the transition to parenthood: Attitudes toward childbearing and competing alternatives. *Social Psychology Quarterly, 64* (2), 101–127.

Barber, J. S. (2001b). The intergenerational transmission of age at first birth among married and unmarried men and women. *Social Science Research, 30*, (2), 219–247.

Barber, J. S., & Axinn, W. G. (1998a). The impact of parental pressure for grandchildren on young people's entry into cohabitation and marriage. *Population Studies, 52*(2), 129–144.

Barber, J. S., & Axinn, W. G. (1998b). Gender role attitudes and marriage timing among young women. *The Sociological Quarterly, 39*(1), 11–32.

Barber, J. S., & Axinn, W. G. (2005). How do attitudes shape childbearing in the United States? In A. Booth & A. C. Crouter (Eds.), *The new population problem: Why families in developed countries are shrinking and what it means*, pp. 59–92. Mahwah, NJ: Lawrence Erlbaum Associates.

Barber, J. S., Axinn, W. G., & Thornton, A. (2002). The influence of attitudes on family formation processes. In R. Lesthaeghe (Ed.), *Meaning and choice: Value orientations and life course decisions* (pp. 45–95). The Hague, the Netherlands: NIDI/CBGS Publications.

Barber, J. S., Pearce, L. D., et al. (2002). Voluntary associations and fertility limitation. *Social Forces, 80*(4), 1369–1401.

Bellah, R. N., Madsen, R., et al. (1985). *Habits of the heart: Individualism and commitment in American life*. Berkeley: University of California Press.

Bengston, V. L. (1975). Generation and family effects in value socialization. *American Sociological Review, 40*, 358–371.

Bronfenbrenner, U. (1979). *The ecology of human development: Experiments by nature and design*. Cambridge, MA: Harvard University Press.

Bumpass, L. L. (1990). What's happening to the family? Interactions between demographic and institutional change. *Demography, 27*, 483–498.

Bumpass, L. L. (2002). Family-related attitudes, couple relationships, and union stability. In R. Lesthaeghe (Ed.), *Meaning and choice: Value orientations and life course decisions* (pp. 162–184). The Hague, the Netherlands: NIDI/CBGS Publications.

Bumpass, L., & Lu, H. (2000). Trends in cohabitation and implications for children's family contexts in the U.S. *Population Studies, 54,* 29–41.

Burr, W. R., Leigh, G., Day, R., & Constantine, J. (1979). Symbolic interaction and the family. In W. Burr, R. Hill, F. Nye, & I. Reiss (Eds.), *Contemporary theories about the family* (pp. 42–111). New York: Free Press.

Campbell, E. Q. (1969). Adolescent socialization. In D. A. Goslin (Ed.), *Handbook of socialization theory and research* (pp. 821–860). Chicago: Rand McNally.

Cherlin, A. J. (1980). Postponing marriage: The influence of young women's work expectations. *Journal of Marriage and the Family, 42,* 355–365.

Cherlin, A. J. (1992). *Marriage, divorce, remarriage.* Cambridge, MA: Harvard University Press.

Chodorow, N. J. (1978). *The reproduction of mothering: Psychoanalysis and the sociology of gender.* Berkeley: University of California Press.

Clarkberg, M. E. (2002). Family formation experiences and changing values: The effects of cohabitation and marriage on the important things in life. In R. Lesthaeghe (Ed.), *Meaning and choice: Value orientations and life course decisions* (pp. 185–215). The Hague, the Netherlands: NIDI/CBGS Publications.

Clarkberg, M. E., Stolzenberg, R. M., & Waite, L. J. (1995). Attitudes, values, and entrance into cohabitational versus marital unions. *Social Forces, 74*(2), 609–632.

Coleman, J. S. (1990). *Foundations of social theory.* Cambridge, MA: Harvard University Press.

Coombs, L. C. (1974). The measurement of family size preferences and subsequent fertility. *Demography, 11*(4), 587–611.

Crimmins, E. M., Easterlin, R. A., & Saito, Y. (1991). Preference changes among American youth: Family, work, and goods aspirations, 1976–1986. *Population and Development Review, 17,* 115–133.

Cunningham, M., Beutel, A. M., Barber, J. S., & Thornton, A. 2005. Reciprocal relationships between attitudes about gender and social contexts during young adulthood. *Social Science Research, 34,* 862–892.

Elder, G. H., Jr. (1977). Family history and the life course. *Journal of Family History, 2*(4), 279–304.

Elder, G. H., Jr. (1978). Approaches to social change and the family. *The American Journal of Sociology Supplement: Turning Points: Historical and Sociological Essays on the Family, 84,* S1–S38.

Festinger, L. (1957). *A theory of cognitive dissonance.* Evanston, IL: Row-Peterson.

Fishbein, M., & Ajzen, I. (1975). *Belief, attitude, intention, and behavior: An introduction to theory and research.* Reading, MA: Addison-Wesley.

Fitch, C. A., & Ruggles, S. (2000). Historical trends in marriage formation. In L. Waite, C. Bachrach, M. Hinden, E. Thompson, & A. Thornton (Eds.), *Ties that bind: Perspectives on marriage and cohabitation* (pp. 59–88). Hawthorne, NY: Aldine de Gruyter.

Gecas, V., & Seff, M. A. (1990). Social class and self esteem: Psychological centrality, compensation, and the relative affects of work and home. *Social Psychology Quarterly, 53,* 165–173.

Glenn, N. D. (1987). Social trends in the United Sates: Evidence from sample surveys. *Public Opinion Quarterly, 51*, S109–S126.

Glenn, N. (1996). Values, attitudes, and the state of American marriage. In D. Popenoe, J. B. Elshtain, & D. Blankenhorn (Eds.), *Promises to keep: Decline and renewal of marriage in America* (pp. 15–33). Lanham, MD: Rowman and Littlefield.

Goldstein, A. P. (1999). *The PREPARE curriculum: Teaching prosocial competencies* (rev.). Champaign, IL: Research Press.

Goode, W. J., (1960). A theory of role strain. *American Sociological Review, 25*, 483–496.

Hout, M., & Greeley, A. (1987). The center doesn't hold: Church attendance in the United States: 1940–1984. *American Sociological Review, 52, 325–345.*

Lesthaeghe, R., & Surkyn, J. (1988). Cultural dynamics and economic theories of fertility change. *Population and Development Review, 14*(1), 1–45.

Lesthaeghe, R. (Ed.). (2002). *Meaning and choice: Value orientations and life course decisions.* The Hague, the Netherlands: NIDI/CBGS Publications.

Marchena, E., & Waite, L. J. (2002). Re-assessing family goals and attitudes in late adolescence: The effects of natal family experiences and early family formation. In R. Lesthaeghe (Ed.), *Meaning and choice: Value orientations and life course decisions* (pp. 97–127). The Hague, the Netherlands: NIDI/CBGS Publications.

Marini, M. M. (1978). The transition to adulthood: Sex differences in educational attainment and age at marriage. *American Sociological Review, 43*, 483–507.

Miller, A. S., & Hoffmann, J. P. (1995). Risk and religion: An explanation of gender differences in religiosity. *Journal for the Scientific Study of Religion, 34*, 63–75.

Moffitt, R. (2005). Remarks on the analysis of causal relationships in population research. *Demography, 42*(1), 91–109.

Morgan, S. P., & Waite, L. J. (1987). Parenthood and the attitudes of young adults. *American Sociological Review, 52*, 541–547.

National Center for Health Statistics. (1973). *100 years of marriage and divorce statistics, United States, 1867–1967.* Rockville, MD: Author.

National Center for Health Statistics. (1977). *Trends in fertility in the United States.* Hyattsville, MD: Author.

National Center for Health Statistics. (2004). *Births, marriages, divorces, and deaths: Provisional data for 2004.* 53(21). Author.

Ogburn, W. F., & Tibbitts, C. (1933). The family and its functions. In W. C. Mitchell (Ed.), *Recent social trends in the United States: Report of the President's research committee on social trends* (pp. 661–708). New York: McGraw-Hill.

Pagnini, D. L., & Rindfuss, R. R. (1993). The divorce of marriage and childbearing: Changing attitudes and behavior in the United States. *Population and Development Review, 2*, 331–347.

Plotnick, R. (1992). The effects of attitudes on teenage premarital pregnancy and its resolution. *American Sociological Review, 57*, 800–811.

Preston, S. H. (1987). The social sciences and the population problem. *Sociological Forum, 2*(4), 619–644.

Raley, R. K. (2000). Recent trends in marriage and cohabitation: The United States. In L. Waite, C. Bachrach, M. Hinden, E. Thompson, & A. Thornton (Eds.), *Ties that bind: Perspectives on marriage and cohabitation* (pp. 59–88). Hawthorne, NY: Aldine de Gruyter.

Rindfuss, R. R. (1991). The young adult years: Diversity, structural change, and fertility. *Demography, 28* (4), 493–512.

Rindfuss, R. R., Swicegood, C. G., & Rosenfeld, R. (1987). Disorder in the life course: How common is it and does it matter? *American Sociological Review, 52,* 785–801.

Schoen, R., Astone, N. M., Nathanson, C. A., Kim, Y. J., & Murray, N. (2000). The impact of fertility intentions on behavior: The case of sterilization. *Social Biology, 47*(1/2), 61–76.

Schneider, C. E. (1985). Moral discourse and the transformation of American family law. *Michigan Law Review, 83*(8), 1803–1879.

Schulenberg, J., Bachman, J. G., Johnston, L. D., & O'Mulley, P. M. (1995). American adolescents' views on family and work: History trends from 1976–1992. In P. Noack, M. Hofer, & J. Youniss (Eds.), *Psychological responses to social change* (pp. 37–64). New York: Walter de Gruyter.

Sherkat, D. E. (1998). Counterculture or continuity? Competing influences on baby boomers. Religious orientations and participation. *Social Forces, 76,* 1087–1115.

Sherkat, D. E., & Ellison, C. G. (1999). Recent developments and current controversies in the sociology of religion. *Annual Review of Sociology, 25,* 363–394.

Smith, T. E. (1988). Parental control techniques: Relative frequencies and relationships with situational factors. *Journal of Family Issues, 9*(2), 155–176.

Teachman, J., Tedrow, L., & Crowder, K. (2001). The changing demography of America's families. In R. Milardo (Ed.), *Understanding families into the new millennium: A decade in review* (pp. 453–465). Minneapolis, MN: National Council on Family Relations.

Thomson, E. (1997). Couple childbearing desires, intentions, and births. *Demography, 34*(3), 343–354.

Thomson, E. (2002). Motherhood, fatherhood and family values. In R. Lesthaeghe (Ed.), *Meaning and choice: Value orientations and life course decisions* (pp. 251–271). The Hague, the Netherlands: NIDI/CBGS Publications.

Thomson, E., McDonald, E., & Bumpass, L. L. (1990). Fertility desires and fertility: Hers, his, and theirs. *Demography, 27*(4), 579–588.

Thornton, A. (1985). Changing attitudes toward separation and divorce— Causes and consequences. *American Journal of Sociology, 90* (4), 856–872.

Thornton, A. (1989). Changing attitudes toward family issues in the United States. *Journal of Marriage and the Family, 51*(4), 873–893.

Thornton, A., Alwin D. F., & Camburn, D. (1983). Causes and consequences of sex-role attitudes and attitude changes. *American Sociological Review 48*(2), 211–21.

Thornton, A., Axinn, W. G., & Teachman, J. (1995). The influence of educational experiences on cohabitation and marriage in early adulthood. *American Sociological Review, 60,* 762–774.

Thornton, A., Axinn, W. G., & Xie, Y. (in press). *Marriage and cohabitation.* Chicago: University of Chicago Press.

Thornton, A., & Fricke, T. E. (1987). Social change and the family: Comparative perspectives from the West, China, and South Asia. *Sociological Forum, 2,* 746–779.

Thornton, A., & Young-DeMarco, L. (2001). Four decades of trends in attitudes toward family issues in the United States: The 1960s through the 1990s. *Journal of Marriage and the Family, 63*(4), 1009–1037.

U.S. Census Bureau. (2005a). *Current population survey, March and annual social and economic supplements, 2004 and earlier.* June 29: Author.

U.S. Census Bureau. (2005b). *2004–2005 statistical abstract of the United States:* Author.

U.S. Census Bureau. (2005c). *School enrollment-Social and economic characteristics of students: October 2003:* Author.

Veroff, J., E. Douvan, & Kulka, R. (1981). *The inner American: A self-portrait from 1957 to 1976.* New York: Basic Books.

Waite, L. J., & Spitze, G. D. (1981). Young women's transition to marriage. *Demography, 18*(4), 681–694.

Waite, L. J., Goldscheider, F. K., & Witsberger, C. (1986). Nonfamily living and the erosion of traditional family orientations among young-adults. *American Sociological Review, 51*(4), 541–554.

6

Continuity and Change:
The Family in Argentina

Georgina Binstock
Centro de Estudios de Población (CENEP)

Argentina has experienced important family transformations in union
formation, union dissolution, fertility, and family roles. Recent decades
have been marked by increases in the age at marriage, marital dissolution, nonmarital births, and cohabitation. Family roles have also been
altered, with women increasingly contributing to the economic support
of their families. This chapter synthesizes what is known about these
changes and places them in the broader context of family and social
trends. Included is a summary of past research on behaviors, values,
attitudes, and beliefs in relation to family life. The period covered is the
second half of the 20th century to the present, with emphasis on the
last decades.

This chapter begins with a brief historical context for Argentina,
followed by a section about legal aspects concerning the family. Next, it
documents changes in family behaviors, including marriage, cohabitation, separation and divorce, fertility, gender roles, and living arrangements, and in family attitudes and values. The chapter closes with some
final reflections on these changes.

ARGENTINA HISTORICAL CONTEXT

Argentina's relatively sparse population of about 37 million people is
highly concentrated, with almost 90% living in urban areas, including
one third in greater metropolitan Buenos Aires. The majority of the
population is Catholic, and the State, although allowing freedom of
religion, economically supports the Catholic Church. In terms of educational attainment, about 1 in 3 adults have completed at least secondary education, and about 75% of teenagers are enrolled in school.

151

Argentina is rebounding from a dramatic economic and political collapse in 2001. Poverty and unemployment rates reached almost 60 and 20%, respectively, in 2002 and although they have been steadily declining, in 2004 the poverty rate was 39% and the unemployment rate was about 12%.

Argentina was a Spanish colony until 1816, when it declared its independence. By the 1880s, after half a century of successive wars, the territory of the country was unified and had the institutional and political structure of a national state. The State began to control and regulate a series of public as well as private aspects of social life, including education, marriage, and public health. These changes were driven by ruling elite's strong commitment to modernize the country in the fashion of Western societies.

Influenced by social Darwinism, the elite's idea of progress contained a strong racial component (Zimmerman, 1992), defining native populations as "barbaric" and European immigrants as "civilized." This ideology translated into the promotion of European immigration and campaigns to decimate indigenous populations. A significant European immigration—consisting primarily of men—at the turn of the 20th century had a great influence in shaping culture and society, especially the growth and urbanization of the population (Table 6.1). The 1869 population of 1.9 million quadrupled by 1914, and then doubled again by 1947 (to almost 16 million).

Another avenue to modernity pursued by the ruling elites was mass education. Free, mandatory, and secular public education was established by law in 1884, resulting in rapid declines in illiteracy rates for both men and women (Table 6.1). By the mid-1940s, there were virtually no gender differentials in illiteracy rates or primary school enrollment, and soon after, women's secondary school attendance was comparable with men's. Starting with the cohorts born in the late 1940s, women showed higher enrollment and graduation rates in all educational levels (Binstock & Cerrutti, 2005).

The process of modernization was already quite advanced by the early 20th century in terms of secular legislation, fertility and mortality levels, literacy rates, and urbanization, with more than half of the population living in urban areas by 1914. The city of Buenos Aires has always been at the forefront on social and demographic trends.[1]

---

[1]An important proportion of the country's population (at least one-third) has been concentrated in Buenos Aires (and later, in its metropolitan areas as well). As a result, national demographic and social trends are largely determined by the behavior of those living in Buenos Aires and its surrounding area (significant regional variations are evident).

TABLE 6.1

Argentina. Selected Demographic Indicators, 1869–2001

					Education**			
Year	% Urban population	% Foreign born	% Illiteracy Men	% Illiteracy Women	Completed elementary or more Men	Completed elementary or more Women	Completed high school or more Men	Completed high school or more Women
1869	26.6	12.1	64.6	78.1	–	–	–	–
1895	37.4	25.4	39.6	20.2	–	–	–	–
1914	52.7	29.9	–	–	–	–	–	–
1947	62.2	16.3	12.1	15.2	–	–	–	–
1960	72.0	13.3	7.4	9.6	46.8	44.2	8.0	6.5
1970	79.0	9.5	6.4	8.1	55.0	53.5	11.9	12.1
1980	82.2	6.8	5.5	6.0	67.0	65.8	17.1	18.4
1991	88.4	5.0	4.5	4.9	77.8	76.6	24.5	27.3
2001	89.9	4.2	2.6	2.6	82.2	82.0	30.8	35.5

**For population 15 years and older. In 1947 it refers to population 20 years and older.
Sources: Urban Population: Torrado (2003) and National Censuses (1895 to 2001).
Foreign-born population: National Censuses.
Illiteracy: Schkolnik and Pantelides (1974); Torrado (2003); and National Census 2001,
Education: Germani (1955) and National Censuses.

Argentina's economy showed a constant growth rate until 1970, with the first growth period, based on extensive land exploitation, lasting until 1930, and the second growth period, based on substituting local production for large-scale industrialization, lasting until 1970. In general, these decades were periods of upward mobility and the consolidation of a large middle class. In the late 1970s the economy started to show clear signs of deterioration, which worsened with the implementation of a series of neo-liberal and structural adjustment policies in the early 1990s. The 1990s witnessed an unprecedented deterioration in income distribution and increase in poverty and unemployment rates (Rapoport, 2000). Poverty rates increased from 21 to 38% between 1991 and 2001, peaked at 58% in 2002, and declined to 38% in 2004.

Over much of its history Argentina has been politically unstable.[2] Since 1930 several military dictatorships ruled the country, alternating with short periods of democratic governments. The last dictatorship

---

[2]In 1912, electoral law established male mandatory and secret voting, and the first presidential election was in 1916. Women had to wait until 1947 to be allowed to vote.

(1976–1983) was characterized by strong censorship and by systematic repression to any opposition. The reestablishment of democracy in 1983 substantially changed the social climate, freedom of the press, and diffusion of ideas.

FAMILY LEGISLATION

During Argentina's colonial times, norms and legislation regarding family matters, including marriage, were guided by the Catholic Church and its canonical principles (Council of Trent). The formal steps for marriage were to make a verbal marriage promise, complete an application at the parish office for the priest to review for any canonical impediment, make the public announcement of the engagement, and hold a marriage ceremony (Frias, 1994; Socolow, 1989). In many cases, the verbal marriage proposal was enough for the couple to initiate sexual relations and even start living together. In 1776, King Charles III of Spain attempted to restrict the power of the Catholic Church (Ciccerchia, 1989; Socolow, 1989) by issuing the *Real Pragmática*[3]—legislation that significantly changed the rules governing marriage. Initially applied only to the White population, but later extended to Blacks and mixed races as well, the *Real Pragmática* was intended to reestablish social order by preventing unwanted behaviors such as mismatched marriages (either in terms of race or economic background) and out-of-wedlock childbearing. This legislation required that people younger than 25 have parental authorization to marry, and was later expanded to allow parents to oppose their children's marriage without specifying the reasons.[4] Parent–child disputes over marriage were moved from ecclesiastical to civil courts (Socolow, 1989). *The Real Pragmática* has been characterized as rigid family legislation that reinforced and consolidated already established racial and economic prejudices (Frias, 1994; Socolow, 1989).

Despite the *Real Pragmática's* efforts to restrict church power, canonical principles continued to regulate family issues in Argentina until the legislation of the Civil Code in 1869. The Catholic family conception and patriarchal family system served as the basis not only for this legislation but also for the legislation to come for most of the 20th century (Torrado, 2003). The new family law continued to (a) designate men as the head of the family, with sole parental authority and jurisdiction, and sole right to administrate family properties, (b) restrict

---

[3]The *Real Pragmática* was issued in 1776 in Spain and extended to America in 1778.
[4]The age limits for parental authorization were lowered in successive legislation with different age thresholds according to sex of the child and father and mother's surviving status.

women's rights, including condemning a wife's adultery more severely than a husband's,[5] and (c) sustain religious marriage and its indissolubility. Although a civil marriage system was enacted in 1888, the indissolubility of the marriage and the subordination of women in the domestic sphere, two fundamental features of canonical legislation (Torrado, 2003), were maintained.

During the 20th century, laws were passed that very slowly began to democratize the family and to equalize women's and men's rights. Among the most important of these laws were women's right (regardless of their marital status) to choose an occupation, to make contracts, and to make use of their own (but not matrimonial) properties (1926); women's rights to vote and hold elected positions (1947); and some legal inheritance rights for children born to unmarried parents (1954).[6]

After the mid-1980s, when democracy was permanently reestablished, other significant legal changes were made that affected marriage and family life. These include shared parental rights (1985), equality of rights between children of married couples and out-of-wedlock children (1985), recognition of health benefits and survivor pension (but not inheritance) rights of partners in consensual unions (1987), free and equal administration of matrimonial patrimony between husbands and wives (1987), and the availability of divorce—with the possibility of remarriage (1987).[7]

Also, with the Constitutional reform of 1994, international treaties that recognize basic human rights, rights for children, and the condemnation of all forms of discrimination against women were given constitutional rank. Same-sex civil unions were recognized in 2003, although only in the city of Buenos Aires, and abortion continues to be illegal.

MARRIAGE

Based on a Catholic conception of family and Western patterns of family formation, Argentina's secular legislation viewed dating and mate selection as personal matters conducted with mutual consent, and marriage as the institutional regulation and legitimization of couples' co-residence,

---

[5]The law also includes a different definition of adultery for men and woman.
[6]See Torrado (2003) for a full review of legal changes during this period.
[7]After civil marriage was established in 1888, divorce was a recurring matter of debate and was occasionally addressed in the House of Representatives. In 1954, during the Peron presidency, divorce was decreed but then revoked a year later when a dictatorial government came into power.

sexual relationships, and childbearing. This ideal type of courtship, marriage, and family organization never fully matched real behaviors. On the contrary, the patriarchal family model and Catholic ethics of the family coexisted from early on with an acceptance of premarital and extramarital sexuality, high levels of illegitimate childbearing, unmarried unions, family disobedience, and households headed by women, particularly among poor families and in rural settings (Ciccerchia, 1989, 1994; Moreno, 1997; Szuchman, 1986).

The traditional conception of the family was translated in the limited way national censuses, conducted since 1869, classified individuals' union status. People were asked whether they were single, married, or widowed, despite the questioners being well informed about the extent to which couples were divorced or lived together without being married. This classification remained unchanged up until 1947, when for the first time a category was included for those separated and divorced. Then in 1960 a category was added to identify those living in consensual unions.

Estimates on marriage age at the turn of the 20th century indicate a range between 26 and 30 years for both native and foreign-born men, between 23 and 27 years for foreign-born women, and between 16 and 21 years for native-born women (Gil Montero et al., 1998).[8] During this period, European immigrants, particularly women, tended to have somewhat different marriage patterns than natives, exhibiting less celibacy, higher rates of marriage (as opposed to consensual unions), later ages at marriage, and lower fertility.

With this immigrant influx, ethnicity was an important factor in the selection of a spouse. New immigrants tended to marry within their nationality (Baily, 1980; Otero, 2000; Szuchman, 1977), a tendency that carried into the second generation, but abated in the third (Otero, 2000). Economic cycles and sex ratio imbalances also influenced nuptiality trends throughout the 20th century.

Although data are not readily available to accurately measure age at first marriage trends for most of the 20th century,[9] all indirect approaches and studies that evaluate marriage timing point to a trend

---

[8]Age at marriage is likely to be somewhat overestimated, particularly for native women, because they more often formed consensual unions.

[9]Generally measured as mean age of people marrying at particular year, or changes in the proportion of people married at each age group. An additional limitation is that until recently vital statistics did not distinguish whether it was a first- or second-order marriage (with the exception of the city of Buenos Aires, where there is available data to distinguish first-order from higher order marriages since 1965).

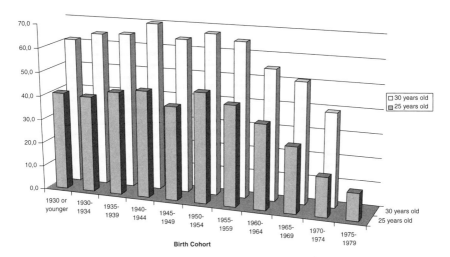

FIGURE 6.1   Buenos Aires City: Cumulative proportion of women who had
their first marriage at selected ages by birth cohort.

toward later ages at marriage in the last decades, particularly among
women (Wainerman & Geldstein, 1994; Sana, 2001; Torrado, 2003;
Mazzeo, n.d.). The 1960 mean age at marriage—24.7 years for women
and 28.2 years for men—had increased by 1 to 3 years (varying by state)
by 1990 (Sana, 2001). Throughout the 1970s and 1980s, the mean age at
first marriage for women and men in the city of Buenos Aires was relatively stable at 25.7 and 28.0 years, respectively. By 1990, age at marriage
had increased to 28.0 and 29.3 among women and men, respectively; this
upward trend continued throughout the 1990s (Mazzeo, n.d.).

A recent study comparing first-marriage timing across cohorts of
women in Buenos Aires found that, beginning with women born in the
1960s, each successive birth cohort married at significantly older ages
(Binstock, 2004). For example, between 60 to 70% of women born
between the 1930s and 1950s were already married by age 30. This
figure declined to 55% among women born in the early 1960s, and to
39% among those born in the early 1970s (Figure 6.1).

COHABITATION

Another important change in union formation patterns is increases in
cohabitation. In 1960, when Argentina's national census included for the

TABLE 6.2
Argentina. Marital Status (Ages 14 and Older) 1869 to 2001

			Marital Status		
Year	Single	Married	Consensual Union	Separated/ Divorced	Widowed
1869	53.0	38.0			9.0
1895	49.0	44.0			7.0
1914	49.0	44.0			7.0
1947	47.0	47.0			6.0*
1960	35.4	54.1	4.3	0.6	5.6
1970	33.9	52.6	5.4	1.6	6.5
1980	31.3	52.9	6.8	2.1	6.9
1991	31.1	47.6	10.4	3.8	7.1
2001	33.9	39.8	14.9	4.8	6.7

Note. For the years 1960, 1970, and 1991, "the unknown" were proportionally distributed.
*For 1947, it includes divorce (Germani, 1955).
Sources: Schkolnik and Pantelides (1974); Germani (1955); National Censuses (1970, 1991, and 2001).

first time an option of "consensual union" to describe marital status,[10] 4.3% of people chose this option. This percentage steadily increased over the years to reach 15% in 2001 (Table 6.2). Although consensual unions are reported more frequently in the poorest regions of the country, they have also increased among other social classes in urban settings, a pattern observed in other Latin American and developed countries as well. In Buenos Aires, the proportion of people in consensual unions grew from 0.8% in 1960 to 5% in 1980 to 11% in 2001.

During much of the past five decades, increases in cohabitation were linked to increases in marital instability. Before the divorce law in 1987, cohabitation was the only alternative to forming a union after ending a marriage. Cohabitation increases are also linked to changes in union formation patterns among young adults. For example, in the city of Buenos Aires, premarital cohabitation went from being a rare event (less than 5% among women born before 1945) to becoming a common experience among more recent cohorts (reaching 45% for the 1975–1979 birth

---

[10]Schkolnik and Pantelides (1974) argued that this does not immediately resolve the problem of the social condemnation, which is principally responsible for the inadequate declaration of the civil status.

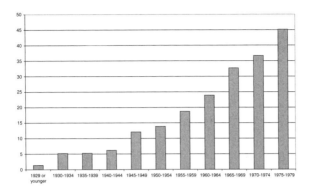

FIGURE 6.2   Buenos Aires City: Proportion of women who cohabited prior to their first marriage by birth cohort.

cohort) (Figure 6.2). Furthermore, cohabitation does not account for all the upswing in marriage postponement first observed among women born in the early 1960s. In other words, recent generations are postponing union formation, be it through marriage or through cohabitation (Binstock, 2004) (Table 6.3).

MARITAL DISSOLUTION

Because the national census did not include a marital status category to designate people separated or divorced until 1947, we do not have census data for years prior to this. From 1947 to 1960, the proportion of people aged 14 and older who reported being separated or divorced was very small (around 0.%). This percentage increased to 2.1 by 1970 and to 4.8 by 2001.[11] In Buenos Aries, divorce and separation were more prevalent than in the general population—increasing from 1% in 1960 to 3% by 1980, and to 8% by 2001.

A recent study on first-marriage dissolution trends among women in the city of Buenos Aires (for which there are statistics prior to 1947) reveals the magnitude and speed of the increase in marital instability (Binstock, 2004). Among women born in the first half of the 1930s, only 1% had divorced by their 5th wedding anniversary and only 7% had divorced by their 20th anniversary. This proportion increased steadily, and among women born in the second half of the 1950s, 8% had divorced

---

[11]These figures are based on census data and include both separated and divorced people. Data is not fully comparable in 2001 because of changes in measurement categories.

TABLE 6.3

Buenos Aires City. Cumulative Proportion of Women Who Had Formed a First Union by Selected Ages by Type of Union and Birth Cohort

	Until 27 years old			Until 30 years old		
	Total	Union	Marriage	Total	Union	Marriage
1930–1939	59.3	5.5	53.8	70.7	6.9	63.8
1940–1949	52.2	7.7	52.2	72.8	9.5	63.3
1950–1954	51.1	9.9	51.1	73.2	12.0	61.2
1955–1959	52.2	10.0	52.2	74.5	12.0	62.5
1960–1964	38.2	14.6	38.2	66.2	20.7	45.5
1965–1969	28.2	22.3	28.2	66.9	30.3	36.3
1970–1974	17.4	28.5	17.4	65.0	40.4	24.6
1975–1979	10.6	34.5	10.6			

Source: Binstock (2005).

by their 5th anniversary and 27% had divorced by their 20th anniversary (Table 6.4). Trends among the younger cohorts suggest that marriage dissolution rates will continue on the rise.

Even after the legalization of divorce, the most common way that people terminated a marriage has been through residential separation, as opposed to legal separation or divorce. In the city of Buenos Aires, divorce rates reached the highest level (between 4 and 6 per thousand) in the years immediately after divorce was legalized in 1987, and have leveled off since 1993 at 2 per thousand.[12]

FERTILITY

Argentina's fertility began to decline by the turn of the 20th century, ahead of most Latin American countries, well before the accessibility of modern contraceptive devices, and without public effort for fertility regulation (Pantelides, 1989; Torrado, 2003). Fertility decline occurred simultaneously with mortality declines in a society undergoing rapid urbanization and incipient industrialization. The spread of mass education and the lower fertility of women from some immigrant groups have been singled out as the main factors to explain overall fertility decline. In fact, European immigrants, followed by the native urban middle class, were

---

[12]Note, however, that although the divorce rate has leveled off, the percentage of divorces with respect to marriages is still increasing (Torrado, 2003).

TABLE 6.4

Buenos Aires City. Cumulative Proportion of Women Who Dissolved Their First Marriage at Selected Marital Durations by Type of Dissolution and Birth Cohort

	Separation			*Widowhood*				*Total*			
	Marital duration (in years)				*Marital duration (in years)*				*Marital duration (in years)*			
	5	10	15	20	5	10	15	20	5	10	15	20
1930–34	1.0	2.3	4.6	6.1	0.0	2.5	5.8	7.4	1.0	4.8	10.4	13.5
1935–39	1.7	4.2	7.3	9.9	0.8	3.0	5.1	5.6	2.5	7.3	12.4	15.5
1940–44	3.3	7.3	10.1	13.7	0.7	1.6	3.8	4.7	4.0	8.9	13.8	18.4
1945–49	5.2	10.4	16.1	20.2	0.6	2.3	4.2	5.7	5.8	12.7	20.3	26.0
1950–54	4.7	12.0	18.7	22.2	0.2	1.5	2.3	2.7	4.9	13.5	21.0	25.0
1955–59	7.8	15.5	21.2	26.9	0.4	0.7	1.2	1.5	8.2	16.2	22.4	28.4
1960–64	6.7	16.4	22.1		0.0	0.5	1.2		6.7	17.0	23.3	
1965–69	12.2	21.0			0.0	0.7			12.2	21.7		

Note. No responses are excluded and represent around 5 percent of women in each cohort.
Source: Binstock (2004).

the ones that initially led this process (Pantelides, 1989, 2002). The fertility decline first started in the city of Buenos Aires and later spread to other provinces. The total fertility rate declined from 7.0 children per woman in 1895, to 5.3 in 1914, to 3.2 in 1947, fluctuating around that level until 1980. Since then, fertility has steadily declined to 2.5 by 2001 (Pantelides, 1989, 2002; Sana, 2001)(Table 6.5).[13]

Presently, fertility levels continue to vary greatly within regions, ranging from a low of 1.6 to a high of 3.5. The city of Buenos Aires stands alone with respect to all aspects of fertility trends, given that it had lower starting fertility levels and earlier fertility decline and that it currently has the lowest fertility rates in Argentina.[14]

---

[13]While overall fertility was declining, adolescent fertility showed an increase from 1960 to 1980, and then started to decline again. The profile of adolescent mothers has also been changing in the last two decades. Between 1980 and 2000 the proportion of teenager mothers who were single increased from 33 to 44% and the proportion in consensual unions rose from 22 to 44%. Teenage mothers in married unions declined from 44 to 11% (Binstock & Pantelides, 2005).

[14]This has led different authors to conclude that there are different fertility transitions by regions (Giusti, 1993), and differential access to efficient contraception and safe abortion (López, 1995).

TABLE 6.5

Argentina: Selected Sociodemographic Indicators, 1869–2001

Year	TFR	Percent Illegitimate Births	Average Household Size	Percent Nuclear Households	Percent Female Headed Households	Women's Labor Force Participation[a]
1869	6.8	—	6.1	—	—	58.7
1895(a)	7.0	21.1	5.5	—	—	41.9
1914(b)	5.3	21.7	5.2	—	—	27.4
1947(e)	3.2	26.4	4.3	—	14.2	23.4
1960	3.1	23.5	4.3	—	16.5	23.3
1970	3.1	—	3.8	58.5	16.5	26.5
1980	3.3	28.4	3.9	58.2	19.2	26.9
1991(c)	2.9	36.1	3.6	64.8	22.4	39.7
2001(d)	2.4	54.7	3.6	63.2	27.7	44.9

Notes:
(a) For illegitimate births it refers to 1900.
(b) For illegitimate births it refers to 1916.
(c) For illegitimate births and TFR it refers to 1990.
(d) For illegitimate births it refers to 1999; for TFR it refers to 2000–2005.
(e) For illegitimate births it refers to 1949.

Sources:

TFR: Pantelides (1989), Sana (2001), and CEPAL (2002).

Illegitimate births: Ministerio de Salud, Sana (2001), and Torrado (2003).

Average household size: Germani (1955) and National Censuses.

Nuclear households: National Censuses.

Female headed households: Arino (1999), Torrado (2003), and National Census (2001).

Women's labor force participation: Recchini de Latters (1974), Mychaszula et al. (1989), and National Census (1991, 2001).

[a]For population 14 years and older. In 1869, 1895, and 1914 it refers to population 10 years and older.

Illegitimate births have traditionally been high in the country, particularly among native women and those in the poorer regions of the country. Fertility declines during the first decades of the 1900s were not accompanied by a decrease in the proportion of out-of-wedlock births. On the contrary, out-of-wedlock births increased from 22 to 28% of all births from 1910 to 1939, with substantial regional variations.

Bunge (1940/1984), in a very influential study, asserted that illegitimate birth levels did not agree with the culture achieved by the country, with the Christian concept of family, and with the "natural order." Illegitimacy was increasing because fertility was declining mainly among better off and educated women, where illegitimacy had never been a concern. In Bunge's words, the decline in fertility was a serious problem, given that "reproduction is being confined to the less privileged sectors and, frequently, biologically less selected" (p. 172). Bunge was successful in making "denatality" a social concern that was reflected in the State's position to promote fertility. Public family planning efforts were not mounted until the mid-1980s, when they became a topic of public debate framed as reproductive rights. Despite strong opposition of the Catholic Church, a national reproductive health law was established in 2002 that provides and guarantees free services in public institutions.[15]

The proportion of out-of-wedlock childbearing ranged from 20 to 30% between 1900 and 1980, and has increased steadily since then, reaching 55% by 1999 (Table 6.5). In Buenos Aires, the proportion of extramarital births increased from 10 to 21 to 42% from 1950 to 1980 to 1999. An important fraction of these increases in extramarital births is due to increases of childbearing by cohabiting couples.

HOUSEHOLD COMPOSITION AND SIZE

Historically, family structure has been predominantly nuclear in Argentina, although there are studies that show the importance of extended or composed arrangements in different times and places (Ghirardi, 1998). By the early 1800s the most common arrangement in the city of Buenos Aires was nuclear (García Belsunce, 1999), with extended arrangements more common among poor families (Szuchman, 1986). During the first half of the 19th century extended arrangements increased among well-off families, reaching the levels found among poor families (Szuchman, 1986). That is, contrary to what modernization theory would predict, "as Porteños edged closer to the modernizing era of the export

---

[15]Prior to the national law, some provinces had local legislation. For instance, in 1988 Buenos Aires implemented the Responsible Procreation Program.

boom economy during the second half of the century, coresidential kinship increased" (Szuchman, 1986, p. 79). Still, nuclear practices were the most common arrangement for married couples in Buenos Aires, with only 3 out of 10 households being shared with kin by 1855. Married couples preferred to retain nucleated patterns, and extended arrangements were formed for economic necessity and adherence to social norms that require caring for elderly parents (Szuchman, 1986).

Caccopardo and Moreno (1997) studied living arrangements in Argentina's interior provinces that had the lowest prevalence of foreign-born people in 1869. They found that 35% of households were nuclear, 15% were extended family (i.e., nuclear with other family members), 15% were composite (i.e., nuclear with additional nonfamily members, usually servants, orphans, temporary employers, or apprentices), and 16% had multiple families in the same household. Average household size ranged from 4.2 to 8.4 members. The authors also found that a significant proportion of single adults were heading nuclear households, reflecting the coexistance of legal marriage and consensual unions as alternatives for family formation. In addition, almost half of households were headed by women, likely reflecting sex imbalance ratios at the time, high male mobility for work and war, and the prevalence of unstable unmarried unions that resulted in women being left alone with a child.

As a result of the expansion of nuclear arrangements and fertility declines, average household size[16] decreased rapidly beginning in the mid-1800s, falling from 6.1 members in 1869, to 4.3 members in 1947, and to 3.6 members in 2001 (Table 6.5). With the exception of Buenos Aires, which decreased at a faster rate, household size declined in all other regions at a similar pace, with regional size differentials associated with income level and urbanization.

The preference for nuclear household arrangements in Argentina increased over the second half of the 20th century, growing from 58.5% of all households in 1970 to 63.2% in 2001 (Table 6.5).[17] However, it is important to point out another pattern within this trend, which Jelin (2005, p. 404) summarizes:

---

[16]Note that census definitions of households have not remained constant over the period under study.

[17]The slight decrease in the proportion of nuclear households from 1991 to 2001 is due to the increase of single-person households. Single-person households peaked in 1947 (16%) and were majority masculine (87%), as a result of immigrants' living arrangements patterns. By 1960, single-person households decreased to 7%, growing steadily to 15% by 2001. This increase is mainly the result of the aging process and women's higher life expectancy. Presently, half of single-person households are among women over 45 years old (Torrado, 2003). The city of Buenos Aires has the highest level of single-person households (25%).

With rising instability of conjugal unions and patterns of remarriage and formation of new unions, there is a large increase in "re-assembled" households—those made up by a (new) couple and children from previous unions. Current statistical data-gathering techniques, however, are not prepared to sort out different types of family processes in household formation. They capture synchronic data, and not the history of family formation behind it, and thus they appear under the "complete" nuclear or extended categories. Such households—and the family links that are created by the new unions—are still not framed within clear legal bodies, and the relationships they produce among their members (beyond the traditional image of the "step-relative") have not yet been typified legally or even in terms of social norms and habits.

As a result of increases in unmarried fertility and marital dissolution, there has been an increase of "incomplete nuclear households," which in most cases consist of a woman and her children (Jelin, 2005; Wainerman, 2003a).

GENDER ROLES

In the patriarchal nuclear model, gender roles are clearly established, with men as the economic providers and women in charge of reproductive and household activities (childbearing, childrearing, and domestic chores). This conception, as we saw earlier, was well reflected in family legislation until very recently.

When mandatory public education was established in 1884, women's education was believed to be fundamental to modernizing the country, yet was not intended to change long-established gender roles (Mead, 1997). Instead, education was viewed as helping women to improve their role in the family and to play a more central role in maintaining social order. At this time, motherhood was being redefined from biological and passive, to scientific, active, and affectionate (Guy, 1998).

Accordingly, gender roles in society were vigorously transmitted through elementary textbooks. Being a woman was synonymous with being a mother and the provider of affection, whereas men were portrayed as economic providers and active participants in society. Women's virtues were to be cultured, refined, respectful, hygienic, and neat, whereas men's virtues were to be smart and active. Women's work outside the home is rarely mentioned, and if so, it is usually in relation to economic necessity or professions that are extensions of their maternal role (Wainerman & Heredia, 1999). Similar conclusions can be drawn from magazines, scientific journals, and congressional debates during the first decades of the 20th century (Wainerman & Navarro, 1979).

This portrait of family life and gender roles greatly contrasted with the reality of Argentina during this period, when a significant proportion of women were engaged in productive activities beyond childrearing and housekeeping. For example, almost 60% of women (ages 10 and older) were working outside the home in 1869, with similar proportions across ages.[18] Women living in rural areas worked in family and nonfamily farms, and women in urban areas were mainly involved in domestic service and manual textile activities. Urbanization and industrialization were accompanied by a decline in female labor-force participation. By 1895 women's labor-force participation had declined to 42%, but it continued to show similar levels across all ages (Recchini de Lattes, 1974).[19] For the next 60 years or so it continued to decline (Table 6.5), but it began to show significant associations with women's marital and childbearing status, and educational level (Recchini de Lattes, 1974; Wainerman, 1979).

Women's labor-force participation began to increase again in the 1960s and rose steeply in the 1970s as a result of the country's economic deterioration and high unemployment rates among men. These new workers were largely middle-aged married women, including those with small children.[20] This increase in women's labor-force participation has been interpreted as mainly an adaptation to the economic crisis rather than a reaction to new opportunities or a process of modernization in a developing society, particularly in the case of less-educated women's participation (Jelin, 2005; Wainerman, 2003a; Wainerman & Geldstein, 1994).

Gender roles have significantly changed since the 1980s, given the increasing proportion of households in which both spouses work or in which women have become the main economic provider (Geldstein, 1994, 1999; Wainerman, 2003a). Additionally, increases in marital separation and single motherhood have resulted in more women bearing the

---

[18]Conceptual definitions and techniques to measure labor-force participation have varied across the period under study. Rates before 1970 shown are estimates by Lattes (1974) to make them comparable with those in 1970 and 1980. These figures are not fully comparable with 1991 and 2001 because of changes in measurement techniques.

[19]In 1907, a specific law for women's work ruled that women should work shorter hours and should have maternity leave and other benefits. The basis of this legislation, though, was the belief that precarious working conditions will affect women's performance of their main role in society: procreation and reproduction of the family (Wainerman & Navarro, 1979).

[20]Female labor-force participation among women ages 25–44 went from around 36 to 54% between 1980 and 1991.

sole responsibility of providing for their children (Geldstein, 1994, 1999). For example, in the metropolitan area of Buenos Aires, the proportion of women who constitute the principal economic household contributor increased from 19 to 27% between 1989 and 1992 (Geldstein, 1994). Increasing education along with economic deterioration has thus significantly altered the profile of working women and their labor trajectories. In recent times, career aspirations are no longer limited to women with a higher education. Moreover, women are now are working in a more stable manner, whether they are single or married, and regardless of their children's ages (Wainerman, 2003a).

Although women are balancing work and household responsibilities, it appears that this is not the case among men. In-depth studies conducted in greater metropolitan Buenos Aires show that women's increasing responsibilities associated with their participation in the labor force have not been balanced by greater involvement of men in domestic tasks (Cerrutti, 2003; Wainerman, 2003b). Men, however, do tend to be more involved in their children's lives and activities than their fathers were (Wainerman, 2003b).

RELIGIOUS AND FAMILY VALUES

The last decades have been significant in terms of changes in family behaviors, particularly in relation to marriage, cohabitation, unmarried childbearing, and divorce—mirroring those observed in Western Europe and other developed countries (Lesthaeghe, 1995; Van de Kaa, 1987). Accordingly, these behavioral transformations have been attributed to significant changes in people's values and beliefs regarding family and gender roles (Sana, 2001). The little empirical evidence on this matter points to a weakening of religion in people's lives and an expansion in the range of behavioral alternatives, and an increase in individual freedom of choice.

Today, the majority of the Argentina population remains Catholic, and a very significant proportion report that they believe in God and consider themselves religious (80%). However, only one quarter attend religious ceremonies on a regular basis, and just 6% declared that they would turn to God or a religious person if they had a difficult matter to resolve. The Catholic Church has been trying to adjust to the new times by adopting strategies to maintain (or gain) members, for example, by increasing the avenues through which Catholic marriages can be annulled, and by organizing counseling groups for remarried individuals. The city of Buenos Aires has the highest percentage of people that consider themselves nonreligious (16%, versus 10% in the rest of the country).[21]

Religiosity has become increasingly a private matter. From the time civil marriage was ruled in 1888 as the only requirement to be legally married, religious marriage ceremonies have become a personal choice. At the turn of the 20th century, about 65% of couples who married in the city of Buenos Aires had a religious (Catholic) ceremony, a proportion that decreased to 50% a century later (Torrado, 2003, p. 280). It is also likely that an important proportion of couples that have a church ceremony do so more for tradition or to please parents rather than because of sacred convictions (López, Findling, & Federíco, 2000). Today it is not uncommon for couples who choose religious wedding ceremonies to have lived together before marriage or to have children.

Available anecdotal data also point to a decline in people's participation in religious ceremonies. A study conducted in the city of Buenos Aires during the 1960s among women aged 25 to 50 found that 20% reported attending religious ceremonies at least once a week and a similar proportion reported never attending (CELADE & CFSC, 1972). Data from the World Values Survey collected 20 years later (in 1983) revealed a similar proportion of women reporting their attendance at religious ceremonies at least once a week, but a larger proportion (31%) reporting that they never attended.[22]

Despite recognizing the importance of family values and attitudes in shaping recent social and family trends in Argentina, scholars have largely neglected this area of research, largely because of the lack of systematic national or regional representative data. One of the few studies on this topic examined the extent to which values and attitudes toward marriage, divorce, childbearing and childrearing, and abortion have changed over the last two decades (Binstock & Cerrutti, 2002). Results of this study are consistent with what has been observed in other societies: Argentineans have expanded the range of individual choice by accepting and supporting a wider range of family behaviors. At the same time, it is also clear that this greater tolerance does not reflect an abandonment of long-established family forms, such as the institution of marriage. People continue to believe that an intact family is the best context for

---

[21]According to a survey ordered by the Episcopal Consulate (Clarin, 11-20-2001).

[22]These figures were estimated to make them comparable with the CELADE and CFSC study, that is, among women 20–50 years old living in Buenos Aires. By 1990 and 1995, the proportion of women declaring never attending religious ceremonies increased to 39 and 44%, but these figures should be taken cautiously, given small sample sizes for each of those years.

children, but they also seem less willing to sacrifice their own well-being and satisfaction to offer that environment. One of the largest changes found in this study was the increase between 1983 and 1995 in the proportion of respondents reporting approval of "women wanting to be single mothers without a stable partner" (from 26 to 60%).

Although characteristics of those living in Buenos Aires, particularly their higher education and lower religiosity, are associated with more tolerant family attitudes, they do not account for all of the attitudinal changes observed during the study period. For example, although women seem to have led the increased emphasis on individual freedom and tolerance in the family arena, men followed this trend more slowly and even countered it with a concomitant increase in their conformity with some long-established values, such as marriage and traditional gender roles (Binstock & Cerrutti, 2002).

Gender differences in attitudinal shifts are hypothesized to be linked to (a) the significant increase in women's economic contribution to household maintenance, with its implications for increasing independence and autonomy, and (b) considerable improvements in women's educational attainment (surpassing that of men), with its influence over a wide range of values and personal expectations. It has also been posited that as women expanded their roles outside and within the family, men felt threatened by their relative lack of power (inside and outside of marriage), and responded by expressing a desire for traditional family patterns that accorded men greater status (Binstock & Cerrutti, 2002, p. 19).

CONCLUSION

In reviewing family trends in Argentina, we have observed that the last several decades have seen important changes in matters of family formation, dynamics, and dissolution. Fewer people are getting married, and those that do are marrying at later ages, having fewer children, and disrupting their marriages more often. Also, more people are choosing to form their first union through cohabitation and to have their children while cohabiting. Women have also altered their role within families by playing a more significant role in the household economy, or by becoming the sole provider. These changes have challenged the patriarchal nuclear family model of a father–husband breadwinner and a mother–wife in charge of reproductive activities, and indicate a major change in marriage as an institution. Furthermore, rather than being short-lived, these trends have continued among the most recent cohorts of young adults.

The significance of these trends, which started in the 1960s, lies not merely in the emergence of the behaviors per se, but also in the social sectors in which they have occurred. As we have shown, for much of the country's history the patriarchal family model and Catholic family values coexisted with premarital and extramarital sexuality, high levels of illegitimate childbearing, and nonmarital unions. Recent changes in family behaviors in Argentina have been linked—as in other societies—to increasing secularization and individualization, to the spread of modern values regarding personal autonomy and fulfillment, and to increasing tolerance to alternative family forms (Binstock & Cerrutti, 2002; Jelin, 2005; Sana, 2001; Wainerman, 2003). Family behaviors such as cohabitation, divorce, and unmarried childbearing, once hidden in mainstream middle-class society, have grown in visibility and acceptance in all social strata during the past four decades.[23]

To understand the context of these changes in family behaviors, it is necessary to highlight the important cultural changes that began during the 1960s. Feijoó and Nari (1996) describe the 1960s as a crucial decade in Argentina for changes in gender roles, particularly for middle-class women. Women during the 1960s achieved a level of autonomy never experienced by earlier generations—attending universities, going out alone, enjoying greater sexual freedom, and using modern contraceptives. During this time, women, particularly those in the middle class, were faced with discontinuities in gender roles and a variety of new female models: the guerrilla, the hippie, the intellectual, the housewife surrounded by electrical appliances, the "modern" mother. In general, the daily lives of the middle classes, less provincial and closer to the world, were influenced by the "American way of life," which included new forms of religion and political activism, new attitudes toward sex and marriage, and even new choices in music and attire (Feijoó & Nari, 1996, p. 11).

Also in the 1960s Argentina television began broadcasting shows that presented nontraditional gender roles or discussed topics such as birth control or racial discrimination alongside more popular soap operas and other shows that portrayed traditional gender roles (Feijoó & Nari, 1996). During this period the mass media also began to spread information on the application of psychoanalysis to child rearing and socialization. The 1960s was also a time of various international cleavages—such as the Cuban revolution and student protests in France—that had a strong influence on con-

---

[23]The middle class in Argentina, and particularly in the city of Buenos Aires, has been very significant, and even more so when compared with other Latin American countries.

solidating socialist movements and increasing the political participation of workers and students in Argentina (Feijoó & Nari, 1996).

Another important element to consider is the inflexibility of the legislation about remarriage. People who had separated from their spouses did not have any option if they wanted to form a new relationship, other than to enter a nonmarital union.[24] This legal limitation, rather than restraining people from forming a new relationship following a marital separation, resulted in an increase in nonmarital unions as an alternative to remarriage. This increase was correlated with changes not only in the values of the couples who chose this nonmarital option, but also in the tolerance afforded this behavior among the friends and relatives of these couples. Given the Catholic Church's firm opposition to divorce and to nonmarital unions, many cohabiting couples may have become less religious or more private in their practice of religious beliefs. Also, the children who were born or raised within consensual unions or with separated parents became socialized within the context of these new religious and family values. As documented, the generation born in the 1960s is the one leading changes in patterns of first-union formation, by choosing to cohabit first rather than directly marry. This is also the generation that leads the recent increase in out-of-wedlock childbearing. Also during this period, the increased labor-force participation of women in response to the income deterioration of their partners and husbands probably had important implications for values of independence and autonomy. Women's increasing education had similar effects, with its more general influences over values, personal expectations, and career aspirations.

In general, social change in Argentina has taken place earlier and in a broader way than legal changes. Clearly, women have experienced the largest transformations. Originally regarded as inferior to men from a legal and cultural point of view, women had to struggle to become active participants in society. Not surprisingly, then, we find that women were more likely than men to embrace attitudes and behaviors that emphasized individual freedom and tolerance in the family arena. Although this trend has been clearly documented for the early 1980s and mid-1990s, it is likely that it started earlier and that it heralds even greater tolerance to alternative family forms.

Argentina during the mid-1980s offered the best scenario from a legal and social point of view for individuals to openly embrace their choices and preferences in family matters. The military dictatorship in power

---

[24]This obviously also involved unmarried people when they were involved with somebody who was previously married.

between 1976 and 1983 implemented a systematic policy of censorship, repression, kidnapping, torture, and disappearance of political opponents, including pregnant woman and teenagers. After democracy was reestablished at the end of 1983, human rights became a major focus of debate in society. As we also documented, major changes in family legislation took place during this time, as well as legal sanctions against all forms of discrimination against women. Elementary school textbooks that had been almost immune to social changes for a century began to portray alternatives to nuclear family forms and traditional gender roles for women (Wainerman & Heredia, 1999). Also, democracy brought censorship to an end in the mass media. Television shows openly discussed any topic and boundaries were slowly and steadily pushed, from subject matter to the language used. Topics such as sexual relationships, out-of-wedlock childbearing and single-parent households, nonmarital cohabitation, divorce, remarriage, and step-families, sexual orientation, prostitution, working couples and working mothers, family violence, contraception, and addictions were all portrayed and discussed in the mass media. During this period, growing proportions of Argentineans were not only being born and raised in alternative family forms, but also being exposed in the larger society to a broad range of alternative family paths.

ACKNOWLEDGMENTS

I thank Edith A. Pantelides for her comments and Carolina Peterlini for her valuable assistance in the preparation of this chapter.

REFERENCES

Ariño, M. (1999). *Hogares y mujeres jefas de hogar: Universos a des-cubrir.* Serie Informes de Investigacion No 2. Buenos Aires: Cátedra Demografía Social, Facultad de Ciencias Sociales, Universidad de Buenos Aires. Unpublished report.
Argentina Ministerio de Salud. (various years: 1980, 1981, 1990, 1999). *Estadísticas vitales: Información básica.* 1980 and 1981, Series 5, No. 23; 1990, Series 5, No. 34; 1999, Series 5, No. 43. Buenos Aires: Dirección Nacional de Estadísticas de Salud, Programa Nacional de Estadísticas de Salud.
Bailey, S. (1980). Marriage patterns and immigrant assimilation un Buenos Aires, 1882–1923. *Hispanic American Historical Review, 60*(1), 32–48.
Binstock, G. (2004). Cambios en las pautas de formación y disolución de la familia entre las mujeres de la Ciudad de Buenos Aires. *Población de Buenos Aires, 1,* 7–14.

Binstock, G. (2005). Transformaciones en la formación de la familia: Evidencias de la Encuesta Anual de Hogares de la Ciudad de Buenos Aires. In Asociación Argentina de Población, *VII Jornadas Asociación Argentina de Estudios de Población* (pp. 1065–1079). Buenos Aires: INDEC-AEPA.

Binstock, G., & Cerrutti, M. (2002). *Changing attitudes towards the family in Argentina, 1980–1995.* Paper presented at the Annual Meeting of the Population Association of America, Atlanta.

Binstock, G., & Cerrutti, M. (2005). *Carreras truncadas: El abandono escolar en el nivel medio en la Argentina.* Buenos Aires: UNICEF.

Binstock, G., & Pantelides, E.A. (2005). La fecundidad adolescente hoy: Diagnóstico sociodemográfico. In M. Gogna (Ed.), *Embarazo y maternidad en la adolescencia. Estereotipos, evidencias y propuestas para políticas públicas* (pp. 77–112). Buenos Aires: CEDES-Ministerio de Salud y Ambiente de la Nación-UNICEF Argentina.

Bunge, A. (1984). *Una nueva Argentina.* Buenos Aires: Hyspamérica. (Original work published 1940.)

Caccopardo, M. C., & Moreno, J. L. (1997). Cuando los hombres estaban ausentes: La familia del interior de la Argentina decimonónica. In H. G. Otero & G. Velázquez (Eds.), *Poblaciones argentinas: Estudios de demografía diferencial* (pp. 13–28). Tandil: PROPIEP.

Centro Latinoamericano de Demografía & University of Chicago Community and Family Study Center. (1972). *Fertility and family planning in metropolitan Latin America.* Chicago: Community and Family Study Center, University of Chicago.

Cerrutti, M. (2003). Trabajo, organización familiar y relaciones de género en Buenos Aires. In C. H. Wainerman (Ed.), *Familia, trabajo y género. Un mundo de nuevas relaciones* (pp. 105–151). Buenos Aires: UNICEF/FCE.

Ciccerchia, R. (1989). Vida Familiar y prácticas conyugales. Clases populares en una ciudad colonial. Buenos aires, 1800–1810. *Boletín del Instituto de Historia Argentina y Americana, 3*(2), 91–109.

Ciccerchia, R. (1994). Familia: La historia de una idea. Los desórdenes domésticos de la plebe urbana porteña, Buenos Aires, 1776–1850. In C. H. Wainerman (Ed.), *Vivir en familia* (pp. 49–72). Buenos Aires: UNICEF/Losada.

Comisión Económica para América Latina y el Caribe. CEPAL. (2002). *Boletín Demográfico: América Latina y el Caribe. Indicadores seleccionados con una perspectiva de género, 70.* Santiago de Chile: CEPAL.

Feijoó, M. C., & Nari, M. (1996). Women in Argentina during the 1960s. *Latin American Perspectives, 23, 1*(88), 7–26.

Frías, S. (1994). La familia en la época hispánica. In C. García Belsunce, César, *La familia: permanencia y cambio.* Buenos Aires: Comisión Arquidiocesiana para la cultura, Comité de Historia, Fundación Mapfre América.

García Belsunce, C. (1999). La Familia. In Academia Nacional de la Historia, *Nueva Historia de la Nacion Argentina 2. Periodo Español (1600–1810)* (pp. 127–148). Buenos Aires: Planeta.

Geldstein, R. N. (1999). *Los roles de género en la crisis: Mujeres como principal sostén económico del hogar.* Cuaderno del Cenep, 50. Buenos Aires: CENEP.

Geldstein, R. N. (1994). Familias con liderazgo femenino en sectores populares de Buenos Aires. In C. H. Wainerman (Comp.), *Vivir en familia* (pp. 143–182). Buenos Aires: UNICEF/Losada.

Germani, G. (1955). *Estructura social de la Argentina: Análisis estadístico.* Buenos Aires: Raigal.

Ghirardi, M. M. (1998, October). *Familia y cambio social en la Argentina a fines del período colonial y comienzos de la vida independiente.* Paper presented at IUSSP Conference Changes and Continuity in American Demographic Behaviours: The Five Centuries' Experience, Córdoba.

Gil Montero, R., Massé, G., Pollero, R., & Teruel, A. (1998, October). *Argentina y Uruguay en los albores del siglo XX. Heterogeneidades intranacionales y homogeneidades transnacionales. Aportes demográficos para su interpretación.* Paper presented at IUSSP Conference Changes and Continuity in American Demographic Behaviours: The Five Centuries' Experience, Córdoba.

Giusti, A. E. (1993). Finalizó la transición de la fecundidad en Argentina? In Conferencia Latinoamericana de Población & PROLAP & Instituto Nacional de Estadística Geográfica e Informática, *IV Conferencia Latinoamericana de Población: La transición demográfica en América Latina y el Caribe* (Vol. II, pp. 243–260). México: Instituto Nacional de Estadística Geográfica e Informática.

Guy, D. (1998). Madres vivas y muertas. Los múltiples conceptos de la maternidad en Buenos Aires. In D. Balderston & D. J. Guy (Comp.), *Sexo y sexualidades en América Latina* (pp. 231–256). Buenos Aires: Paidós.

Jelín, E. (1994). Familia, crisis y después.... In C. H. Wainerman (Ed.), *Vivir en familia* (pp. 23–48). Buenos Aires: UNICEF/Losada.

Jelin, E. (2005). The family in Argentina: Modernity, economic crisis, and politics. In B. N. Adams & J. Trost (Eds.), *Handbook of world families* (pp. 391–413). Sage.

Lattes, A. E. (1974). El crecimiento de la población y sus componentes demográficos entre 1870 y 1970. In Z. Recchini de Lattes & A. E. Lattes (Eds.), *La población de Argentina* (pp. 29–66). Buenos Aires: INDEC.

Lesthaeghe, R. (1995). The second demographic transition in Western countries: An interpretation. In K. O. Mason & A. M. Jense (Eds.), *Gender and family change in industrialized countries* (pp. 17–62). Oxford: Claredon Press.

López, E. (1995). Fecundidad, práctica anticonceptiva y tamaño de la familia: Un estudio en madres del conurbano de Buenos Aires. In AEPA (Ed.), *II Jornadas Argentinas de Estudios de Población* (pp.141–159). Buenos Aires: AEPA y Honorable Senado de la Nación.

López, E., Findling, L., & Federico, A. (2000). Casarse o no casarse? Imágenes sobre la formacion de familias. *Sociedad, 16,* 153–173.

Mazzeo, V. (n.d.). *Comportamiento de la nupcialidad en la ciudad autónoma de Buenos Aires: período 1890–1999.* Buenos Aires: Dirección General de Estadística y Censos.

Mead, K. (1997). Gendering the obstacles to progress in positivist, Argentina, 1880–1920. *Hispanic American Historical Review, 77*(4), 645–675.

Moreno, J. L. (1997–1998). Sexo, matrimonio y familia: La ilegitimidad en la frontera pampeana del Rio de la Plata, 1780–1850. *Boletin de Instituto de Historia Argentina y Americana "Dr. Emilio Ravignani," 16 & 17*, 61–82.

Mychaszula, S., Geldstein, R., & Grushka, C. (1989). *Datos para el estudio de la participación de la población en la actividad económica. Argentina, 1947–1980.* Buenos Aires: CENEP.

Otero, H. (2000). *Endogamia e integración de inmigrantes en la Argentina moderna. Balances y perspectivas desde un enfoque regional.* Paper presented at Seminario sobre Población y Sociedad en América Latina, Salta.

Pantelides, E. A. (1989). *La fecundidad argentina desde mediados del siglo XX.* Cuaderno del CENEP, 41. Buenos Aires: Centro de Estudios de Población.

Pantelides, E. A. (2002). Completing the fertility transition: The case of Argentina. In N. Unidas (Ed.), *Completing the fertility transition* (pp. 333–342). New York: United Nations.

Rapoport, M. (2000). *Historia económica, política y social de la Argentina (1880–2000).* Buenos Aires: Ediciones Macchi.

Recchini de Lattes, Z. (1974). Población económicamente activa. In Z. Recchini de Lattes & A. E. Lattes (Eds.), *La población de Argentina* (pp. 149–172). Buenos Aires: INDEC.

Sana, M. (2001). La segunda transición demográfica y el caso argentino. In AEPA, *V Jornadas Argentinas de Estudios de Población* (pp. 141–159). Luján: Universidad Nacional de Luján & AEPA.

Schkolnik, S., & Pantelides, E. A. (1974). Los cambios en la composición de la población. In Z. Recchini de Lattes & A. E. Lattes (Eds.), *La población de Argentina* (pp. 67–93). Buenos Aires: INDEC.

Socolow, S. (1989). Aceptable partners: Marriage choice in colonial Argentina, 1778–1810. In A. Lavrin (Ed.), *Sexuality and marriage in colonial Latin America* (pp. 209–247). Lincoln: University of Nebraska Press.

Szuchman, M. (1977). The limits of the melting pot in urban Argentina: Marriage and integration in Córdoba, 1869–1909. *Hispanic American Historical Review, 57*(1), 24–50.

Szuchman, M. (1986). Household structure and political crisis: Buenos Aires, 1810–1860. *Latin American Research Review, 21*(3), 55–93.

Torrado, S. (2003). *Historia de la familia en la Argentina moderna (1870–2000).* Buenos Aires: Ediciones de La Flor.

Van de Kaa, D. J. (1987). Europe's second demographic transition. *Population Bulletin, 42*(1), 1–58.

Wainerman, C. H. (1979). Educación, familia y participación económica femenina en la Argentina. *Desarrollo Económico 18*(72), 511–537.

Wainerman, C. H. (2003a). La reestructuración de las fronteras de género. In C. H. Wainerman (Ed.), *Familia, trabajo y género. Un mundo de nuevas relaciones* (pp. 55–104). Buenos Aires: UNICEF/FCE.

Wainerman, C. H. (2003b). Padres y maridos. Los varones en la familia. In C. H. Wainerman (Ed.), *Familia, trabajo y género. Un mundo de nuevas relaciones* (pp. 199–224). Buenos Aires: UNICEF/FCE.

Wainerman, C. H., & Geldstein, R. (1994). Viviendo en familia: Ayer y hoy. In C. H. Wainerman (Ed.), *Vivir en familia* (pp. 183–235). Buenos Aires: UNICEF/Losada.

Wainerman, C. H., & Heredia, M. (1999). *¿Mamá amasa la masa? Cien años en los libros de lectura de la escuela primaria.* Buenos Aires: Editorial de Belgrano.

Wainerman, C. H., & Navarro, M. (1979). *El trabajo de la mujer en la Argentina: Un análisis preliminar de las ideas dominantes en las primeras décadas del siglo XX.* Cuaderno del CENEP no. 7. Buenos Aires: CENEP.

Zimmerman, E. A. (1992). Racial ideas and social reform: Argentina, 1890–1916. *Hispanic American Historical Review, 72*(1), 223–246.

7

Family Change in Iran: Religion, Revolution, and the State

Mohammad Jalal Abbasi-Shavazi
Department of Demography, University of Tehran

Peter McDonald
Demography and Sociology Program,
Australian National University

This chapter examines dynamics and change in the Iranian family during the 20th century, especially subsequent to the Islamic revolution in 1979. Two main questions are addressed: To what extent has the family changed over these years in Iran? And how have ideas affected change? We begin by describing historical family values and customs and discuss the changes that have taken place. Next, social structural changes are discussed and consideration is given to the extent to which family dynamics and change have been influenced by structural changes or ideational forces. In particular, we focus on the roles of religion, revolution, and the state in family dynamics, continuity, and change, and discuss the elements of family life that have continued unchanged throughout the years.

The institution of family in Iran has been influenced by values and perceptions from the pre- and post-Islamic eras and has changed in response to sociocultural, political, and economic changes over the last two centuries. The crucial periods for transformation of family attitudes and behaviors were the periods before and after the Islamic Revolution. The study describes a complex mosaic of individual and family change and persistence. At the level of the family, several dimensions of family life have remained fairly constant, whereas others have changed dramatically. The most important individual change in recent decades is the increased level of education across cohorts, stimulated by the egalitarian nature of the revolution. The timing of marriage has also shifted toward higher ages, particularly for girls, and fertility behavior and attitudes of women have changed considerably. Change within the family has tended to be stronger at the level of the individual couple. This includes decisions about the number of children to have and attitudes about gender roles within the relationship. As attention shifts from the internal or intimate to the external or public aspects of family, change becomes more muted. This is due to the official regulations regarding the public role of women. Marriage with relatives remains common with little change across time, although attitudes have changed. The study concludes that political forces have played a fundamental role in enhancing or restraining social change in relation to the family.

IDEALIZED MORALITY AND FAMILY CHANGE

In relation to family change, McDonald (1994) has argued that an idealized family morality is a fundamental component of the culture of all societies. Because family organization is at the core of all societies, it is a component of the society's definition of itself, its identity. Consequently, change in family organization can be expected to be slow and measured. Nevertheless, as globalization proceeds and education levels increase and as communication brings the world and its ideas to everyone's doorstep, the forces of change are ever-present. The extent to which societies will be open to change will vary according to the degree to which deviation from the idealized morality is tolerated. Western societies in the past 30 years have been marked by a new surge in toleration of individual behaviors that in earlier periods would have been considered unacceptable. Directly and indirectly, Western secular democracy is now promoted to the world through the process that is called *Westernization.*

Westernization does not necessarily proceed in a hegemonic way. In particular, little variation from the idealized family morality has occurred in countries where the family system is reinforced by a strong social morality—where variation from the ideal is deemed to be illegal, antisocial, or contrary to the teachings of the prevailing religion. In these countries, the ideal is policed by the strong, formal institutions of the society, principally the institutions of religion and the state. Where the ideal is rigidly enforced, as in postrevolutionary Iran, family change cannot be predicted well from changes in the characteristics of individuals such as changes in education, occupation, or economic well-being, because the individual is constrained from operating outside the prevailing idealized morality. In such circumstances, it is pointless to seek to distinguish between changes that are "structural" and changes that are "ideational" because ideology is structure and structure is ideology.

Family change must be interpreted within a framework that is political: how much and what type of change in family organization will be acceptable to the ruling authorities. Individuals can experiment with the boundaries of change and find that in some areas, these boundaries are relatively flexible whereas in others they are rigid. In contemporary Iran, the boundaries are defined or interpreted by religious authorities. Change may proceed in some aspects of family life because the change is not viewed as a threat to idealized family morality. For example, birth control and a small family size are accepted, whereas cohabitation or sexual relations outside marriage are anathema. During the period of the Shah, Westernization, in its milder form of 30 years ago, was given greater rein. Although many interpretations of the Islamic revolution are possible, many Iranians today believe that the revolution reversed the excessive encroachment of Westernization on Iranian idealized morality.

Thus, changes in the Iranian family need to be interpreted not in a conventional Western sociological framework of structure and ideology but in terms of the interpretation of idealized morality by religious and state institutions, an altogether more political approach. This does not mean that social dynamism is not possible. Iranians now are much more highly educated than in the recent past and are consequently more open to social change. They have a strong desire for better economic outcomes for their families and a belief that these should be attainable. However, change must proceed within the political context, a context in which structure and ideology are largely indistinguishable.

We begin this chapter with a review of the Iranian family from a historical perspective, emphasizing how family change has occurred along with political changes. We then discuss contemporary forces for change in family organization in Iranian society and present information from surveys and censuses on the areas of family life that have changed and not changed. We draw conclusions in the final section.

THE IRANIAN FAMILY: A HISTORICAL PERSPECTIVE

The Iranian Family until the 1900s

The institution of the family in Iran has influences from long-standing Islamic values and prescriptions, the 1960s and 1970s modernization efforts, the Islamic Revolution, 8 years of the Iran–Iraq war, and the recent efforts toward economic development. In this section, we provide a brief overview of the organization of the family with particular attention to the 20th century.

The original Muslim family in Iran was patrilineal, endogamous, and male-dominated. Islam places strong emphasis on family and considers it the foundation of the society. According to Islam, girls and boys become mature at ages 9 and 14 years, respectively, and they should perform their religious duties from these ages. They also should establish their families at an early point. The woman has a right to property, wealth, and inheritance, but not equal to that of men. Both men and woman have equal rights for nurturing children. Monogamy is the main pattern of marriage in Islam. However, polygamy is allowed if the man can afford it (up to four wives) and can treat his wives with justice. Temporary marriage is allowed, with the duration of marriage specified at the time of the contract, but there is no right of inheritance from temporary marriages (Bahmani, 2000, p. 28).

The principal characteristics of the Iranian family in the past were endogamy, preferred marriage between paternal cousins, equality of brothers under the laws of inheritance, residence of married sons with their parents, early marriage, and the possibility of polygamy (Behnam, 1985, p. 555). The family in Iran was an autonomous unit of production and consumption, and patrilineal and patriarchal in nature. The eldest male of the family (grandfather, father, eldest son, uncle) was the patriarch and family authority and power was vested in him. Apart from gender, hierarchy within the family was built on respect due to age and experience.

Marriage concerned not only two individuals but also potentially two lineages. Because marriage played a pivotal role in the maintenance of the social system based on the kinship network, the community retained control over this important transaction. Endogamy, especially cousin marriage, was the preferred form of marriage. Endogamy provides a greater knowledge and assurance about the characters of the bride and groom, it ensures that lineage property is maintained within the lineage, it makes divorce difficult because of the implied threat to lineage solidarity, and it protects the patriarch from potentially dissident outsiders. Early marriage was common for girls and boys, and marriage was universal. Early marriage for girls was preferred because it ended a family's economic responsibility for its girl children and because it reduced the potential for the shame of a pregnancy before marriage (Ezazi, 1995, p. 55). The relationship between husband and wife was patriarchal and the wife was required to demonstrate respect for her husband. The fact that polygamy was allowed meant that women were always insecure. Intimacy between the couple was somewhat restrained and all family members had ascribed duties in life according to conventional (and differentiated) roles for men and women. Men had a unilateral right to divorce, although the rate of divorce was low. Children belonged to the father after divorce, in both permanent and temporary marriages (Bahmani, 2000, pp. 29–36). Fertility was high due to the fear of infant mortality, the need for security in old age, fear of being alone, and the productive role of children. Boys were preferred to girls.

Iranian women in the first quarter of the 1900s occupied an inferior position in society. Educational opportunities for women were extremely limited. Although little data exist on the education of women, one source states that by 1925 only 3% of all Iranian women were literate (Rahman, 1957, p. 27). Women could neither vote nor hold political positions. Most women seemed to have accepted their inferior status and believed this to be their fate (Sansarian, 1985, p. 88). The family mode of organization covered all aspects of its members' lives. The most important of these aspects were procreation, the socialization of children, food production, the building of homes, the use of leisure time, health and medical care, and the protection and defense of the whole family, individually and collectively (Nassehi-Behnam, 1985, pp. 557–558).

The form of the family in Iran remained unchanged for many centuries. However, the end of the 19th and the beginning of the 20th century were marked by a great influx of ideas that were accompanied by significant transformations in the family, especially among elite families who had contacts with the West. During the period 1895–1925, Iran was opened to the West, the society moved toward industrialization, feudalism weakened, and a state apparatus was developed. The rural economy was largely replaced by a cash economy, and foreign as well as internal investments were encouraged. This industrial investment needed human resources, and thus rural people moved to cities. Migration from rural to urban areas followed by migration to the West brought about social changes that affected family life. With economic prosperity, urbanization, and exposure to other ways of life, the household production economy gradually disappeared and the importance of the lineage as an economic unit began to wane. Thus, in this period of history, change in family structure was accepted as the bonds in the extended family became less economic in orientation. Nevertheless, the patriarch retained most of his power over other family members, the position of women remained at a very inferior level, and the Islamic codes of family behavior were enforced.

Change during the Pahlavi Regime (1925–1979)

During the 54 years of Pahlavi rule of Reza Shah (1925–1941) and Mohammad Reza Shah (1941–1979), Iran experienced major social and economic changes, not least in the area of family life. In the 1920s, Reza Shah enacted laws to increase the minimum legal age at marriage to 14 years for girls, passed a compulsory education act, and, following Kamal Ataturk, attempted to force women to abandon the veil.

Vatandoost (1985, pp. 107–114) singled out three major initiatives between 1935 and 1967 by these monarchs that affected the general status of Iranian women. The first was a 1935 decree by Reza Shah banning the public use by women of the *chador* (the veil). During his 16 years of absolute rule, Reza Shah took major steps to centralize power and to achieve a degree of Westernization and modernization. In his efforts to provide an impression of Iran as a modern nation, he tried to abolish all visible symbols of the past, such as the veil and the native attire for men, and to replace them with Western dress and headgear. However, these initiatives were made with little attention to religious sensitivities; as a result, the veil ban policy, for example, was not rigidly enforced at the local level.

The second major initiative was a decree by Mohammad Reza Shah granting Iranian women the right to vote as well as to run for and hold public office. In 1963, Mohammad (Md.) Reza Shah outlined a six-point reform program, known as the *Shah's White Revolution referendum*, that consisted of: (a) land reform, (b) nationalization of forests, (c) sale of shares of government-owned industries (to finance land reform), (d) profit-sharing with workers to prevent the exploitation of labor, (e) formation of the literacy corps, and (f) amendments to election laws granting voting rights to women. However, the *ulama* (religious teachers) believed that there were hidden motives behind the Shah's White Revolution. They believed that any initiative by the Shah, who was regarded as pro-United States, could only be self-serving and, in the long run, this would mean a further loss of Iran's independence (Vatandoost, 1985, pp. 113–114).

The third initiative of the Shah period was the 1967 legislation entitled the Family Protection Law, which granted certain rights to Iranian women by attempting to create legal obstacles to the exercise by men of a unilateral privilege to multiple marriages and to terminating a marriage at will (Vatandoost, 1985, p. 107). The law did not replace the 1931 Civil Law or the 1938 Marriage Law, but adapted these laws according to the needs of the society as determined by Md. Reza Shah. The law reduced the unilateral right of men to divorce, and polygamy became subject to the consent of the first wife. Women were also given the right to divorce. The custody of the children after divorce was subject to the agreement of the couple, and in cases of dispute between the two, the court had the right to make the decision based on the best interests of the children. According to the law, men had to get the written permission of the first wife to marry a second wife. However, the ages at marriage for boys and girls were not changed in the 1967 Family Protection Law. Work opportunities for women were increased and as a result women's employment increased to around 14% by 1976 (Vatandoost, 1985, p. 114).

Changes similar to these were made in other Islamic countries around the same time—for example, the 1974 Marriage Act in Indonesia. However, in Iran, these laws were abolished following the Islamic Revolution in 1979. The fact that opposing laws prevailed successively in Iran indicates that what was important was not social attitudes but the power of the state.

In 1971, a conference was organized by the Ministry of Health and the Iran Women's Organization to discuss a family planning program. There were discussions about increasing the age at marriage as well as other issues related to the amendment of the 1967 Family Protection Law. The Society of Women Lawyers criticized the law for giving the right to men to marry a second wife even with the first wife's agreement. As a result, in 1974, the *Majlis* (the Islamic Council) amended the 1967 Family Protection Law. One of the amendments was the increase in age at marriage for girls to 18 and for boys to 20. However, the court could give permission to marry if the girl was physically and mentally sound and she was not younger than 15. The law further limited the right of men to take a second wife by subjecting that right to eight other conditions (Bahmani, 2000, pp. 39–43). These amendments were not implemented fully, but their symbolic value was important, indicating that some of women's marriage rights were officially recognized (Hoodfar, 1995, p. 107; Makhlouf Obermeyer, 1994, p. 46).

Some of these legal changes may have been successful to the extent that they were initiated in response to changing values—for example, increasing the age at marriage for girls and boys. However, some of the initiatives, including the banning of the veil, received criticism and resistance within the society, especially by religious leaders, as they were regarded as top-down Western-oriented reforms. Vatandoost (1985, p. 125) argued that the lack of success of Reza Shah's and Mohammad Reza Shah's efforts in changing the status of Iranian women was chiefly due to their equation of social reform with modernization, and modernization with Westernization. He noted that Reza Shah was convinced that even Western attire was necessary for social reform. He believed:

The traditional Islamic beliefs and institutions were incompatible with a realization of the country's goals, and were therefore expendable. Similarly, his son was unable to differentiate between reform and

Westernization, for in his autobiography he clearly presents the need for Westernization as a welcome ordeal.

The Effects of the 1979 Islamic Revolution

The 1979 Islamic Revolution was in some ways a response or a resistance to the initiatives by Reza Shah that were considered Western and/or non-Islamic. The revolution brought about major sociocultural, political, and legal changes that affected many areas of social life in Iran, including family life.

Soon after the revolution, the Islamic government emphasized domesticity and motherhood as the main roles of women, and reversed some of the policies initiated during the Shah's regime. The main legal changes after the Islamic Revolution in the area of marriage were the reduction of age at marriage, eliminating the limitations on polygamy, and the provision of financial support for new couples. Immediately after the Islamic Revolution, the 1967 and 1974 Family Protection Laws were annulled, and the judiciary system was ordered to use only laws aligned with *Sharia* law (the legal system inspired by the Koran, the Sunna, and older Arabic law systems). Later, in 1982, Imam Khomeini, the leader of the revolution, decreed his dissatisfaction with the laws of the Shah period and ordered the courts to substitute laws according to *fatwa* (judgments issued by Islamic judges on specific contemporary issues). For example, according to the 1931 Law, the minimum ages at marriage for girls and boys were 15 and 18, respectively, but according to *fatwa*, the minimum ages at marriage for girls and boys were 13 and 15 respectively, and marriage for girls at an earlier age was left to judicial discretion based on an assessment of the girl's maturity. Courts could give permission for marriage for ages as early as 10 and 11 if the girl had started her menstruation (Bahmani, 2000, pp. 46–63).

The *hijab* (veil) became compulsory and women were required to wear *chador* (a full-length, loosing fitting black garment covering a woman's clothing) and a special form of dress in public areas and offices. Primary, secondary, and high schools were segregated for boys and girls. The presence of women in offices was discouraged and employment opportunities for women became more restricted. As a result, the female employment rate decreased from 14% in 1976 to 7% in 1986.

However, contrary to Western expectations, an egalitarian spirit prevailed in the streets during this period of the Revolution. Both during and after the Revolution, males and females alike joined in the demonstrations, marches, and strikes that culminated in the establishment of the Islamic Republic of Iran. This visible participation of women presented a

TABLE 7.1
The Literacy Rate for Women Aged 15–19 to 25–29, Iran, by Rural and Urban Areas

Age groups	1966		1976		1986		1996	
5 years	Urban	Rural	Urban	Rural	Urban	Rural	Urban	Rural
15–19	57.7	5.4	75.4	19.8	85.8	53.0	96.9	86.4
20–24	41.2	2.7	59.4	10.1	75.8	36.5	93.8	77.9
25–29	29.5	1.4	49.4	4.9	65.5	22.0	89.5	65.4

Note. Sources: Statistical Centre of Iran, various censuses.

new image of the female, and women themselves began recognizing their strength in numbers (Touba, 1985, p. 131).

Education is one of the main factors of social change, and operates to promote family change in many ways. One of the main social changes in the 20th century, and particularly over the past two decades, has been the expansion of mass education in Iran. Children of all social classes have access to education. The literacy rate has increased dramatically in both urban and rural areas (see Table 7.1). For example, the literacy rate for women aged 15–19 in urban areas increased from around 57% in 1966 to around 97% (almost universal) in 1996. The improvement in rural areas has been more dramatic, increasing from only 5% in 1966 to 86% in 1996.

In 1998, around 52% of those admitted to government universities were girls. The figure increased to 57% in 1999 and then to 62% in 2001 (Abdollahyan, 2001). These increases in educational attainment for Iranian girls mean that marriage and childbearing are often delayed into the early twenties. Studies suggest that aspirations and expectations of women in postrevolutionary Iran have also risen considerably (Kian-Thiebaut, 2002; Mir-Hosseini, 2002; Shadi-Talab, 2001). This has led to the improvement of the status of women at least within the family, and women have increased their role in family decision making. Shadi-Talab (2001, p. 54) concluded that "the expansion of education throughout the country and to all families, has resulted in the presence of an educated girl beside a very illiterate mother; the former tried to encourage the older woman to express herself and participate in decision-making." Increased literacy has contributed to women's confidence, and has increased women's perceptions that they have options in many aspects of their lives, particularly women in rural areas, who had been much constrained by past gender inequities (Hoodfar, 1996).

Attitudes toward female employment outside the home have also changed (Mohseni, 2000). Of the 73% of women aged 15–49 surveyed by the authors in 2002 who said they would prefer their daughters to continue their education after high school rather than to marry early, 62.5% said that this was so that their daughters could find a job in the future. A vast majority of women surveyed believed that women should work outside the home to have financial autonomy and also to contribute to the family's income (Abbasi-Shavazi, McDonald, & Hosseini-Chavoshi, 2003). Another recent action has been the provision of military training to females, and they have been permitted to join law enforcement agencies. These activities were restricted for women immediately after the revolution. However, despite dramatic changes in women's education and reported preferences for work outside the home, women's paid employment remains low in Iran.

Since the revolution, women have gained more freedom within the household and in specific forms of social activity, such as classes for reciting quran and prayer meetings. *Rozeh* and *Sofreh* are two examples of ceremonies organized and attended by women of all ages. In addition to recitation and prayer, broader social and political issues are discussed at these meetings. For example, the Ministry of Health has taken advantage of these meetings to promote family planning. The meetings have also been exploited for political purposes. Given the nature of these gatherings, most husbands and the government encourage women to attend. On the other side of change, women activists and feminists have also taken advantage of these meetings in the past (Touba, 1985, p. 132). This suggests that those in authority consider that women have a vote and an influence that is independent of their husbands' position.

Other recent signs of change in this area include the publication of several weekly magazines and academic journals that publish articles on women's affairs. There was also an improvement in the status of women after the 1997 presidential election of Mohammad Khatami. Women's participation in this election was very significant and Khatami initiated various programs for women's empowerment. He appointed a woman as the deputy to the President and Head of the Environment Organization. He also appointed an advisor to the President for women's affairs. There are several women activists in social as well as political fields, notably Shirin Ebadi, the Nobel Peace Prize winner in 2003. A number of women representatives have also been elected to the parliament and to rural-city councils. Several nongovernmental organizations are active in women's affairs and work very closely with women and the government to improve the status of women in Iran. These women, as noted by Hoodfar (1995, p. 106), have questioned prescribed gender roles and the male interpretation of the proper "Islamic role" for women, and have encouraged the government to introduce reforms in the areas of marriage, divorce, and education. The 2005 election of a conservative government may see some of these more liberal directions reversed, again emphasizing the importance of politics in social change.

CONTEMPORARY FORCES OF CHANGE IN THE IRANIAN FAMILY

Industrialization, Urbanization, and Westernization

The previous section documents the importance of political shifts upon the changing forms of the Iranian family. In this section, we turn to the effects of structural changes such as urbanization and industrialization, as well as to the emergence and influence of new ideas, or ideational effects. Socioeconomic changes have affected family models, particularly in urban areas. Nassehi-Behnam (1985, p. 560) referred to broken nuclear families as a new consequence of rural migration to cities in search of work. Men from rural areas left their wives and children in the village and went to the cities for work. With the movement of young migrants from rural areas, the national mode of production changed from farming to manufacturing. Agricultural production lost its importance and young people became less interested in farming, which consolidated the movement to cities. Also, mechanization of farms lowered the need for labor in rural areas, and thus the productive value of children declined for families. These changes contributed to the decline of the patriarchal and extended family in rural areas. Family changes in urban areas have been different from those in rural areas. Housing problems, along with other issues in urban areas, mitigate against co-residence of the extended family.

Family modes of organization in any society are important in shaping people's attitudes and behavior toward family formation and reproduction. For example, the family in the past was based on a household economy in which all family members contributed to household production. The process of socialization also took place within the family. In such circumstances, the family was responsible for the protection of its members. Ladier-Fouladi (2002), analyzing social welfare and the family in Iran, notes that, from the 1950s, economic modernization, urbanization, and growing school enrollment, particularly, in towns and cities, began very slowly to shift some of its long-held family responsibilities, although the relatively late involvement of the state in the field of social protection meant that the family retained its central support functions and power of control for many years (Ladier-Fouladi, 2002, pp. 362–365). She notes that, more recently, social and religious foundations have taken over some functions of the family and the local networks that would otherwise have continued to support their members. By their influence on the organization of the family, these foundations helped to undermine the principle of family interdependence and favored the emergence of the autonomous individual or couple. Nevertheless, state-funded social welfare has not developed to the extent that it will supplant the family mode of protection at the couple and individual levels. The family remains the paramount source of economic and emotional support.

To what extent have ideas contributed to family and family change in Iran? In his *Idea of Modernization in Iran*, Azadarmaki (2001) argued that the changes in contemporary Iran were more ideational than structural, political, or historical. Azadarmaki (2001, p. 150) concluded that

> modernization was imported, western, influenced by capitalism, and against social traditions, but while imported, it emerged as an ideology in Iran and became a tool for intellectuals or politicians to fight against social and cultural traditions. Given the fact that the idea of modernization was imported and people were not willing to accept it, this provided a crisis situation and led to un-development rather than development.

In the introductory remarks in *Women and the Family in Iran*, Fathi (1985, p. 5) described the zeal of Westernization during the Pahlavi regime as Europeanization, which led to excesses and blind imitation among some segments of Iranian society:

> The relationship between men and women in Iran has been influenced, especially in the present century, by western ideas and ways of life. Although some writers argue that western idea and practices have influenced only the upper and upper-middle classes, this is not so. During the fifty years of the Pahlavi regime, the western-educated and -oriented segment of the society was given disproportionate power and influence. These were the technocrat, bureaucrats, army officers, teachers, and journalists, whose influence reached far beyond their social class position. The members of this elite group even became role models for their subordinates, students, and readers.... However, despite the efforts of intellectuals..., a satisfactory accommodation between the western and indigenous cultural elements has not yet been achieved in Iran, and probably not in most Muslim societies. (Fathi, 1985, p. 5)

Fathi (1985) also expressed the view that "modernization and westernization from above" adopted by the Pahlavi regime "had its staunch and popular opponents," and thus, the uprising of 1979 and the creation of the Islamic Republic were responses to the reality that accommodation between Western and indigenous cultural elements had not been achieved.

Aghajanian (1997) argued that the accelerated adoption of communication and mass media and technology, including computers with access to the Internet and television programs through satellite antennae, has contributed to the acceptance of Western ideals among younger generations of Iranians. For example, Saroukhani and Navaie (2002, pp. 132–138) found that around 95% of women in Tehran watched TV for 1 to 3 hours during normal days, and around 45% listened to radio. Aghajanian (1997) noted that the adoption of Western ideas in all aspects of life by young generations will be a continued source of stress on the family. This will also reinforce the existing gender-based conflict, as young generations of women will be exposed to the gender-egalitarian values of Western culture. Expansion of transport has also been an important factor in convergence of behaviors, thus affecting family and fertility behaviors and attitudes.

Therefore, it seems that ideas have contributed to the transformation of family values and culture in Iran in recent decades, and with the advancement of communication technology, undoubtedly, the contribution of ideas on changes in attitudes and behavior of couples toward the family will continue in the future. Nevertheless, we concur with the conclusions of both Azadarmaki and Fathi, who emphasize the importance of political institutions as filters for ideology. Ideology does not take the form of a free movement. Westernization is indeed always a force of change, but its impact is filtered lightly or heavily by the nature of the political group holding power in the country.

The Structures of Religion

The structures of religion have taken on considerable importance in the diffusion or suppression of new ideas since the revolution. After the revolution, all accepted directions, whether liberal or conservative in the Western sense, have been considered to be Islamic. There has been little religious opposition to any legal or administrative changes coming from the top, as religious leaders have a considerable role in policymaking in postrevolutionary Iran. Mosques and Friday prayers throughout the country have become sources of propagation of the decisions made at the top on any political or social issue. Friday prayers are held in each city every week and the Imams receive a bulletin indicating important social news or any political decision made by the leader, government, or parliament that may affect people's lives and the country in general. Thus, political decisions are presented by the Imams with justifying religious arguments. This is backed by dissemination in the following days in newspapers and media broadcasts. Access to mass media in general and TV and radio in particular has increased substantially, and has become almost universal in recent years. These approaches have contributed to ideational change and convergence of behaviors and ideals after the revolution, but all were driven by political agendas.

The generally held view in the West has been that Iran is influenced by religious leaders and fundamentalists who are against development plans. However, some of the development plans in postrevolutionary Iran have surprised international observers. "Education and health for all" is an example of the programs that have brought about major social changes in recent decades. Whatever the direction, development plans have been implemented according to the Iranian-Islamic style, a style that selectively and rigidly filters Western influences. For example, Western observers have been critical of the segregation of the sexes in schools as well as the compulsory wearing of the *hejab*—considering these regulations to be against human rights. The Islamic authorities in Iran, however, argue that these regulations are based on cultural and religious sensitivities that must be observed if the goal of increased levels of education and social standing for women are to be achieved. And, indeed, the literacy rate and the level of education of women have increased substantially. Women's status has also been moved forward through the use of the nationwide health network to promulgate and provide access to family planning. On the other hand, women's employment outside the family circle has reversed its direction since the revolution.

The advancement of higher education in postrevolutionary Iran is noteworthy. All universities were closed down immediately after the revolution. The reason was to prepare textbooks and curriculums according to Islamic ideology. However, the universities were reopened after a few years and government investment in higher education was increased considerably. Although Iran was isolated from the West in the late 1980s, the government provided around 5,000 scholarships for students to complete their postgraduate studies in other countries, particularly in England, Canada, and Australia. Most of these graduates have returned and are employed in various universities in all provinces of Iran. In addition to the government universities, a private university (Free-Islamic University) has been established, has been expanded into different levels (undergraduate and postgraduates), and has branches in all provinces of Iran. Every province has at least two government universities (medical and nonmedical) as well as a Free-Islamic University. The aspiration for higher education for children has become a widespread norm among Iranian families.

FAMILY DYNAMICS AND CHANGE IN CONTEMPORARY IRAN

In this section, we describe family dynamics and change in Iran over the last two decades. Besides the Iranian decennial censuses, the surveys conducted by the authors in recent years are used to demonstrate continuity and change in the elements of family in Iran.

Nuptiality Change in Iran: 1976–1996

Marriage patterns have changed in Iran over the last two decades. The extent of change was greater during the period 1986–1996 than in the earlier decade, 1976–1986. Table 7.2 shows the female singulate mean age at marriage and the percentage never married by age for women for Iran from 1966 to 2000. As can be seen from the table, the mean age at first marriage for Iranian women increased slightly from 19.5 in 1976 to 19.7 years in 1986. This was followed by a sharp increase from 19.7 to 23.1 years from 1986 to 2000.

Interestingly, counter to this trend, the government of the Islamic Republic of Iran has consistently encouraged early marriage since 1979. Despite the campaign for early marriage, age at first marriage increased during this period. In 1966, 54% of women were never married by ages 15–19. This figure rose to 66% by 1976. Then the early marriage policies after the revolution temporarily slowed the long-term trend, and the proportion never married for ages 15–19 remained stable until 1986. However, this was followed by a sharp rise from 1986 to 1996 and again to 2000. The proportion of never-married women at ages 15–19 increased substantially to 84% by 2000. The changes in marriage patterns applied in both rural and urban areas of Iran. In rural areas, the female mean age at first marriage increased from 19.7 in 1986 to 22.1 in 1996, whereas in the urban areas the figure rose from 20.1 to 22.0.

Despite the increase in mean age at marriage, universality remains one of the major characteristics of the Iranian marriage pattern. Marriage is strongly supported by both religion and tradition in Iranian society. As a result, the majority of women get married before age 30 and the vast majority of women (99%) get married by their early 40s.

TABLE 7.2

Singulate Mean Age at Marriage (SMAM) and Percentage Never Married: Women Aged 15–19 to 35–39, 1966 to 2000, Iran

Age Group	1966	1976, SMAM 19.5	1986, SMAM 19.7	1996, SMAM 22.1	2000, SMAM 23.1
15–19	54.1	65.7	65.7	82.1	83.5
20–24	13.4	21.4	25.8	39.5	47.1
25–29	3.8	6.8	9.4	14.8	20.8
30–34	1.7	2.7	4.6	6.4	9.3
35–39		1.3	2.6	3.2	4.1

Note. Sources: Doroudi Ahi (2001) and Ministry of Health and Medical Education (2002).

Nevertheless, the percentage of women never married at ages 30–34 increased from 1.7% in 1966 to 9.3% in 2000, indicating the potential for a small movement away from universal marriage. In the contemporary marriage market, because of the huge increase in births in the early 1980s, many young women are finding it difficult to find husbands from among the smaller older cohorts of men born in the 1970s. Many women from this generation may not marry.

Fertility Decline in Iran

The first family planning program in Iran was officially implemented during the period 1966–1976. Fertility decreased from around 7.7 births per woman in 1966 (Amani, 1970) to around 6.0 in 1976, but then rose to 7.0 in 1980 soon after the revolution. Despite the postrevolutionary pronatalist ideology, the high fertility regime was short-lived, and fertility started to decline by the mid-1980s. It fell from 6.8 births per woman in 1984 to 6.3 in 1986 and further to around 5.5 in 1988. The decline was slow until the government population policy was reversed and a new family planning program was officially inaugurated in December 1989. Fertility fell sharply thereafter, to below 2.8 in 1996, more than a 50% decline in 6 years. The recent estimates show that the TFR had declined further to 2.2 in 2000. The fall in fertility has been observed in all provinces and rural and urban areas of Iran, and in recent years some provinces have experienced fertility below an average of two children per woman (Abbasi-Shavazi & McDonald, 2005, 2006).

Variations in Attitudes and Values Relating to the Family

To study the variation across Iran in attitudes and values related to the family, the authors conducted a survey in 2002 in four very diverse provinces of Iran. Results from this study are used in the remainder of the chapter.

The four provinces are (a) Sistan and Baluchistan, located in the southeastern part of Iran and sharing borders with Afghanistan and Pakistan, (b) West Azarbaijan in the northwest of the country with common borders with Iraq and Turkey, (3) Gilan, to the northwest of Tehran on the Caspian Sea, and (4) Yazd, in the central desert region of Iran. The selected provinces cover a range of ethnic and religious differences. Sistan and Baluchistan is populated mainly by Baluchi, whereas West Azarbaijan contains two large ethnic groups, Turks and Kurds. The people living in the two other provinces are mainly Persians. Furthermore, a considerable proportion of the population in both Sistan and Baluchistan and West Azarbaijan are Sunni Muslims, whereas the population in Yazd and Gilan is predominantly Shiites. Sistan and Baluchistan has the lowest level of socioeconomic development whereas Gilan and Yazd approach the highest levels of socioeconomic development in the country. It should also be noted that Gilan and Yazd, despite their relatively similar socioeconomic characteristics, have different social values and attitudes. People in Yazd are known for being religious, whereas people in Gilan are considered more liberal in terms of values and attitudes. A study of Iranian values and attitudes (Ministry of Culture and Islamic Guidance, 2002) showed that people in Yazd placed more emphasis on religion in their daily lives than did Iranians as a whole. Selection of a diverse set of provinces allows for consideration of varying institutional settings.

All provinces except Sistan and Baluchistan reported low fertility ideals, with 60–75% of women reporting two children as the ideal. In Sistan and Baluchistan, a sizeable minority, around 40%, still expressed an ideal of four or more children. At the other extreme, in Gilan, around 20% of women expressed an ideal of only one child. Furthermore, the ideal number of children across cohorts of women married from 1960 to 2000 varied little, with these women, many of whom had a large number of children, expressing low fertility ideals. Even in Sistan and Baluchistan, most women disagreed that "having many children would increase the family's income."

Mate Selection and Marriage to Relatives

Ezazi (1997, p. 102) argued that in contemporary Iran, despite the effects of urbanization and industrialization on family values, the state and society have little bearing on individual rights in relation to marriage and provide couples with little support. The family has the main influence and provides the main support. Thus, financial elements of marriage are still important in marriage ceremonies, and instead of the state, the family must support children who wish to marry. This means that families seek a high dowry for their daughters to assist the couple to establish their family after marriage. Also, this is considered as an investment in case of divorce. Ezazi (1997, p. 103) concluded that these conditions and relationships are the main obstacles to the emergence of the nuclear family in its sociological meaning because the roles and relationships between men and women are determined by the values associated with dowry.

Marriage with a relative has been one of the main characteristics of the Iranian family (Abbasi-Shavazi, McDonald, and Hasseini-Chavoshi, 2006; Abbasi-Shavazi and Torabi, 2006). The ideal choice has been marriage to first and second cousins, and it is common for newborns to be betrothed to one of their cousins. In the four provinces studied, little or no change was found across women married from 1960 to 2000 in the incidence of marriage with a cousin. Cousin marriage stands at more than 70% in Sistan and Baluchistan, at over 40% in Yazd province, at around 30% in West Azarbaijan, and around 22% in Gilan. Sistan and Baluchistan consists predominantly of Baluchi people (around 70%), who belong mainly to the Sunni Sect of Islam, among whom the practice of cousin marriage is particularly high (Table 7.3). Yazd is considered to be a conservative society where people emphasize religion and conservative aspects of family life, but the level of education and other development indicators are high as compared with other provinces in Iran. Although Yazd, known as *Darol-ebadah*, or "home of prayer," has undergone major social changes in recent years, many aspects of family life and attitudes have remained unchanged.

TABLE 7.3

Marriage with a Relative: A Comparison of Own Behavior with Current Attitude, Women Married from 1980 Onward, Four Provinces of Iran, 2002

Province	Actually Married a Relative (%)	Agree That It Is Better to Marry a Relative (%)
Gilan	22.1	9.3
West Azarbaijan	31.3	21.3
Yazd	42.2	18.2
Sistan and Baluchistan	77.1	62.7

Note. Source: Iran Fertility Transition Survey (2002).

Despite the continued high incidence of marriage with a relative, Table 7.3 shows a shift in attitude away from this practice, except in Sistan and Baluchistan. The disjunction between personal behavior and attitude toward marrying a relative is particularly strong in Yazd, suggesting that the large increases in education and economic development in that province may lead to future changes in the rate of cousin marriage.

Divorce

Divorce has been uncommon historically in Iranian society. However, there existed a unilateral right for divorce for men before the approval of the 1967 Family Protection Law. Saroukhani (1997), in his study *Divorce: A Study on the Reality and Its Causes*, analyzed the level and trend of the divorce rate in Iran by province. He showed that the divorce rate had been very low in Iran until the 1974 amendment to the Family Protection Law that gave women the right to divorce—after which it climbed to its highest rate (Saroukhani, 1997, p. 36). Nassehi-Behnam (1985, p. 560) posited that three main factors contributed to a higher rate of divorce in urban than rural areas of Iran: better employment opportunities for women, not only in conventional women's jobs such as teaching and medical assistantships but also in the industrial and service sectors; promulgation of new laws and modification of regulations to attract the female work force to the sectors of production that provide women with the opportunity to improve their social and economic status; and higher tolerance in urban society for the breaking of civil and religious contracts such as marriage. However, the rate of divorce fell again during the 1980s, as did women's market employment, and has remained low since that time.

CONCLUSION

The chapter set out to examine family dynamics and change, and the extent to which structural changes or ideas have affected family life trends in Iran. We reviewed historical and contemporary forces for change in family values and behavior, concluding that although both structural and ideational forces had been important, the major fluctuations in values and behaviors had been conditioned by the wide political swings in Iran. When politics predominate, we concluded, structure becomes ideology and ideology becomes structure. We then described family dynamics and change in recent decades with an emphasis on postrevolutionary Iran. Here we found both radical change (a remarkable fall in fertility, later marriage) and surprising continuity (marriage with a relative, low divorce rates). We found no evidence of the emergence of

Western behaviors such as cohabitation outside marriage or births before marriage. Indeed, punishments for these behaviors remain very severe. Again, for the most part, we interpret these changes in the political context of idealized family morality. As a result of the rise of mass education and the expansion of mass communication by way of access to electricity in all areas of Iran, expectations have become more uniform. This has had the effect of hastening change or solidifying conservatism, depending on the position of the ruling authorities.

We have observed a complex mosaic of individual and family change and persistence. The most important individual-level change in recent decades is the increased level of education across cohorts, stimulated by the revolution. It should be noted that schools for boys and girls were mixed during the Shah's period, and because this was regarded as un-Islamic by religious leaders, schools became segregated by gender after the revolution. However, women's education was also particularly encouraged and, as a result, has increased substantially since the revolution.

The timing of marriage has also shifted toward higher ages, particularly for girls, and fertility behavior and attitudes of women have changed considerably. Change within the family has tended to be stronger at the level of the individual couple. This includes decisions about the number of children to have and gender roles within the couple relationship. Despite these changes, some aspects of family at the societal level have remained the same. Arranged marriages and family support and control of individuals within the family have remained largely intact. However, as Nassehi-Behnam (1985, p. 561) concluded, the principal change that can be observed in this domain is the tendency for blood ties to be replaced by relationships created by marriage. The vertical authority of the patriarch over family members is being replaced by parent–children relationships in which the (adult) children have much greater independence and even some authority. The principal driving force for this change is urbanization. However, the dominance of men over women is still apparent both within the family and in the broader society. Nevertheless, new women-only social and political structures have emerged that provide women with much greater power than they have held in the past.

Under the strong political regimes that have characterized Iran for most of the last century, the long-standing idealized morality remains strong unless the political structure is tolerant of the spread of new ideas. Western ideas were tolerated under the Shah governments, but, as history shows, the ensuing change was too rapid relative to the prevailing idealized morality. The ensuing Islamic Revolution swung the political weight behind conservatism, and because the revolution change has been closely scrutinized and permitted only when it appears to provide no threat to the prevailing morality. Thus, women's education was able to flourish but not women's employment. Fertility was able to fall to very low levels but was constrained rigidly to childbearing within marriage. The promise of a more liberal approach under the Khatami government was not realized, and once again, Iran in 2005 has a very conservative government that will exercise rigid control over the forces of Westernization. The political structure operating in the shadow of an idealized morality remains the dominant paradigm of social and family change in Iran.

REFERENCES

Abbasi-Shavazi, M. J. (2002). *Recent changes and the future of fertility in Iran.* Presented to the Expert Group Meeting on Continuing Fertility Transition, Population Division of the United Nations, New York.

Abbasi-Shavazi, M. J., & McDonald, P. (2005). *National and provincial level fertility trends in Iran, 1972–2000* (No. 94). Canberra: Australian National University.

Abbasi-Shavazi, M. J., McDonald, P. and Hosseini-Chavoshi, M. 2006, Modernization and the cultural practice of consanguineous marriage: Case study in four provinces of Iran, Paper presented at the 2006 European Population Conference, 21–24 June, Liverpool.

Abbasi-Shavazi, M. J., McDonald, P., & Hosseini-Chavoshi, M. (2003). *Changes in family, fertility behaviour and attitudes in Iran* (No. 88). Canberra: Australian National University.

Abbasi-Shavazi, M. J., & Torabi, F. 2006. Levels, trends and patterns of consanguineous marriage in Iran, *Journal of the Population Association of Iran,* 1(2): 61–88.

Abdollahyan, H. (2004). The generations gap in contemporary Iran. *Journal of Wealth Trends, 44,* 78–85.

Aghahanian, A. (1997). Family and family change in Iran. In C. B. Hennon & T. H. Brubaker (Eds.), *Diversity in families: a global perspective.* New York: Wadsworth.

Amani, M. (1970). *Births and fertility in Iran.* Tehran: University of Tehran. (Persian)

Azadarmaki, T. (2001). *The idea of modernization in Iran.* Tehran: Tehran University Press. (Persian)

Bahmani, E. (2000). *Confrontation of family with modernism with emphasis on legal aspects.* Unpublished master's thesis in sociology, University of Tehran, Tehran. (Persian)

Behnam, D. (1985). The Muslim family and the modern world: Papers from an international symposium. *Current Anthropology, 26*(5), 555–556.

Doroudi Ahi, N. (2001). *Marriage and sex imbalance in ages at marriage: Marriage squeeze in Iran, 1966–1996.* Unpublished master's thesis in demography. University of Tehran, Tehran. (Persian)

Ezazi, S. (1997). *Sociology of family: With emphasize on the role, structure, and function of the family in contemporary world.* Tehran: Roshangaran and Women Studies. (Persian)

Fathi, A. (1985). Introduction. In A. Fathi (Ed.), *Women and the family in Iran* (pp. 1–10). Leiden: E. J. Brill.

Hoodfar, H. (1995). Population policy and gender equity in post-revolutionary Iran. In C. M. Obermeyer (Ed.), *Family, gender, and population in the Middle East* (pp. 105–135). Cairo: American University in Cairo.

Hoodfar, H. (1996). Bargaining with fundamentalism: Women and the politics of population control in Iran. *Reproductive Health Matters, 8,* 30–40.

Kian-Thiebaut, A. (2002). Women and the making of civil society in post-Islamist Iran. In E. Hooglund (Ed.), *Twenty years of Islamic revolution: Political and social transition in Iran since 1979* (pp. 56–73). Syracuse: Syracuse University Press.

Ladier-Fouladi, M. (2002). Iranian families between demographic change and the birth of the welfare state. *Population: English Edition, 57*(2), 361–370.

Makhlouf Obermeyer, C. (1994). Reproductive choice in Islam: Gender and state in Iran and Tunisia. *Studies in Family Planning, 25*(1), 41–51.

McDonald, P. (1994). Families in developing countries: Idealised morality and theories of family change. In L. Cho & M. Yada (Eds.), *Tradition and change in the Asian family* (pp. 19–28). Honolulu: East West Center.

Ministry of Health and Medical Education. (2002). *Iran demographic and health survey.* Tehran.

Mir-Hosseini, Z. (2002). Religious modernists and the "women question." In E. Hooglund (Ed.), *Twenty years of Islamic revolution: Political and social transition in Iran since 1979* (pp. 74–95). New York: Syracuse University Press.

Mohseni, M. (2000). *Study of knowledge, attitudes, and socio-cultural behaviours in Iran.* Tehran: Author. (Persian)

Nassehi-Behnam, V. (1985). Change and the Iranian family. *Current Anthropology, 26*(5), 557–562.

Rahman, M. (1975). Movement for the emancipation of women in Persia. *Bulletin of the Institute of Islamic Studies, 1,* 26–39.

Sansarian, E. (1985). Characteristics of women's movement in Iran. In A. Faithi (Ed.), *Women and the family in Iran* (pp. 86–106). Leiden: E. J. Brill.

Saroukhani, B. (1997). *Divorce: A study on the reality and its causes.* Tehran: Tehran University Press.

Saroukhani, B., & Navaie, J. (2002). *Family in Tehran: Identity and main characteristics.* Tehran: Author. (Persian)

Shadi-Talab, J. (2001). Iranian women: Rising expectations. *Critical Middle Eastern Studies, 14*(1), 35–56.

Touba, J. R. (1985). Effects of the Islamic revolution on women and the family in Iran. In A. Fathi (Ed.), *Women and the family in Iran* (pp. 131–147). Leiden: E. J. Brill.

Vatandoost, G. R. (1985). The status of Iranian women during the Pahlavi regime. In A. Fathi (Ed.), *Women and the family in Iran* (pp. 107–130). Leiden: E. J. Brill.

Social Change and Marriage in Vietnam: From Socialist State to Market Reform

Rukmalie Jayakody
Department of Human Development and Family Studies
Population Research Institute
Pennsylvania State University

Vu Tuan Huy
Institute of Sociology
Vietnam Academy of Social Sciences, Hanoi, Vietnam

Major social, political, and economic changes have occurred in Asia over the past few decades, and these changes are likely to substantially impact key institutions, including the family. Vietnam, in particular, has experienced profound changes during the past century, including prolonged periods of war, socialist collectivization, political reunification, a shift from a centrally planned to a market-based economy, and an extensive opening to the outside world. Additionally, major policy initiatives designed to affect basic aspects of family life, including mate selection and marriage, gender relations, and family size, have been adopted by the Vietnamese government. Although speculation on the effects of these changes is common, little systematic, empirically based research has been conducted into the nature and extent of family change and the major influences on it. A major problem has been a lack of baseline data, which has made it difficult to determine the extent to which family patterns and relations have actually changed in response to social changes, and to gauge how the combination of wartime and revolutionary experiences, socialist ideology, market reforms, and the exposure to Western ideas and media have affected Vietnamese families.

We have been able to examine some of these issues using recently available data from the Red River Delta Family Survey (RRDFS). The objective of the RRDFS was to document and explain changes in the Vietnamese family that have taken place within the context of major social changes and events occurring over the past four decades. In examining family changes, we focus on the central messages from the government about family ideals and behavior, and explore how they have been translated and transmitted to ordinary individuals. We high-light the role of socialist ideology in dictating family behavior and the dissemination of this ideology. Additionally, we examine the impact of market reforms and globalization on the government's messages and how these recent changes have impacted family attitudes and behavior. Also considered is the role of increased industrialization and urban-ization that has occurred after renovation policies were passed in the mid–late 1980s.

We begin by providing background information on Vietnam, high-lighting some of the major events of the 20th century and reviewing what is known about Vietnamese families through the period of French colonization. We use this information, gathered from historical docu-ments, anthropological accounts, and prior research, to develop a por-trait of Vietnamese families in the past. We then assess potential sources of change to these family patterns. In particular, we examine changes in government policies and family laws as explanations for some of the changes observed in our data.

VIETNAM: A BRIEF HISTORY

Vietnam is the second most populous country in Southeast Asia (behind Indonesia) and the thirteenth most populous in the world (Barbieri, Allman, San, & Thang, 1996). Its 80 million people are highly concentrated in the fertile deltas and coastal plains, particularly the Red River Delta in the North (1,180 persons/km^2) and the Mekong Delta in the South (408 persons/km^2), which together account for 57% of the population (Central Census Steering Committee, 1999). Vietnam remains primarily an agricultural society; agriculture is the largest sector in the economy, accounting for about a quarter of the gross domestic product (Central Institute for Economic Management, 1999) and employs 63% of the labor force. Reflecting this agricultural base, 73% of the population lives in rural areas, although the pace of urbanization is increasing. Per capita income is around $550 (World Bank, 2005). The majority ethnic group is the Viet Kinh, comprising 83% of the popula-tion, with the other 17% made up of 56 different ethnic minority groups, who mainly reside in mountainous areas in the north and central areas of Vietnam. The Viet Kinh are the focus of this research.

Vietnam has experienced long periods of foreign conquest, including more than 1,000 years of Chinese domination that lasted until the end of the 10th century and that had a significant impact on Vietnam's administration, educational system, literature, language, and culture (Taylor, 1983). However, the greatest influence was on the Vietnamese elite, who had the most contact with the Chinese, with far less influence among the common people (Cima, 1989).

Vietnam was further transformed in the 19th century with French colonization, and in 1878 the country was divided into three areas: Cochinchina (southern Vietnam), Annam (central Vietnam), and Tonklin (northern Vietnam). The French brought with them an introduction to Western education, and their rule also heralded the start of industrialization, urbanization, and commercial agriculture. Under the leadership of Ho Chi Minh, the Democratic Republic of Vietnam declared independence from the French in 1945, leading to 9 years of armed struggle. The Geneva Accord, signed in 1954, ended French control and called for a temporary division of the country, with the southern half ruled from Saigon by Ngo Dinh Diem's regime, with heavy U.S. support, and Ho Chi Minh's party ruling northern Vietnam from Hanoi (Duiker, 1995).

The North and South had distinctly different economic structures. The current research focuses on families in the North. Given the different economic and political situations experienced by the North and the South, we should expect families to have responded differently to many changes experienced in the 20th century. The Democratic Republic of Vietnam in the North focused on building a socialist economy whereas the South followed a modified capitalist model. The North faced substantial agricultural problems due to its lack of mechanization, and per capita rice production in the North was one of the lowest in Asia (Duiker, 1995). Ho Chi Minh's government focused on efforts to establish state ownership and to collectivize. By the 1960s, collectivization was well underway and 80% of families in lowland districts belonged to semi-socialist or fully socialist collective organizations. By 1965, 90% of the industrial and agricultural sector was under state or collective ownership (Duiker, 1995). Food production gradually grew but never reached targeted goals, and food shortages were common.

Direct U.S. aid to South Vietnam began soon after the Geneva Accord, and in January 1955 American advisors began arriving to train South Vietnamese troops. President Kennedy increased support for the Diem regime in 1961, and in response, communist-armed units in the South were unified into the People's Liberation Armed Forces (Cima, 1989). The escalation of war began in 1963, and after years of fighting, the Agreement on Ending the War and Restoring Peace was signed in Paris on January 1973.

In April 1975 the war officially ended, the last American troops left Saigon, and the country was unified under the communist government of former North Vietnam into the Socialist Republic of Vietnam. The economy faced substantial problems during this post-reunification period, including a poor infrastructure, insufficient capital, excessive bureaucratic controls, high inflation, and massive foreign debt. Reunification was followed by a decade of economic crisis. The country's economic growth rate in the latter half of the 1970s was an unimpressive 0.4%. State industrial control and land collectivization resulted in low production and the country relied heavily on aid from its socialist allies.

Responding to this economic crisis, the Sixth National Congress of the Communist Party introduced its policy of *doi moi* (renovation) in 1986. In contrast to reform systems undertaken by the former Soviet Union and Eastern European states, which centered on political reform, Asian socialist countries have concentrated on economic liberalization and growth (Norlund, Gates, & Dam, 1995). The reform process in Vietnam began after China adopted reforms in 1978. Extensive restructuring occurred in three interrelated areas: (a) transforming the administratively planned economy into a market economy; (b) establishing international economic relations, particularly with non-Soviet countries; and (c) mounting bureaucratic reforms aimed at eliminating corruption, increasing efficiency, and establishing law-based governance. Similar to efforts in China and the former Soviet Union, agricultural decollectivization and free-market reforms were the centerpiece of reform efforts. Vietnam's post-*doi moi* economic growth has been impressive: The gross domestic product began growing by nearly 9% annually; inflation fell from 400% in 1988 to 17% in 1994; the country went from being a rice importer to the second largest rice exporter (behind Thailand); poverty rates fell from 55% in 1993 to 37% in 1998[1]; and living standards markedly improved (Haughton, Haughton, & Phong, 2001; Lamb, 2002).

Although *doi moi* brought about substantial economic improvement in the lives of many Vietnamese, evidence indicates that problems also

---

[1]The poverty measure takes into account the cost of buying enough food to provide 2,100 calories/day/person, with some provision for nonfood items; the rates for 1993 and 1998 are adjusted for inflation (Haughton, Haughton, & Phong, 2001).

emerged with the economic transition. Many argue that the position of women has deteriorated, both in terms of employment and education (Asia Development Bank, 2002; Desai, 2001; Werner, 2002), and that their position in the family has declined (Long, Le Ngoc Hung, Truitt, Le Thi Phuong Mai, & Dang Nguyen Anh, 2000) as son preference has grown post *doi moi* (Belanger & Khuat Thu Hong, 2002; Goodkind, 1995). Although most Vietnamese have enjoyed improvements in living standards, increasing inequality, particularly between urban and rural areas, is also apparent. Social service provision, established and publicly provided under the centrally planned government, has declined or disappeared—a reduction that has important implications for the extent to which families have had to pick up where the state left off.

THE FAMILY IN VIETNAM

One problem with assessing family change in Vietnam is the lack of available baseline data. Social science research on families is a relatively new endeavor. Most of what we know about families prior to colonization comes from examining dynasty codes that specified inheritance rules and laws on family behavior. It is uncertain the extent to which these codes were applied to all families, or whether they were followed only by elite families. The war years, first for independence from France and then for reunification, disrupted any attempts at family research. Information on families from this period also results from examining laws, notably the Marriage and Family Law of 1959.

Post reunification, little social science research of any sort was conducted, although a few village-focused studies are available. Notable among these is the longitudinal, in-depth study of Hai Van, a commune in the Red River Delta, that examines family organization, household production, and division of labor (Houtrat & Lemercinier, 1984). However, Hai Van is unique in that it is a predominantly Catholic community in a country with less than a 6% Catholic population. It was not until the 1980s that social science research centers were established (Fahey, 1998) and research on families began.[2] To assess the extent of change, we provide a summary of what is known about Vietnamese families in the past.

Although Vietnam belongs to Southeast Asia geographically, many argue that culturally it is closer to East Asia, with its Confucian culture and a kinship system similar to China, Taiwan, and South Korea (Belanger, Oanh, Jianye, Thuy, & Thank, 2003). The resemblance of Vietnamese

---

[2]The first census for the country as a whole was conducted in 1979, although the results were never published.

kinship to China is not surprising, given the 10 centuries of Chinese domination (Krowolski, 2002). Compared to China, however, Confucianism is more varied in Vietnam, due in part to its geographic proximity to the Southeast Asian region and its late adoption of Confucianism. Although Confucianism emerged in China beginning in 770 BC, it was not adopted by the Vietnamese elite until the 10th century and even later by the larger society (Frenier & Mancini, 1996). Also, Vietnamese culture is influenced by Buddhism, Taoism, and its own indigenous cultural systems, and a notable feature is the relatively high status of women compared with China. Even during the Colonial period, French observers wrote eloquently about the strong position of Vietnamese women as opposed to Chinese women (Belanger et al., 2003; Frenier & Mancini, 1996; Insun Yu, 1994).

Despite its diversity, Vietnamese society has been dominated by Confucian ideology and the clearest principle underlying kinship is linearity. Information on precolonial Vietnamese kinship patterns comes from the Le Code, which operated during the Le Dynasty from 1428 to 1788. Examination of this code shows clear evidence of patriliny in Vietnam for over 500 years. It is unclear, however, whether this kinship system is something indigenous to Vietnam or a remnant of Chinese rule (Haines, 1984). Following patriliny, the second principle evident in this code is seniority. In terms of kinship, seniority was determined by age and sex, and documented the nature of relationships between husbands and wives and parents and children (Haines, 1984). However, compared to China, the Le Code appears to be much less male centered. For example, daughters were allowed to inherit property along with sons, and children could not claim their inheritance until their mother, not just their father, had died (Bryant, 2002).

The extent of Confucian influence is still debated, but it appears that its influence in Vietnam was less than in China (Woodside, 1971). The majority opinion is that the patriarchal family served as the basic social institution, with Confucianism framing social norms in terms of duties and obligations of family members (Belanger & Khuat Thu Hong, 1996; Jamieson, 1986; Krowolski, 2002; Liljestrom & Lai, 1991). The emphasis was on the welfare of the family group, rather than individual autonomy. Special reverence was given to the family's ancestors, and the family cult, or the cult of ancestors, held to the belief that after death the spirits of the departed continued to influence the living. If the ancestors received proper spiritual nourishment then the family would receive their ancestor's protection and good wishes. Lack of veneration for the ancestors may result in their disfavor and lack of protection. The line on ancestor worship passed through males, and a senior male was needed to oversee preparation for ancestor celebrations and worship. This resulted in a strong son preference, a preference reinforced by postmarital residence with the husband's family and inheritance standards that strongly favored sons (Jamieson, 1986). In fact, the continuity of the family line passed through the *first son*. The inequality of daughters relative to sons in this context of patriliny, ancestor worship, and family inheritance is illustrated by the adage: "Having a single son means that you have descent, while having ten daughters does not" (Mai Huy Bich, 1991).

Marriage was considered a social contract and was arranged by parents through intermediaries. Following the Le dynasty, the Gia Long dynasty code made even more explicit the role of parents in marriage. Article 49 states that marriage is legal only when it is approved by the senior male in the kinship hierarchy (Vu Manh Loi, 1991). Arranged marriage seems to have been stricter among the rich, with more freedom of mate choice among the poor (Insun Yu, 1994). Additionally, unlike in China, the young adults themselves were often consulted in making the final choice of a spouse (Belanger & Khuat Thu Hong, 1996). Fostering filial piety was of overriding importance in childrearing (Cima, 1989). The strength of patrilineage is also evident in the common practice of newly married couples residing with the groom's parents immediately after marriage.

Evidence indicates that these Vietnamese family patterns described here were maintained until the August Revolution in 1945 (Minh Huu Nguyen, 1995). Thus, we use these characterizations of Vietnamese family life as our baseline for assessing change since then. Substantial evidence suggests that this family form has changed significantly over the past six decades, particularly in the North, where traditional ideas were challenged by party doctrine, the demands of war, collectivization, population resettlement, mass mobilization of men and women for the war effort, and the increased movement of women into the labor force (in large part, to take up positions left vacant by men who joined the war effort). For instance, communists labeled as feudal the notion that the family was the primary focus of individual loyalty. The 1986 *doi moi* (renovation policies) may have led to further change through emphasis on modernization, industrialization, and urbanization, and the concomitant increasing exposure to media images and Western attitudes.

In assessing the extent of family change, we focus on three aspects of marriage: (a) spousal selection, (b) wedding customs and ceremonies, and (c) postmarital living arrangements. Given what we know about families in the past (pre-1945), arranged marriage appears to have been the norm (although sometimes with the couple's approval); the uses of horoscopes, matchmakers, bride- and groom-wealths,[3] and elaborate wedding ceremonies were common; and couples were expected to live with the husband's parents after marriage. To assess change from our baseline—the pre-socialist family traditions and practices described earlier— we use retrospective data from three marital cohorts in the Red River Delta (the fertile delta region in the north): a cohort marrying between 1963 and 1971 (just prior to and during Vietnam's war for reunification), a cohort marrying between 1977 and 1985 (representing the post-reunification period), and a cohort marrying between 1992 and 2000 (well after the passage of renovation policies in 1986).

SOURCES OF CHANGE: GOVERNMENT POLICIES

Many theories of family change have been offered, including those high-lighting changes in the modes of production, increases in education, and the effects of industrialization and urbanization (Goode, 1963; Thornton & Fricke, 1987). Indeed, Vietnam has experienced, or is experiencing, dramatic changes in all these areas. Although we do not discount the importance of these potential influences on family change, we examine here the impact of the emerging and evolving socialist state and its laws and decrees. We also look at how these changing laws and decrees have been used by the government to respond to various social changes and to influence individual families. In particular, the Marriage and Family Law, originally passed in 1959 and then reissued in 1988 and 2000, illus-trates how government policies have responded to and exerted influence on the family.

Although many political and social leaders made Vietnamese indepen-dence the primary goal following French occupation, they also sought to modernize the country. Rising to prominence in his efforts to end French rule, Ho Chi Minh founded and led the Communist Party with indepen-dence and modernization as key goals. Commonly referred to as Uncle Ho, he remains a beloved figure and is identified mainly as a nationalist, rather than as a communist, leader. His writing and studies of his work indicate he sought Marxism primarily because he viewed it as the most effective way to modernize the country (Duiker, 2001; Minh, 2001). Ho Chi Minh believed that for the country to modernize, Vietnamese families needed to abandon feudal vestiges and resist bourgeois influences. In fact, from the time of Ho Chi Minh to the present, the government has

---

[3]In Vietnam, the bride- and groom-wealths appear to be given by each family to the young couple.

continued to focus on family behavior as a crucial component of Vietnam's efforts to modernize. Through decrees, laws, and propaganda, the government's goals for family behavior have been specified. Through mass organizations and state media these state messages have been transmitted to families and individuals throughout society. Vietnam's political structure, with its effective dissemination of national policies to the local level, greatly aided in this transmission. The Communist Party, the Youth League, and particularly the Vietnam Women's Union (VWU), were very effective in broadcasting state messages.

The 1945 August Revolution began the drive for fundamental changes in family behavior deemed necessary for Vietnam's modernization. Along with calls for independence and freedom, the Constitution of the New Democratic and Republic State of 1946 also contained directives for families, with statements condemning young age at marriage and encouraging marriages based on love rather than family arrangement (Vu Manh Loi, 1991). When the communists assumed power in the South in 1975, their focus was on social development and reunification. Family changes were seen as critical to social development and the state attacked the notion of family as the primary focus of individual loyalty and the "feudal" aspects of traditional families (Bryant, 2002). Elaborate alters and ceremonies for ancestors were labeled as wasteful and superstitious (Kleinen, 1999); parental authority was challenged when some children publicly denounced parents during land reform (Hy V. Luong, 1989)[4]; and arranged marriages were attacked in state messages. In particular, the 1959 Law of Marriage and the Family contained several directives on family behavior, all focused on the family changes necessary for modernization. The following is an example.

> The socialist family is one in which the husband and wife are equal, take care and help each other to progress, and are actively involved in the construction of socialism and the defense of the country, and together raise their children as useful citizens of society. ...Individuals should strive to develop good customs and habits of our nation, wipe out backward practices and vestiges of feudal marriage and family regimes, and oppose influence of bourgeois marriage and family patterns (cited in Vu Manh Loi, 1991).

This law, passed in the North in 1959 and enacted in 1960, sharply contrasts with the Family Law passed by the Southern government in 1959, which instead sought to strengthen parental authority over children,

---

[4]These measures were not as radical as those in China, like the Cultural Revolution.

reinforce Confucian morality and ancestor worship rites, and make legal separation extremely difficult and divorce almost impossible (Zhang & Locke, 2001). After reunification in 1975, the Northern law was imposed on the entire country.

Subsequent policies, notably the 1988 and the 1996 Marriage and Family Law and the Strategy for Family until 2010, further specified family behavior needed for modernization and also illustrated how state messages have adapted to meet different modernizing needs. When examining the extent of changes in arranged marriage, wedding customs and ceremonies, and postmarital living arrangements, we rely on these state policies and the mechanisms used to transmit these policies to individuals as explanations for observed behavioral changes.

DATA

We use as our baseline the characteristics provided earlier on presocialist families—that is, family and marriage behavior from before the 1945 August Revolution—and then use data from the 2003 Red River Delta Family Survey (RRDFS) to assess the extent of change from this baseline description. The RRDFS consists of a representative sample of 1,296 currently married individuals. To measure changes over time and the influence of historical time on life course trajectories, three purposively chosen marriage cohorts were targeted for interviews, with each cohort corresponding to an important historical period in Vietnam's recent history:

1. The War Cohort—married between 1963 and 1971, the period just prior to and during Vietnam's war for reunification when the country was still divided into two governments. For the North, this period is marked by aggressive collectivization efforts and mass mobilization.
2. The Reunification Cohort—married during 1977 and 1985, the early postunification period when economic hardship and social upheaval were most severe and when a centrally planned economy was pervasive. Economic growth was stagnant during this period and food shortages were common.
3. The Renovation Cohort—married between 1992 and 2000, the years when economic reforms and the opening of Vietnam to global influences were well underway. Even though *doi moi* was passed in 1986, it was not until the early 1990s that these reform efforts were put into place and noticeable change was evident.

The survey contains extensive information about marriage and family behaviors, and includes factors that could exert influence on these behaviors over time, including place of origin and place of residence (e.g., rural vs. urban), educational background of respondents and their spouses, and the composition and size of family of origin. The sample was selected using a stratified multistage cluster sampling approach. The 1,296 respondents were equally divided between husbands and wives, rural and urban settings, and the three marriage cohorts. Based on the targeted sample size, the sample design called for drawing respondents from nine urban districts and nine rural districts. Within each district, three communes (or wards, the urban equivalent of the commune) were selected and within each commune two villages were selected. Within each village, 12 respondents were selected.

We asked individuals for information about events and experiences in the past. Age is controlled by asking people to report experiences at a similar position in the life course, in our case at the time of marriage and during the first years of childrearing. Individuals are categorized according to their marriage cohort, with the cohort serving as the historical marker. Differences in experiences or behaviors across the marriage cohorts are attributed to historical change. Although this approach can separate historical effects from age effects, we cannot distinguish historical change as being due to period effects or cohort effects. That is, when we use marriage cohort as our historical marker, each successive marriage cohort is also associated with a different period, so that period and cohort are confounded. An additional concern in analyses using cross-sectional data to examine social change is selectivity. Because our sample criteria require currently married couples, our oldest cohort is likely to be less representative of the population, as both individuals in the couple must still be alive. That is, people who married during the war cohort but subsequently died were not selected. Our sampling criteria specified only the marital cohorts for selection, and did not specify an age range for members of each cohort. Table 8.1 presents some descriptive information on our sample, including respondents' mean age and age range, as well as mean age at marriage and marital age range by sex and cohort.

FAMILY CHANGE

We begin by examining aspects of marriage for our three cohorts, beginning with the extent to which marriages were primarily arranged by parents or by the young couple themselves. The extent of arranged marriages, and whether this has changed over time, was assessed using the following

TABLE 8.1
Current Age and Marital Age of Respondents (Years)

	War		Reunification		Renovation	
	Male	Female	Male	Female	Male	Female
Current mean age	60.13	56.36	47.65	44.04	33.23	28.48
Current age range	49 to 76	49 to 66	34 to 66	36 to 55	24 to 52	19 to 48
Mean age at marriage	25.27	21.55	25.52	22.25	26.43	21.51
Marital age range	15 to 44	17 to 29	15 to 42	16 to 31	18 to 45	16 to 34

question: "How was your spouse chosen? Was the decision mainly yours, your parents, or both?" Response categories included: (a) arranged mainly by parents or family, (b) arranged by parents but with my approval, (c) I chose my spouse, but consulted my parents, and (d) I chose my spouse without influence from my parents. The first panel in Table 8.2 displays these results and indicates that marriages arranged mainly by parents or family are rare among all three cohorts. Parentally arranged marriages were more prevalent among the war cohort, with 3.5% of individuals in this marital cohort indicating that their marriage was primarily arranged by their parents or family. Marriages in which the parent or family was primarily responsible, but where the child was consulted were more common—8.1% among the war cohort, 3.5% among the reunification cohort, and 1.9% among the renovation cohort. It is this type of marriage, initiated by parents but with children's approval, that appears to most closely resemble the presocialist family pattern in Vietnam. Among all three cohorts the most common arrangement was for the marriage to be initiated by the young couple, with approval from their parents.

The low prevalence of parental marriage arrangements is not surprising given our earliest cohort, the war cohort, married after strong government messages against arranged marriage were communicated and after the passage of legislation making arranged marriages illegal. Therefore, our war cohort already represents change from the baseline, the presocialist family.

The 1946 Constitution laid the foundations for the abolition of arranged marriage, arguing that this practice hindered women's equality. Subsequent decrees further emphasized free-choice marriage. For example, Decree 97, passed in May 1950, recognized the rights of children in their own marriage decisions. Cadres from the Vietnam's Women's

TABLE 8.2

Cohort Changes in Marriage (%)

	War Cohort	Reunification Cohort	Renovation Cohort
How was your spouse chosen?			
Arranged mainly by parents or family	3.5	0.5	0.9
Arranged by parents, with R's approval	8.1	3.5	1.9
R chose spouse, with parental approval	76.8	85.5	88.2
R chose spouse, without parental influence	11.4	10.6	8.8
What was served at the wedding ceremony?			
Snacks only	42.3	21.7	3.5
Meal only	29.7	35.5	45
Both snacks and a meal	27.8	42.8	51.5
What kinds of gifts were given?			
No presents	10.7	0.5	0.2
Mostly in-kind	72.9	72.3	9.5
Mostly in cash	9.7	16.5	83.1
Equally in cash and in-kind	5.7	7.6	6.7
Advice from fortune teller/horoscope			
On spouse compatibility	4.9	8.5	22
On determining an auspicious wedding day	20.4	28.9	54.6
Receiving bride-wealths and groom-wealths			
Received neither	70.8	61.8	30.6
Received a dowry only	9.3	13.7	19.0
Received a bride-wealth only	9.5	9.3	7.6
Received both a dowry and a bride-wealth	10.4	15.3	42.8
Who did you live with right after marriage?			
With husband's family	54.1	66.3	71.8
With wife's family	7	3.9	3.0
Independently	35.2	28.2	25.0
Other	3.2	1.4	0.2

Union (VWU) and the Communist Party focused on "educating" people to the benefits of free-choice marriages during the late 1950s and throughout the 1960s. In 1959 the North passed the Law of Marriage and Family, which outlawed arranged marriages. In an often-quoted speech at a meeting on the Draft Law on Marriage and Family, Ho Chi Minh said, "to enjoy concord in matrimonial life, marriage must be based on genuine love" (Minh, 1967).

In addition to spousal choice, we also examined cross-cohort changes in other aspects of marriage, including the type of ceremony, the use of fortune tellers and horoscopes leading up to the marriage, and the provision of bride- and groom-wealths. Although the 1959 law focused on abolishing arranged marriage and polygamy, establishing gender equality, and protecting women and children (i.e., declaring freedom from abuse), it also influenced these other aspects of marriages and weddings. Traditional and elaborate wedding ceremonies and the provision of bride- and groom-wealths were also labeled wasteful and thus banned in the 1959 law. Instead, the State organized simple weddings, with the objective of undermining the family's role and eliminating social class inequalities (Belanger & Khuat Thu Hong, 1996). In addition, the customs of seeking advice from fortune tellers and horoscopes were labeled superstitious, and individuals and families were told to abandon these practices. We examine whether the law was as successful in curbing these other marital customs as it was in reducing parental arranged marriages.

An area of continuity across our three cohorts is that of the marriage ceremony itself. Regardless of cohort, almost all individuals had a formal marriage ceremony of some sort (results not shown)—only 2.3% of the war cohort, 2.5% of the reunification cohort, and 0.5% of the renovation cohort reported that they had no formal wedding ceremony. Although formal ceremonies are common among all three cohorts, the elaborateness of these ceremonies, in terms of food served and gifts given, varies substantially. Table 8.2 shows these cross-cohort variations among couples who had a formal wedding ceremony. The increasing tendency for weddings to include meals—either alone or in combination with snacks—suggests a move from more simple to more elaborate ceremonies over time. For example, serving snacks only was the most common food choice among the war cohort (42.3%), declining to 21.7% among the reunification cohort and to only 3.5% among the renovation cohort. Concomitantly, serving a meal (alone or with a snack) rose from just over half (57.5%) among the war cohort, to 78.3% among the reunification cohort, to 96.5% among the renovation cohort.

The nature of wedding gifts has also changed (see Table 8.2). Receiving no gifts at all has been the minority experience for individuals in all three cohorts, but it has become increasingly uncommon over time, with 10.7% of the war cohort receiving no gifts for their wedding, compared with only 0.5% of the reunification cohort and 0.2% of the renovation cohort. A shift in the type of gifts given is also apparent.

Receiving mostly in-kind gifts, such as a hammock, a mosquito net, or a cooking pot, was common for the war and reunification cohorts (72.9% and 72.3% respectively), but dropped to only 9.5% among the renovation cohort. Cash gifts have supplanted in-kind gifts as the norm among the most recent cohort (83.1%, compared to 9.7% for the war cohort and 16.5% for the reunification cohort, report receiving mostly cash gifts). Although cooking pots were common in the past, today's wedding guests arrive with red envelopes stuffed with crisp new bills.

Although the transition to cash gifts seems indicative of the new market economy, Vietnamese are far from abandoning presocialist wedding customs. Rather than decreasing, the use of fortune tellers and horoscope readers to consult about either the compatibility of the couple or an auspicious date for the ceremony has increased sharply over time (see Table 8.2). Regardless of cohort, the use of fortune tellers or horoscope readers (such as a local monk) is more commonly used to determine an auspicious wedding date than to consult on the appropriateness of the match. Seeking advice on the appropriateness of the match increased across the three cohorts from 4.9% to 8.5% to 22%. Seeking advice on an auspicious wedding day increased from 20.4% to 28.9% to 54.6%.

A sharp increase in the provision of bride- and groom-wealths is also evident (see Table 8.2). Couples in the war cohort appear to have heeded the government's message to avoid these payments—about 71% of couples in the war cohort received neither. Bride- and groom-wealths were not common among the reunification cohort either, where 62% received neither. In contrast, the renovation cohort appears to have readopted these customs, with only 31% of this most recent cohort received neither. Across the three cohorts, receiving only a groom-wealth increased from 9.3% to 13.7% to 19%; receiving only a bride-wealth declined slightly from 9.5% to 9.3% to 7.6%. Receiving both increased from 10.4% to 15.3% to 42.8%. Bride- and groom-wealths, banned by the 1959 Marriage and Family Law in the North as vestiges of the feudal system, seem to have been abandoned by many families during the war and reunification period only to resurge among the renovation marriage cohort, whose families may have been more willing to ignore these government directives.

Another important aspect of Vietnamese families is postmarital living arrangements. According to Vietnamese custom, co-residence of the newly married couple with the groom's parents was considered obligatory, at least until another brother marries and joins the parental household. If there are multiple sons, the eldest son is expected to stay with the parents (Pham Van Bich, 1998). We might expect change across our three cohorts on postmarital living arrangements for several reasons. First, the socialist regime emphasized children's autonomy and independence from parents, and therefore we should expect declines in co-residence after marriage. Additionally, researchers such as Goode (1963) have proposed that a variety of factors, including the spread of schooling, increased urbanization, and exposure to Western ideas and attitudes, will result in the adoption of more Western-type family practices, including more nuclearization of families and less co-residence. On the other hand, increased urbanization may result in lower housing availability and higher housing costs, resulting in increases in postmarital co-residence among our renovation cohort.

A decline in postmarital co-residence may signal a weakening in this custom, while an increase may point to greater economic need. However, if economic reasons, rather than kinship customs, are driving postmarital co-residence, then we would expect to see co-residence among both the husband's parents and wife's parents, because economic reasons would make little differentiation between the two. Our results reveal two important findings. Not only has the proportion of young couples co-residing with the husband's family increased over the three cohorts—from 54.1% to 66.3% to 71.8%—but the proportion living with the wife's parents has declined—from 7.0% to 3.9% to 3.0%. This increase in co-residence with the husband's family is not merely a function of rising housing costs associated with urbanization. The custom has not only increased in both urban and rural areas, but it has become more common in rural areas. For the renovation cohort, 62% of urban respondents and 82% of rural respondents lived with the husband's parents after marriage (results not shown).

EXPLANATIONS FOR CHANGE

Our results indicate substantial changes across the three cohorts in customs surrounding marriage. Rather than providing a consistent picture on the direction of change, our results indicate some changes away from presocialist patterns whereas other changes indicate a return and some changes back to these patterns. With respect to arranged marriage, there has been a clear decline in parents taking the lead in their children's marriage decisions. At the same time, evidence of increasing children's autonomy is lacking in that seeking parental approval of a marriage partner remains important, and in fact, appears more common for our most recent cohort. Also, the custom of living with the husband's parents after marriage appears to have been strengthened, with more young couples in the renovation cohort following this custom than those in the two earlier marriage cohorts.

In trying to understand changes observed across our three cohorts, we focus on explanations involving the changing nature of the socialist state, its goals for modernization, and the extent of its reach into individual families. Modernizing the country remains a common refrain among today's government leaders, and current propaganda and media messages emphasize the benefits of and need for modernization. Marriage and family behavior have remained central to modernization efforts.

As discussed, the 1959 Marriage and Family Law contained several directives on family behavior, including encouraging free-choice marriages, prohibiting bride- and groom-wealths and large wedding feasts, and discouraging the use of fortune tellers and horoscope readers. The law was aimed at all levels of society and was disseminated from cities to the most remote villages. As evidenced by our data, the government directives and the law seem to have been quite effective in reducing many of the targeted behaviors. The war cohort demonstrated lower levels of all marriage-related behavior examined compared to our other two marital cohorts. In part, this was achieved by the highly politicized nature of families that had evolved during this wartime period. Family behavior became very publicly visible and salient at this time of collectivization, increasing the pressure to conform to directives that emphasized the community and deemphasized the role of family. Also, family functions were increasingly adopted by collective institutions. For example, the economic functions of families were completed by cooperatives and factories, which provided its members with almost all necessities of living, including jobs, income, children's education, and housing. The collective organizational structure and wartime climate produced a highly politicized environment where behavior was monitored by neighbors and coworkers. To act or think in any way outside the prescribed manner was viewed as unpatriotic and against the war effort.

Additionally, the Vietnam Women's Union (VWU), a mass organization that was given the task of seeing that the dictates of the 1959 Marriage and Family Law were enforced, carried the statutes of this 1959 law through collectives and local administrative levels. The VWU was founded as part of the Fatherland Front in 1930 and continues to operate at the commune, district, provincial, and national levels. The VWU has responsibility for representing women and family issues,[5] and with its mass membership and local-level influence, this organization was very

---

[5]The VWU is our primary research partner in the field. Prior to data collection, for each commune, province, and district in our sampling frame, we meet with the VWU, explain our study, and sought their assistance. The groups have been invaluable in providing us with introductions to the community, providing guides and sometimes transportation to respondent houses, providing office space to serve as a central location for interview teams, and so on.

effective in communicating the objectives of the new law to all levels of society, and helping to implement and enforce it. The efforts of the VWU, combined with the environment during collectivization, led to high levels of adherence with the law. Our result showing low levels of parentally arranged marriages indicates their effectiveness.

The VWU remains an important institution today. Currently, its membership exceeds 11 million, or over 50% of all Vietnamese women age 18 and over (Asia Development Bank, 2002; Asia Development Bank, 2002; Long, Henderson, Mai, & Haub, 2000; United Nations Development Program, 1996). In 1988 the Government Decree No. 163 was passed to ensure that the VWU be consulted and involved in any discussions, plans, or policies relating to women and children at all government levels (United Nations Development Program, 1996) and under *doi moi* the VWU has become one of the nation's chief institutions sponsoring economic development and carrying forth the message of modernization to the local levels (Werner, 2002). Additionally, as a result of its large membership and long reach, foreign organizations often collaborate with VWU to push issues of gender. In particular, the Swedish International Development Agency (SIDA) is a very active partner, stressing a cross-cutting awareness of gender issues and gender equity at even the most remote local levels.

The politicized nature of daily life, the influence of collectives, and the VWU's ubiquitous impact may also explain the relatively lower prevalence of bride- and groom-wealths, elaborate wedding ceremonies, and cash gifts during the earlier (war and reunification) cohorts. Additionally, messages of children's independence and autonomy from parents likely contributed to the lower prevalence of co-residence with the husband's parents after marriage in the earlier cohorts. The nature of state support across the three cohorts is also an important explanation for changes in postmarital living arrangements.

During collectivization, the State, rather than the family, was responsible for providing employment and housing. Many young couples lived separately from parents in order to receive land and housing subsidies from cooperatives and government agencies (Hung, 2002). Under the strong socialist state, young families were able to achieve economic independence from parents and have a separate residence. Indeed, this was encouraged as a way to weaken parental control over children, seen by the state as essential for modernization. Renovation policies have resulted in reproductive and productive tasks being shifted back to the household. Additionally, economic liberalization has been accompanied by withdrawal of state support in vital areas (Tuyen, 1999). As state support has receded, young couples are increasingly turning to their families for housing assistance, and postmarital co-residence has increased. Not only are young couples looking to their parents for housing assistance, but also for child care help. The state-supported kindergartens and crèches prevalent during the war and reunification cohort disappeared after renovation. The limited availability of child care, and the exorbitant price of the services that did exist, resulted in young couples turning to their families for child care.

Renovation (*doi moi*) led to a weakening of state influence over individuals and families. Today, Vietnamese are no longer dependent on government rationing for food and housing, and as the nongovernment economic sector has grown, the proportion of government employees has declined. The decline in state services also means less reliance on government. Along with the economic changes, people are talking about a *doi moi* of attitudes, referring to increased independence from the state and more independence in thought and action (Templer, 1999). After renovation, citizens were less strict in their adherence to state dictates. Although this weakening of government control can readily be seen in our renovation cohort's marriage/wedding behaviors—increased provisions of bride- and groom-wealths, increased use of fortune tellers and horoscope readers, and increases in large wedding celebrations—some signs of weakening were evident in the reunification cohort as well.

As state control over individuals' lives declined across cohorts, families increasingly and openly went back to customs practiced for centuries in presocialist Vietnam, a tendency best illustrated in the resurgence of lavish wedding ceremonies and feasts. The state continues to issue decrees against this and media messages continue to discourage it. For example, the government recently issued a directive that government employees are not allowed to organize fancy wedding feasts and ceremonies for themselves or their children. Despite continuity and even new emphasis in directives on this issue, few people appear to be listening. Hanoi and Ho Chi Minh City (formerly Saigon) are filled with wedding shops where brides can rent fancy white, Western-style wedding dresses for their wedding receptions. Photographers and videographers have enjoyed a booming business as demand for professional pictures and videos of marriage and engagement ceremonies has grown. Wedding banquets, previously organized at home, have become common in hotels and restaurants.

Our explanations for the changes observed across the three marriage cohorts center on changing policies and shifting government interest in enforcing those policies. Some changes, such as wedding elaborateness (serving meals rather than only snacks), the receipt of cash gifts, and the provision of bride-wealths and groom-wealths, may reflect economic changes rather than policy changes. That is, Vietnam has enjoyed improvements in the standard of living since economic renovation policies were passed and many Vietnamese have more disposable income. We do not discount the importance of economic improvements, but view economic explanations alone as insufficient for understanding the differences across cohorts. Although improving economics are likely to play a role, changes in policy are also important for understanding changes in mating and marriage.

THE FAMILY, MODERNIZATION, AND VIETNAM TODAY

Government messages about family behavior have changed with the transition to the market economy and the decline in social provision. Modernization remains an important goal, and family change continues to be seen as essential for modernization. However, the specific messages about modernization are changing. Modernization is defined primarily in economic terms and is viewed as good and desirable. When asked, "Do you think that modernization would be good for Vietnam?" 65% responded that it would be "very good"; 32% said "somewhat good"; and only 1% said "not good at all." A random subsample of respondents was also asked open-ended questions about what modernization meant. Overwhelmingly, the responses defined modernization in economic terms.

Vietnam's current government messages on modernization are intertwined with ideas on economic development. Just as the original socialist state during the 1950s saw a clear role for families in modernizing efforts, today's socialist state also emphasizes the importance of family behavior. However, today's messages on modernization make a clear distinction between economic modernization, which is desired and good, and the Westernization of the family, which is viewed with caution. The state conveys that although Vietnamese should strive for modernization economically, but they should retain their traditional family base. This message can be seen in the 2000 Marriage and Family Law, which added an article encouraging all family generations to help care for one another and in fact established the duty of individuals to provide care for family members. Rather than intergenerational independence, as earlier government edicts had directed, the 2000 law focused on the significance of extended families and mutual obligation among family members (Vu Manh Loi, 2000). This law seems to recognize that in today's Vietnam, which largely lacks government support for elder care or child care, it is important to the social and economic fabric that family members can rely on and will provide support to one another.

In addition, perhaps in reaction to a series of newspaper articles claiming that Vietnam's university students and other young adults had begun cohabiting at high rates as they do in Western Europe and the United States, the 2000 Marriage and Family Law[6] added a stipulation against cohabitation: "To protect marriage and family system, males and females who live together without marriage are not recognized by law."

Concern over perceptions of dramatic increases in cohabitation went even further with the establishment of the mobile licensing program. In this program, state representatives in mobile units (vans) go door to door in urban areas, looking for couples who are not legally married. When these couples are found they are educated on the benefits of legal marriage and are encouraged to register their marriage. The mobile vans carry all the necessary documents for registration.

This concern over rampant cohabitation has not been supported by evidence, however. In fact, in a series of interviews we conducted in local communes and wards, we found low levels of cohabitation. Also, the small percentage of cohabiting couples does not, as the government fears, represent individuals who are testing or trying out marriage. Although these couples have not legally registered their marriages, they are considered married in the eyes of the couple, their family, and the community. In most instances, these couples had engagement and wedding ceremonies attended by family and community members, but had not officially registered their marriage. In the past there were strong incentives to register. For example, after registering, the collective commune, or ward would often provide a couple with some gifts, such as a hammock or mosquito net. Additionally, marriage registration was needed to obtain housing, jobs, food rations, and other goods and services. These advantages to registering no longer exist.

CONCLUSION

Vietnam continues to experience dramatic changes. Although Vietnam's economic growth slowed as a result of the Asian economic crisis in the latter 1990s, the recovery appears well underway. The average gross national product (GNP) growth rate was 7% between 2000 and 2002, with higher growth expected in the next few years (Li, 1996).

---

[6]Cohabitation was first mentioned in the 1986 Marriage and Family Law, but the 2000 law was more explicit.

However, problems associated with economic growth are also evident. For example, unemployment in rural areas grew to 30% in 1999
(compared to 7.4% in urban areas). In a recent survey conducted by a
mass organization for Vietnamese peasantry, 75% of young peasants
chose leaving the countryside as their main aspiration in life (Khuat
Thu Hong, 2003). In the midst of these shifts, the government continues to emphasize its modernization messages. The potential for these
changing opportunities and challenges to impact Vietnamese families
is substantial, particularly given the country's age structure: 53% of
the population is under the age of 25 and 30% are under the age of 15.
This group of 40 million young people is facing increasingly uncertain
times with changing educational structures and opportunities, a
faster pace of urbanization, new economic structures, and growing
exposure to global influences, in particular to Western messages and
media. How they and their families will adapt to these changes, and
how the government will respond, are yet to be seen.

REFERENCES

Asia Development Bank. (2002). *Women in Vietnam*. Manila: Regional and
   Sustainable Development Department and Mekong Department, Asian
   Development Bank.
Barbieri, M., Allman, J., San, P. B., & Thang, N. M. (1996). Demographic trends in
   Vietnam. *Population: An English Selection, 8*, 209–234.
Belanger, D., & Khuat Thu Hong. (1996). Marriage and the family in urban North
   Vietnam, 1965–1993. *Journal of Population, 2*(1), 83–111.
Belanger, D., & Khuat Thu Hong. (2002). Too late to marry: Failure, fate, or for-
   tune? Female singlehood in rural north Vietnam. In J. Werner & D. Belanger
   (Eds.), *Gender, household and state: Doi Moi in Vietnam* (pp. 89–110). Ithaca,
   NY: Cornell Southeast Asia Program.
Belanger, D., Oanh, K. T. H., Jianye, L., Thuy, L. T., & Thank, P. V. (2003). Are sex
   ratios at birth increasing in Vietnam? *Population, 58*(2), 231–250.
Bryant, J. (2002). Patrilines, patrilocality and fertility decline in Viet Nam. *Asia-
   Pacific Population Journal, 17*(2), 111–128.
Central Census Steering Committee. (1999). *The 1999 census of Vietnam at a
   glance*. Hanoi: Gioi Publishers.
Central Institute for Economic Management. (1999). *Vietnam's economy in
   1998*. Hanoi: Education Publishing House.
Cima, R. J. (Ed.). (1989). *Vietnam: A country study*. Washington, DC: Federal
   Reserve Division, Library of Congress.
Desai, J. (2001). *Vietnam though the lens of gender: Five years later. Results
   from the second Vietnam Living Standards Survey*. Food and Agriculture
   Organization of the United Nations, Regional Office for Asia and the Pacific.

Duiker, W. J. (1995). *Vietnam: Revolution in transition*. Boulder, CO: Westview Press.

Duiker, W. J. (2001). *Hi Chi Minh: A life*. Hyperion.

Fahey, S. (1998). Vietnam's women in the renovation era. In K. S. M. Stivens (Ed.), *Gender and power in affluent Asia* (pp. 222–249). New York: Routledge.

Frenier, M. D., & Mancini, K. (1996). Vietnamese women in a Confucian setting: The causes of the initial decline in the status of East Asian women. In K. Barry (Ed.), *Vietnam's women in transition* (pp. 21–37). New York: Macmillan.

Goode, W. J. (1963). *World revolution and family patterns*. New York: Free Press.

Goodkind, D. M. (1995). Vietnam's one-or-two-child policy in action. *Population and Development Review, 21*(1), 85–111.

Haines, D. W. (1984). Reflections of kinship and society under Vietnam's Le dynasty. *Journal of Southeast Asian Studies, 15*(2), 307–314.

Haughton, D., Haughton, J., & Phong, N. (Eds.). (2001). *Living standards during an economic boom: Vietnam 1993–1998*. Hanoi: Statistical Publishing House.

Houtrat, F., & Lemercinier, G. (1984). *Hai Van: Life in a Vietnamese commune*. Zed Books.

Hung, L. N. (2002, June). *The patterns of fertility decline and family changes in Vietnam's emerging market economy: Factors and policy implications*. Paper presented at the Internation Union for the Scientific Study of Population, Bangkok, Thailand.

Hy V. Luong. (1989). Vietnamese kinship: Structural principles and socialist transformation in northern Vietnam. *Journal of Asian Studies, 48*, 741–756.

Insun Yu. (1994). *Law and Vietnam society in the 17th and 18th century*.

Jamieson, N. (1986). The traditional family in Vietnam. *Vietnam Forum, 8*(Summer–Fall), 91–150.

Khuat Thu Hong. (2003). *Adolescent and youth reproductive health in Vietnam: Status, issues, policies and programs*. Policy Report. Hanoi: Center for Social and Economic Development.

Kleinen, J. (1999). *Facing the future, reviving the past: A study of social change in a Northern Vietnamese village*. Singapore: Institute for Southeast Asian Studies.

Krowolski, N. (2002). Village household in the Red River Delta: The case of Ta Thanh Oai, on the outskirts of the capital city, Hanoi. In J. Werner & D. Belanger (Eds.), *Gender, household and state: Doi moi in Vietnam* (pp. 73–88). Ithaca, NY: Cornell Southeast Asia Program.

Lamb, D. (2002). *Vietnam, now*. New York: Public Affairs.

Li, T. (1996). *Peasants on the move: Rural–urban migration in the Hanoi region*. Occasional Paper No. 91. Institute for Southeast Asian Studies.

Liljestrom, R., & Lai, T. (Eds.). (1991). *Sociological studies on the Vietnamese family*. Hanoi: Social Science Publishing House.

Long, L. D., Henderson, L. N., Mai, L. T. P., & Haub, C. (2000). *The doi moi generation: Coming of age in Vietnam today*. Hanoi: Population Council.

Long, L. D., Le Ngoc Hung, Truitt, A., Le Thi Phuong Mai, & Dang Nguyen Anh. (2000). *Changing gender relations in Vietnam's post doi moi era*. Paper presented at the Policy Research Report on Gender and Development, Working Paper Series No. 14.

Mai Huy Bich. (1991). A distinctive feature of the meaning of reproduction in Confucian family tradition in the Red River Delta. In R. Liljestrom & T. Lai (Eds.), *Sociological studies on Vietnamese families* (pp. 49–56). Hanoi: Social Science Publishing House.

Minh, H. C. (1967). *On revolution: Selected writings, 1920–1966.* New York: Praeger.

Minh, H. C. (2001). *Selected writings, 1920–1969.* University Press of the Pacific.

Minh Huu Nguyen. (1995). *Age at first marriage in Vietnam: Patterns and determinants.* Unpublished working paper, University of Washington, Seattle.

Norlund, I., Gates, C., & Dam, V. C. (Eds.). (1995). *Vietnam in a changing world:* Nordic Institute of Asian Studies.

Pham Van Bich. (1998). *The Vietnamese family in change: The case of the Red River Delta.* Surrey, England: Curzon Press.

Taylor, K. (1983). *The birth of Vietnam.* Berkeley: University of California Press.

Templer, R. (1999). *Shadows and wind: A view of modern Vietnam,* New York: Penguin.

Thornton, A., & Fricke, T. E. (1987). Social change and the family: Comparative perspectives from the West, China, and South Asia. *Sociological Forum, 2*(4), 746–778.

Tuyen, N. N. (1999). Transitional economy, technological change and women's employment: The case of Vietnam. *Gender, Technology and Development, 3*(1), 43–64.

United Nations Development Program. (1996). *Gender and development briefing kit.* Hanoi: Author.

Vu Manh Loi. (1991). The gender division of labor in rural families in the Red River Delta. In R. Liljestrom & T. Lai (Eds.), *Sociological studies on the Vietnamese family* (pp. 149–164). Hanoi: Social Science Publishing House.

Vu Manh Loi. (2000). Marriage, family, and women. In T. D. Luan (Ed.), *Social development in Vietnam: A sociological overview in 2000* (pp. 23–32). Hanoi: Social Sciences Publishing.

Werner, J. (2002). Gender, household, and the state: Renovation (doi moi) as social process in Vietnam. In J. Werner & D. Belanger (Eds.), *Gender, household and state: Doi moi in Vietnam* (pp. 29–47). Ithaca, NY: Cornell Southeast Asia Program.

Woodside, A. (1971). Ideology and integration in post-colonial Vietnamese nationalism. *Pacific Affairs, 44*(4), 487–510.

World Bank. (2005). *World Bank development indicators.* Washington, DC: World Bank.

Zhang, H. X. & Locke, C. (2001). *Rights, social policy, and reproductive well-being: The Vietnam situation.* Research paper, School of Developmental Studies, University of East Anglia, Norwich, England.

9

The Relevance of Ideational Changes to Family Transformation in Postwar Japan

Makoto Atoh
Waseda University

This chapter examines how an ideational approach is useful for explaining changes in demographic aspects of families in Japan after World War II. It focuses on two aspects of postwar Japanese families: structural aspects of families, such as family size and composition, and demographic events, such as marriage, fertility, and divorce. The changes in family structure in postwar Japan can be summarized by shrinkage (smaller family sizes) and simplification. As discussed later, these changes occurred in the context of postwar revisions to the Civil Code that changed the legal norms of families.

As for changes in the dynamic or vital events of families in the postwar years, only limited discussion is possible on the role played by ideational factors before the mid-1970s because of the scarcity of nationally representative survey data on family values and norms in this period. After the mid-1970s, a relatively numerous series of nationally representative surveys containing similar questions permit a better examination of the relevance of ideational factors for family changes in Japan.

POSTWAR CHANGES IN DEMOGRAPHIC ASPECTS OF JAPANESE FAMILIES

Families are defined here as social systems constructed by relatively small number of kin members having conjugal and parent–child relationships with the purpose of raising group well-being (Morioka et al., 1987).

Two demographic aspects of families are of interest here: demographic structure and dynamic events. Family structure is defined by both family size (number of members) and family composition (attributes of members, especially their kin relations). Dynamic events are occurrences that transform family structure, such as marriage (or partner-making), births, deaths, divorces and separations, the home leaving of children, and the joining and leaving of other members. Families in Japan have changed dramatically since the end of World War II in their demographic aspects as well as in their other social and economic aspects, but in this paper we will focus on the former.

Changes in Family Structure

In postwar Japan, family structure changed in terms of the shrinkage of household size and the simplification of kin relationships of household members. First, according to population censuses, which have been undertaken every 5 years since 1920, except 1945, the average household size was stable at about 5 persons between 1920 and 1955, after which it began a steady decrease, reaching 2.7 in 2000 (NIPSSR, 2005). As shown in Table 9.1, the percentage of households of more than 5 persons decreased from 55% to 12% between 1955 and 2000. Today, the average household size in Japan is 2.7 persons, quite similar to that of most Western societies.

Second, reduced family size was caused by the simplification of kin relationships of household members, together with fertility decline. In prewar Japan, household kin relationships were often rather complex because a married son (particularly the eldest son) generally lived in his parents' home even after his marriage. But between 1955 and 2000, the percentage of complex households (comprising kin members other than nuclear family members) decreased from 37% to 14% (Table 9.1), primarily because more married sons (or daughters) tended to leave their parents' home in adulthood to establish their own households. Although the proportion of nuclear family-type households has remained around 60% to 65% between 1955 and 2000, the percentage of single households has increased dramatically from about 4% to 26% in this period. This family structural change in the postwar Japan—often called the "nucleation" of the family—considerably simplified household kin relationships (Atoh, 1993).

Changes in Dynamic Events of Families

From the viewpoint of changes in dynamic events of families, the postwar years may be divided into three periods that correspond to changes in

TABLE 9.1

Average Household Size and Percentage Distribution of Households by Household Size, Proportion of Complex Households, and the Proportion of Elderly People Living Together with Their Children: Japan

Year	Average Household Size (Persons)	Percent Distribution Households by Size			Percent of Complex Households	Percent Elderly (65 or More) Living with Children
		1	2–4	5 or more		
1920	4.89	5.8	43.0	51.3	38.2	—
1925	4.87	—	—	—	—	—
1930	4.98	5.5	41.7	52.9	—	—
1935	5.02	—	—	—	—	—
1940	4.99	—	—	—	—	—
1950	4.97	5.4	40.9	53.7	—	—
1955	4.97	3.5	41.9	54.6	36.5	—
1960	4.54	5.3	47.2	47.5	34.7	86.8
1965	4.05	8.1	54.7	37.2	29.2	—
1970	3.70	10.8	60.6	28.6	25.4	78.7
1975	3.45	13.5	63.3	23.2	22.3	—
1980	3.33	15.8	63.2	21.0	20.7	69.8
1985	3.23	17.5	62.4	20.1	19.8	65.5
1990	3.06	20.2	62.6	17.2	17.8	60.5
1995	2.88	23.1	62.4	14.5	15.9	55.9
2000	2.71	25.6	62.6	11.8	13.9	50.5
2005						

Source: Bureau of Statistics, Population Census.

the total fertility rate. These are: (a) 1947 to the late 1950s, when a short-term baby boom was followed by a precipitous fertility decline; (b) the end of the 1950s to the mid-1970s, when fertility remained almost constant at around replacement level; and (c) the mid-1970s to the present, when fertility continuously declined to below-replacement levels (see Figure 9.1).

During the initial postwar fertility transition, the total fertility rate declined from more than 4.0 to around 2.0, brought about mainly by family limitation among married couples and partly by the rise in marriage age (Otani, 1993). Between 1950 and 1960, marital fertility rates declined by 44% (NIPSSR, 2005). Completed family size also decreased

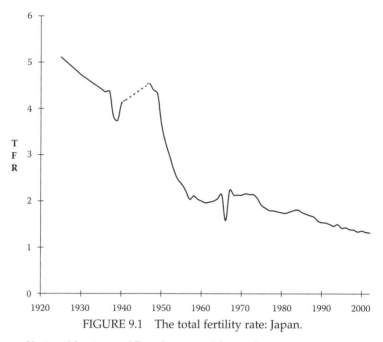

FIGURE 9.1   The total fertility rate: Japan.

Source: National Institute of Population and Social Security Research (2005).

dramatically, from 5.0 children ever born for the 1901-1905 birth cohort of married women, to 4.1 children for the 1911-05 birth cohort of married women, to 2.3 children for the 1928-32 birth cohort of married women (NIPSSR, 2005). Also, the average age at first marriage rose by 1.4 years for men and 1.3 years for women between 1950 and 1960. After temporarily increasing just after World War II, the divorce rate returned to its prewar declining trend.

During the second postwar fertility phase, the total fertility rate remained between 2.0 and 2.1 (Figure 9.1) and all the dynamic events, such as marriage, divorce, and childbearing, were relatively stable. Between 1960 and 1975, the average age at first marriage remained around 24.5 years old for women and around 27.0 for men; the never-married proportions for both men and women in their early 30s remained low at about 11–14% and 8–9%, respectively, and nearly universal marriage prevailed. The general marital fertility rate declined only moderately, from 109% (per thousand) to 93%, during this period. Although the divorce rate started its long-term increasing trend, the crude divorce rate was merely 1.1% even in 1975, one of the lowest among the developed countries (Council of Europe, 2005).

In the period of below-replacement fertility, the total fertility rate first sank below replacement level in 1974 and continued to decline subsequently, reaching 1.3 in 2003 (Figure 9.1). The direct cause of such fertility decline was the postponement of childbearing, which was largely attributable to the postponement of marriage (Atoh, 1992; Kaneko, 2005; Otani, 1993). Between 1975 and 2000, the age-specific fertility rate declined from 107% to 40% for women 20 to 24 years old and from 190% to 100% for women 25 to 29 years old. Thus the contribution of these age groups to all births also declined in this period, from 25% of all births in 1975 to 14% in 2000 for women aged 20–24, and from 53% to 40% for women aged 25–29 (NIPSSR, 2005). During the same period, the mean age at first birth for women rose from 25.8 to 28.0 years. Similar fertility declines due to the postponement of childbearing, as observed in Japan during this period, were also observed in Western societies in the 1970s (Council of Europe, 2005).

Changes in marriage age and proportions marrying were the main causes for the postponement of childbearing. Between 1975 and 2000, the mean age at first marriage increased from 24.7 to 27.0 years for women and from 27.0 to 28.8 years for men, whereas the proportion of never married rose dramatically from 21% to 54% for women in their late 20s and from 8% to 27% for women in their early 30s. In addition, the rise in the divorce rate accelerated. The crude divorce rate doubled from 1.1% to 2.1% between 1975 and 2000 (Figure 9.2), reaching the average level of developed countries (Council of Europe, 2005). The rapid rise in the divorce rate in this period is probably related somewhat to declining fertility through its effect on the proportion of currently married women.

Another reproductive behavior that changed dramatically in this period is sexual behavior among unmarried young people, although its effect on fertility is unclear. Sexual activity among unmarried young people, particularly among girls, was rare until the middle of the 1970s, but has increased gradually since then. According to surveys undertaken by the Japan Association of Sex Education (JASE) between 1974 and 1999, the proportion of students who had ever had sexual intercourse rose from 10% to 27% for males and from 6% to 24% for females in high school, and from 23% to 63% for males and from 11% to 51% for females in college (JASE, 2000). But the current levels of sexual activity among young people in Japan are much lower than those in the Western societies where cohabitation is prevalent.

Although marriage, childbearing, and sexual activity among unmarried youth have changed dramatically during this period, other dynamic family events have remained relatively consistent. For example, completed fertility for married women decreased only from 2.3 to 2.2

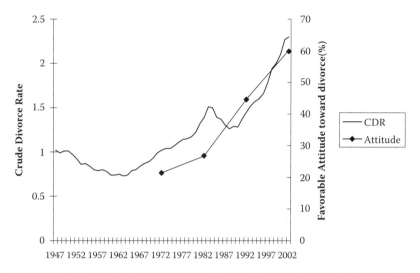

FIGURE 9.2   The crude divorce rate and favorable attitude toward divorce (%).
Source: NIPSSR (2004) and BGE (2003).

births per woman between those of the 1928–1932 birth cohort and those
of the 1953–1957 birth cohort. However, in more recent cohorts of married women aged 30–34, the mean number of children ever born declined
more substantially: from the 2.0 for 1953–1957 birth cohort to 1.5 births
for the 1968–1972 birth cohort (NIPSSR, 2003a). Another area of relative
consistency is in cohabitation and extra-marital fertility. According to a
series of the National Fertility Surveys undertaken by the NIPSSR for
never-married respondents aged 18 to 34 (called NIPSSR's S-survey hereafter), the proportion of those who were currently cohabiting increased
only modestly from 0.9% to 2.3% for males and from 0.7% to 2.4% for
females between 1987 and 2002 (NIPSSR, 2003b). The proportion of extramarital births, although it has increased gradually since the mid-1970s,
was still rare in 2002, at only 1.9% (NIPSSR, 2005). This is conspicuously
lower than levels found in Western societies, where the proportion of
extramarital births was between 10% (Austria) and 64% (Iceland) in 2003
(Council of Europe, 2005).

FAMILY AND ECONOMIC CHANGES IN POSTWAR JAPAN

Family changes in the postwar Japan, at least such demographic
aspects of family changes as described earlier, are, of course, very much
related to dramatic social and economic changes in postwar Japan.

Three social and economic factors are particularly important for both the shrinkage of family size/simplification of household composition and fertility transition/fertility decline below replacement level: (a) economic development, industrialization, and the development of an employee-centered society, (b) heightened regional migration and urbanization, and (c) the rise in college enrollment rates and accompanying gender revolution.

Economic Development, Industrialization, and the Coming of an Employee-Centered Society

Japan's labor force, by industry, has changed dramatically in postwar Japan. The proportion of workers in the primary industry, which was 49% in 1950, has continuously decreased, reaching 14% in 1975 and only 5% in 2000. Although the proportion of workers in the secondary industry showed a moderate increase from 22% in 1950 to around 30–34% thereafter, the proportion in the tertiary industry increased from 30% in 1950, to 52% in 1975, to 64% in 2000 (NIPSSR, 2005). Such industrialization and the development of the service economy were accompanied by the decreasing proportion of self-employed and family workers and the increasing proportion of employees. The proportion of employees increased from 34% in 1950, to 69% in 1975, to 83% in 2000 (NIPSSR, 2005). Industrialization and the coming of an employee-centered society supposedly weakened the value of children as family labor force (Leibenstein, 1957), which lowered the necessity of having large families or two-generation households and, in turn, possibly contributed to the prevalence of small families and the simplification of household composition.

Continuous economic growth caused by industrialization, especially rapid economic growth in the 1960s, gave rise to an affluent society in Japan: Per capita income increased 4.2 times between 1955 and 1975 (Hashimoto, 2000). The ability to accumulate individual assets and rely on more benevolent social security benefits, especially for medical care and old-age pension, weakened the dependency of the elderly on their families, which may have been conducive to smaller and simplified families.

Regional Migration and Urbanization

Industrialization promotes regional migration. Particularly in the period of rapid economic growth between the mid-1950s and early 1970s, young people seeking jobs migrated from rural areas to urban areas or toward the three largest metropolitan areas, Tokyo, Nagoya, and Osaka.

After this rapid economic growth period, such migration flow continued, although at a weaker pace (NIPSSR, 2005). In addition, because
population age structure in urban areas and the three largest metropolitan areas became comparatively younger than that in rural areas or
nonmetropolitan areas, the natural increase (births minus deaths) of
the former became larger (Atoh, 2000). Thanks to positive social
increase as well as larger natural increase, the proportion living in
urban areas or in the three largest metropolitan areas steadily
increased. Between 1950 and 2000, the proportion of the total population living in these areas increased from 37% to 79% and from 37% to
51%, respectively (NIPSSR, 2005). Rural to urban migration of young
people and their inclination to live in single households and, when married, to form nuclear-family households in urban areas contributed to
the increase in the proportion of smaller and simpler households. On
the other hand, households in rural areas where only parents and
grandparents remained were nucleated after losing grandparents, and
subsequently became single households after one parent was lost,
which also contributed to the shrinkage and simplification of the average households. In addition, because marriage in large metropolitan
areas consistently occurred at later ages than in other areas (NIPSSR,
2005), growing urbanization and the concentration of population in the
three largest metropolitan areas contributed to the rise in the proportion single households, the postponement of marriage and childbearing, and the decline in fertility.

Rise in Educational Levels and Gender Revolution

Greater affluence led to higher levels of educational attainment in the
postwar Japan. The high school enrollment rate increased dramatically
in the 1950s and 1960s and reached about 90% for both sexes by 1975.
The college enrollment rates, including two-year colleges mainly for
female students, also began increasing in the 1960s, reaching about 50%
for both sexes by 2004 (NIPSSR, 2005). In addition, the number of high
school graduates who study at two-year specialized training schools
has recently increased (MEST, 2003). These increases in educational
attainment, particularly since the 1960s, led to lower fertility through
their effect on the marriage market.
    Since the late 1970s, the high school enrollment rate for women has
surpassed that of men, and women's college enrollment rates have surpassed men's since the late 1980s. Analyses of population census data
show that higher levels of education for women are associated with
larger proportions who never marry (but the reverse is true for men)

(Bureau of Statistics, 2002a). It is certain that women's greater access to secondary and higher education led to their postponement of marriage and childbearing. Women also gained power in the economic sphere, with labor force participation rates increasing for women who were in their late 20s and 30s during this period, and wage differentials by gender shrinking since the mid-1970s (MHLW, *Basic Statistical Survey on Wage Structure*, each year). This gender revolution, or sex role revolution (Davis, 1990), may have contributed to the postponement of marriage and childbearing through increases in the opportunity cost of child care (Ogawa & Mason, 1986) and increasing divorce rates in this period.

IDEATIONAL AND FAMILY CHANGES 1: FAMILY NUCLEATION

Revision of the Civil Code

Japan enacted the modern Civil Code in 1898 and revised it dramatically in 1947 just after World War II. The transition from the old Civil Code to the new Civil Code meant a radical change in the basic family (type) model as a legal norm. The central family type in Japan during the old Civil Code was the stem family system, and the "Samurai" family model, the most rigid type of stem family system, was codified. It was characterized by the following four points:

1. The household head, usually a grandfather or a father, had legal power to decide the registered family membership of each family member.
2. Any marriage required the consent of the household head.
3. The eldest son (the heir) had the right of complete inheritance.
4. The heir had the obligation to support the parents (ACFH, 1996).

Under this family model, the eldest son was expected to get married and live in his parents' household, be subject to their demands, support them economically after their retirement, and take care of them when they needed long-term care.

The new constitution, which was based on the principle of individual dignity and gender equality, was enacted under strong influence from the General Headquarters (GHQ) of the American Occupation Forces. The new Civil Code enacted "the egalitarian nuclear family model" (Todd, 1999), which (a) abolished legal power of household heads over family members, (b) left marriage decisions to those who were marrying, and (c) gave wives the right to partially inherit their husband's property and gave sons and daughters equal rights to inherit from their parents

(ACFH, 1996). However, this new code retained a provision that obligated sons and daughters to support their parents, if needed.

One phenomenal impact of this drastic revision of the Civil Code was the change from arranged to romantic-love marriage, as shown in retrospective data on marriage type from a series of National Fertility Surveys undertaken by the National Institute of Population and Social Security Research (NIPSSR). These surveys (called NIPSSR's M-surveys hereafter)—which focused on currently married women aged 18 to 49—found that although at least 70% of marriages held before World War II were reportedly arranged marriages, this proportion fell to less than 7% by 2000 (NIPSSR, 2003a). Another major change was that women's status grew within the family as a result of their acquisition of legal rights of inheritance.

Next, we examine the effects of these changes in the family model in the Civil Code on the structure and functions of families.

Normative and Behavioral Change in the Generational Relationship

In the typical nuclear family model, children are expected to leave their parents' home after they graduate from school and/or take their first job, and to form a separate household when they get married. Old parents are expected to live on their own income (e.g., pension benefits), to live as independently as possible, and to move to an assisted-living institution if their independent lives are difficult to sustain.

Living Arrangements. According to Japan's population censuses, the proportion of elderly aged 65 or over living with their children has declined by about 1% per year, from 87% to 51%, between 1960 and 2000 (Table 9.1). However, the results of the Mainichi Newspaper's nationally representative surveys (called Mainichi surveys hereafter), conducted almost biennially between 1950 and 2000, found stability in some living arrangement behavior. These surveys showed that the proportion of ever-married women aged under 50 who lived with their parents (mostly their parents-in-law) after they married remained around 35% between 1963 and 2000, except in the 1970s when it dropped to around 25% (PPRC, 2000). The main reason for the stability of co-residence rates for newlyweds in the 1980s and 1990s seems to be that the proportion of never-married people increased disproportionately among residents of large metropolitan regions, where co-residence inclination was relatively weak.

TABLE 9.2

"What Do You Think about the Way of Having Contact with Children and Grandchildren in Old Age?"

Country	Year	1. Live Together	2. Meet Sometimes to Enjoy Dinner and Chatting	3. Meet Occasionally to Enjoy Chatting	4. No Contact	5. DK/NA
			Way of Having Contact			
Japan						
	1981	59.4	30.1	7.1	1.1	2.3
	1986	58.0	33.7	5.8	1.5	1.0
	1990	53.6	37.8	6.0	0.9	1.7
	1995	54.2	38.0	5.6	0.8	1.4
	2000	43.5	41.8	6.6	0.9	7.2
Korea		38.4	46.2	10.4	1.0	4.0
Germany		14.9	60.5	14.1	0.7	9.8
Sweden		5.0	64.6	24.7	0.1	5.6
U.S.		8.7	66.2	20.8	0.5	3.9

Source: Cabinet's Office (2001).

A series of international comparative surveys on the elderly (called ICE surveys hereafter), undertaken every 5 years between 1980 and 2000 by the Cabinet's office (renamed from the Prime Minister's Office after January 2001), showed that the proportion of respondents aged 60 or over who thought it preferable to live with their children and grandchildren had decreased from 59% in 1981 to 44% in 2000. However, as Table 9.2 shows, this is still much higher than comparable proportions in Western countries such as Germany, Sweden, and the United States, where the proportions of elderly wanting to co-reside with their children/grandchildren ranged from 9% to 15% in 2000 (Cabinet's Office, 2001).

Another series of surveys, undertaken by the Section for the Elderly People, Prime Minister's Office, in 1981, 1987, and 1992 (called SEP surveys hereafter), showed a similar declining trend in co-residence preference among two groups of respondents—the elderly aged 60 and over and married people aged 30 to 49. However, preference for co-residential living was consistently about 10% higher for the elderly respondents on the assumption that they were feeble or their spouse died (SEP, 1993). Additionally, the majority of elderly that preferred co-residence (80–85%) desired to live with their sons' families (usually the eldest son's family), suggesting the robustness of the patrilinear stem family norm.

Living Expenses at Old Age. According to Mainichi surveys, the proportion of ever-married women under 50 who said that they would depend on their children for their living expenses in old age decreased continuously between 1950 and 2000, from about 60% to 10% (PPRC, 2000). The proportion of the elderly respondents aged 60 or more expressing the same view in ICE surveys decreased from 19% to 8% between 1981 and 2000 (Cabinet's Office, 2001). This decline in the normative expectation to depend on children's economic support in old age may be explained, at least in part, by Japan's rapid economic growth in this period, which has enabled most elderly people to live on their own assets and public pension benefits.

Long-Term Care. Norms on long-term care for disabled parents have experienced only modest changes. In an SEP survey in 1974, a group of respondents aged 30 to 49 and a group aged 60 to 74 were asked: "Who will take care of the daily life of bedridden elderly parents?" Results indicate that 86% of the younger group and 88% of the older group selected "children" or "mainly children" and the rest selected "children and society," "mainly society," or "society" (SEP, 1975). Similarly, in SEP surveys in 1981, 1987, and 1992, the two respondent groups were asked: "Who should take care of bedridden elderly parents?" As shown in Table 9.3, about 95% of the group aged 30–49 years and about 90% of the group aged 60-plus years chose "mainly families" or "families are central, but they should be supported by welfare measures" in all three survey years (SEP, 1993), with the proportion selecting the latter increasing gradually among both groups. In the same three surveys—in answer to the question of "Whom do you ask for long-term care if you got bedridden?"—the clear preference for the elderly male respondents was "their marital partner," whereas the elderly female respondents chose "daughters-in-law" first, followed by "marital partners" and "daughters." Between 1981 and 1992, however, the proportion of elderly women choosing "daughters-in-law" decreased and the proportion choosing "marital partners" increased (SEP, 1993).

In each Mainichi survey from 1960 to 2000, the same question was asked of ever-married women: "What do you think about the fact that children take care of their elderly parents?" Although the proportion of those who chose "It is a good custom" decreased steadily from 35% to 15% over the entire period, the proportion of those who chose "It is

TABLE 9.3
"Who Should Take Care of Bedridden Elderly Parents?": Japan

Year	Type of Respondent	1. Mainly Such Family Members as Spouse and Children	2. Families Are Central, but Complemented by Welfare Measures	3. Mainly Welfare Measures Such as Home Helper	4. Elderly Home	5. DK
1981	E	79.7	13.1	1.9	2.0	3.4
	Y	72.6	24.1	0.9	1.0	1.4
1987	E	73.3	17.1	1.7	4.9	2.9
	Y	62.6	32.2	1.7	2.0	1.9
1992	E	67.2	22.2	2.8	4.4	3.4
	Y	55.7	37.5	2.3	2.8	1.7

Note. The question was asked to two groups of respondents: those ages 60 and over (E), and those ages 30–49 (Y). Source: SEP (1993).

children's natural obligation" increased between 1960 and 1985 but then suddenly decreased during the late 1980s, during which time the proportion who chose "It is unavoidable because of insufficient welfare facilities and systems" and "I don't think it is a good custom" increased (PPRC, 2000). It is ambiguous whether such a phrase as "take care of elderly parents" used in the Mainichi surveys means physical care and/or financial support. Abrupt changes in the response trend to this question in the late 1980s, however, may have been affected by the emerging social and political importance of long-term care in Japan during this period.

The Legal Ideal and Japanese Families

How did the postwar change in Japan's family model as explicated in the Civil Code, from the stem family model to the nuclear family model, affect norms and behavior related to the structure and functions of Japanese families? As for marriage, romantic-love marriage became prevalent, although parents' consent to partner choice is still tacitly regarded as important. In terms of gender shifts, the wife's inheritance rights and females' equal inheritance rights among siblings were legally as well as substantively established. Thus, as far as marriage and inheritance are concerned, we could say that the legal ideal of the nuclear family became substantiated into Japanese families.

On the other hand, although norms and behavior related to living arrangements changed gradually and steadily, co-residence rates and norms remain much stronger in Japan than in the Western societies where the nuclear family system has been the social norm for centuries (Hajnal, 1982; Todd, 1999). In addition, although postwar norms and behavior related to economic support for elderly parents weakened very dramatically, probably due to the improved individual assets and public pension benefits available to the elderly, norms and behavior related to elderly parents' dependence on family members for long-term care when needed weakened only modestly and remain very strong. Thus, in terms of living arrangements as well as long-term care, the norms of the stem family system persist, or the "emotional nucleation" of the family has only partially occurred.

In Japan, the public long-term care insurance system was introduced in 2000, by which the elderly have access to various low-cost long-term care services in the form of either home care or institutional care (MHLW, 2000). It remains to be seen whether such newly introduced public insurance systems will lessen the degree of elderly dependence on family care, resulting in less co-residence and greater "emotional nucleation of families" (Caldwell, 1982).

IDEATIONAL AND FAMILY CHANGES 2: BELOW-REPLACEMENT FERTILITY

Changing Norms on Dynamic Demographic Events

Little data on how norms changed with dynamic family events are available for the period of fertility transition during the 1950s and the subsequent period of replacement-fertility up to the early 1970s. Therefore, it is difficult to trace how these norms have changed with the inception of two-child families within the context of late and nearly universal marriage and low divorce rates. For the period of below-replacement fertility since the mid-1970s, however, there are relatively abundant data from series of nationally representative surveys undertaken by several organizations.

Sexual Behavior among Single Youth. Between 1974 and 1999 the rate of college students having experienced sexual intercourse increased from 23% to 63% for males and from 11% to 51% for females. However, even in 1977, 68% of the 18- to 24-year old respondents in a survey taken by the Section for the Youth, Cabinet's Office (ICY Surveys, hereafter), agreed that "It does not matter whether young people have sex with a lover before marriage"—a proportion that remained stable thereafter (SY, 1999). These data suggest that the change (increase) in young people's tolerance for premarital sex well preceded the change in actual sexual behavior

Marriage Institution. Despite a continuous rise in the proportion of single youth and the delay in marriage, there were still very few who thought lightly of marriage or rejected marriage institution itself. But tolerance to celibacy expanded slightly in this period.

Although the proportion of single respondents aged 18 to 34 in NIPSSR's S-survey who said "I do not intend to get married in my life" remained about 5% between 1982 and 2002, the proportion who agreed that "It is OK for me to remain single until I can meet an ideal partner" increased from about 40% to about 50% between 1987 and 2002 (NIPSSR, 2003b).

In two opinion surveys on women's life undertaken by the Prime Minister's Office in 1972 and 1987, respondents aged 20 or over were asked how women felt about marriage versus singlehood. The proportion favoring the opinion that "Women would rather get married" decreased from 84% to 79% for male respondents and from 80% to 70% for females in this period (PRS, 1973, 1987). According to similar surveys conducted by the Cabinet's Office, the proportion agreeing that "It does not matter whether one gets married or not, because it should be freely chosen" increased from 66% to 84% for males and from 58% to 79% for females between 1992 and 2002 (BGE, 2003; PRS, 1993). Furthermore, in ICY surveys, although very few young people have agreed that "One would rather not get married," the proportion holding the opinion that "One should get married" or "One would rather get married" decreased from 77% to 69%. Additionally, those agreeing that "It is OK even if one does not get married" increased from 13% to 26% between 1982 and 1997 (SY, 1999).

Cohabitation. According to ICY's survey, less than half of respondents in the United States, Germany, France, the United Kingdom, and Sweden agreed with the opinion that "One would rather get married" in 1998 (SY, 1999)—an attitude clearly related to the increase in cohabitation and extramarital births since the 1970s in the Western societies.

However, in Japan, NIPSSR's 2002 S-survey showed that only about 2% of single respondents aged 18 to 34 were currently cohabiting (NIPSSR, 2003b). In addition, the proportion of extramarital births in Japan was less than 2% in 2002, although it has been very gradually increasing since the middle of the 1970s (NIPSSR, 2005). In spite of such low prevalence rates of cohabitation and extramarital births, the norm on cohabitation seems to be changing steadily. According to Mainichi surveys, the proportion of women aged 20 to 49 who felt that cohabitation was acceptable increased from 40% to 49% between 1994 and 2004 (Atoh, 2005; PPRC, 2000). It is not yet certain whether such attitudinal change will lead to behavioral change.

Divorce. The strong negative attitude toward divorce prevailed until the beginning of the 1980s, but tolerance for divorce has increased since then. According to a series of opinion surveys for respondents aged 20 to 59 undertaken by Cabinet's Office, the proportion of women who agreed that divorce should be an option for those dissatisfied with their spouses remained around 20% to 30% between 1972 and 1982, but rose to 45% in 1992 and 60% in 2002 (Figure 9.2). Although women of all ages have become more tolerant toward divorce since the beginning of the 1980s, younger women have more permissive attitudes than older women. Male respondents, who have also grown more tolerant in their attitudes toward divorce over this period, nevertheless have been consistently less accepting than women. As shown in Figure 9.2, this normative change on divorce occurred in parallel with a dramatic rise in the divorce rate. Compared with such countries as Sweden, Germany, and the United Kingdom, however, Japanese people are much less accepting of divorce (BGE, 2003; PRS, 1973).

Preferences for the Number of Children. Among cohorts of currently married women who have completed their childbearing since the 1970s, little change has occurred in the number of children ever born. However, since the early 1990s, the average number of children born to women currently married less than 10 years has declined (NIPSSR, 2003a). Preference for number of children has changed in a way that is similar to fertility behavior. According to NIPSSR's M-survey for married women aged 18 to 49, between 1977 and 1997 the average ideal number of children remained at about 2.6 children (after having declined from 2.8 children in 1972), and the average intended number of children decreased only modestly, from 2.2 to 2.1 (after having remained stable at this level since 1972) (NIPSSR, 2003a). NIPSSR's S-survey showed, however, that the average desired number of children decreased gradually from 2.3 to 2.1 for single men and from 2.3 to 2.0 for single women between 1982 and 2002 (NIPSSR, 2003b).

IDEATIONAL CHANGE IN NONFAMILIAL ASPECTS

Drawing on a series of opinion surveys continuously undertaken since either the 1950s or 1970s, we now examine postwar ideational changes in terms of (a) values and goals for personal life, (b) religious views, (c) views on the nature and materialism, and (d) gender role attitudes. In examining such ideational changes, the two postwar periods, that is, that of fertility transition and replacement fertility and that of below-replacement fertility, are focused on.

Values and Goals for Personal Life

In a series of quinquennial surveys undertaken by the Institute of Statistical Mathematics between 1953 and 1998 (called ISM surveys hereafter), respondents aged 20 or over were asked: "What is the most important thing for you?" (ISM, 1999). As shown in Figure 9.3, the lowest ranked choices over the entire period of 1953 to 1998 were "traditional family system, ancestors" and "nation, society." For the period between 1953 and 1973, "life, health, self" and "love, soul" increased, and "children" and "money, property" decreased. For the period between 1973 and 1998, "families" increased considerably, surpassing all other categories, which showed declining trends.

   Several questions in the ISM surveys compared individual happiness with the status of Japan. Between 1953 and 1968 the proportion who agreed that "It is only when Japan improves that individuals become happy" decreased and the proportion who agreed that "Japan becomes better only when individuals become happy" increased somewhat, although no clear trend has emerged since 1973 (ISM, 1999).

   A question in the ISM surveys asked respondents to choose two important values from among "filial piety, payment of a favor, respect of individual rights, and respect of freedom." From 1963 to 1998 the proportions choosing "filial piety" have been always the largest and have increased, ranging between 60% and 70%, and the proportions choosing any of the other three values have remained at about 40% to 50% in every survey (ISM, 1999).

   Judging from the response pattern to the three questions in the ISM surveys, between the 1950s and the middle of the 1970s, allegiance to or identification with a society or a nation weakened, with a concomitant increase in the importance attached to personal life. It seems,

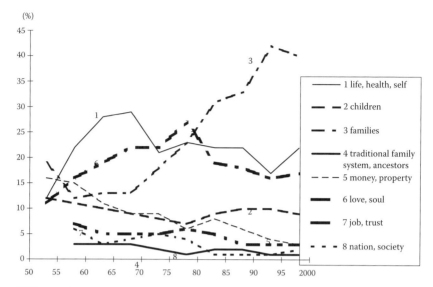

FIGURE 9.3   "What is the most important thing for you?" Source: ISM (1991).

however, that this change does not mean an increase in the kind of strong individualism characterizing Western cultures—in which rights and freedom of individuals are regarded as the highest value—but rather an increase in respect for personal life connected with family life.

This shift away from valuing the society/nation in lieu of valuing elements of personal life during the period leading up to the mid-1970s may have been largely a reflection of larger changes in postwar Japan. Just after World War II, under the strong influence of the American occupational forces, the valuation of both the imperial Japan and the legalized traditional family system of the prewar years was negated and the new legal system, based on the principle of respect for individual rights, was introduced.

The ideational shifts that followed these institutional changes, demonstrated by responses in the ISM surveys, may have influenced the trend toward two-child families via the rapid growth of family planning during this period—characterized mainly by induced abortion (legal or illegal) in the 1950s and by contraception in the 1960s (Atoh, 2000). In the prewar years people were encouraged to have large families for the glory of their nation and the continuation of their traditional family system, but in the postwar years people felt free to decide their family size according to their own economic conditions and personal preferences, and availed themselves of the means to control their procreation.

After the middle of the 1970s, however, ISM surveys did not show any clear trend in views on the valuation of individuals versus society, except stronger respect for family life. Other series of opinion surveys revealed two different trends on this question. On one hand, a series of public opinion surveys on Japanese society undertaken annually by the Cabinet's Office (POSJS surveys) showed no clear trend between 1977 and 2002 in the response pattern for respondents aged 20 and over to the question "To what extent do you like your country?" (PRS, 2003). Similarly, ICY surveys of young respondents showed little significant change in response pattern to the question "Are you proud of your own country?" On the other hand, the same ICY survey showed a significant increase in affirmative responses to the question "Do you want to contribute to your own country?" beginning around 1990 (SY, 1999). Also the POSJS surveys showed an increase around 1990 in the proportion of respondents (in a forced-choice question) selecting "People should pay more attention to their nation or their society" over "People should put more emphasis on the achievement of fruitful personal life" and a concomitant increase in the proportion indicating they "want to contribute to their society" (PRS, 2003).

Therefore, it is not clear how public opinion may have changed in terms of the relative importance placed on individualism versus social responsiveness since the middle of the 1970s. Even if the desire to contribute to a society or a nation was actually strengthened during the 1990s, it is not clear how this may have related to changes in dynamic family events such as rising proportions of single young people, an increasing tendency to postpone marriage and childbearing, and rising divorce rates. The trend toward the valuation of a society or a nation seems to be not harmonious with the idea of the second demographic transition theory that individuation, implying weakened interests in a nation, is connected with radical family change (Lesthaeghe et al., 1988).

Views on Religion

To a lesser extent than other postwar changes in values, the importance of religion in daily life has gradually weakened in Japan over the past five decades. The proportion of ISM survey respondents who said they held religious belief or faith fell from 35% in 1958 to 29% in 1998. Also, those who gave an affirmative answer to the question "Do you venerate your ancestors?" gradually decreased from 77% in 1953 to 60% in 1998 (ISM, 1999). In the ICY survey, those who replied "It is (very or

242 ATOH

fairly) important" to the question "How important is a religion to your life?" dropped from 41% in 1977 to 30% in 1997 (SY, 1999). The value placed on religion has gradually weakened in postwar Japan, but the changes were not necessarily distinguished in the period of fertility transition or below-replacement fertility. In this regard, the assertion that secularization is related to the second demographic transition (Lesthaeghe et al., 1988; Van de Kaa, 1987) is applicable to Japan only to a limited extent, if at all.

Views on Environment and Postmaterialism

ISM survey respondents were asked which opinion they agreed with on the relationship between man and nature: "Man should obey nature in order to get happiness"; "Man should use nature in order to get happiness"; or "Man should conquer nature in order to get happiness" (see Figure 9.4). Although between 1953 and 1968 those who chose "conquer nature" increased from 23% to 30%—making this choice second to "use nature" (40% in 1968)—between 1968 and 1998 "conquer nature" decreased to 6% and "obey nature" increased from 19% to 49%, becoming the first choice (Figure 9.4) (ISM, 1999). Also, in a series of public opinion surveys on daily living undertaken annually by the Public Relations Section of the Cabinet's Office between 1972 and 2003, respondents were asked: "Which do you think is more important, emotional or spiritual affluence or material affluence?" In the early 1970s, responses were balanced at about 40% each, but since then the proportion choosing "emotional affluence" has increased to about 60% today (PRS, 2004).

The outcome of these two series of surveys reveals that although people had a strong belief in technological progress (shown by stronger preference for "conquer nature") and strong aspirations for economic development (shown by stronger preference for "material affuluence") in the period of rapid economic growth (1950s through the mid-1970s), they came to think of nature or the natural environment as important and to seek emotional fulfillment after Japan became an economically affluent society (Sakamoto, 2000). In this regard, the view in the second demographic transition theory that postmaterialism is related to radical changes of family formation could be applicable to the period of below-replacement fertility in Japan (Inglehart, 1977; Van de Kaa, 1987).

Views on Gender Roles

It is very difficult to identify when views on gender role division began to take root in Japan. This may have originated in premodern Japan, but

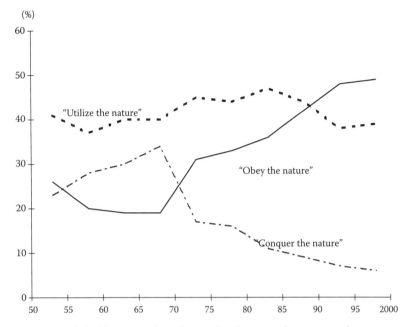

FIGURE 9.4   Views on the relationship between humans and nature.
Source: ISM (1999).

it was clearly consolidated during the period of rapid economic growth when the portion of employed workers increased and, as a result, the separation between workplaces and homes began to take place for a large number of people. According to a series of surveys on women and gender equality undertaken by the Cabinet's Office (ICW surveys), more than 80% of both male and female respondents aged 20 to 59 gave an affirmative reply in 1972 to the statement, "Men work outside, women keep the home." By 2002, however, that figure had fallen to 47% among men and 37% among women (BGE, 2003; PRS, 1973). When comparing women's responses by age group, older respondents in all survey years consistently show greater support for the gender role division, with all age groups declining to a similar extent over the entire period (see Figure 9.5). The same trend is also apparent in the results of ICY surveys, in which those in favor of the gender role division decreased from 50% in 1977 to 18% in 1997 (SY, 1999). Comparing such results for Japan with surveys of Western societies, Japan was far behind the Western societies in terms of an egalitarian view on gender roles in the 1970s, but is now fairly comparable (BGE, 2003; SY, 1999).

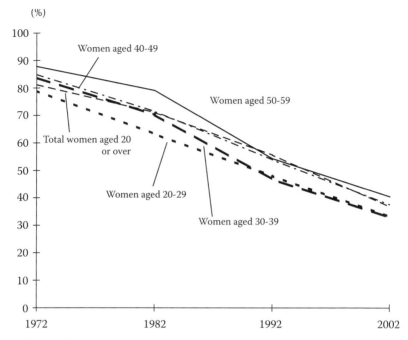

FIGURE 9.5   The proportion of women, by age, agreeing with "Men work outside, women keep the home." Source: BGE (2003).

In ICW surveys and other similar national surveys, respondents were asked their opinions on women's occupational work. As shown in Figure 9.6, in 1972, 39% of surveyed women thought that women would rather not be engaged in occupations at all, or if they were, would rather quit after marriage or after the birth of their first child; 40% thought that women would rather quit an occupation while raising children, but resume it after the children were grown; and only 12% thought that women would rather continue to work through marriage and childrearing (PRS, 1993). In subsequent ICW surveys, "quit and resume" responses remained at about the same levels but "continue" responses increased, reaching 41% of all female respondents in 2002. Thus, about 80% of all female respondents came to believe that women would rather have an ongoing occupation, with time out when raising their children (Figure 9.6). No clear response patterns have emerged by age group, and "continue" responses have increased similarly for all the

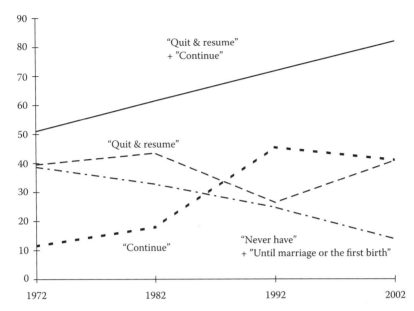

FIGURE 9.6   "What do you think about women's occupational work?"
Source: PRS (1993) and BGE (2003).

age groups. Also, male respondents were consistently less likely than females (by about 10%) to choose either the "continue" or "quit and resume" responses. The proportion of female respondents that currently favors continual occupational work for women in Japan (41%) is lower than corresponding proportions in such developed countries as Sweden, the United States, Germany, and the United Kingdom, which all stood at more than 50% in 2002 (BGE, 2003).

As was shown earlier, the change in views on gender roles has been very rapid and dramatic since the 1970s. This is in sharp contrast with the very slow change in observed gender role behavior. According to a series of time-use surveys undertaken by the Bureau of Statistics, the proportion of all activity time men spent on child care and household chores increased only modestly, from 6% to 9%, between 1991 and 2001 (Bureau of Statistics, 2002b), and represents a considerably smaller effort in this area than has been found in Western societies, where these proportions are consistently more than 20% (UNDP, 1995). Wives, even if they are employed, do most of the household chores and child care in Japan today. Furthermore, NIPSSR's M-survey revealed that among currently married women who were born in the 1960s, the proportions having full-time work and no work were about 70% and 1%, respectively, before their marriage, about 40% and 30% just after marriage, and about 16% and 70% just after having their first child—a pattern very similar to the one found among counterparts born in the 1950s (NIPSSR, 2003a). This implies that, at most, only one out of four women continue their full-time job after their marriage and first birth, today.

The ISM's surveys have asked the question, "If you were to be born again, which sex would you prefer to be, male or female?" Men have shown little change in their response: About 90% have consistently responded that they wished to be reborn male. Among women, about 64% wished to be reborn male in 1958, but this proportion decreased steadily, dropping to 42% in 1973 and to 28% in 1998 (ISM, 1999). Also, the NIPSSR's M-survey has asked about preferred gender composition for children. From 1982 to 2002, the results revealed a clear transition from favoring boys to favoring girls. Among married women who considered three children as ideal, for example, 62% favored "two boys and one girl" and 36% favored "one boy and two girls" in 1982. However, the pattern reversed in 2002 to 42% and 55%, respectively (NIPSSR, 2003a).

The change in rebirth gender preference among female respondents probably reflects the strengthening of women's social and economic position and the weakening of the social regulation of women's behavior, in both public and private spheres. The change in gender composition preferences for children among married women probably reflects the changing social trends described earlier; the changes in female inheritance rights, along with the weakening of the norm of the patrilinear stem family system; and women's increasing desire to have girls as chatting partners as well as future caregivers.

In sum, the change in views on gender roles since the middle of the 1970s, that is, the negation of the fixed gender role division, and women's stronger aspiration for career work and increased girl preference, are very rapid and dramatic. Indeed, such change in views on gender roles went along with the rise in women's educational levels and the increase in women's gainful employment, but the ideational change is faster than the behavioral change, particularly if looking at the change in men's role in family matters. The larger the gap between women's expectation for more balanced gender roles and the reality of much less balanced ones, the more discouraged and hesitant are women to get married. Hence this situation seems to be strongly connected with a very drastic change in dynamic events of families in the period of below-replacement fertility.

CONCLUSION

This chapter has examined how ideational factors are related to family changes in the postwar Japan, that is, the shrinkage of the family size and simplification of the family structure that had continued consistently following postwar years and changes in dynamic or vital events of families, especially fertility decline to below-replacement level and its relevant changes since the middle of the 1970s up to now.

First, the shrinkage and simplification of families were caused not only by fertility decline but also by "family nucleation" in postwar Japan, as measured by the decrease in the proportion of complex households and in the proportion of the elderly people living together with their children. It is certain that such family nucleation was related to the rise in employed workers due to industrialization, with large-scale migration of young people from rural to urban areas and/or toward the three largest metropolitan areas and urbanization. But, in addition, the revision of the legal family model in the Civil Code from the stem family type to the nuclear family type after World War II possibly played the role of promoting, behaviorally and normatively, family nucleation. According to a series of numerous surveys, norms on economic support for old parents have dramatically weakened and norms on co-residence of old parents with their children have moderately but steadily weakened in postwar years.

Will such behavioral and normative changes lead Japanese families to "the emotional nucleation of families" (Caldwell, 1982) prevalent in the Western societies? In contrast with economic support and living arrangement, norms on long-term care of old parents by their children have weakened only modestly in postwar years, and filial piety is regarded as more important than the respect of individual rights even today. This suggests that the stem family norm, although weakened partially, will continue to affect family behavior of Japanese people in the future. This might be the other aspect of the significance of the ideational factor for family change.

Second, changes in dynamic events of families in Japan, particularly in the period of below-replacement fertility, are similar to those in the Western societies since the 1960s, which are sometimes called "the second demographic transition." They may be, of course, related to social and economic changes, such as the advent of an affluent society, the rise in educational levels, and the rise in women's labor force participation. But ideational factors may have played the role also for this phenomenon. It was found that although normative changes occurred in tandem with behavioral changes with regard to such dynamic events as marriage, family size, and divorce, normative change preceded by far the behavioral one with regard to premarital sex and cohabitation.

Ideational changes on nonfamilial aspects of a society were examined, which were asserted by the proponents of the second demographic transition theory to be relevant to the changes in dynamic events in the Western societies since the 1960s (Lesthaeghe et al., 1988; Van de Kaa, 1987). Although changes toward individuation have not explicitly occurred and those toward secularization have not been conspicuous since the mid-1970s, the values included in postmaterialism, such as those stressing the importance of environment and emotional affluence, have been elevated since the mid-1970s in Japan, as was asserted by the second demographic transition theory.

The ideational factor regarding gender roles was also examined. Since the mid-1970s, people, particularly women, have become more likely to negate traditional gender role division and to be supportive of women's occupational roles even after childbirth. Also, at least among women, girl preference surpassed boy preference and the positive evaluation of the female sex was strengthened. All these ideational changes regarding gender roles occurred in parallel with some parts of behavioral changes, such as absolute and relative rise in women's educational levels and the increase in their gainful employment, having resulted in changes in dynamic events of families.

Will ideational changes regarding gender roles lead furthermore to marriage and birth dearth and keep the lowest low fertility in Japan? The recent comparative analyses of developed countries show that the more gender-equal, behaviorally and normatively, the higher is fertility, and that Japan is one of the countries that are less gender-equal, as well as having lower fertility (Brewster et al., 2000; Chesnais, 1996). The behavioral change regarding gender roles is considerably more gradual than their ideational change, as is shown typically in the scarcity of men's involvement in family matters, especially child care (Atoh, 2000). Such a large gap between women's expectation and the reality regarding gender roles may have been conducive to lowest low fertility. This may suggest that if behavioral changes on gender roles catch up with ideational changes on them, the latter will not necessarily bring down fertility further in Japan.

REFERENCES

Association of Comparative Family History. (Ed.). (1996). *Encyclopedia of families.* Tokyo: Kobundo.

Atoh, M. (1992). The recent fertility decline in Japan: Changes in women's role and status and their policy implication. In Population Problems Research

Council, the Mainichi Newspapers (PPRC) (Ed.), *The population and society in postwar Japan* (pp. 51–72). Tokyo: The Mainichi Newspapers.
Atoh, M. (1993). Demographic studies of families. In K. Morioka et al. (Eds.), *Development of family sociology* (pp. 32–36). Tokyo: Baifukan.
Atoh, M. (2000). *Contemporary demography.* Tokyo: Nihon-hyoronsha.
Atoh, M. (2005). Changing family norms and lowest-low fertility. In The Population Problems Research Council, the Mainichi Newspapers (Ed.), *Family norms in the age of lowest-low fertility* (pp. 11–42). Tokyo: Mainichi Newspapers.
Brewster, K. L., et al. (2000). Fertility and women's employment in industrialized countries. *Annual Review of Sociology, 26,* 271–296.
Bureau of Gender Equality (BGE), Cabinet's Office. (2003). *International comparative survey on gender equality.* Author.
Bureau of Statistics, Ministry of General Affairs. (2002a). *Report on population census, 2000.* Author.
Bureau of Statistics, Ministry of General Affairs. (2002b). *Report on the basic survey of social life: Time use data. Author.*
Cabinet's Office (2001). *Summary of the international comparative survey on the daily living and views of the elderly people.* Author.
Caldwell, J. C. (1982). *Theory of fertility decline.* New York: Academic Press.
Chesnais, J. C. (1996). Fertility, family, and social policy in contemporary Western Europe. *Population and Development Review, 22*(4), 729–739.
Council of Europe. (2005). *Recent demographic developments in Europe, 2004.* Strasbourg: Author.
Davis, K. (1990). Wives and work: The sex role revolution and its consequences. *Population and Development Review, 10*(3), 397–417.
Hajnal, J. (1982). Two kinds of pre-industrial household formation system. *Population and Development Review, 8*(3), 449–494.
Hashimoto, J. (2000). *The economic history of the contemporary Japan.* Tokyo: Iwanamisyoten.
Inglehart, R. (1977). *The silent revolution: Changing values and political styles among Western politics.* Princeton, NJ: Princeton University Press.
Institute of Statistical Mathematics. (1999). *Studies on Japanese nationality, 10th national survey 1998.* Institute of Mathematical Statistics Report, No.75.
Japanese Association of Sex Education (2000). Report on the 5th National Survey on Sexual Behavior of the youth. Tokyo: Shogakukan.
Kaneko, R. (2004). Demographic mechanism of declining fertility below replacement level. In H. Ohbuchi et al., (Eds.), *Demography of below-replacement fertility* (pp. 15–36). Tokyo: Harashobou.
Leibenstein, H. (1957). *Economic backwardness and economic growth: Studies in the theory of economic development.* New York: John Wiley & Sons.
Lesthaeghe, R. J., et al. (1988). Cultural dynamics and economic theories of fertility change. *Population and Development Review, 14*(1), 1–46.
Ministry of Education, Science and Technology. (2003). *A summary of statistics on education.*

Ministry of Health, Labor and Welfare (MHLW). (2000). *The white paper on health, labor and welfare 2000.*

Morioka, K., et al. (1987). *New family sociology* (rev. ed.). Tokyo: Baifukan.

National Institute of Population and Social Security Research. (2003a). *Report on the 12th Japanese national fertility survey 2002: Marriage process and fertility of Japanese married couples.* Author.

National Institute of Population and Social Security Research. (2003b). *Summary of the national fertility survey for single youth, 2002.* Author.

National Institute of Population and Social Security Research. (2005). *Demographic Statistics, 2005.* Author.

Ogawa, N., & Mason, A. (1986). An economic analysis of recent fertility in Japan: An application of the Butz–Ward model. *Jinkogaku-Kenkyu, 9,* 5–15.

Otani, K. (1993). *The analysis of fertility in the contemporary Japan.* Kyoto: Kansai University Press.

Population Problems Research Council, the Mainichi Newspapers. (2000). *The population of Japan: Its trajectory of the postwar 50 years (Survey results from the 1st to the 25th Mainichi Newspapers' national opinion surveys on family planning).* Tokyo: JOICFP.

Public Relations Section, Prime Minister's Office. (1972). *The public opinion survey on women.* Author.

Public Relations Section, Prime Minister's Office. (1973). *The public opinion survey on women.* Author.

Public Relations Section, Prime Minister's Office. (1987). *The public opinion survey on women.* Author.

Public Relations Section, Prime Minister's Office. (1993). *The public opinion survey on gender equality.* Author.

Public Relations Section, Cabinet's Office. (2003). *Public opinion survey on Japanese society.* Author.

Public Relations Section, Cabinet's Office. (2004). *Public opinion survey on daily living.* Author.

Sakamoto, Y. (2000). How has the Japanese way of thinking changed? A half century of the statistical survey of the Japanese national character. *Proceedings of the Institute of Statistical Mathematics, 48*(1), 3–33.

Section for the Elderly People, Prime Minister's Office. (1975). *Summary of the survey on the support for the elderly parents.* Author.

Section for the Elderly People, Prime Minister's Office. (1993). *Report on the survey on daily living and long-term care of the elderly people.* Author.

Section for the Youth, Prime Minister's Office. (1999). *Report on the 6th International Comparative Youth Survey.* Author.

Todd, E. (1992). *L'Invention de L'Europe, Edition du Seuil* (trans. into Japanese by H. Ishizaki). Tokyo: Fujiwarasyoten.

United Nations Development Plan. (1995). *Human development report 1995.* Author.

Van de Kaa, D. J. (1987). *Europe's second demographic transition. Population Bulletin 42(1).* Population Reference Bureau.

10

The Influence of Ideational Dimensions of Social Change on Family Formation in Nepal

William G. Axinn
Dirgha J. Ghimire
Jennifer S. Barber
Population Studies Center
University of Michigan

As recently as the early 1970s, much of rural Nepal remained a subsistence agricultural society, with most social activities organized within families, and family formation patterns the same as they had been for centuries. Dramatic change between 1975 and 1995 in some rural areas spurred the spread of wage labor employment, schools, markets, transportation, government services, and the mass media. In 1995 we launched the Chitwan Valley Family Study (CVFS) to document the rapid social changes occurring in rural Nepal and investigate their influence on marital and childbearing processes. By 2005 the CVFS generated more than two dozen studies of factors influencing the timing of marriage, the arrangement of marriage, family size preferences, the timing of first birth, and the use of contraception to end childbearing—dimensions of family formation that have changed dramatically in Chitwan Valley. Two important explanations for these changes are role conflict between new nonfamily activities and marriage/childbearing, and the rising costs of childrearing. However, these cost-benefit or microeconomic explanations are not sufficient to explain the full extent of family change in Chitwan. The evidence accumulated thus far also points toward ideational dimensions of social change as a particularly important influence on changes in marital and childbearing behavior. In this chapter we review that evidence, formulate a framework for understanding ideational influences on family behavior, and identify future steps for research in this area.

We begin with a theoretical framework designed to link together the wide range of mechanisms connecting social change to family change and variation. This framework identifies three types of mechanisms affecting family change and variation: changes in the costs and benefits of family behavior, the diffusion of new ideas about family behavior, and childhood experiences that produce long-term personality change. Drawing on results from several studies using data from the CVFS, we summarize the evidence from Nepal that points toward ideational mechanisms of family change.

This summary identifies three types of empirical evidence. The first type is evidence of a relationship between childhood community context and early life experiences on the one hand, and adult family formation decisions on the other hand. This relationship is consistent with hypotheses about personality traits that may be formed early in childhood. The second type is evidence of a relationship between experiences that provide access to new ideas, particularly exposure to the mass media, and family formation behavior. This evidence also points toward ideational mechanisms that probably link macro-level social changes to micro-level family formation behavior. The third type of evidence is relationships between community context and access to new ideas on the one hand, and attitudes and preferences about family formation behavior on the other hand. New attitudes and preferences about family formation behavior constitute a key mechanism through which ideational changes influence these behaviors.

THEORETICAL FRAMEWORK

Social Change and Family Organization

The modes of social organization framework considers a wide array of social changes and their potential influence on individuals and families (Thornton & Fricke, 1987; Thornton & Lin, 1994). The framework builds on previous research that focused exclusively on the family mode of *production* (Caldwell, 1982; Lesthaeghe & Wilson, 1986) and extends it to modes of *social organization* across a variety of domains: consumption, residence, recreation, protection, socialization, procreation, and production. Historically, most of these activities of daily living were organized within the family (Ogburn & Nimkoff, 1955; Thornton & Fricke, 1987). As social changes created new nonfamily institutions to organize these activities, they increasingly took place outside the family (Coleman, 1990). This continuum—from social activities organized inside to outside the family— provides a useful construct in understanding social change and the family.

Our choice of this framework is rooted in the premise that improvements in transportation and communication, increasing monetization of the economy, and growth of the population increase the division of labor in society. Durkheim argued that these factors increase the number of people who interact with one another, or the "moral density" of society (1984, p. 257). The modes of social organization framework argues that changes in transportation, communication, and monetization affect not only production, but a wide variety of other social activities as well, which in turn influence the social organization of families. As activities of daily living increasingly take place outside the home and away from families, the structure of social interactions changes, altering social relationships with both family members and others outside the family. This reorganization of family life is the key link between macro-level social changes and micro-level outcomes in family-building behaviors (Axinn & Yabiku, 2001).

Family Organization and Family Formation Behavior

The modes of social organization framework can be used to integrate and expand on existing explanations of family formation behavior. Theoretical work linking social change to family formation behavior has mainly focused on two sets of explanations: (a) microeconomic explanations, which emphasize the impact of changes in the costs and benefits of marriage and childrearing, and (b) ideational explanations, which emphasize the impact of changes in the diffusion of beliefs and preferences related to marriage and childbearing. The modes of social organization framework incorporates both perspectives, to which we add a largely unexplored mechanism: personality development (Axinn & Yabiku, 2001).

Costs and Benefits of Family Formation. Microeconomic theories of family formation processes, sometimes referred to as "demand" theories, focus on the costs and benefits of marriage and childrearing (Becker, 1991; Easterlin & Crimmins, 1985; Lesthaeghe & Surkyn, 1988; Notestein, 1953; Willis, 1973). Recent theoretical work by sociologists also emphasizes this perspective. For example, Coleman explicitly links the reorganization of family life to individuals' childbearing and childrearing behaviors via the costs and benefits of childrearing (Coleman, 1990). As nonfamily organizations and institutions (what Coleman calls corporate actors) grow, they remove responsibilities from the family for activities it once performed: production (p. 580), education (p. 581), food preparation (p. 587), and care of the aged (p. 584). The key is that when these activities happen within the household, they create positive externalities to marriage and childrearing for household members. For example, while the aged are cared for in the family home, they also can oversee young children. Similarly, when parents' productive activities occur near the home, spouses provide needed labor and children can assist with the simpler tasks. These positive externalities keep the costs of marriage and childrearing low. However, when these social activities shift to specialized corporate actors, the positive externalities begin to disappear, which increases the costs and decreases the benefits of marriage and childrearing. This shift motivates individuals to delay marriage and limit fertility (Coleman, 1990, p. 585).

Earlier theories of demographic change contain many ideas similar to Coleman's. For example, Notestein argued that the reorganization of social activities outside the family reduces parents' motivations to have children. He wrote that fertility transitions began in settings that "stripped the family of many functions in production, consumption, recreation, and education" (Notestein, 1953, p. 16). Caldwell's intergenerational wealth flows theory of fertility decline is also similar to Coleman's claim that the reorganization of care for the elderly outside the family reduces the motivation to have children. When social change reduces the value of children, intergenerational flows of wealth reverse and flow from parents to children. This reversal, argues Caldwell, induces fertility declines (Caldwell, 1982). Thus, these theories use the social organization of the family to link macro-level social changes to individual-level childbearing behavior. Or, as Coleman says, "The new corporate actors are specialized and narrow purpose entities, constitutive of a structure marked by a high division of labor, and have no place for childrearing" (Coleman, 1990, p. 579).

Note that in this theory of family change, individuals are assumed to be aware of their self-interest and make decisions about marriage and childbearing to maximize it within a shifting set of social circumstances. This is an important contrast to theories arguing that changes in marriage and childbearing occur in response to individuals' growing awareness of self-interest (Kasarda, Billy & West, 1986).

Diffusion of New Ideas. Different from perspectives that emphasize the costs and benefits of marriage and childrearing, diffusion perspectives stress social interactions as the key to family change. New patterns of social interaction change the patterns of communication among individuals and facilitate the spread of new ideas about family formation. This perspective was fueled by the empirical observation that patterns of fertility decline overlapped with ethnic, language, and religious groupings, suggesting that patterns of communication may have shaped childbearing behavior (Anderson, 1986). Additional evidence showed that factors believed to be closely related to the costs of childrearing did not explain fertility decline (Bongaarts & Watkins, 1996; Cleland & Wilson, 1987).

The spread of many types of new ideas has been linked to delayed marriage and reduced childbearing. These include information about contraception (Knodel, 1987), preferences for smaller families (Caldwell, 1982; Lightbourne, 1984), higher consumption aspirations (Easterlin, 1987; Freedman, 1979), and secular and individualistic attitudes and preferences in general (Bumpass, 1990; Lesthaeghe & Surkyn, 1988; Lesthaeghe & Wilson, 1986). Social change via this type of diffusion requires a fundamental change in social interaction—that is, individuals must somehow come into contact with these new ideas and sources of information. Multiple potential mechanisms of change have been suggested, including social networks that guide the informal spread of information or gossip networks (Watkins, 1991; Watkins & Danzi, 1995); the spread of Western ideas through colonial education systems (Caldwell, 1982); increased migration, travel, and tourism (Bongaarts & Watkins, 1996; Freedman, 1979); and contact with mass media (Bongaarts & Watkins, 1996).

The modes of social organization framework is consistent with both microeconomic and diffusion theories of family change. For example, the reorganization of social activities may alter the costs and benefits of marriage and childrearing and thereby stimulate individual-level changes in behavior, as asserted by most microeconomic theories (Bulatao & Lee, 1983; Easterlin & Crimmins, 1985). However, a reorganization of activities may also alter the group of people with whom individuals interact and thereby facilitate the spread of alternative ideas, which is consistent with ideational diffusion theories (Cleland & Wilson, 1987; Montgomery & Casterline, 1993). Thus the modes of social organization framework incorporates both microeconomic change and the diffusion of ideas as mechanisms of fertility change. This characteristic of the framework is particularly useful, as both sets of changes are likely to exert important influences on marriage and childbearing behavior (Lesthaeghe & Surkyn, 1988).

Long-Term Personality Development. The framework also suggests an overlooked mechanism linking social change to family formation behavior: personality development (Axinn & Yabiku, 2001). Recent theoretical advances demonstrate how the social organization of families in early childhood affects children's long-term personality development (Yabiku, Axinn, & Thornton, 1999). Social activities organized around the family integrate family members, which affects the environment in which children are raised. Empirical evidence confirms the long-term impact of family integration in childhood on adult self-esteem, and theory predicts similar long-term influences on attitudes, values, and preferences related to family formation (Axinn & Yabiku, 2001; Yabiku, Axinn, & Thornton, 1999). Specifically, when individuals have high levels of family integration in childhood, they are likely to prefer earlier family formation and larger families. The complementary prediction is that when social change removes activities from the family, family integration decreases, stimulating preferences for smaller families and later family formation. This mechanism of social change is ideational in nature, but rather than working through the diffusion of new ideas among adults, it occurs in childhood with the social organization of the family shaping personality development (Axinn & Yabiku, 2001).

Because it emphasizes the timing and sequencing of both macro-level historical changes and micro-level individual experiences, the life-course perspective is extremely valuable for illuminating the empirical differences among our hypotheses (Elder, 1977, 1983). Timing is important because different mechanisms work through different periods in an individual's lifetime. The personality mechanism just described suggests that social context affects the social organization of families, which influences personality development in children and subsequently affects their family formation behavior in adulthood. Mechanisms affecting the perceived costs and benefits of marriage and childrearing operate during adulthood, whereas ideational mechanisms may operate in adulthood with the spread new ideas about marriage and fertility (e.g., gossip networks—Watkins, 1991), or in childhood through exposure to information that alters attitudes and preferences for the long term (e.g., school books depicting families with only two children—Caldwell, 1982).

An interesting issue is the interplay between personality mechanisms developed in childhood and adult contemporary context. The research literature on attitudes and behavior recognizes that a key reason attitudes and preferences do not necessarily translate into consistent behavior is real constraints associated with circumstances at the time of behavior (Ajzen, 1988). For example, in our setting a woman who lived nearby a school in her childhood may place a high value on sending her own children to school, but if she does not have access to nearby schools in adulthood, when she has children, her behavior may not be consistent with those values. Thus, it may be reasonable to expect that the effect of current adult context is more important than childhood context. On the other hand, the attitudes and preferences formed in childhood may be particularly important factors in adult decision making. Work by Elder (1974) suggests long-term influences of childhood experiences, even in the presence of very different adult contexts. Thus, we expect there to be independent effects of childhood and adult contexts on adult decision making (Axinn & Barber, 2001; Axinn & Yabiku, 2001).

APPLYING THE MODES OF SOCIAL
ORGANIZATION FRAMEWORK

Application of the modes of social organization framework requires knowledge of the starting state of family versus nonfamily social organization and attitudes toward family formation (Thornton & Fricke, 1987; Thornton & Lin, 1994). From these initial characteristics, the context-specific consequences of social change can be predicted. This differentiates the framework from most demographic transition theories, which imply that parents will always desire fewer children when social activities become organized outside the family (Caldwell, 1982; Coleman, 1990; Notestein, 1953). This unilineal outcome, however, is not necessarily a universal consequence of changes in family organization. The consequence of reorganizing social activities outside the family is likely to depend on both the social context and the specific social activity being reorganized. For example, in low-fertility settings with many activities organized outside the family, such as the United States, the reorganization of childcare outside the family may increase fertility (Presser, 1986; Rindfuss, 1991). Before predicting the consequences of specific social changes using the family organization framework, we describe the setting and the family changes that characterize it.

Setting

The study area is the Western Chitwan Valley located in South-Central Nepal. Because poverty and topographical barriers have delayed the spread of new nonfamily organizations and institutions in Nepal (Blaikie, Cameron, & Seddon, 1982), the vast majority of social activities were organized within the family until very recently (Fricke, 1986). Chitwan is a wide flat valley nestled in the Himalayan foothills at approximately 450 feet above sea level, 100 miles southwest of Kathmandu, the country's capital. Until the early 1950s, Chitwan was covered by virgin forests, infested with malaria-carrying mosquitos, and inhabited by dangerous fauna ranging from poisonous snakes to Bengal tigers. Beginning in the mid-1950s, with assistance from the U.S. government, the Nepalese government began a program to clear the forests, eradicate malaria, and distribute land to settlers from the higher Himalayas. Our study examines social change in a 92-square-mile area of Western Chitwan that was cleared and settled.

New roadways through the valley were major sources of social change. Although rich soils, flat terrain, and new opportunities drew many farmers into the area, the valley remained a remote, isolated frontier until the late 1970s. The first all-weather road into Chitwan was completed in 1979, linking Chitwan's largest town, Narayanghat, to cities in Eastern Nepal and India. Two other important roads followed: one west, linking that town to the western portion of Nepal, and another north, linking Chitwan to Kathmandu. Because of Narayanghat's central location, by the mid-1980s this once-isolated town became the transportation hub of the country. This change produced a rapid proliferation of government services, businesses, and wage labor jobs in Narayanghat that spread throughout Chitwan (Pokharel & Shivakoti, 1986). The population of this valley continued to grow via both immigration and natural increase (Central Bureau of Statistics, 1987; Tuladhar, 1989).

Within the lifetimes of many of its current residents, the social organization of Chitwan has changed greatly. In the late 1950s there were virtually no employment opportunities, market places, schools, health posts, or transportation services. Now bus service through the valley provides access to the wage labor opportunities and commerce of Narayanghat. Commercial enterprises, such as grain mills and new retail outlets, are now scattered throughout Chitwan, as are a range of government services, including schools, agricultural cooperatives, police posts, and health posts. For the hundreds of small farming communities in the Western Chitwan Valley, these changes have significantly transformed the local context.

Contextual Change. Our research on how contextual changes influence family formation behaviors is explicitly designed to capitalize on this transformed local setting. Our life-course perspective motivated us to design methods to measure neighborhood context that emphasize the timing and sequencing of contextual change. To that end, we designed and collected data using a Neighborhood History Calendar, which measures the timing and sequencing of important changes and events in the history of each neighborhood (Axinn, Barber, & Ghimire, 1997).

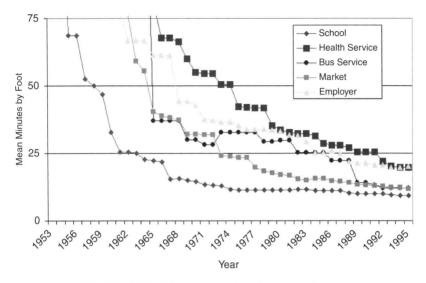

FIGURE 10.1   Change over time in mean minutes
by foot to the nearest public service.

Our innovative Neighborhood History Calendar approach provides a comprehensive set of temporally detailed measures of local-level contextual change and variation. The measures are extremely flexible, allowing us to document change and variation in many ways. For example, in Figure 10.1 we present the history of change in the community infrastructure of Chitwan Valley: historical time increases along the x axis, and travel time in minutes increases on the y axis. The lines represent, across 43 years, the time required to reach the nearest school, health service, bus service, market, or employer, averaged across all 171 neighborhoods in the study area. The declining slopes of these lines indicate that the average time to walk to each of these services has declined dramatically over the recent history of Chitwan Valley, and the differences among the lines indicate which of these changes spread through the valley first, second, and third.

These neighborhood history data can also be used to calculate measures of the temporal order of change in many different metrics, including the number of services available in any year, the number of years of exposure to each service within a particular distance, the temporally changing geo-weighted measures of the services available within the entire study area, or the most common temporal sequence of the appearance of these services within a particular distance.

Family Change.   Nepal has been characterized by dramatic changes in family formation behaviors in recent years, as well. The beginning of fertility decline is quite recent in Nepal, falling from a total fertility rate (TFR) of 5.1 in 1991 to 4.6 in 2001 (His Majesty's Government, 2001; K.C., 2003; Suwal, 2001). Prior to these changes, Nepal's TFR had been stable at around 6 for as long as records are available (Banister & Thapa, 1981; Tuladhar, 1989). Little direct historical evidence addresses past family size preferences for the Nepalese population or the population that now inhabits Chitwan, but there are some indications that the groups who now inhabit Chitwan preferred large families and did not desire to limit their family sizes (Fricke, 1986; Gurung, 1980; Hitchcock, 1966; McFarlane, 1976). The fertility transition that began in the 1990s is mirrored in several other family formation transitions, such as marital timing and arranged marriages (Ghimire et al., 2006; Yabiku, 2002).

Our life-course perspective motivated us to design methods to measure family formation processes and related experiences that emphasize the timing and sequencing of these experiences. Analyses of a wide range of topics have demonstrated the importance of life history data for untangling complex demographic processes (Freedman, Thornton, Camburn, Alwin, & Young-Demarco, 1988). Life history calendars are invaluable for collecting detailed retrospective data because they assist respondents' recall of the timing of life events (Axinn, Pearce, & Ghimire, 1999). We used these calendars to measure the timing of important experiences including marriage, childbearing, contraceptive use, labor-force participation, education, children's education, child mortality, mobility, and living arrangements.

The measures from these life history calendars demonstrate substantial change over time in many key dimensions of family formation behavior. In Figure 10.2 we show the proportion of married individuals who participated in the selection of their spouse by the year of marriage. The clear upward trend shows a steady increase over the past 60 years, with participation in spouse selection climbing from none of the respondents married between 1936 and 1945 to more than half of those married between 1986 and 1995.

Participation in spouse selection is not the only feature of marriage that is rapidly changing. Figure 10.3 displays the mean age at first marriage for different marriage cohorts. This figure shows a dramatic rise in age of marriage, with mean age climbing from just 15 years for respondents married between 1956 and 1965 to nearly 21 for those married between 1996 and 2002.

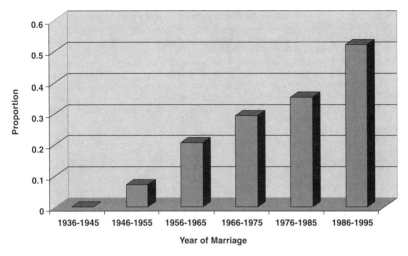

FIGURE 10.2   Proportion of married persons who participated in spouse selection.

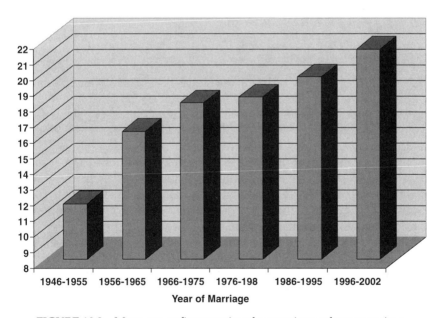

FIGURE 10.3   Mean age at first marriage by marriage cohort over time.

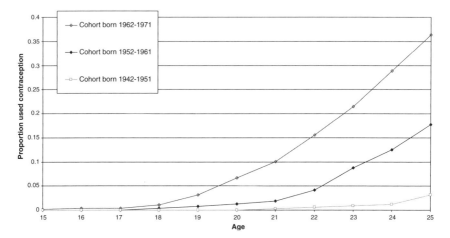

FIGURE 10.4   Cohort differences in the cumulative proportion of women with
at least one child who have ever used a contraceptive to stop childbearing
(sterilization, IUD, Norplant, Depo-Provera, or spouse sterilization).

Contraceptive behavior has also changed dramatically in Chitwan. In
Figure 10.4 we show the proportions of women with at least one child,
by age cohort, who have ever used a permanent contraceptive method.
Among the cohort born in 1942–1951 (ages 45–54 in 1996), less than 5%
had used contraception to terminate their childbearing by age 25. Yet
among the cohort born in 1962–1971 (ages 25–34), more than 35% had
used contraception to terminate their childbearing by age 25. Of course,
many in the 1942–1951 birth cohort eventually went on to use birth control (49% by age 45), but the large differences across cohorts demonstrate a tremendous change in the pace of adopting contraception.

As one would expect, the mean total number of children ever born
per woman has decreased as the use of permanent contraceptives has
increased. For women born in 1942–1946 the average per woman was
6.4, but for women born in 1952–1956 it was 4.9—a significant drop for
only a 10-year age difference.

Thus, recent decades in Chitwan have been characterized by dramatic changes in the arrangement of marriage, the timing of marriage,
the use of contraception, and childbearing.

Empirical Predictions

In this setting, we expect community-level changes in access to nonfamily organizations and institutions, such as markets, schools, health care, and transportation, to result in the reorganization of production, consumption, residence, recreation, protection, and socialization outside the family. As these activities of daily living are reorganized outside the family, we expect the costs and benefits of marriage and childrearing, the diffusion of new ideas, and long-term effects on personality will each change in ways that will promote later marriage, greater spousal selection, later first births, and more fertility-limiting behavior. Many specific mechanisms are likely to work together to produce these consequences (Axinn & Barber, 2001; Axinn & Yabiku, 2001; Ghimire, 2003; Pearce, 2000; Yabiku, 2002). For our purposes, we focus on three areas that implicate ideational mechanisms in reshaping marital and childbearing behavior in this setting: the independent effects of childhood community context, the mechanisms of access to new ideas, and the factors promoting new attitudes and preferences.

Childhood Community Context. As discussed earlier, childhood nonfamily experiences are likely to produce relatively stable attitudes and preferences that are less positive toward marriage and childbearing. In this setting we predict that early childhood access to and experiences with nonfamily services will delay marriage and limit fertility in adulthood. Because childhood context is likely to be similar to adult community context, and observed consequences of adult community context may reflect cost-benefit mechanisms rather than ideational mechanisms, observation of an effect of childhood context that is *independent* of adult context is essential to provide evidence for ideational mechanisms. One set of CVFS results we present focuses directly on these independent effects of childhood community context.

Access to New Ideas. As discussed earlier, most changes in community context and individual experience are likely to have both cost-benefit and ideational consequences for family behavior. Education is a clear example. Learning in schools is obviously a mechanism for the spread of new ideas (Axinn & Barber, 2001; Caldwell, 1982; Thornton, 2001), but access to education can also alter the cost-benefit trade-off of marriage and childbearing (Axinn & Barber, 2001; Becker, 1991; Easterlin & Crimmins, 1985). Separating these two mechanisms of educational effects on family formation is a daunting task. We examine education, but we also describe CVFS results from studies of the consequences of mass media exposure and experience with new group organizations. Although media exposure and group participation both undoubtedly have important cost-benefit consequences, these mechanisms of access to new ideas also implicate ideational mechanisms.

New Attitudes and Preferences. Finally, the ethnographic literature on Nepal indicates that the vast majority of the Nepalese population has for centuries held positive attitudes toward early marriage, arranged marriage, early childbearing, large families, and unlimited fertility (Acharya & Bennett, 1981; Bennet, 1983; Fricke, 1986; Gurung, 1980; Hitchcock, 1966; McFarlane, 1976; Messerschmidt, 1976). Factors that promote new ideas about these dimensions of family formation are important mechanisms for promoting changes in related behaviors. Because ample evidence from other settings indicates that attitudes like those held historically in Nepal have a dramatic impact on subsequent marital and childbearing behavior (Axinn & Thornton, 1992a, 1992b, 1993; Barber, 2000, 2001; Barber & Axinn, 1998a, 1998b), we also investigate the factors associated with countervailing attitudes—that is, positive attitudes toward later marriage, self-selection of spouses, later first births, smaller families, and contraception to limit childbearing.

RESEARCH DESIGN

Our research is explicitly designed to capitalize on the variance in Chitwan's community context in investigating the influence of nonfamily organizations and experiences on family formation behaviors. Both theoretical arguments and empirical evidence have failed to produce consistent conclusions regarding which contextual levels are relevant to family formation behavior. Dyson and Moore (1983) suggest that different regional environments, defined in terms of North and South Indian kinship regimes, shape fertility, and contraceptive use behavior. Entwisle and Mason (1985), who operationalize social setting at the national level, note similar effects. Others have located contextual effects on fertility at the community level (Entwisle, Casterline, & Sayed, 1989; McNicoll, 1980, 1984). In our study of family formation behavior, we operationalize context at an extremely local level—the neighborhoods in which individuals interact when conducting daily activities. By studying variation across neighborhoods within a single valley, our design focuses on this local level contextual variation and excludes variation at higher levels of context.

The households of Chitwan are organized in distinct *tols*, or neighborhoods, which are separated from other neighborhoods by farm lands. The neighborhoods vary in distance from the valley's urbanized center (Narayanghat) and from other infrastructure changes such as new roads, schools, or health posts. The neighborhoods vary from those characterized by a great deal of change to those with little evidence of recent change (Shivakoti & Pokharel, 1989). Furthermore, the timing of changes varies a great deal among the neighborhoods in Chitwan. These variations provide an opportunity to examine the influence of many differences in local context on family formation behaviors.

As described earlier, our life-course perspective motivated us to design methods to gather reliable data on community-level event histories and individual-level life histories. These methods are described in detail elsewhere (Axinn et al., 1997, 1999). Although somewhat rare for settings like Nepal, our study also included multiple measures of individual attitudes and beliefs regarding marriage, childbearing, contraceptive use, and related issues. Measurement of these subjective phenomena required a great deal of intensive ethnographic research, focus-group analysis, and survey pretesting. As we discuss later, our research to date demonstrates that our measures of community characteristics are strongly associated with these measures of individual attitudes and beliefs (Barber, 2004).

RESULTS

Our results emanate from more than a dozen distinct studies conducted during the last 10 years that focus on the timing of first marriage, the arrangement of marriage, the timing of first birth, and the timing of contraceptive use to limit fertility. All analyses of timing of events (marriage, birth, and contraceptive use) feature hazard models drawing on measures from the life history calendar and estimated using techniques designed to correct standard errors for within-neighborhood clustering (Barber, Murphy, Axinn, & Maples 2000). Readers interested in learning more about the specific techniques used to estimate these models or other details of the studies themselves can consult our original work, as cited later. Our focus here is on summarizing the substantive results, which we do in the order of our predictions already described.

Childhood Community Characteristics

Several studies based on data from the CVFS demonstrate significant independent effects of childhood community context on adult family formation behavior. We begin our summary of these results by presenting findings from Axinn and Barber's 2001 study of mass education and fertility limitation. In this study the authors evaluate a wide range of links between the spread of mass education and decisions to use contraceptive methods to limit childbearing. They estimate multilevel discrete-time hazard models of using contraception to stop childbearing, controlling for many exogenous factors (see Axinn & Barber, 2001).

They find that living within a 1-hour walk of a school during childhood substantially and significantly raises the odds of limiting childbearing in adulthood. Women who lived near a school during their childhood were 41% more likely than those who did not to adopt a permanent contraceptive method during any 1-year period. Their analyses also show that the influence of having lived near a health post or a bus service is not independent of having lived near a school. When these three measures are included in the same model, the influence of schools remains statistically significant, but the influence of health posts and bus service declines dramatically, rendering them statistically insignificant.

Axinn and Barber (2001) also find that childhood community characteristics have statistically significant effects that are independent of the effects of current community characteristics. In particular, living near a school during childhood increases a woman's likelihood of fertility limitation regardless of whether she lives near a school as an adult. This suggests that childhood educational opportunities and adult educational opportunities may influence contraceptive use via different mechanisms (Axinn & Barber, 2001). For instance, it could be that living near a school during childhood affects a woman's attitudes and educational expectations for her children, whereas living near a school during adulthood mainly affects the actual chances that a woman can send her children to school. This is consistent with other research indicating that exposure to social change during childhood alters attitudes toward marriage, but exposure to social change during adulthood does not (Barber, 2004). This is particularly interesting in the Nepalese context, where many women exposed to schools during their childhood were not able to attend. Thus, their childhood exposure to school may have affected their *attitudes* toward education (particularly toward educating their children), but did not affect their own educational attainment.

Overall, Axinn and Barber find that the spread of mass education has a strong influence on the transition from unlimited childbearing to birth control-limited childbearing and operates through multiple mechanisms. They show that childhood access to schools, having an educated husband, access to schools in adulthood, and sending one's children to school all have substantial effects on women's propensity to limit their childbearing through permanent contraceptive use. Furthermore, these effects are largely independent of one another, and thus represent a large cumulative effect on women's contraceptive use.

Axinn and Yabiku (2001) conduct a parallel study using these same data, but investigating a broader range of nonfamily organizations and services. Estimating models analogous to those described above, they also find that childhood community context has long-term effects on fertility limitation that are not explained by adult experiences or adult community context. That is, exposure to nonfamily organizations and services in childhood significantly increases the odds of using contraceptives to terminate childbearing in adulthood (Axinn & Yabiku, 2001).

Exposure to schools and other nonfamily organizations in childhood may well alter attitudes, values, and beliefs in a direction likely to increase fertility limitation. Strong theory and empirical evidence lead us to expect that attitudes, values, and beliefs formed early in life will remain influential across the life span (Alwin, 1994; Alwin & Krosnick, 1991). To the extent that this childhood environment alters women's views of childbearing and childrearing, it may be part of the explanation for the observed long-term impact of childhood social context. Direct measurement of values and expectations will be necessary to document such mechanisms. Of course, other complex mechanisms may also be at work.

Access to New Ideas

As discussed earlier, access to new ideas is another potentially powerful mechanism of family change. A number of studies based on data from the CVFS demonstrate significant independent effects of access to the new ideas on adult family formation behavior. In particular these studies focus on three important sources of the new ideas: schooling, mass media, and interaction with people outside of the family. Although education in schools is an obvious mechanism for the spread of new ideas (Axinn & Barber, 2001; Caldwell, 1982; Thornton, 2001), we focus on summarizing CVFS results from studies of media exposure and group participation because it is difficult to separate the ideational and cost-benefit consequences of schooling (Axinn & Barber, 2001).

We begin by presenting findings from Ghimire, Axinn, Yabiku and Thornton's 2006 study of premarital nonfamily experiences and spouse choice. In this study the authors investigate the consequences of a wide array of premarital nonfamily experiences on the degree of participation in choice of first spouse. Although historically in Nepal virtually all marriages were arranged by parents, as shown Figure 10.2 (given earlier), there has been dramatic change over time in participation in the selection of a spouse.

Of 2,832 ever-married respondents interviewed in the CVFS, 65% reported that their first marriages were solely arranged by parents/ relatives and 35% reported they either participated to some degree or solely chose their spouse. Instead of using a dichotomy of arranged marriage versus individual choice, Ghimire et al. (2006) treat the choice of a spouse as continuum, focusing on the level of respondent partici- pation in the choice of spouse. To estimate multivariate models of this ordinal measure, Ghimire et al. (2006) use an ordered logistic regression estimation technique.

Among the six nonfamily experiences investigated, exposure to media and participation in youth clubs both have independent signifi- cant effects on the degree of participation in spouse choice. The odds of participating at a higher level of spouse choice were 54% higher for those who scored at the top of the media exposure index than for those who scored at the bottom. Likewise, those who participated in youth clubs were 46% more likely to have a higher level of participation in spouse choice than those who did not. Despite the explanatory value of youth club participation, however, the analyses conducted by Ghimire et al. (2006) go on to demonstrate that increased exposure to mass media accounted for the vast majority of the cohort change in young people's participation in the choice of their spouse.

Studies of marriage timing using the CVFS data echo these results. In his multilevel discrete-time hazard model analyses of marriage timing, Yabiku (2005, 2006) found that exposure to media has a strong negative effect on the rate of marriage. For example, women who watched television before their marriage married at rates 36% lower than women who had not. He found similar effects for seeing a movie in a cinema hall, and also found that merely living near a cinema hall or having neighbors who watched televi- sion or saw movies decreased respondents' rate of marriage.

Results from CVFS studies of media exposure and childbearing behavior are just as strong. In their study of the role of mass media in fertility limitation behavior, Barber and Axinn (2004) use the CVFS data to estimate multilevel hazard models of contraception to terminate childbearing analogous to those discussed above. Here, however, they investigate the various ways that mass media exposure may influence the decision to terminate childbearing, controlling for the largest pos- sible set of potentially exogenous factors.

Barber and Axinn (2004) begin by constraining media exposure to the period before marriage. Their results show that a wife's premarital exposure to radios and movies is significantly associated with higher rates of adopting a permanent contraceptive method. They also find a large cumulative relationship between multiple types of premarital media exposure and adopting a permanent contraceptive method. For example, individuals exposed to three sources have .38 higher log-odds of adopting a permanent contraceptive method than individuals exposed to one source. Finally, they show that the correlations between adopting a permanent contraceptive method and exposure to radios and movies are independent—that is, exposure to radios is associated with a higher rate of adopting a permanent contraceptive method regardless of exposure to movies, and vice versa. Next, Barber and Axinn investigate lifetime media exposure. Here too they find strong positive correlations between exposure and adopting permanent contraception—and these correlations are substantially larger than those found for media exposure before marriage.

These effects are not only *statistically* significant, they are also indicative of a *substantive* relationship between media exposure and permanent contraceptive use. In fact, the media exposure effects are as large as many of the other effects in their models, including those for husband's education, wife's labor-force participation, husband's parents' labor-force participation, and current as well as childhood neighborhood characteristics.

Another set of CVFS results focuses on the effects of voluntary association groups. Barber, Pearce, Chaudhury, and Gurung (2002) hypothesize that multiple mechanisms act to produce positive associations between participating in voluntary association groups and adopting a permanent contraceptive method, including social support, personal empowerment, economic incentives, and motivation to adopt new attitudes. Many of these mechanisms rely on direct group participation. For a couple to gain social support or receive economic incentives from a group, for instance, at least one member of the couple must participate. The potential impact of these mechanisms is demonstrated by their finding that direct participation is strongly associated with permanent contraceptive use (see Table 2 in Barber et al., 2002). Other change mechanisms, however, such as exposure to new attitudes and increased information, may operate due to the mere presence of a voluntary association, regardless of whether either member of the couple actually participates. The positive effect on contraceptive use of living near a voluntary association, regardless of participation, demonstrates the potential effect of these types of mechanisms (see Table 3 in Barber et al., 2002). Thus, overall, their results provide strong support for a relationship between voluntary associations and permanent contraceptive use, but the presence of both individual- and neighborhood-level effects does not allow them to distinguish between the different types of mechanisms. They also investigate the separate effects of five types of voluntary associations: women's groups, youth groups, agricultural groups, credit groups, and other groups. Their results suggest that all types of voluntary associations may be equally likely to influence permanent contraceptive use.

Similar to the CVFS findings for the effects of mass media, the effects of the presence of groups on contraceptive use may implicate ideational mechanisms of social change. Although the effects of mass media are somewhat stronger and more consistent for both marital arrangement and contraceptive use, both mass media exposure and group participation are potentially important mechanisms of access to new ideas. Based on results from the CVFS to date, it appears that exposure to the mass media is likely to be a more important overall ideational mechanism producing family change.

New Attitudes and Preferences

Finally, as discussed earlier, the ethnographic literature on Nepal indicates that the vast majority of the Nepalese population has held positive attitudes toward early marriage, arranged marriage, early childbearing, large families, and unlimited fertility for centuries (Acharya & Bennett, 1981; Bennet, 1983; Fricke, 1986; Gurung, 1980; Hitchcock, 1966; McFarlane, 1976; Messerschmidt, 1976). Factors promoting new ideas about these dimensions of family formation constitute important mechanisms for promoting changes in family formation behaviors. A number of studies using the CVFS data have documented factors associated with attitudes and preferences that differ from these historical norms. We begin by summarizing Barber's (2004) study of community context and attitudes toward marital behaviors.

Barber investigates seven different marriage-related attitudes among men and women: intercaste marriage, divorce, widow remarriage, child marriage, arranged marriage, mother-in-law obedience, and polygyny. Each of these attitudes is measured with an ordinal scale and Barber uses multilevel OLS (ordinary least squares) regression to estimate multivariate models of factors predicting variation in these attitudes.

She finds consistent evidence that the number of nonfamily institutions to which an individual was exposed during childhood is associated with more individualistic attitudes toward marriage. Individuals who were exposed to schools, employment opportunities, markets, and/or bus services are significantly more negative toward child marriage, arranged marriage, mother-in-law obedience, and polygyny, and are significantly more tolerant of intercaste marriage, divorce, and widow remarriage.

The magnitude of these effects is substantial. For example, individuals who lived near a school, employer, market, and bus service score, on average, .09 lower on the measure of attitude toward child marriage than do individuals who lived near only one of those nonfamily institutions. This is slightly more than 10% of one standard deviation on the scale measuring this attitude (see Barber, 2004). The influence of these nonfamily institutions is even more dramatic in the case of attitudes toward divorce. Individuals who lived near all four of the nonfamily institutions score, on average, .15 higher on the measure of acceptance of divorce than do individuals who lived near only one of the nonfamily institutions. This is 17% of a standard deviation on this scale.

Barber (2004) also investigated the extent to which the relationship between childhood social context and attitudes toward marriage exists net of both individuals' and neighbors' subsequent behaviors. She found that some portion of the relationship is independent of subsequent behaviors. The remaining portion of the relationship for attitudes toward divorce is particularly strong, and there is an important residual relationship on attitudes toward polygyny as well. These residual relationships suggest that mere exposure or other aspects of proximity to nonfamily institutions can influence individual attitudes, regardless of whether an individual or his or her neighbors are actually able to take advantage of that nonfamily institution's goods or services (Barber, 2004).

Barber and Axinn's (2004) study of mass media exposure and childbearing, described briefly earlier, also investigated the influence of media exposure on attitudes and preferences toward three dimensions of childbearing: large families, son preferences, and contraceptive use. Overall, they found strong relationships between lifetime media exposure and attitudes toward these dimensions of childbearing, measuring influence in multiple ways. Exposure to more types of mass media is associated with lower scores on the Coombs scale (preferred number of children) and less agreement with the two statements about the virtue of a large family and the bane of childlessness. Individuals who were exposed to one more source of mass media than their peers scored, on average, .38 fewer points on the Coombs scale. In other words, individuals with lifetime exposure to movies, television, and newspapers scored 1.14 points lower—nearly half of a standard deviation—than individuals exposed to none of these media sources (see Barber & Axinn, 2004). Similarly, agreement with the statement "Having many children is better than being rich" is lower among those exposed to mass media, although this is statistically significant only among men. Thus, men exposed to radio, movies, and TV have 1.44 lower log-odds of agreement (vs. disagreement) than men exposed to none of these sources. More media exposure is also associated with less agreement with the statement "A man with no children cannot go to heaven," but it is also statistically significant only among men. Men exposed to radio, movies, and TV have 1.65 lower log-odds of agreement than men exposed to none of these sources. Media exposure is also associated with weaker preferences for sons over daughters. Individuals exposed to radio, movies, and TV have 1.02 lower log-odds than their counterparts of agreeing with the common Nepali saying "One son, what son? One eye, what eye?" Finally, mass media exposure is associated with positive attitudes toward contraception. Exposure to an additional mass media source is associated with a .33 increase in the log-odds of *disagreeing* with the statement "A vasectomized man cannot be blessed by God." And individuals exposed to movies, television, and newspapers have .93 higher log-odds of agreeing with the statement "Everyone should use family planning."

Neighborhood characteristics that may be indicators of media exposure are also related to attitudes toward childbearing and contraceptive use. Net of whether they saw a movie in a theater before they were married, individuals who live far from a movie theater prefer larger families and have stronger son preference. To investigate the sensitivity of the results to changes in model specification, Barber and Axinn (2004) estimate many different variations of these models. Those tests all produce substantively comparable results. Their findings are consistent with the idea that as individuals are exposed to more sources of mass media, they become less positive toward large families, feel less like they must have at least one son, and become more accepting of contraceptive use as a way to achieve those desires.

Overall, these studies show that childhood social context is strongly related to attitudes toward marriage and mass media exposure is strongly related to attitudes toward childbearing. Living near nonfamily institutions during childhood is associated with individualistic attitudes toward marriage, or positive attitudes toward individual rather than family control of marriage. Living in a community with access to mass media and personal experience with mass media are associated with more positive attitudes toward small families, weaker son preferences, and more positive attitudes toward contraceptive use. Thus the same childhood community factors and access-to-new-ideas factors that influence family formation *behavior* in these settings also influence family formation *attitudes*.

Researchers using the CVFS have not yet had the opportunity to determine either the influence of these attitudes on subsequent family formation behavior or the extent to which variations in attitudes explain the overall effects of childhood community context and media exposure on behavior. Clearly these are important next steps in this program of research. In the meantime, the evidence summarized here, demonstrating strong associations with family formation attitudes, suggests a promising avenue for future research on the ideational mechanisms linking social change and variation to family formation behaviors.

CONCLUSION

Together, various studies using data from the CVFS have found strong empirical evidence that ideational mechanisms of social change are linked to long-term changes in marital and childbearing behaviors. The evidence we summarize here focuses on the effects of childhood community context, access to new ideas through mass media and groups, and new attitudes and preferences about family formation behavior. Each of these bodies of evidence fit together into a picture of ideational mechanisms of social change that are operating in concert with other mechanisms of social change.

Scholars have long explored the relative importance of early versus current environments on behavior (Alwin & Thornton, 1984; Elder, 1974; Mannheim, 1952), and evidence from the CVFS is consistent with the conclusion that both have strong effects in our setting. A number of scholars have argued that in spite of possible long-term consequences of childhood environments, contemporary circumstances are a more important determinant of behavioral choices (Kohn, 1983; Ryder, 1965). Theoretical perspectives on fertility that focus on the costs and benefits of childrearing are closely tied to this view (Becker, 1991; Coleman, 1990; Easterlin & Crimmins, 1985; Notestein, 1953). In the microeconomic view of childbearing behavior, childbearing behavior is influenced by the cost-benefit trade-offs perceived at the time of childbearing decision making. This implies that fertility decisions are effected by community characteristics in adulthood rather than community characteristics when the decision maker was a child. Some of the results from the CVFS constitute evidence in support of this idea—contemporary nonfamily context and children's education are two important examples (Axinn & Barber, 2001; Axinn & Yabiku, 2001).

Of course, childhood circumstances may simply predict later adult circumstances. The fact that the effects of childhood community context do not diminish once CVFS studies add measures of adult context is evidence against this hypothesis. The enduring and independent effects we found of childhood neighborhood context on adult childbearing decisions run counter to purely microeconomic explanations of fertility. The documentation of important effects of mass media and group participation on both marital and childbearing outcomes also points toward non-microeconomic explanations (Barber & Axinn, 2004; Barber et al., 2002; Ghimire et al., 2006). A number of sociologists have advanced various types of diffusion theories, generally stressing social interactions as key social changes that produce family change, as alternatives to perspectives that emphasize the costs and benefits of family formation (Anderson, 1986; Bongaarts & Watkins, 1996; Cleland & Wilson, 1987). Because the diffusion of new ideas may work through both childhood and adult processes, it is difficult to use differences in timing across the life course to adjudicate between ideational diffusion and microeconomic processes. However, our evidence of independent effects of childhood contextual circumstances clearly points toward an ideational process that is separate from adult cost-benefit comparisons: the early development of long-term attitudes and preferences (Axinn & Yabiku, 2001).

This mechanism has been overlooked in nearly all previous studies of macro-level social change and individual family formation behavior. The modes of social organization framework we use here draws our attention to this mechanism because recent research has demonstrated that the social organization of families in childhood has long-term effects on individual personality (Yabiku et al., 1999). Social activities organized around the family tend to integrate family members. Theory predicts that (a) high levels of family integration in childhood stimulate preferences for earlier family formation and larger family sizes, and (b) social changes that remove activities from the family reduce family integration and stimulate preferences for smaller families and later family formation (Axinn & Yabiku, 2001; Yabiku et al., 1999). This mechanism of social change is ideational in its nature, but it differs from mechanisms that rely on the diffusion of new ideas among adults. This mechanism implicates the social organization of families in childhood and how it shapes the long-term personality characteristics. Mass media exposure and participation in group organizations may operate in similar ways.

This mechanism is consistent with more recent theoretical work in economics that predicts early context forms individual preferences and tastes that endure across life (Becker, 1996), and later context represents the constraints in which individuals reveal their preferences. This work posits that even as they encounter new circumstances and experiences, individuals may cling to past preferences simply because it is too costly to derive new ones (Becker, 1996, p. 127). The enduring effects of childhood circumstance are central to Easterlin's theories of childhood socialization, cohort size, economic opportunity, and fertility (Easterlin, 1987). Thus, ideational mechanisms of change linked to individual personality are neither antithetical to microeconomic perspectives on family formation behavior, nor unheard of among the economists most closely associated with the application of microeconomic theory to family formation behavior. In fact, if researchers are to explain how social change affects family formation behavior, we will almost certainly need to integrate both microeconomic and ideational perspectives. Although many pose these two sets of family theories as competing alternatives, these social processes probably work closely together, reinforcing each other over time (Lesthaeghe & Surkyn, 1988).

The modes of social organization framework is a fundamental theoretical tool for studies of family formation behavior because it can generate empirical predictions across a wide variety of substantive domains, and permits the construction of family formation hypotheses that incorporate both microeconomic theories (Bulatao & Lee, 1983; Caldwell, 1982; Easterlin & Crimmins, 1985) and ideational theories (Anderson, 1986; Cleland & Wilson, 1987; Montgomery & Casterline, 1993). Equally important, the framework identifies other key mechanisms of social change that have not been applied in studies of family formation behavior, such as the influence of family social organization on social integration and childhood personality development (Axinn & Yabiku, 2001; Yabiku et al., 1999). It is an ideal tool for studies of the link between macro-level contextual change and individual behavior because it explicitly links macro-level social change to individual family formation behavior via the social organization of the family (Axinn & Yabiku, 2001; Thornton & Fricke, 1987; Thornton & Lin, 1994). This has emerged as a fundamental element of a broad range of theories linking social change to families (Caldwell, 1982; Coleman, 1990; Freedman, 1979; Lesthaeghe & Wilson, 1986; Notestein, 1953). In sum, it is a flexible framework that can address a broad set of research problems for both sociologists and other social scientists and represents an important step forward in theoretical reasoning regarding the links between family and social change.

ACKNOWLEDGMENTS

The authors thank all the scientists who participated in the planning and execution of the Chitwan Valley Family Study, including Arland Thornton, Tom Fricke, Ganesh Shivakoti, Lisa Pearce, Scott Yabiku, Dan Hill, Steve Heeringa, Douglas Massey, Susan Murphy, Stephen Mathews, Jeanne Spicer, and Ann Biddlecom. We also thank all the field staff of the

Population and Ecology Research Laboratory and the Institute for Social and Environmental Research in Nepal who conducted the many different data collections of the CVFS. We also thank the support staff of the Institute for Social Research for their effort to execute these data collections, conduct data analyses, prepare the manuscripts cited in this chapter, and prepare this chapter. Thanks too to the many respondents in Nepal who gave generously of their time. Finally, we thank the Demographic and Behavioral Sciences Branch of the NICHD for its generous support of many different data collection and data analysis phases of the CVFS (1R01 HD32912, 1 R01 HD33551, and 5 R37 HD039425). Special thanks to Heather Gatny and Sara Brauner. All errors and omissions in this chapter are the responsibility of the authors.

REFERENCES

Acharya, M., & Bennett, L. (1981). *Rural women of Nepal: An aggregate analysis and summary of eight village studies.* Kathmandu: Tribhuvan University.

Ajzen, I. (1988). *Attitudes, personality, and behavior.* Chicago: Dorsey Press.

Alwin, D. F. (1994). Aging, personality, and social change: The stability of individual differences over the adult life span. In D. L. Featherman, R. M. Lerner, & M. Perlmutter (Eds.), *Life-Span development and behavior* (pp. 135–185). Hillsdale, NJ: Lawrence Erlbaum Associates.

Alwin, D. F., & Krosnick, J.A. (1991). Aging, cohorts, and the stability of sociopolitical orientations over the life span. *American Journal of Sociology, 97,* 169–195.

Alwin, D. F., & Thornton, A. (1984). Family origins and the schooling process: Early versus late influence of parental characteristics. *American Sociological Review, 49,* 784–802.

Anderson, B. A. (1986). Regional and cultural factors in the decline of marital fertility. In A. J. Coale & S. C. Watkins (Eds.), *The decline of fertility in Europe* (pp. 293–313). Princeton, NJ: Princeton University Press.

Axinn, W. G., & Barber, J.S. (2001). Mass education and fertility transition. *American Sociological Review, 66*(4), 481–505.

Axinn, W. G., Barber, J. S., & Ghimire, D. J. (1997). The neighborhood history calendar: A data collection method designed for dynamic multilevel modeling. *Sociological Methodology, 27,* 355–392.

Axinn, W. G., Pearce, L. D., & Ghimire, D. (1999). Innovations in life history calendar applications. *Social Science Research, 28,* 243–264.

Axinn, W. G., & Thornton, A. (1992a). The influence of parental resources on the timing of the transition to marriage. *Social Science Research, 21,* 261–285.

Axinn, W. G., & Thornton, A. (1992b). The relationship between cohabitation and divorce: Selectivity or causal influence? *Demography, 29*(3), 357–374.

Axinn, W. G., & Thornton, A. (1993). Mothers, children, and cohabitation: The intergenerational effects of attitudes and behavior. *American Sociological Review, 58*(2), 233–246.

Axinn, W. G., & Yabiku, S. (2001). Social change, the social organization of families, and fertility limitation. *American Journal of Sociology, 106*(5), 1219–61.

Banister, J., & Thapa, S. (1981). *The population dynamics of Nepal.* Honolulu: East-West Population Institute.

Barber, J. S. (2000). Intergenerational influences on the entry into parenthood: Mothers' preferences for family and nonfamily behavior. *Social Forces, 79*(1), 319–348.

Barber, J. S. (2001). Ideational influences on the transition to parenthood: Attitudes toward childbearing and competing alternatives. *Social Psychology Quarterly, 64*(2), 101–127.

Barber, J. S. (2004). Community social context and individualistic attitudes toward marriage. *Social Psychology Quarterly, 67,* 236–256.

Barber, J. S., & Axinn, W. G. (1998a). The impact of parental pressure for grandchildren on young people's entry into cohabitation and marriage. *Population Studies, 52*(2), 129–144.

Barber, J. S., & Axinn, W. G. (1998b). Gender role attitudes and marriage timing among young women. *The Sociological Quarterly, 39*(1), 11–32.

Barber, J. S., & Axinn, W. G. (2004). New ideas and fertility limitation: The role of mass Media. *Journal of Marriage and the Family, 66,* 1180–1200.

Barber, J. S., Murphy, S., Axinn, W. G., & Maples, J. (2000). Discrete-time multilevel hazard analysis. *Sociological Methodology, 30,* 201–235.

Barber, J. S., Pearce, L. D., Chaudhury, I., & Gurung, S. (2002). Voluntary associations and fertility limitation. *Social Forces, 80*(4), 1369–1401.

Becker, G. S. (1991). *A treatise on the family.* Cambridge, MA: Harvard University Press.

Becker, G. S. (1996). *Accounting for tastes.* Cambridge, MA: Harvard University Press.

Bennet, L. (1983). *Dangerous wives and sacred sisters.* New York: Columbia University Press.

Blaikie, P., Cameron, J., & Seddon, D. (1982). *Nepal in crisis.* Delhi: Oxford University Press.

Bongaarts, J., & Watkins, S. C. (1996). Social interactions and contemporary fertility transitions. *Population and Development Review, 20,* 639–682.

Bulatao, R., & Lee, R. (1983). *Determinants of fertility in developing countries.* New York: Academic Press.

Bumpass, L. L. (1990). What's happening to the family? Interactions between demographic and institutional change. *Demography, 27,* 483–98.

Caldwell, J. C. (1982). *Theory of fertility decline.* New York: Academic Press.

Central Bureau of Statistics. (1987). *Population monograph of Nepal.* Kathmandu, Nepal: His Majesty's Government.

Cleland, J., & Wilson, C. (1987). Demand theories of fertility transition: An iconoclastic view. *Population Studies, 41,* 5–30.

Coleman, J. (1990). *Foundations of social theory.* Cambridge, MA: Harvard University Press.

Durkheim, E. (1984). *The division of labor in society.* New York: Free Press.

Dyson, T., & Moore, M. (1983). On kinship structure, female autonomy, and demographic behavior in India. *Population and Development Review, 9*(1), 35–60.

Easterlin, R. (1987). *Birth and fortune.* Chicago: University of Chicago Press.

Easterlin, R. A., & Crimmins, E. M. (1985). *The fertility revolution: A supply–demand analysis.* Chicago: University of Chicago Press.

Elder, G. H., Jr. (1974). *Children of the great depression: Social change in life experience.* Chicago: University of Chicago Press.

Elder, G. H., Jr. (1977). Family history and the life course. *Journal of Family History, 2,* 279–304.

Elder, G. H., Jr. (1983). The life-course perspective. In M. Gordon (Ed.), *The American family in social-historical perspective* (3rd ed., pp. 54–60). New York: St. Martin's Press.

Entwisle, B., Casterline, J., & Sayed, H. (1989). Villages as contexts for contraceptive behavior in rural Egypt. *American Sociological Review, 54,* 1019–1034.

Entwisle, B., & Mason, W. M. (1985). Multilevel effects of socioeconomic development and family planning programs on children ever born. *American Journal of Sociology, 91*(3), 616–647.

Freedman, D., Thornton, A., Camburn, D., Alwin, D., & Young-Demarco, L. (1988). The life history calendar: A technique for collecting retrospective data. *Sociological Methodology, 18,* 37–68.

Freedman, R. (1979). Theories of fertility decline: A reappraisal. *Social Forces, 58,* 1.

Fricke, T. (1986). *Himalayan households: Tamang demography and domestic processes.* Ann Arbor, MI: UMI Research Press.

Ghimire, D. J. (2003). *The social context of first birth timing in Nepal.* Unpublished PhD dissertation, University of Michigan.

Ghimire, D. J., Axinn, W. G., Yabiku, S. T., & Thornton, A. (2006). Social change, premarital nonfamily experiences and spouse choice in an arranged-marriage society. *American Journal of Sociology.*

Gurung, H. B. (1980). *Vignettes of Nepal.* Kathmandu: Sajha Prakashan.

His Majesty's Government. (2001). *Statistical year book of Nepal 2001.* His Majesty's Government, National Planning Commission Secretariat, Central Bureau of Statistics, Ramshah Path, Thapathali, Kathmandu.

Hitchcock, J. T. (1966). *The Magars of Banyan Hill.* New York: Holt, Rinehart, and Wilson.

Kasarda, J. D., Billy, J. O. G., & West, K. (1986). *Status enhancement and fertility: Reproductive responses to social mobility and educational opportunity.* Orlando, FL: Academic Press.

Knodel, J. (1987). Starting, stopping, and spacing during the early stages of fertility transition: The experience of German village populations in the 18th and 19th centuries. *Demography, 24,* 143–162.

Kohn, M. L. (1983). On the transmission of values in the family: A preliminary formulation. *Research in Sociology of Education and Socialization, 4,* 3–12.

Lesthaeghe, R., & Surkyn, J. (1988). Cultural dynamics and economics theories of fertility change. *Population and Development Review, 14,* 1–45.

Lesthaeghe, R., & Wilson, C. (1986). Modes of production, secularization and the pace of fertility decline in western Europe, 1870–1930. In A. Coale & S. C. Watkins (Eds.), *The decline of fertility in Europe* (pp. 261–292). Princeton, NJ: Princeton University Press.

Lightbourne, R. E. (1984). *Fertility preferences in Guyana, Jamaica, and Trinidad and Tobago, from the World Fertility Survey 1975–1977: A multiple indicator approach.* Voorburg, Netherlands: International Statistical Institute.

Mannheim, K. (1952). The problem of generations. In D. Kecskemeti (Ed.), *Essays in the sociology of knowledge* (pp. 286–323). London: Routledge and Kagan.

McFarlane, A. (1976). *Resources and population: A study of the Gurungs of Nepal.* Cambridge: Cambridge University Press.

McNicoll, G. (1980). Institutional determinants of fertility change. *Population and Development Review, 6,* 441–462.

McNicoll, G. (1984). Notes on the local context of demographic change. In *Fertility and the family: Proceedings of the Expert Group on Fertility and Family* (pp. 411–426). New York: UN.

Messerschmidt, D. A. (1976). Ecological change and adaptation among the Gurungs of the Nepal himalaya. *Human Ecology, 4,* 167–185.

Montgomery, M. R., & Casterline, J. B. (1993). The diffusion of fertility control in Taiwan: Evidence from pooled cross-section time-series models. *Population Studies, 47,* 457–479.

Notestein, F. W. (1953). Economic problems of population change. In *The economics of population and food supplies* (pp. 13–31). Proceedings of the Eighth International Conference of Agricultural Economics. London: Oxford University Press.

Ogburn, W. F., & Nimkoff, M. F. (1955). *Technology and the changing family.* Boston: Houghton Mifflin.

Pearce, L. D. (2000). *The multidimensional impact of religion on childbearing preferences and behavior in Nepal.* Unpublished PhD dissertation, Pennsylvania State University, University Park.

Pokharel, B. N., & Shivakoti, G. P. (1986). *Impact of development efforts on agricultural wage labor. Rural Poverty Paper Series* No. 1. Winrock, Nepal.

Presser, H. B. (1986). Changing values and falling birth rates. *Population and Development Review, 12*(suppl.), 196–200.

Rindfuss, R. R. (1991). The young adult years: Diversity, structural change, and fertility. *Demography, 28,* 493–512.

Ryder, N. B. (1965). The cohort as a concept in the study of social change. *American Sociological Review, 30,* 843–861.

Shivakoti, G. P., & Pokharel, B. N. (1989). Marketing of major crops in Chitwan: A case study of six village panchayats. Research Report Series No. 8, Winrock, Nepal.

Suwal, J. V. (2001). Socio-cultural dynamics of first birth intervals in Nepal. *Contribution to Nepalese Studies, 28*(1), 11–33.

Thornton, A. (2001). The developmental paradigm, reading history sideways, and family change. *Demography, 38*(4), 449–465.

Thornton, A., & Fricke, T. (1987). Social change and the family: Comparative perspectives from the West, China, and South Asia. *Sociological Forum, 2*(4), 746–79.

Thornton, A., & Lin, H. S. (1994). *Social change and the family in Taiwan.* Chicago: University of Chicago Press.

Tuladhar, J. M. (1989). *The persistence of high fertility in Nepal.* New Delhi: Inter-India Publications.

Watkins, S. C. (1991). *From provinces into nations: Demographic integration in Western Europe, 1870–1960.* Princeton, NJ: Princeton University Press.

Watkins, S. C., & Danzi, A. D. (1995). Women's gossip and social change: Childbirth and fertility control among Italian and Jewish women in the United States. *Gender and Society, 9*, 469–90.

Willis, R. (1973). A new approach to the economic theory of fertility behavior. *Journal of Political Economy, 81*, 14–64.

Yabiku, S. T. (2002). *Social organization and marriage timing in Nepal.* Unpublished PhD dissertation, University of Michigan, Ann Arbor.

Yabiku, S. T. (2005). The effect of nonfamily experiences on age of marriage in a setting of rapid social change. *Population Studies, 59*(3), 339–354.

Yabiku, S. T. (2006). Neighbors and neighborhoods: Effects on marriage timing. *Population Research and Policy Review, 25*(4), 305–327.

Yabiku, S. T., Axinn, W. G., & Thornton, A. (1999). Family integration and children's self-esteem. *American Journal of Sociology, 104*, 1494–1524.

11

Family Change in Turkey: Peasant Society, Islam, and the Revolution "From Above"

Bernard Nauck
Daniela Klaus
Department of Sociology
Chemnitz University of Technology
Chemnitz, Germany

Turkey is a very interesting case for the study of diversity and change in family systems. The following analysis describes how three cultural layers have contributed to this diversity and change: Turkey's history as a peasant society, the religious influences of Islam in a basically heterogeneous setting of the Ottoman Empire, and the cultural revolution in the process of modern nation building. Together, these three layers have helped to create the exceptional cultural heterogeneity and family life seen in Turkey today.

In the first part of the analysis, the implications of these cultural layers for family and kinship regimes in Turkey are described, setting the ground for an analysis of recent changes in Turkish families and their relationship to changes in the larger social structure. Two shifts are examined in particular: changes in the spousal relationship and related gender issues, and changes in intergenerational relationships and related fertility trends. For this purpose, various data sources are used, including public vital statistics and results from social surveys. In many cases, however, the availability of representative data on families in Turkey beyond vital statistics is rather limited, especially with regard to a systematic observation of social change.

THREE CULTURAL INFLUENCES ON THE CONTEMPORARY
TURKISH FAMILY AND KINSHIP SYSTEM

Asia Minor, or Anatolia as it is called nowadays, of which present-day Turkey predominantly consists, has been invaded and occupied by a series of ethnic groups throughout history, a few of which include the Greeks, Macedonians, Persians, Arabs, Armenians, Kurds, Turkmen, and the Norman crusaders. The Turkmen, pastoral nomads originating from Central Asia, were relative latecomers, invading Anatolia in several waves from the 6th century onward (Güvenc, 1994). This history has led to an amalgamation and coexistence in Turkish society of various cultural influences and traditions, the resulting heterogeneity of which makes Turkey an interesting but difficult case for the study of cultural bases of family systems. Moreover, knowledge about the social history of the family in Anatolia, which takes these various influences into account, is fragmented and still in its embryonic stage. These caveats can be considered as we trace the origins of the family life forms found in present-day Turkey to three essential cultural factors in history.

Influence of the Peasant Society

The first and most influential factor is that, until modern times, the majority of the population on the territory of the Turkish state has been a segmented rural peasant society. The resulting kinship system is characterized by patrilineal descent, endogamy with preferred marriage between cousins according to the exchange principle of cross-cousin marriage (Lévi-Strauss, 1993), equality of brothers in inheritance, and patrilocality of extended family households as the principle unit of subsistence economy. These family characteristics serve as efficient institutional regulations for securing the necessary workforce within the production unit and the necessary production factor—land—across generations for the lineage. However, this peasant society has always coexisted with a variety of minorities, especially in the urban areas and along the coast, who specialize in income resources—for example, the Greeks in trading and fishing, the Jenissary in military service, and some Kurdish tribes in nomadic shepherding.

This ethnic pluralism, together with regional differences in predominance of urban and rural cultures, has led to the antagonistic situation that two fundamentally different conceptions of marriage coexist: the "patrilineal descent" and the "affinal" regime.

The Regime of Patrilineal Descent. In the rural parts of Turkey, a conception of marriage prevails that is based on an exchange of goods and human capital within or between kinship systems, with the logical consequence that the families of origin having a strong influence on the partner-selection process and that the prime loyalty goes to the community of descent in comparison to the conjugal relationship. Family formation in rural Turkey is characterized by these kinds of arranged marriages, by early marriage in the absence of any necessity of economic independence, by patrilocal residence after marriage, and by a nearly total inclusion of the population into marriage.

Contrary to popular views, these characteristics are not the result of Islamic influences, but instead can be traced back to pre-Islamic times. In fact, these characteristics show strong parallels to the non-Islamic societies of the Balkans and of the northern rim of the Black Sea, and are fundamentally different from the "Central European" neolocal pattern of family formation (Anderson, 1980; Duben, 1985a; Hajnal, 1965). As described by Bastug (2002), the patrilocal household in Turkey is

> the joint residence of a minimal patrilineage and is headed by the senior male. Property is for the most part held in common and viewed as the property of the lineage. The children of the males will be members of the patrilineage and their sons will remain in the household after marriage. Daughters of the household ... will leave their natal household at marriage to join that of their husbands, and their children will be members of their husbands' lineages. (p. 102)

Many "custom law" regulations of marriage, family, and kinship from the rural traditions of what is now Turkey can be traced back more than 2,000 years, and have remained stable in their basic principles of patrilineal organization. However, significant changes in the marriage system occurred when the tribally organized Turkmen nomads began to settle around 1000 A.D. and engaged in agricultural production. The nomadic Turkmen tribes were strictly exogamous—that is, people with a common male ancestor within seven generations were not allowed to marry—which made the payment of bride-wealth in exchange for giving away a daughter a necessity. With the process of settlement, however, exogamy was replaced by endogamy, reestablishing the marriage between close relatives as the preferred form (Bastug, 2002, p. 103).

Some of the Turkish "custom law" regulations contradict markedly codified Islamic law, especially those in regard to the payment of bride-wealth to the woman's family of origin and the exclusion of women from heritage (Ortayli, 1985). All types of heritage, varying from the oldest son as the single inheritor, to the equal distribution of family estate among all male descendants, to the equal distribution, regardless of the sex of the offspring, are evident for Turkey throughout the Ottoman

Empire. However, the main type of family dissolution involves, in connection with the patrilocal residence of the male descendants, the preservation of property and decision-making power in the hands of the patriarch until his death, and his establishment as the public representative of the entire family (his wife, his unmarried daughters, his male offspring with their wives and children). In the case of the patriarch's death, the family dissolves. The sons typically inherit equal shares of the family property and become patriarchs of their own families. The widow of the former patriarch lives in one of her sons' households, preferably with her eldest son (Duben, 1985a; Schiffauer, 1987).

These rules of inheritance proved to be stable until well into the 20th century, as they did not, before then, contribute to the scattering of land ownership and thus the increasing poverty of the rural population. This stable situation was endorsed by two factors: the availability of land and the low mean life expectation. Land availability existed because property rights were based on common law and related to cultivation: The family that cultivated a piece of land was the acknowledged owner. Because large pieces of uncultivated land surrounded rural villages, these could be taken into possession in response to changes in family size and available workforce. Another decisive influence on these inheritance patterns was the high mortality rate until the beginning of the 20th century (Coale & Demeny, 1966). Duben (1985a) describes this effect on family life:

> 64% of children reached the age of 1, but only 47% reached the age of 20. That is, roughly half of all children born probably never lived to marry and have children of their own. If the expectation of life for males at age 20, which we can take as the age at first marriage for males, was 36, and if we calculate the probability of giving birth to a son occurring roughly four years after marriage, then we can conclude that only about 35% of all fathers had a chance of being alive to witness the marriage of their first born son. Most fathers would have been dead eight years before the happy event, and most sons would have come into their inheritance early in life and might have lived in a simple family household once their siblings were grown and married. (p. 125)

This family system has always implied extensive variation during the family life cycle in regard to household size and the complexity of the family structure. These variations depend especially on the age at marriage, the number of male descendants who reach marriage age, and the dying age of the patriarch. In any case, the time span in which families have complex, extended structures is limited. Accordingly, the proportions of extended family household never dominated in any historical period and never exceeded one-third of the households during the last four centuries.

The Bilinear-Affinal Regime.   In urban and coastal parts of Turkey, the widely accepted conception of marriage is based on romantic love— with freedom to choose one's marriage partner and an emphasis on the conjugal relationship—and it generally occurs within a bilineal kinship system (with a rather weak influence given to the respective families of origin). In fact, this form of marriage—the so-called Western European marriage pattern (Hajnal, 1965)—can be traced back historically and culturally to the *urban societies* of ancient Greece (Goody, 1990), and thus to the territory that is now Turkey. It may be concluded from some indications that this family type has survived in the urban centers of Western Anatolia, where the Greek influence remained strong throughout the existence of the Ottoman Empire. Accordingly, the existence of this marriage type in Turkey is not to be seen as a result of recent social developments alone, but of long-lasting cultural antagonisms.

Indeed, this coexisting "affinal" kinship regime is in many ways the opposite of the dominating descendance regime, as it is based on monogamy and exogamy, cognatic descent and kindred, and neolocality (and thus nuclear families), instead of polygamy and endogamy, unilineal descent and lineages, patrilocality, and extended households.

Influence of Islam

A second influential factor, which in the literature is not always systematically separated from the heritage of peasant society, is Islam. The first Turkish tribes adopted Islam in the 7th century, and by the year 1000 most of the Turkish population in Anatolia was Islamic (Bastug, 2002). Since 1517, the sultan has been the religious leader, and until 1924, the caliph ruled as the head of the state with spiritual powers (Ahmad, 1993, p. 52ff.). Islam had, at least during the long historical period of the existence of the Ottoman Empire, legally enforced and legitimated some specific family forms, such as polygamy and sex segregation with the beginning of maturity. Islam also successfully fought against any ancestor worship—as Judaism and Christianity also did. This contributed considerably to the destruction of the powerful lineages of the nomadic Turkmen, as it removed the cultural base for the remembrance of common ancestors and created the ground for smaller patrilineal units of intergenerational solidarity.

Under Islamic law the husband was allowed not only to marry up to four women but also to purchase as many female slaves as he wanted and to cast off his wife. Contrary to the institutional regulations of lineage and patrilinearity related to rural subsistence economy, Islam considered women to have an individual right to property and inheritance independent of their marriage relationship. Accordingly, the Moslem religion forbade the bride's father or other kin from appropriating the bride-wealth and left it entirely in the hand of the woman to be given in marriage. Islamic law also demands that the bride-wealth be documented in the marriage register and be paid in two parts as an endowment: one part on the occasion of the marriage, the other part out of the inheritance in case of divorce or if the husband dies (Ortayli, 1985, p. 96).

Although these parts of Islamic law were adopted to a large extent in the cities, the custom law of patrilineal inheritance prevailed in the villages. It has to be considered, however, that several smaller schools of belief have coexisted during the Ottoman Empire in the territory that is now Turkey, each having its own normative guidelines for marriage and family. Two of these are represented by the Sunites and Alevites, with the Alevites having a more liberal worldview and a stronger emphasis on women's entitlements and less sex segregation. In addition, other religious minorities such as Greek Orthodox Christians and Jews lived according to their own legal systems and maintained their own family regulations. In fact, not much is known about the specifics of Islamic traditions in Turkish family life. As most of the knowledge about Islamic families is either based on religious or legal studies or on Arabic families (Goody, 1990, p. 361ff.), it is quite uncertain to what extent it was adopted in Turkish society.

Influence of Kemalist Reforms

Finally, the foundation of the Turkish Republic in the 1920s also influenced the modern family structure in Turkey. This event not only established a secular state according to the principles of Western democracies, including the division of power between legislative, executive, and jurisdiction branches, it also initiated a "cultural revolution from above," as the founder, Kemal Atatürk, imposed on the Turkish society a series of legal reforms without any preparatory phase. The Kemalist revolution was intended from the beginning to be part of a process of Westernization (Garbcilik) (Caporal, 1982, pp. 197f.) that would pave the way for Turkey to become an advanced civilization driven by the ideas of developmental idealism (Thornton, 2005, p. 134ff.).

The flavor of this Westernization and modernization movement can be seen in Atatürk's rhetoric of the period: "There are different countries, but there is only one civilization. Prerequisite for the progress of a nation is to participate in this one civilization" (Aksan, 1981, p. 31); "The civilized world is far ahead of us. We have no choice but to catch up.... We shall adopt...works of Western civilization. Uncivilized people are doomed to be trodden under the feet of civilized people" (Mango, 2004, p. 438). In his famous "long speech" (*nutuk*) to the delegates of the Republican Party in 1927, Atatürk stressed that the reform of the family law, a strategic part of his program of Westernization, would "lift the nation to a level it deserves in the civilized world."

In this sense, "Westernization" meant for Atatürk also the adoption of the nuclear family model according to the bourgeois family ideal, with a division of labor between spouses but a strong emphasis on the importance of women's roles. As pointed out by Arat (1994, p. 60ff.), Atatürk's many speeches confirm the high value he assigned to women "as productive and reproductive forces."

- "If it is found to be sufficient to have only one of the two sexes that compose a society equipped with the contemporary needs. More than half of that society would remain weak. ... Therefore, if knowledge and technology are necessary for our society, both our men and women have to acquire them equally" (Atatürk, 1952, p.151).
- "I would emphasize again that apart from their public responsibilities they bear, women have the highly important duty of being successful mothers. ... Women must be highly qualified so that they may educate the next generation in all the attributes it will need to function properly in the contemporary world and in our society" (Kemal Atatürk in Konya 1923, in Taskiran, 1976, p. 56).
- "The highest duty of women is motherhood. If one realizes fully that education of both, boys and girls, starts in infancy, the importance of motherhood becomes evident" (Kemal Atatürk in Izmir 1923, in Taskiran 1976, p. 59).

In 1926, the national assembly passed a civil code, which was practically a complete adoption of the Swiss civil code. In the same year, it proceeded similarly with the Italian penal law, and in 1929, the German code of criminal procedure was adopted. This legal reform implied and was accompanied by the following measures.

- The prohibition of "religious" gowns in public and the enforcement of "Western" dress for civil servants (1925).
- The introduction of the Gregorian calendar, the 24-hour clock, and the Latin alphabet (1926).

- The introduction of monogamy and state-registered marriage as the only legal form of marriage (1926).
- The introduction of the active and passive right of female voting (1926/1934).
- Coeducation in middle schools (1927) and high schools (1934).
- The abolishment of Islam as state religion (1928).
- Compulsory secular schooling for boys and girls, and the prohibition of religious schools (1928).
- Sunday as a weekly public holiday (1934).
- The introduction of family names (1934).

The new civil code abolished religious jurisdiction and Islamic family law (Seriat). The consent of both partners was a requirement for marriage; only civil marriage ceremonies and legal forms of divorce were officially recognized; one-sided disownment of the wife by the husband and polygamy were made illegal; and women were granted property and inheritance rights (Abadan-Unat, 1987; Karasan-Dirks, 1980). The penal code also followed European trends in pronatalistic population policy and outlawed abortion (penal code of 1926) and sterilization (penal code of 1936). With the Law of Public Health of 1930, the government aimed at increasing the number of births and decreasing the number of deaths, with a target population of 50 million. In this context, the import, production, and sale of contraceptives were forbidden.

The legal age of marriage was increased to 18 years for men and 17 years for women. Interestingly, in 1938 it was again reduced to 17 and 15 years, respectively, because the new regulation was hardly enforceable nationwide. However, the new civil code left the superior position of husbands largely untouched (as was the case in those European countries at that time, from which the code was adopted). For instance, women could not take outside work or travel abroad without the permission of the male head of the household. The Kemalist reform thus did not eliminate legal sex inequalities—not only because the implemented Swiss civil code did not aim for equal opportunities for men and women, but also because "state feminism" (Arat, 1994, p. 59) pursued the improvement of the women's situation just as far as the women's (re)productive importance served to enhance the Westernization of the country. The push to increase female educational participation was, for the most part, intended to expand the state's influence in socialization via mother-to-child promulgation of the Kemalist ideology, and to improve women's ability to "raise the next generation of men" (Arat, 1994, p. 60). In fact, the family policy under Atatürk pursued more generally the weakening of the patriarch's influence on behalf of a higher state control over families.

The "women issue" is a political arena where the antagonisms of peasant society ("Turkism"), Islam, and Kemalism have clashed. As the most prominent feminist Turkish social scientist points out: "Current debates on women continue to express the tensions between Westernization, Islam, and Turkism, and one cannot help but note the persistence of both the concerns expressed and the imagery used to express them. The issues of women's dress and conduct are still used by the state to signify political intent, although women nowadays increasingly appear as active participants and militants in causes concerning them" (Kandiyoti, 1989, p. 144).

These three influential factors did not supersede or merge entirely with one another, but instead retained some separate impacts on marriage and the family. This has led to diverging developments and, in contemporary Turkey, a variety of coexisting family types with sometimes antagonistic norms. The persistence (or even the predominance) of elements of a peasant culture in the modern Turkish family structure is not surprising, given the peasant culture's long history and its underpinning of the evolution of stable family structures in the territory of Turkey (Ortayli, 1985, p. 104).

The institutional antagonisms to be found in the Turkish family and kinship system are thus mainly the result of "ideational" influences: the overlay of Islamic influences and Kemalist reforms on the long-time patrilineal regime, which had been evolutionary stable under the conditions of subsistence economy. At least for the Kemalist revolution, these influences have been both direct and indirect. The direct influences resulted from changes made to the civil and penal codes of Turkey's legal system and their (partial) enforcement; the indirect, amplifying effects resulted from changes in the population structure, including life expectancy, migration, education, and labor-force opportunities, as discussed in the next section.

Although empirical evidence is hardly available, it can be additionally assumed that the educational system, especially higher education, also has direct effects on family change through exposure of students to Westernization. High proportions of the teaching staff of Turkish universities get their academic training and their degrees in Anglo-Saxon countries; the curricula of schools and universities follow the principles of individualism, secularism, and rationalism; and the elite universities follow American models—teaching in English and often from American textbooks. This Western influence is seen in the teaching of the Turkish social sciences, for example, which typically follow the interpretations of family sociology represented by Engels (1884/1970), Durkheim (1921), Ogburn (1928), Parsons (1943), or Goode (1963), who related consensual marriage to "modernization" and to the division of production and reproduction in the process of industrialization. This interpretation supports the conceptual framework of Kemalist reforms in particular and the "developmental paradigm" in general (Thornton 2005), holding out the family structure of urban Turkey as a success story of modernization and disregarding the more recent results of research in the history of family since Hajnal (1965, 1982).

SOCIETAL CHANGES SINCE NATION BUILDING

Diverging Family Types

One political consequence of the imposed Kemalist reforms was that the legitimation of many political measures in the population was always weak and challenged by opposing political movements. Although the state was organized as a strongly centralized bureaucracy and based on considerable military power—which was, in fact, the backbone of democracy and legal principles over the decades—the state has never been able to enforce its legal principles throughout its entire territory. Thus, the notoriously weak state has contributed considerably to the antagonistic coexistence of different family types in the 20th century.

For example, the introduction of a minimal marriage age and the necessity of consent between the bride and the groom has not eliminated early and arranged marriages, and the refusal of the state to acknowledge noncivil marriages has not eliminated religious weddings. Moreover, religious ceremonies are considered by a large part of the population to be a legitimate substitute for, rather than merely a preliminary or subsequent addition to, the ceremony at the registry office. In some rare cases this form of marriage is also associated with polygamy, which is still followed, although at a decreasing frequency, in some population groups. In the Kurdish part of the population, polygamy frequently takes the form of the *levirat*, that is, the marriage of a brother's widow (Yalcin-Heckmann, 1991). A side effect of the existence and tolerance of polygamous marriages is that extramarital involvements among urban males are to some extent indistinguishable from rural polygamy and thus much easier to legitimate in public. Religious ceremonies are also increasingly chosen by young couples in urban regions to legitimize their sexual relationship without submitting themselves to any legally binding commitments or being forced to initiate civil divorce proceedings if the relationship ends.

The most frequent reason for the preference of religious marriages (habitualized-traditional behavior aside) is, however, that it allows the families of origin to ignore the minimal age requirement and significantly increase their influence over the marriage arrangements. The lack of state recognition of such marriages eliminates legal regulation of such practical matters as lineage, insurance benefits, and inheritance, which increases the dependence of the young married couple on stable relationships to the respective families of origin. Various practices of the state (e.g., campaigns encouraging couples to "legalize" their relationships by postregistering their religious marriages) and of other involved parties (including the paternal adoption of children born outside of a legal marriage and quite complicated donations within the kinship system) aim to harmonize the de jure and de facto situations of religious marriages. Frequently, the postregistration of a religious marriage happens after the minimal age of marriage is reached. These differences between religious and registered marriages contribute considerably to discrepancies between the age-at-first-marriage statistics derived from register data, which capture only civic marriages (with concomitant age minimums), and demographic survey data, which capture both religious and civic marriages (see Table 11.1).

Differences in family forms were further increased by considerable population growth, which resulted from decreasing mortality in combination with stable high fertility, and which led to extensive regional and international migration.

Population Growth

The first census of the Turkish Republic in 1927 counted 13.6 million inhabitants (State Institute of Statistics, 2003, p. 45ff.). The pronatalistic policy of this period reflected the significant population losses and high infant mortality resulting from the liberation war at the beginning of the 20th century. As Shorter (2000) describes the situation:

> Turkey was still a long way from having a population adequately balanced by gender, age composition, and marital relationships within families, signified by proportions widowed, unmarried, and married. Individual families probably were aware of imbalances, such as too many dependents and not enough males to plow and enlarge the fields. Widowhood was a serious matter, amounting to 23% of adult women (age 20 and over) in 1935. In 1927, it had been as high as 30% in the Western provinces. (p. 107)

TABLE 11.1
Family-Related Indices

Year	Age of Women at First Marriage — Register Data	Age of Women at First Marriage — Survey Data	CMR	Percentage — Married	Percentage — Divorced	Percentage of Divorces — Divorces of Childless	Percentage of Divorces — In First Year of Marriage	Age of Women at First Birth	TFR
1930	19.5[a]	x	6.30[d]	x	x	x	x	x	x
1935	19.7[a]	x	5.50[d]	68[e]	0.5[f]	66[h]	x	x	x
1940	19.9[a]	x	7.90[d]	x	x	59[h]	5[h]	x	6.7[m]
1945	20.1[a]	x	9.20[d]	66[e]	0.5[f]	61[h]	8[h]	x	6.6[m]
1950	19.7[a]	x	9.50[d]	67[e]	0.8[f]	62[h]	6[h]	x	6.9[m]
1955	18.1[a]	x	9.50[d]	71[e]	0.8[f]	62[h]	7[h]	x	6.5[m]
1960	19.2[a]	15[c]	7.70[d]	73[e]	0.8[f]	56[h]	10[h]	x	6.2[n]
1965	19.6[a]	16[c]	7.30[d]	72[e]	0.8[f]	52[h]	9[h]	x	5.8[n]
1970	19.9[b]	17[c]	7.10[d]	61[e]	0.7[f]	55[h]	11[h]	20[k]	5.7[n]
1975	20.1[b]	18[c]	6.80[d]	59[e]	0.7[f]	53[h]	12[h]	20[k]	5.1[n]
1980	20.7[b]	19[c]	8.30[d]	61[e]	0.7[f]	46[h]	12[h]	21[k]	4.4[n]
1985	21.5[b]	19[c]	7.30[d]	60[f]	0.7[f]	46[h]	11[h]	22[l]	3.6[n]
1990	22.0[b]	20[c]	8.20[d]	61[f]	0.8[f]	44[h]	13[h]	x	3.0[n]
1995	22.2[b]	20[c]	7.60[d]	x	x	45[h]	13[h]	x	2.6[n]
2000	22.0[b]	x	6.8[d]	60[g]	1.1[g]	44[l]	19[l]	x	2.5[n]

Note. Sources: [a]State Institute of Statistics, 2001, p. 5. [b]Council of Europe, 2001. [c]Authors' calculation based on the Turkish Demographic Health Survey (THDS), 1998. [d]CMR= crude marriage rate, State Institute of Statistics, 2001, p. 28. [e]State Institute of Statistics, 2004, pp. 27, 59. [f]State Institute of Statistics, 2001, p. 14, population aged 15 and older. [g]State Institute of Statistics, 2004, p. 39. [h]State Institute of Statistics, 2001, p. 30ff. [l]State Institute of Statistics, 2004, p. 65. [k]Council of Europe, 1987, p. 69. [l]Council of Europe, 1995, 43. [m]Shorter, and Macura, 1982, p. 32. [n] State Institute of Statistics, 2003b.

The child mortality rate (between 0 and 5) was as high as "27% of births, and an average life expectancy of 35 years (1935–1940). For those who lived to the age of five, the average expectation of remaining life was 50 years" (Shorter, 2000, p. 116). Within 20 years (by 1955), life expectancy increased to 60 for women and 62 for men (Shorter & Macura, 1982). Stable high fertility together with increased life expectancy led to a fast increase in population size, which almost doubled, to 24 million, by 1955 (State Institute of Statistics, 2003, p. 45ff.).

Migration

One consequence of the population growth within the second half of the 20th century was that it pushed the customary rules of inheritance to their limits, providing fewer and fewer opportunities for patrilocal residence of all-male descendants and their families and pushing them into a massive out-migration into the urban centers and to foreign countries. This process was fueled by large regional disparities in industrialization and an imbalance in the allocation of workplaces. The internal migration took place mainly from rural to urban and from the east to the west (Western Turkey was much more industrialized), resulting over the past 50 years in large decreases of the rural population and especially of Eastern Anatolian rural areas. This area-specific depopulation occurred despite a nationwide fertility rate well above the replacement level and a population that grew to 68 million by 2000 (State Institute of Statistics, 2003, pp. 45ff.). Today, the majority of the population of Turkey lives in urban agglomerations. Although in 1927 about 76% of the total population was rural, by 2000 the share had declined to 35% (State Institute of Statistics, 2003, p. 45ff.).

About one-half of the urban population in Turkey today is comprised of rural immigrants (Kagitcibasi & Sunar, 1992). They typically enter the urban metropolises via building houses "within one night" in extensive squatter areas (*gecekondu*) on public property, where they live sometimes for generations. In these settlements, the Turkish custom law of landownership survives somehow in a transformed way, as it makes use of the basic principle that those who own the land make use of it. Amnesties by the state occur on regular bases (and are thus highly anticipated by the inhabitants); they transform this custom law practice into the "legal" ownership of real estate. The same happens when the users of a particular piece of land can "prove" that they have cultivated it for a certain period of time. This practice, however, is becoming less common.

Because rural migrants in urban metropolises normally maintain strong social ties to their regions of origin and due to the common chain migration, which means that family members or members from the former neighborhood frequently follow the initial rural-to-urban migrants (Erder, 2001, p. 122), the migration process has only partially resulted in an urbanization of the family lifestyle. In fact, migration has primarily led to greater visibility of the differences between previously segmented and regionally separated population groups. This has contributed considerably to an increase in social tensions, whereas marriages between the respective population groups remain on a very low level (Gündüz-Hosgör & Smits, 2002).

Labor Market

Until recently, the economic structure of Turkey remained rather unchanged, as the distributions of workplaces in the respective sectors show. From 1935 until 1960, about 80% of the workplaces were to be found in the agricultural sector, and the rest were divided up equally between industry and the service sector (Buhbe, 1996, p. 244ff.; World Bank, 1984, p. 258). By 2000, the distribution of workplaces has changed to 48% in the agricultural sector, 18% in the industrial, and 34% in the service sector (State Institute of Statistics, 2003, p. 55). With continuing population growth, the urban labor market now faces the problem of a growing labor force accompanied by a stagnation of the economy since the recession in the middle of the 1980s. Because women are particularly disadvantaged in this labor market competition, as they are less educated than their male counterparts (Ergöcmen, 1997, p. 86ff.; Özbay, 1985, p. 128f.), many do not work outside their homes. However, low-income families are often dependent on the female's income (Özbay, 1985, p. 133; Sönmez, 1996), which means that these women are frequently restricted to the informal sector—to unqualified jobs with bad working conditions, poor salary, and exclusion from social insurance (Ecevit, 1988; Kazgan, 1985, p. 88ff.; Özbay, 1988).

Education

Despite the overall increase of the educational level over the past several decades, the weakness of the Turkish State preserved the existing inequalities in educational attainment. The introduction of compulsory schooling with the foundation of the republic resulted in a strong decrease in illiteracy rates (Ergöcmen, 1997, p. 85; Tansel, 1998, p. 2). In

1935, the literacy rate of females of six years and older was 10% compared with 29% among males; by 2000 literacy rates had increased considerably for both females and male—to 81% and 94%, respectively—but the gender gap clearly remains (State Institute of Statistics, 2003, p. 49).

In addition to gender inequalities, educational participation varies in Turkey by residence and social status as well. In 1999, about 82% of children aged 6 to 14 years attended school in cities compared with 74% in rural areas (State Institute of Statistics, 2000). As the introduction of compulsory schooling was not enforced in all regions with the same intensity, the opportunity for secondary schooling also differs markedly by region and social status. This differential opportunity has increasingly polarized the life chances of rural and urban women, in particular, and their dependency on their families of origin or their husbands. Although the women in the rural parts of Eastern Turkey (where the Kurdish population is prevalent) have gained least from educational expansion, the female descendants of the middle and upper classes in the urban metropolises have experienced the strongest gains in educational degrees. According to the combined results of the Turkish Demographic and Health Surveys (TDHS) from 1993 and 1998 (Hacettepe University Institute of Population Studies, 1994, 1999):

> About one quarter of the Kurdish males and more than 70% of the Kurdish females have not completed primary education. For the Turks these percentages are 7 and 22 percent, respectively. Only 2.8 percent of the Kurdish males and 0.5 percent of the Kurdish females have more than secondary education, against more than 10 percent of the Turkish males and almost 5 percent of the Turkish females. (Gündüz-Hosgör & Smits, 2002, p. 424)

The impact of both the structural changes in Turkish societies and the ideational factors of Kemalist reforms on two aspects of family systems—spousal relationships and intergenerational relationships—is discussed next.

THE SPOUSAL RELATIONSHIP

Modes of Marriage

Even in recent years arranged marriages have remained quite common in Turkey. Calculations based on the TDHS of 1993 and 1998 (see Figure 11.1) indicate that about 50% of all first-married women in the most recent marriage cohort available (1989–1998) have an arranged marriage,

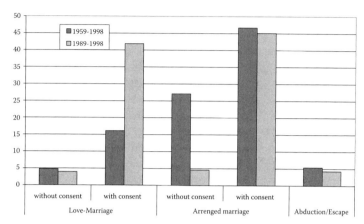

FIGURE 11.1   Modes of first-marriage of Turkish women by marriage cohort.

Source: Authors' calculations based on the TDHS of 1993 and 1998.

compared to 46% with a couple-initiated marriage. However, we also see change over time in the significantly larger proportion of family-arranged marriages (74%) for the 1959–1968 marriage cohort displayed in Figure 11.1. Systematical variations by region of residence, degree of urbanization, and education are also identifiable. The *affinal marriage regime* with its prime solidarity in the spousal unit is widely accepted among the better educated parts of the urban population, for whom the autonomous choice of a marriage partner and a marriage of consent are seen as essential components of the legitimation of romantic love. The *patrilineal marriage regime of descent,* with its prime solidarity in intergenerational relationships, is especially widespread in the rural population, the Middle, North, South, and Eastern Anatolian provinces, as well as among the less educated (migrants) in the Turkish metropolises.

Within the patrilineal marriage regime, marriages regulate the allocation of female labor between the communities of descent. Female descendants leave their household community after marriage and are substituted by daughters-in-law, if possible. Two institutional regulations exist to balance the interests of the communities of descent (Lévi-Strauss, 1993): the payment of bride-wealth, and reciprocal marriages. The *payment of bride-wealth* means a material transfer from the family of origin of the groom to the family of origin of the bride (*baslik*). Similar to recent changes in family-arranged marriages, the payment of bride-wealth experienced a tremendous decline in frequency, with the percentage dropping from 48% to 18% over the 30 years of observation. This custom also varies substantially by region and education, which is another strong indication for the unequal distribution of the two marriage regimes. Looking at the marriage cohort 1989–1998, bride-wealth was paid for 53% of women from the eastern part of Turkey compared to 16% in the west, and for 52% of women without any education compared to 3% of women with at least a secondary education. Bride-wealth payments are a major subject of the negotiations between the family of the bride and the family of the groom, typically represented by third parties. The tradition of the so-called matchmakers prevents the loss of honor in case the negotiations break down.

Probably stemming from the custom of nomadic tribes in Eastern Anatolia, there also exists the institution of marriage by abduction, that is, wedding without the permit of the families of origin and without bride-wealth payments. This does not always take place against the will of the bride, who may see this as an opportunity to escape from the control of her family of origin in creating "facts." This may also occur when a marriage desired by both future spouses is in danger because of the amount of bride-wealth, because of an inferior position in the rank order of the to be married siblings, or because of the parents' prohibition of marriage in general (Özgen, 1985)—for example, if they do not want to lose members of their female labor force. Figure 11.1 (fifth column) suggests the continued existence of this custom today, although only around 4% of the marriages surveyed were formed in this manner.

As the allocation of female labor force is the major purpose of arranged marriages in peasant societies, strong incentives for *reciprocal marriages* are created. Reciprocity can either be achieved by the exchange of brides between communities of descent or by marriage within one community of descent. In fact, marriages among close relatives, especially in the form of cross-cousin marriages, are very common in Turkey. According to the data from the TDHS of 1993 and 1998, around 25% of the first marriages of the surveyed women are between relatives, and 15% of these are to the son of an aunt or an uncle. Again, the percentage is significantly higher in East Turkey, where it amounts to 38%, and among women without any education, where the proportion is 36%, with obvious ethnic differences: According to the TDHS data for 1993, 39% of married Kurds and 21% of married Turks had marriages with relatives, and 86% of married Kurds and 73% of married Turks had arranged marriages (Gündüz-Hosgör & Smits, 2002).

If a large part of a population follows the descent marriage regime, sustaining consequences for the structure of the marriage market are inevitable. Not only are the criteria of partner selection affected, but also the marriage chances and the marriage process even of those parts of Turkish society that do not follow this marriage regime. Parental control interests with respect to the matchmaking process contribute to the high marriage rate in Turkey, which, in turn, increases incentives for early marriage. Any delay in partner selection reduces significantly the subsequent potential partner supply on the marriage market. This results in an early and highly standardized marriage process driven by the search for partners for the sons, the substitution of daughters by daughters-in-law, and the descendants' own interest in a status-oriented, successful marriage. In particular, the frequent *hypergamy* (upward status mobility via marriage) of young and physically attractive women reinforces the early marriage and its standardization. The marriage process is accelerated even further, because a considerable part of the partner selection process is already performed prematurely by arranged marriages between the families of origin and thus many potential female partners are withdrawn from the marriage market. As an overall result, women in Turkey are a scarce, highly valued good on a highly inflexible marriage market (Nauck, 2001), which results in a rather stable marital behavior illustrated by the statistics presented in Table 11.1.

By the mid-20th century a peak of marital inclusion was reached, with a very high marriage rate (9.5) and a relatively low mean age of women at first marriage (about 18 years in 1955 for registered marriages). This almost total inclusion into marriage is partly a result of a process of recovery subsequent to the human losses caused by the wars during the first quarter of the 20th century. Also, as shown in Table 11.1 (column 5), today nearly two-thirds of the population aged 15–49 is married. Correspondingly, remaining unwed or cohabiting hardly exists (Ataca, Kagitcibasi, & Diri, 2005, p. 98), and the proportion of divorced remained stable at a very low level (column 6) throughout the period examined. That many of these divorces occurred among the childless (column 7)—until the mid-20th century, about two-thirds of couples applying for a divorce had no children— suggests infertility as a main reason for divorce. The procreation of descendants traditionally has been deemed second in importance only to the allocation of female labor in terms of the purpose of marriage. The recent increase of parents getting divorced may signal changing modes and meanings of marriage, as does the increasing percentage of divorces within the first year of marriage. In 2000, 19% of registered divorces took place within the first 12 months of marriage (column 8), with "incompatibility" cited 94% of the time as the legal reason for divorce (State Institute of Statistics, 2004, p. 65). It may be assumed that increased expectations in marital quality, together with the absence of premarital relationships, have increased early divorces. Moreover, Turkish statistics register many more women than men as having the status of "divorced," reflecting the much higher acceptability of remarriage for men than for women (Sunar & Fisek, 2005).

Although available data demonstrate that modes of marriage have changed toward greater self-determination for the future spouses, the institution of marriage has maintained its utmost importance in Turkey throughout the past 70 years, and the situation within the marriage has proven to be rather resistant to change. The still widespread patrilineal descendent regime constitutes an advanced hierarchical structure in which the patriarch is considered to be the authority of the family and is entitled to make all decisions. This implies not only a strong status differentiation in favor of the elder descendants, but also to the advantage of the males. Thus, the spousal relationship is signified by the subsidiary status of women with respect to prestige and power (Fisek, 1993; Kagitcibasi, 1982a; Kandiyoti, 1988; Sunar, 2002).

Marital Power and Interaction

Gender inequalities are extensively studied in Turkey. Numerous papers depict the improving but still unequal female participation in education and the paid labor market and thus women's slow status increase since Atatürk's reforms (Ecevit, 1988; Erman, 2001; Kagitcibasi, 1982a; Kandiyoti, 1977, 1982, 1988; Kiray, 1976; Kuyas, 1982; Özbay, 1985, 1988). Several studies deal explicitly with changing sex roles, decision-making arrangements, intrafamily division of labor, and interspousal communication (Ataca & Sunar, 1999; Basaran, 1985; Bolak, 1988, 1997; Ergöcmen, 1997; Erman, 2001; Fox, 1973; Imamoglu & Yasak, 1997; Kagitcibasi, 1985; Özbay, 1988; Olson, 1982; Olson-Prather, 1976). The culture of peasant society has brought about a unique sex-specific allocation of labor, based on clear definitions of men's and women's work. As male members of the household are not supposed to perform certain female tasks, these cannot be transferred between genders, which makes female labor much more flexible than male labor, and makes it therefore necessary to find replacement for female laborers in case of out-marriage (Schiffauer, 1987). However, slight modifications toward a more egalitarian relationship are observed as the wife is no longer a "silent partner" (Nauck, 2002, p. 33).

Female enhancements in education and employment, as well as urban residence, not only shifted some of the power within the marriage to the wives, and therefore increased their involvement in decision making (Fox, 1973, p. 728), but also initiated the emergence of more cooperative arrangements of intrafamilial division of labor in urban contexts (Ataca & Sunar, 1999; Özbay, 1988). Nevertheless, a sharp distinction of traditional gender roles remains the norm throughout Turkish society: "Male decision making in the family is widespread,

300 NAUCK AND KLAUS

communication and role sharing between spouses is limited, indicating well-differentiated and non-overlapping sex roles" (Kagitcibasi, 1982a, p. 12). These gender roles result in a great workload for employed women when attempting to combine both family and occupational interests (Kagitcibasi & Sunar, 1992). "The fact that fully 48.9% of academic women, and 29.8% of women in high-level academic administrative posts, are single, compared to 38.15% and 3% respectively for men, is an index of this conflict" (Sunar & Fisek, 2005, p. 175). If the wife has a paid job, it is common practice to hire servants to take care of the household, rather than increase the husband's involvement. This practice is based on the availability of cheap unqualified female labor, especially from rural–urban immigrants in the *gecekondus*, which has contributed significantly over the past several decades to the higher proportions in Turkey of female professionals in the fields of engineering, law, medicine, and higher education than in any other Western European country (Öncü, 1985).

A unique feature of Turkish marriage is the "duofocal family structure." As Olson (1982) describes this:

There is no strong single center of intra-familial relationships. Instead, each adult tends to be the focus of his/her own rather separate social network. Thus, in a "nuclear" family in which the conjugal role-relationships are highly separated, there are two "foci"—the husband and the wife. (p. 36ff.)

Even spouses in modern settings show quite distinct spheres of activity, and thus the time they spend together is very restricted. The preference for same-sex interactions is also obvious for the youth, who choose rather decidedly for friends of the same sex (Hortacsu, 1989). Despite small variations with respect to urbanization, education, and historical time, the pattern of separate, same-sex social networks is stable and prevalent.

This separation of networks corresponds with the comparably low importance of marriage as compared to preexisting intergenerational relationships. This results in a situation where social relationships between members of the opposite sex typically include members of the family of origin only, in the case of husbands, for example, his own sisters and especially his own mother: Olson contends that for a man, it is probable that "the most intimate cross-sex relationship he will ever have is the one he has with his mother both as a young boy and as an adult—a relationship which will probably be more intense and more important in several ways than the one he will develop with his wife"

(Olson, 1982, p. 50). This duofocal family structure corresponds to the sex segregation in public and is also coherent with the normative system of Islam.

THE INTERGENERATIONAL RELATIONSHIP

Fertility

Contrary to the moderate changes in marriage, fertility has transformed dramatically during the second half of the 20th century. Although in the early years of the Turkish republic a pronatalist population policy was followed, within several decades the government recognized the far-reaching consequences of population growth (Tezcan, 2004), and began in 1965 to enforce the distribution and application of (modern) birth control (Population Planning Law 1965) and in 1983 repealed the prohibition on abortion. Mother and childcare centers and family planning training centers were established and the South-East Anatolian project was created to target regions nationwide with the highest fertility and lowest knowledge of family planning.

As illustrated in Table 11.1, the total fertility rate (TFR) has steadily decreased since the mid-century, from a high of 6.9 in 1950 to 2.5 in 2000—only a little above the replacement level. For the mean age at first birth, the limited years in which data are available (1970 to 1985) show an increase in the age of first motherhood, from 20 to 22 years. Likewise, the proportion of women who did not give birth to at least one child by the age of 20 increased over time, as calculations based on the TDHS of 1998 reveal. In the birth cohort 1948–1952 the share is about 48% and rises to 63% for the 1973–1977 cohort. These differences in women's age at childbirth nearly disappear for higher parities, suggesting a trend toward a postponement of first birth and a shortening of the birth interval between the first and the second child thereafter. Although the birth of a second child remains very common, the most significant change in fertility behavior occurs with regard to higher parity births, with the younger birth cohorts showing a significantly lower probability of having more than two children. Also, educational and regional differences do not show up before the birth of the third child, with mothers who have above-average education or are from the western parts of Turkey having a much lower probability of having more than two children. Even for the youngest cohorts of mothers in the TDHS of 1998, no evidence is found for an increase in lifetime childlessness.

Value of Children

The decrease in having more than two children, together with stable low childlessness, has been explained by the changing value of children (VOC) in Turkey (Kagitcibasi, 1982a, 1982b; Kagitcibasi & Esmer, 1980; Nauck, 1997, 2005). A study from the 1970s (Kagitcibasi, 1982b) found three dimensions of the value of children in Turkey: psychological, social, and economic (p. 52), which translate into the utility of children for stimulation and affect; for social esteem and status; and for work, instrumental help, and insurance. The interplay of the psychological and the economic-utilitarian value of having children is most significant for the understanding of fertility behavior in Turkey. Mainly in agrarian regions of Turkey, children were seen as a source of manpower for contributing to the family income via working in the fields or helping in the family-owned business. In the same sense, and particularly given Turkey's inadequate insurance system, children were an essential source of security against the risks of life such as unemployment, illness, and old age. The economic-utilitarian value of children served as a strong incentive for high parities, as the unit costs of raising children decrease with each additional child, whereas the manpower benefits increase. The psychological value of children follows a different logic: One or two children can provide as much stimulation and affect as four or more children. Thus, the saturation point for maximizing psychological utility is reached much earlier. Accordingly, shifts in the VOC should have a significant impact on fertility behavior.

The high salience of an economic-utilitarian value of children in Turkish society is strongly related to two cultural institutions: the absence of welfare state regulations that would provide social insurance for families, and the patrilineal regime of descent, which reinforce the economic-utilitarian value of children, as it is based on lifelong intergenerational solidarity, with the younger generation working for the elderly. As female descendants in patrilineal kinship systems leave their parents' household after marriage, this obligation is mostly the responsibility of the sons. Thus, boys were traditionally favored over girls, even by mothers. In the VOC survey of 1975, 75% of the female and 93% of the male respondents showed a preference for boys (Kagitcibasi, 1982a, p. 169); whereas in 2002 this sex preference had practically vanished in the case of women, with only 41% of the mothers in 2002 indicating a boy preference (Ataca et al., 2005, p. 109). The economic-utilitarian value of the past was also reinforced by the custom law regulations of land ownership. As non-kin-based employment relationships were virtually unknown, especially in rural Turkey, additional children were the only

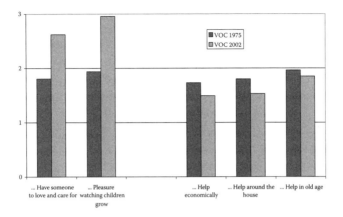

FIGURE 11.2   Changing value of children between 1975 and 2002.

Source: Authors' for calculations based on the VOC data of 1975 and 2002.

source to increase manpower and thus to cultivate additional land—a family strategy that began to lose its efficiency in the mid-20th century.

As shown in Figure 11.2, the value of children shifted in Turkey between 1975 and 2002,[1] with moderate decreases in the importance of children for household and economic help and a smaller decrease in their importance for helping prior family generations in old age. The generational differences are highly significant ($p \le .01$) for all three variables. This value change is viewed as a key motivation for the overall reduction of fertility, because only a high economic-utilitarian value of children is related to high parity. However, aside from the historical decrease in fertility, considerable differences exist not only between urban (TFR in 2003 = 2.1) and rural (TFR = 2.7) areas but also between the regions. According to the TDHS of 2003, fertility is highest in the eastern parts of Turkey (TFR = 3.7), and decreases as one moves to the west, where the rate is lowest (1.9) (Koc & Özdemir, 2004, pp. 46 and 48). Differences in the reported economic-utilitarian VOC correspond to these fertility variations by degree of urbanization. Using an index of the three items presented in Figure 11.2 (economic help, household help, help in old age), a significant higher rating is seen (in 2002) for respondents living in rural settings (2.1) than in urban settings (1.6) (results not shown).

---

[1]The VOC-study from 1975 surveyed a Turkish sample of 1485 women (Kagitcibasi, 1982b). Nearly 30 years later 622 women of the same age-range were surveyed in 2002 (Kagitcibasi & Ataca, 2005).

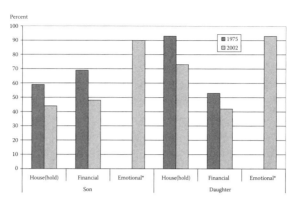

FIGURE 11.3   Changing expectations toward adult children.

Source: Authors' calculations based on the VOC data of 1975 and 2002; * not surveyed in 1975.

As shown in Figure 11.3, the expectations toward adult children also declined with respect to instrumental and financial assistance. For mothers in 1975, significant proportions expected contributions from their sons for long-term help in the household (59%) and financial contributions (69%). Three decades later, the percentages decreased to 44% and 48%, respectively. Similar trends are shown for adult daughters, but still the data reveal significant gender differences. Daughters are more often expected to provide instrumental help, whereas sons are expected to provide financial resources. The female descendants are more seldom involved in paid employment than the males, instead tending to work as unpaid (family) workers in the (family-owned) businesses and farms. In addition, they are expected to perform a variety of household chores that males do not tend perform, including child care and care for the elderly. Despite the apparent drop in daughters' instrumental obligations, mothers in 2002 continued to expect their support to a high degree (73%).

Contrary to this decrease in the economic-utilitarian value of children of the past several decades, the psychological value increased. This may be more of a relative increase in salience than a substantial value shift, because children's utilitarian value decreased in importance. Accordingly, the parent–child relationship offers pleasure, gratification, challenge, and fun, with no significant variation between regions, age groups, or educational levels. This increased salience is illustrated by the changes in the respective percentages shown in Figure 11.2. In 1975, respondents' assignment of emotional importance to having children (i.e., having someone to love and care for; getting pleasure from watching children grow) was in the middle range. In 2002, these variables were gauged at nearly the maximum level. Figure 11.3 confirms the importance placed on the emotional benefit of (grown-up) children in 2002 (although no comparison data is available for 1975), with around 90% of the mothers expecting emotional support from their adult children. Thus, as over time children in Turkey have come to be valued less for their economic value and more for their psychological value, fertility has declined correspondingly, whereas childlessness has remained low and stable (Kagitcibasi, 1982a; Klaus et al., in press; Nauck, 1997).

Childrearing Practices

The institutional constitution of the family, inherent in the descent regime and the corresponding value of children, implies parents' dependence on the functioning of intergenerational relationships across the entire life course. When economic-utilitarian value and lifelong loyalty are expected of offspring, parental control is very important. Among the qualities parents wished for their children in 1975, obedience was mentioned most frequently (60%), whereas independence and self-esteem were named least frequently (18%) (Kagitcibasi, 1982b). In 2002, no change was found with regard to the importance of obedience, but independence and self-reliance were rated much higher.

Several comparative studies have illustrated that the childrearing style of Turkish parents is characterized by protective behavior in the early years and by high authoritative control in late childhood and adolescence (Kagitcibasi, 1982b, 1996; Nauck, 1989). Respect for the father's authority increased throughout childhood, leading to a marked emotional distance in young adulthood. For their part, Turkish fathers often see their role as establishing and reinforcing strict behavioral rules for the children by means of a detached authority. Under this family system, adult children are expected to continue to show respect toward their fathers and to consult them on important decisions. Mothers, who tend to express ongoing and open affection for their children (Kagitcibasi, Sunar, & Bekman, 1988), have often taken the role of the mediator in the relationship between their husbands and the older children (Kiray, 1976). However, in face of the changing value of children, corresponding to a decrease in prevalence of the patrilineal descent family structure, parents have shifted toward a greater appreciation for autonomy and expressiveness in their children (Kagitcibasi, 1982b, 1996; Nauck, 1989; Sunar, 2002).

According to the concept of "culture of relatedness" (Kagitcibasi, 1996), two patterns of intergenerational relationships can be distinguished in Turkey: material interdependence and emotional interdependence. Ataca and colleagues (2005, p. 99) have found that the former is more common in rural and lower income/education strata whereas the latter is increasingly more common among urban middle classes. As the emotional value of children has becomes more apparent, parents not only prefer fewer children, but their relationship is also marked by greater emotional closeness and intimacy. Intergenerational relationships in particular, and the family- and kinship-based network in general, thus remain an important source of emotional solidarity throughout life.

CONCLUSION

The region currently encompassed by the Turkish state has experienced in- and through-migration of various populations for millennia, including the Greeks, Macedonians, Persians, Arabs, Armenians, Kurds, Turkmen, the Norman crusaders—to name just a few. Anatolia has always been at the crossroads of various cultural influences, which were preserved and developed because of the policy of the Ottoman Empire to allow each ethnic group their cultural autonomy, including autonomy in law and religion. This policy resulted in the well-known scattered ethnic picture not only of the Balkans, but of Anatolia as well, however well hidden behind and suppressed by the unifying "Turkism" since the republican nation building in the first half of the 20th century.

The resultant coexistence of antagonistic kinship systems and the high variability in family types and household structures in Turkey do not allow for simple generalizations or a unifying picture of "the" Turkish family. The primary variability of family forms in Turkey, however, remains within the range of the northern rim of the Mediterranean. In fact, as stated by Bastug (2002, p. 108):

> Many aspects of Turkish kinship show far more similarity to kinship patterns in Spain, France, Italy, and Greece than they do to the enduring patrilineal descent system of most of the Arab Middle East and much of the Arab Mediterranean littoral. They also resemble patterns in the Mediterranean region more than those of the original Turkic pattern still normative in Central Asia.

The most obvious similarities are to the patrilineal descent regime with a strong emphasis on personal intergenerational solidarity, but without the "political" organization of large tribal structures that are typical of the pastoral nomads of the Turkmen, Kurds, and Arabs.

In any case, the development of Turkish family and kinship systems is an outstanding example of the path dependency of cultural regulations. In the Turkish case, intergenerational relationships are the basic units of solidarity and result in strong intergenerational ties in both the patrilineal and the bilinear kinship systems. This is not only a major prerequisite for cultural continuity and stability over generations, but it also has important implications for the societal structure in general. Because extended family structures are often the primary means of redistributing material resources and offering personal care, community- and state-based institutions often lack legitimacy and are typically regarded with distrust—if they are not eventually exploited for the benefits of one's own extended family network. Thus, the production of public goods is typically in jeopardy, which results in the weakness of the state, as stated at the beginning. One major consequence of this predominance of kinship-based solidarity is the strong dependence of the individual status on the family resources in social and economic capital, as many mechanisms of redistribution between social strata are missing. Although some families were able to accumulate those resources over several generations, the vast majority of the population continuously has to struggle with poverty, whereas a middle-class remains rather small. Thus, it is highly likely that the ongoing predominance of the descendance regime will continue to contribute to a rather stable system of social inequality with relatively low status mobility and tremendous status differences.

REFERENCES

Abadan-Unat, N. (1987). The family in Turkey—Aspects from the structural and legal point of view. *Zeitschrift des Deutschen Orient-Instituts, 28*, 66-82. [in German]

Ahmad, F. (1993). *The making of modern Turkey.* New York: Routledge.

Aksan, A. (Ed.). (1981). *Mustafa Kemal Atatürk—From speeches and conversations.* Heidelberg, Germany: Julius Groos. [in German]

Anderson, M. (1980). *Approaches to the history of the Western family 1500–1900.* London: MacMillan.

Arat, Z. F. (1994). Kemalism and Turkish women. *Women & Politics, 14,* 57–80.

Ataca, B., Kagitcibasi, C., & Diri, A. (2005). The Turkish family and the value of children: Trends over time. In G. Trommsdorff & B. Nauck (Eds.), *The value of children in cross-cultural perspective. Case studies from eight societies* (pp. 91–119). Lengerich, Germany: Pabst.

Ataca, B., & Sunar, D. (1999). Continuity and change in Turkish urban family life. *Psychology and Developing Societies, 11,* 77–90.

Atatürk, K. (1952). *Atatürk's speeches and statements* (Vol. 2). Ankara, Turkey: Türk Inkilap Tarihi Enstitüsü. [in Turkish]

Basaran, F. (1985). Attitude changes related to sex roles in the family. In T. Erder (Ed.), *Family in Turkish society. Sociological and legal studies* (pp. 167–182). Ankara, Turkey: MAYA.

Bastug, S. (2002). The household and family in Turkey: An historical perspective. In R. Liljeström & E. Özdalga (Eds.), *Autonomy and dependence in the family. Turkey and Sweden in critical perspective* (pp. 99–115). Istanbul: Swedish Research Institute.

Bolak, H. (1988). Towards a conceptualization of marital power dynamics: Women breadwinners and working-class household in Turkey. In S. Tekeli (Ed.), *Women in modern Turkish society: A reader* (pp. 173–198). London: Zed Books.

Bolak, H. (1997). Marital power dynamics: Women providers and working-class households in Istanbul. In J. Gugler (Ed.), *Cities in the developing world: Issues, theory, and policy* (pp. 218–232). Oxford, UK: Oxford University Press.

Buhbe, M. (1996). *Turkey. Politics and contemporary history.* Opladen, Germany: Leske & Budrich. [in German]

Caporal, B. (1982). *Evolution of Kemalism and emanzipation of women.* Ankara, Turkey: Türkiye Is Bankasi Kültür Yayinlari. [in Turkish]

Coale, A. J., & Demeny, P. (1966). *Regional model life tables and stable populations.* Princeton, NJ: Princeton University Press.

Council of Europe. (1987). *Recent demographic developments in the member states of the council of Europe.* Strasbourg, France: Author.

Council of Europe. (1995). *Recent demographic developments in Europe.* Strasbourg, France: Author.

Council of Europe. (2001). *Demographic yearbook 2001.* Strasbourg, France: Author.

Duben, A. (1985a). Nineteenth and twentieth century Ottoman-Turkish family and household structures. In T. Erder (Ed.), *Family in Turkish society. Sociological and legal studies* (pp. 105–126). Ankara, Turkey: MAYA.

Duben, A. (1985b). Turkish families and households in historical perspective. *Journal of Family History, 10,* 75–97.

Durkheim, E. (1921). La famille conjugale. *Revue philosophique, 41,* 1–14. [in French]

Ecevit, F. Y. (1988). The status and changing forms of women's labour in the urban economy. In S. Tekeli (Ed.), *Women in modern Turkish society: A reader* (pp. 81–88). London: Zed Books.

Engels, F. (1970). *The origin of family, private property and the state* (9th ed.). Berlin, Germany: Dietz. [in German] (Original work published 1884)

Ergöcmen, B. A. (1997). Women's status and fertility in Turkey. In Institute of Population Studies (Ed.), *Fertility trends, women's status and reproductive expectations in Turkey: Results of further analysis of the 1993 Turkish demographic and health survey* (pp. 79–104). Ankara, Turkey: Institute of Population Studies.

Erman, T. (2001). Rural migrants and patriarchy in Turkish cities. *International Journal of Urban and Regional Research, 25,* 118–133.

Fisek, G. O. (1993). Life in Turkey. In L. L. Adler (Ed.), *International handbook of gender roles* (pp. 438–451). Westport, CT: Greenwood Press.

Fox, G. L. (1973). Another look at the comparative resources model: Assessing the balance of power in Turkish marriages. *Journal of Marriage and the Family, 35,* 718–730.

Fox, G. L. (1975). Love match and arranged marriage in a modernizing nation: Mate selection in Ankara, Turkey. *Journal of Marriage and the Family, 37,* 180–193.

Goode, W. J. (1963). *World Revolution and Family Patterns.* New York: Free Press.

Goody, J. (1990). *The oriental, the ancient and the primitive. Systems of marriage and the family in the pre-industrial societies of Eurasia.* Cambridge, UK: Cambridge University Press.

Gündüz-Hosgör, A., & Smits, J. (2002). Intermarriage between Turks and Kurds in contemporary Turkey. Inter-ethnic relations in an urbanizing environment. *European Sociological Review, 18,* 417–432.

Güvenc, B. (1994). *Turkish identity. History of Turkish origins.* Ankara, Turkey: T. C. Kültür Bakanligi. [in Turkish]

Hacettepe University Institute of Population Studies. (1994). *1993 Turkish demographic and health survey.* Ankara, Turkey: Institute of Population Studies.

Hacettepe University Institute of Population Studies. (1999). *Turkish demographic and health survey 1998.* Ankara, Turkey: Institute of Population Studies.

Hajnal, J. (1965). European marriage patterns in perspective. In D. V. Glass & D. E. C. Eversley (Eds.), *Population in history* (pp. 101–143). Chicago: Aldine.

Hajnal, J. (1982). Two kinds of preindustrial household formation system. *Population and Development Review, 8,* 449–494.

Hortacsu, N. (1989). Targets of communication during adolescence. *Journal of Adolescence, 12,* 253–263.

Imamoglu, E. O., & Yasak, Y. (1997). Dimensions of marital relationships as perceived by Turkish husbands and wives. *Genetic, Social and General Psychological Monographs, 123,* 211–233.

Kagitcibasi, C. (1982a). Sex roles, values of children, and fertility. In C. Kagitcibasi (Ed.), *Sex roles, family, and community in Turkey* (pp. 151–180). Bloomington: Indiana University Press.

Kagitcibasi, C. (1982b). *The changing value of children in Turkey.* Honolulu, HI: East–West Center.

Kagitcibasi, C. (1985). Intra-family interaction and a model of family change. In T. Erder (Ed.), *Family in Turkish society* (pp. 149–165). Ankara, Turkey: MAYA.

Kagitcibasi, C. (1996). *Family and human development across cultures. A view from the other side.* Mahwah, NJ: Lawrence Erlbaum Associates.

Kagitcibasi, C., & Ataca, B. (2005). Values of children and family change: A three-decade portrait from Turkey. *Applied Psychology: An International Review, 54,* 317–337.

Kagitcibasi, C., & Esmer, Y. (1980). *Development, value of children, and fertility: A multiple indicator approach.* Istanbul, Turkey: Bogazici University.

Kagitcibasi, C., & Sunar, D. (1992). Family and socialization in Turkey. In J. L. Roopnarine & D. B. Carter (Eds.), *Parent–child socialization in diverse cultures* (pp. 75–88). Norwood, NJ: Ablex.

Kagitcibasi, C., Sunar, D., & Bekman, S. (1988). *Comprehensive preschool educational project: Final report.* Ottawa, Canada: International Development Research Center.

Kandiyoti, D. (1977). Sex roles and social Change: A comparative appraisal of Turkey's women. *Signs, 3*, 57–73.

Kandiyoti, D. (1982). Urban change and women's roles in Turkey: An overview and evaluation. In C. Kagitcibasi (Ed.), *Sex roles, family, and community in Turkey* (pp. 101–120). Bloomington: Indiana University Press.

Kandiyoti, D. (1988). Patterns of patriarchy: Notes for an analysis of male dominance in Turkish society. In S. Tekeli (Ed.), *Women in modern Turkish society: A reader* (pp. 306–319). London: Zed Books.

Kandiyoti, D. (1991). Women and the Turkish state: Political actors or symbolic pawns? In N. Yuval-Davis & F. Anthias (Eds.), *Women–nation–state* (pp. 126–149). Houndmills, UK:

Karasan-Dirks, S. (1980). *Die türkische Familie zwischen Gestern und Morgen.* Hamburg, Germany: Orient-Institut. [in German]

Kazgan, G. (1985). Der sozio-ökonomische Status der Frauen in der türkischen Wirtschaft. In N. Abadan-Unat (Ed.), *Die Frau in der türkischen Gesellschaft* (pp. 77–117). Frankfurt, Germany: Dagyeli. [in German]

Kiray, M. B. (1976). The changing roles of mothers: Changing intra-family relations in a Turkish town. In J. G. Peristiany (Ed.), *Mediterranean family structures* (pp. 261–271). London: Cambridge University Press.

Klaus, D., Suckow, J., & Nauck, B. (in press). The value of children in Palestine and Turkey—Differences and its consequences for fertility. *Current Sociology, 55.*

Koc, I., & Özdemir, E. (2004). Fertility. In Hacettepe University Institute of Population Studies (Ed.), *Turkey demographic and health survey 2003* (pp. 45–58). Ankara, Turkey: Institute of Population Studies.

Kuyas, N. (1982). Female labor power relations in the urban Turkish family. In C. Kagitcibasi (Ed.), *Sex roles, family, and community in Turkey* (pp. 181–206). Bloomington: Indiana University Press.

Lévi-Strauss, C. (1993). *Elementary structures in kinship.* Frankfurt, Germany: Suhrkamp. [in German]

Mango, A. (2004). *Atatürk.* London: John Murray.

Nauck, B. (1989). Intergenerational relationships in families from Turkey and Germany. An extension of the "value of children" approach to educational attitudes and socialization practices. *European Sociological Review, 5,* 251–274.

Nauck, B. (1997). Social change, migration, and family formation of Turkish women. In B. Nauck & U. Schönpflug (Eds.), *Familien in verschiedenen Kulturen* (pp. 162–199). Stuttgart, Germany: Enke. [in German]

Nauck, Bernhard. (2001). Intergenerational relationships and marriage regimes: Theoretical considerations of the structure of marriage markets and match making for Turkey and Germany. In T. Klein (Ed.), *Partnerwahl und Heiratsmuster. Sozialstrukturelle Voraussetzungen der Liebe* (pp. 35–55). Opladen, Germany: Leske & Budrich. [in German]

Nauck, B. (2002). Families in Turkey. In R. Nave-Herz (Ed.), *Family change and intergenerational relations in different cultures* (pp. 11–48). Würzburg, Germany: Ergon.

Nauck, B. (2005). Changing value of children: An action theory of fertility behavior and intergenerational relationships in cross-cultural comparison. In W. Friedlmeier, P. Chakkarath, & B. Schwarz (Eds.), *Culture and human development. The importance of cross-cultural research to the social sciences* (pp. 183–202). Hove, UK: Psychology Press.

Öncü, A. (1985). The Turkish woman in qualified professions. In N. Abadan-Unat (Ed.), *Die Frau in der türkischen Gesellschaft* (pp. 183–200). Frankfurt, Germany: Dagyeli. [in German]

Özbay, F. (1985). The consequences of education on the Turkish woman in rural and urban areas. In N. Abadan-Unat (Ed.), *Die Frau in der türkischen Gesellschaft* (pp. 118–145). Frankfurt, Germany: Dagyeli. [in German]

Özbay, F. (1988). Changes in women's activities both inside and outside the home. In S. Tekeli (Ed.), *Women in modern Turkish society: A reader* (pp. 89–111). London: Zed Books.

Özgen, E. (1985). Early marriage, brideprice and abduction of women. In T. Erder (Ed.), *Family in Turkish society. Sociological and legal studies* (pp. 313–349). Ankara, Turkey: MAYA.

Ogburn, W. F. (1928). The changing family. *Publications of the American Sociological Society, 23,* 124–133.

Olson, E. A. (1982). Duofocal family structure and an alternative model of husband–wife relationship. In C. Kagitcibasi (Ed.), *Sex roles, family, and community in Turkey* (pp. 33–72). Bloomington: Indiana University Press.

Olson-Prather, E. (1976). Family planning and husband–wife relationships in Turkey. *Journal of Marriage and the Family, 38,* 379–385.

Ortayli, I. (1985). The family in Ottoman society. In T. Erder (Ed.), *Family in Turkish society. Sociological and legal studies* (pp. 93–104). Ankara, Turkey: MAYA.

Parsons, T. (1943). The kinship system of the contemporary United States. *American Anthropologist, 45,* 22–38.

Schiffauer, W. (1987). *The peasants of Subay. Life in a Turkish village.* Stuttgart, Germany: Klett-Cotta. [in German]

Shorter, F. (2000). Turkish population in the Great Depression. *New Perspectives on Turkey, 23,* 103–124.

Shorter, F. C. & Macura, M. (1982). *Trends in fertility and mortality in Turkey, 1935–1975.* Washington, DC: National Academic Press.

Sönmez, M. (1996). *The two faces of Istanbul: Transformation from 1980 to 2000.* Ankara, Turkey: Arkadas. [in Turkish]

State Institute of Statistics. (2000). *Household and labor force survey 1999.* Ankara, Turkey: Printing Division.

State Institute of Statistics. (2001). *Statistical indicators 1923–1998.* Ankara, Turkey: Printing Division.

State Institute of Statistics. (2003). *Census of population: Social and economic characteristics of population.* Ankara, Turkey: Printing Division.

State Institute of Statistics. (2004). *2004 Turkey's statistical yearbook.* Ankara, Turkey: Printing Division.

Sunar, D. (2002). Change and continuity in the Turkish middle class family. In R. Liljeström & E. Özdalga (Eds.), *Autonomy and dependence in the family: Turkey and Sweden in critical perspective* (pp. 217–237). Istanbul, Turkey: Swedish Research Institute.

Sunar, D., & Fisek, G. O. (2005). Contemporary Turkish families. In U. Gielen & J. L. Roopnarine (Eds.), *Families in global perspective* (pp. 169–184). Boston: Allyn & Bacon.

Tansel, A. (1998). *Determinants of school attainment of boys and girls in Turkey.* Center discussion paper No. 789. New Haven, CT: Yale University, Economic Growth Center.

Taskiran, T. (1976). *Women in Turkey.* Istanbul, Turkey: Redhouse Yayinevi.

Tezcan, S. (2004). Introduction. In Hacettepe University Institute of Population Studies (Ed.), *Turkey demographic and health survey 2003* (pp. 1–16). Ankara, Turkey: Institute of Population Studies.

Thornton, A. (2005). *Reading history sideways. The fellacy and enduring impact of the developmental paradigm on family life.* Chicago: University of Chicago Press.

World Bank. (1984). *World development report 1984.* New York: Oxford University Press.

Yalcin-Heckmann, L. (1991). *Tribe and kinship among the Kurds.* Frankfurt, Germany: Lang.

12

Conclusion

William G. Axinn
Population Studies Center and Department of Sociology
University of Michigan

Rukmalie Jayakody
Department of Human Development and Family Studies and the
Population Research Institute
Pennsylvania State University

Arland Thornton
Population Studies Center and Department of Sociology
University of Michigan

We close this volume concerning ideational perspectives on family change around the world with a brief review of some of the key findings from the previous chapters. We then focus on the research priorities flowing from what we know now and consider next steps for research on ideational influences on the family. Finally we close by encouraging other scientists and scholars to pursue research on ideational influences on family change more aggressively.

KEY LESSONS FROM RESEARCH AROUND THE WORLD

The chapters in this volume have focused on family change around the world, highlighting the historical and cultural circumstances unique to various countries and the impact of ideational forces on family change in these contexts. Rather than producing uniform change, as some globalization of families discussions suggest, the interaction of ideational forces with unique historical and cultural circumstances results in important variations. Although family change may be common to many countries around the world and many countries share similar ideational frameworks, substantial variability in both remains, and there is seldom uniformity in behavior and thought.

Chapters 2 and 4 highlight broad ideational changes resulting in family change throughout Europe and the world. In chapter 2, Thornton and colleagues discuss an ideational factor in family change, developmental idealism, that they consider especially important in influencing family change around the world. Using Argentina and Nepal as examples, they document the extent to which ordinary people believe and accept the propositions of developmental idealism and related aspects of developmental thinking. In chapter 4, Lesthaeghe and Surkyn focus on the implications for family change of what they call the second demographic transition—or the disconnection between marriage and procreation and the diversity of living arrangements other than marriage. Lesthaeghe and Surkyn demonstrate the emergence of these patterns of behavior and values in the 1950s, particularly in Western Europe, and then their diffusion to Southern and Eastern Europe. Mirroring many of the changes in Western Europe, the United States also experienced an emergence of individualistic ideas and attitudes toward family behavior. In chapter 5, Axinn, Emens, and Mitchell draw from a large volume of evidence from the United States to demonstrate the close associations between macro-level ideational shifts and subsequent micro-level changes in family formation attitudes and beliefs.

The chapters in this volume have identified several mechanisms for the spread of ideational beliefs. Religion, in various forms, has been an important mechanism of ideational change in Africa, Argentina, Iran, and Turkey. Although religion is a common factor in all these countries, the nature of religion's influence on family change varies. Chapter 3 on Africa and chapter 6 on Argentina illustrate the impact of the spread of Christianity. Although Islam was the first religion imported to Africa, Christian religions, in conjunction with other mechanisms of ideational change, exposed Africans to new ideas about family structure and relationships. More recently, Anglo-American-inspired Pentecostal movements are having a substantial impact. In Argentina, Catholic conceptions of marriage and Western family patterns have played a central role.

Religion, this time in the form of Islam, has been important in Iran and Turkey, although in Iran it does not appear to be the main motivator of change. Instead, religion circumscribes the parameters of change in Iran, with religious authorities allowing change to proceed in aspects of family life not viewed as threatening to the idealized morality. For example, as described in chapter 7, the use of birth control and limiting family size are viewed as acceptable, even desirable, whereas cohabitation and sexual relations outside of marriage are not. In this way, religion in Iran has been important both for the diffusion of some new ideas and for the suppression of others. Islam has also played an important role in Turkey. As discussed in chapter 11, Islam has a long history in Turkey, with some Turkish groups adopting Islam by the 8th century. This chapter also highlights urban–rural differences in family patterns, noting, for example, that although Islamic law was largely followed in cities, patrilineal inheritance prevailed in the villages.

Several chapters illustrate the top-down impact of laws and policies on ideational change. In Iran, Vietnam, and Turkey, state politics and political regimes defined the goals for family behavior. In Turkey, the Kemalist revolution in the first part of the 20th century imposed a series of legal reforms, and the reform of family law was identified as an important strategy to achieve social and economic goals. Among the changes brought about by the new civil code was the requirement for both partners to consent to a marriage, an increased age at marriage for men and women, and an emphasis on women's equality, particularly in terms of education, inheritance, and property rights. This mirrors the changes in Vietnam brought about by the Communist Party and its belief that family changes were needed for economic success. As described in chapter 8, Vietnam's 1958 Marriage and Family Law also called for the abolishment of the arranged marriage custom, increased the legal age of marriage, and emphasized women's equality. In Iran as well, political forces have played a fundamental role in enhancing and restraining social change. For example, the Family Protection Law of 1967 gave women the right to divorce, eliminating men's unilateral divorce rights. Men were now also required to obtain consent from their first wife before marrying a second wife. These laws were abolished after the Islamic Revolution in 1979. The quick succession of these opposing laws in Iran demonstrates the importance of state power, and not necessarily social attitudes, in shaping social change.

Chapter 3 on Africa and chapter 10 on Nepal show how mass media serve as powerful agents of change by introducing new family ideas and models. Television and other media sources have exposed Africans to depictions of marriages established by individuals rather than by family strategies. In Nepal, access and exposure to new ideas via the mass media are shown to influence attitudes and preferences about family formation behavior. In their discussion of developmental idealism in chapter 2, Thornton and colleagues also identify the power of the mass media in explaining family ideas and behavior.

RESEARCH PRIORITIES

The chapters of this book provide a summary of evidence from around the world that ideas are part of the package of factors that shape family continuity, change, and variation. The findings of studies described in these chapters—and of dozens of others from around the world that did not find their way into these chapters—all point toward ideational change and variation as an important influence on family change and variation. The empirical evidence of this relationship is now substantial. Although social science is virtually never conclusive, and all studies have limitations, by varying the approaches used and the settings across many different studies, social science does cumulate to accepted conclusions regarding strong associations and influences in the empirical world (Axinn & Pearce, 2006; Rosenbaum, 2001). Ideational influence on family change and variation is one of those conclusions.[1]

However, like all research that advances our knowledge of the world, research documenting this relationship has left us with as many questions as answers. What types of ideas influence family change? What are the sources of these ideas? Under what conditions do these ideas have the greatest influence? The chapters in this book speak somewhat to these questions, and conversations among the authors and their colleagues have stimulated speculation regarding their answers or the research that would be required to find those answers. We devote the remainder of this chapter to what we believe are the most important of these questions.

WHICH IDEAS SHAPE FAMILY CHANGE AND VARIATION?

The chapters in this volume and the bodies of research they reflect provide a good deal of information about which ideas may be important influences on family change and variation. Extremely little research evaluates the *relative* influence of different ideas on family behaviors, but the existing research does at least point toward ideas that are likely to be highly influential. In the sections that follow we summarize the most likely of these.

Attitude–Behavior

The social sciences have managed to generate many different theoretical models for understanding the influences of ideas on behavior. They are

---

[1]For example, although we cannot randomly assign ideas to individuals to determine the consequence for family behaviors, like the accepted consequences of cigarette smoking or consumption of high volumes of certain foods, the evidence of ideational influences on family change and variation is now so great that it cannot be ignored.

both too numerous and too broad to review here, spanning every discipline including anthropology, economics, political science, psychology, and sociology (Becker, 1996; Caldwell, 1982; Coleman, 1990; Geertz, 1973; Inglehart, 1997; Lesthaeghe & Surkyn, 1988; Schwartz, 2001; Schwartz & Bilsky, 1987, 1990). Fishbein and Ajzen's theories of reasoned action and planned behavior from social psychology are among the most widely used in studies of family change and variation (Ajzen, 1988; Fishbein & Ajzen, 1975). These frameworks point to the ideas most closely associated with the behavior of interest as the most influential. So, for example, ideas about childbearing should have the greatest influence on childbearing behavior. Chapters in this book (especially chaps. 5, 7, 8, and 9) summarize a great deal of evidence consistent with this prediction.

An important extension of these frameworks draws on the theory of role conflict (Goffman, 1982) to argue that ideas closely related to behaviors that conflict with family behaviors may also be strong influences on family behavior, sometimes stronger than ideas associated with the behavior itself (Barber, 2001). So, for example, ideas about the importance of educational attainment may delay marriage or childbearing. Some empirical evidence, mainly from the United States, is consistent with this prediction, but it remains an understudied area of research concerning ideational influences on family change and variation. It also opens the door to reasoning and research on the full breadth of ideas that may influence family change and variation, beyond ideas closely associated with the behavior in question.

Individualism

As social scientists have sought to understand the relationship between ideas and family change they have also investigated broader, more general ideas than those closely tied to specific family or competing behaviors. Perhaps the ideas receiving the greatest attention are those concerned with individual freedom and autonomy as contrasted with communal orientations favoring obedience to authority. Lesthaeghe and his colleagues have argued that declining religiosity, increased secularism, and other variations in orientations toward individualistic and materialistic pursuits are essential components in explaining changing family behavior in Western Europe (Lesthaeghe, 1983; Lesthaeghe & Neels, 2002; Lesthaeghe & Surkyn, 1987; Lesthaeghe & Wilson, 1986). In this volume (chap. 4), Lesthaeghe and Surkyn extend these lines of thinking beyond Western Europe, to Eastern Europe and other parts of the world. Lesthaeghe and other scholars have focused on ideas favoring individual-oriented pursuits as a key influence on family change in North America

(Bumpass, 1990; Lesthaeghe & Neidert, 2006). These explanations link U.S. trends in premarital sex, cohabitation, out-of-wedlock childbearing, and divorce to well-documented trends favoring independence and autonomy over conformity and obedience (Alwin, 1984, 1988, 2001). Numerous other studies of Western Europe and North America draw on this potential of increasing individualistic orientations as an explanation of specific family changes.

A key limitation of this body of research is the nearly exclusive focus on Europe and North America. Relatively little research has explored the effects of changes in individualistic orientations on family changes in Asia, Africa, and Latin America. New research to fill this gap is an important priority. And even in Europe and North America, these studies have not benefited from the same micro-level longitudinal research designs and measures used in studies linking family behaviors to closely related attitudes, because the key micro-level longitudinal studies of beliefs and behaviors generally have included few or no measures of general orientations toward individualistic pursuits. This limitation leaves us knowing relatively little about how specific dimensions of individualistic ideas shape subsequent family behaviors independent of structural influences and the potential reciprocal influences of experiences on these orientations. Thus, even in Western Europe and North America, micro-level longitudinal studies measuring multiple dimensions of individualistic orientations over time are a high research priority.

Developmental Idealism

One of the most recent ideational explanations of family change and variation focuses on developmental idealism. Thornton (2001, 2005) argues that the Western model of family life has been important outside the West, at least partially because it is intricately related with the ideas of development that have permeated Western thought for thousands of years and, in recent centuries, have been disseminated in many non-Western places. In chapter 2 of this volume, Thornton, Binstock, and Ghimire discuss the developmental idealism model and demonstrate that it is widely understood and used among people in everyday life in Argentina and Nepal. Thornton (2001, 2005) argues that the worldwide dissemination of these ideas has been crucial in changing family systems around the world.

This body of thought provides a specific set of ideas that may be especially important in shaping family change and variation. It also provides strong reasons why ideas favoring individual freedom and autonomy may be making advances relative to ideas favoring community and obedience to authority. However, virtually no research links change in individualistic orientations in Europe and North America to the spread of developmental idealism to other parts of the world, or to revisions in aspects of developmental idealism, such as which behaviors are considered the most "developed." New research in these areas is a high priority for understanding both the links between individualism and developmental idealism and the links between ideational change within Europe and North America and ideational changes spreading through other parts of the world.

In fact, the emergence of developmental idealism as a specific set of ideas fueling the spread of Western family behaviors around the world is so recent that although extensive macro-level evidence demonstrates its importance, little micro-level empirical evidence has yet been documented. Although chapter 2 summarizes some recent evidence, documentation among ordinary people of the spread of developmental idealism, change over time in developmental idealism, and the association between developmental idealism and subsequent family behaviors is virtually nonexistent. Clearly, research in this area is a high priority for improving our understanding of developmental idealism.

Thornton's work on developmental idealism shows how the day-to-day comparisons people make within and across societies help to spread new ideas and behavior. As individuals identify people they want to be more like, either in terms of material conditions or in other ways, they also identify differences between their own behavior or ideas and the behavior or ideas of these others. These comparisons may lead people to try to adopt the behavior or ideas of these others under the—likely false—premise that this emulation will produce the conditions they hope to achieve. Research into this basic psychology of day-to-day human interaction is likely to promote both a better understanding of the way developmental idealism influences family behavior, and the ways individuals choose which ideas they adopt.

The Most Influential Ideas

Each of these sets of ideas has been implicated by past theory and research as a potentially important source of influence on family behavior. All are strong candidates for new research. Those about which we know the least are probably the strongest candidates. To learn which among these are the strongest influences on behavior will require measurement of all of them in a common study design that allows explicit comparison. This comparative research also deserves high priority. Of course, such research is likely to reveal that different sets of ideas are more influential on some behaviors than others, in some populations than in others, or under some conditions than others. We return to these questions of the conditions shaping the relationships between ideas and family behavior after quickly reviewing the potential sources of ideational change and variation.

WHAT CREATES CHANGE AND VARIATION IN THESE IDEAS?

Given the evidence that change and variation in ideas influence family behaviors, another fundamental question concerns the sources of these changes and variations in ideas. Social research has identified many potential sources; we review some of the most compelling here.

Diffusion and Adaptation

Theories of diffusion and adaptation in the social sciences may go back as far as the social sciences themselves. At their root is psychological theory about how individuals learn attitudes, beliefs, and preferences from others with whom they come into some type of social contact, including parents, peers, coworkers, and strangers in a public setting (Mead, 1934). The others with whom an individual spends the most time, or who are most closely associated with the individual, are expected to have the greatest influence on the individual's ideas. Research on change and variation in social networks is closely linked to work on diffusion and adaptation of family ideas. Social networks are believed to be an important conduit through which ideas spread. Social networks may be formed around common languages or religions (Anderson, 1986), common geographic locations (Montgomery & Casterline, 1993), or specific types of social interactions, such as gossip networks (Bongaarts & Watkins, 1996). In many ways, change and variation in social networks and the social interactions they produce are at the root of virtually all hypotheses about the sources of change and variation in ideas.

For example, these mechanisms immediately implicate residential change, travel, and migration as potential mechanisms of ideational diffusion because they move individuals into social interactions with new sets of people, speeding the diffusion of ideas. Thus, theories of fertility change point toward urbanization or even contact with tourists as potential ideational mechanisms of behavioral change (Caldwell, 1982; Freedman, 1979).

Although diffusion through social networks can give individuals access to new ideas, diffusion itself does not explain why individuals adopt some ideas and not others. Individuals are likely to adopt ideas to which they have the greatest exposure, or that come from particularly significant social others, such a parents (Barber, 2000; Mead, 1934). However, other social forces may also shape which ideas are most likely to be adopted. We turn to these forces next.

Nonfamily Organizations

Of course, organizations group people together so that changes in organizations produce changes in the associated individuals. Research on family change provides substantial evidence that the proliferation of new nonfamily organizations is associated with significant changes in family behaviors (Axinn & Yabiku, 2001; Thornton & Fricke, 1987; Thornton & Lin, 1994). Moreover, this same research identifies the spread of new ideas as a likely mechanism linking these changes in social organizations to changes in family behavior (Axinn & Yabiku, 2001; Thornton & Lin, 1994). Both previous research and the chapters of this book point toward a variety of different mechanisms linking specific non-family organizations to the spread of new ideas. We review those briefly here.

Governments, Policies, and Programs. By endorsing specific ideas, enacting them in laws or public policy, and creating programs to support them, government organizations can be among the most influential in spreading new ideas that affect family behavior. Chapters 7 and 8, on Iran and Vietnam, exemplify the role of national government in creating ideational change related to the family. International governance organizations may also play such a role—both chapters 1 and 2 touch on the role of the United Nations in spreading Western ideas around the world.

Religion. A great deal of research on family change and variation addresses the role of religious organizations in influencing ideas about family life. Several chapters touch on this subject, particularly chapters 4, 7, and 11. Most religions advocate some family behaviors, such as marriage or childbearing, and restrict others, such as premarital sex, out-of-wedlock childbearing, or divorce. Variations in participation in these religions, or in beliefs in the religion itself, are likely to produce significant variation in family-related ideas.

Media. As the reach of the mass media has grown, so has investigation of its role in influencing family change and variation (Casterline et al., 1996). Much of this research focuses on how the mass media spread new ideas about the family or new ideas about pursuits that conflict with specific family behaviors (Barber & Axinn, 2004; Casterline, Lee, & Foote, 1996). Chapter 10 of this book provides some evidence from Nepal that the spread of mass media is associated with family change and variation, and that ideational change may be the mechanism for this connection. Other chapters also touch on the potential role of mass media in spreading new ideas (chaps. 2, 3, 8, and 10). It is quite likely that changing access and exposure to the mass media affect change and variation in ideas about the family.

Education. Most research on education treats educational organizations as specifically designed to promote ideational change. Teaching in classes may overtly focus on challenging the ideas students bring to the classroom or on exposing students to new ideas. The social interactions in educational organizations may also promote the development of new ideas (Alwin et al., 1991; Newcomb, 1943). As a result, the proliferation of educational organizations is almost always associated with family change and variation, with ideational mechanisms implicated in furthering this connection (Axinn & Barber, 2001; Caldwell, 1982; Thornton, 2005; Thornton & Lin, 1994).

Economic Change. The research literature has often examined the extent to which ideas mediate the relationship between economic conditions and behavior. Although there are important theoretical and empirical reasons to believe that ideational influences on family life can be independent of economic factors (Barber et al., 2002; Thornton, 2005), economic change and material conditions are likely to influence the adoption of specific ideas. Economic conditions may make some ideas more advantageous than others, or may change the scope of ideas individuals consider. For example, as discussed in chapter 4, it has been argued that as income and consumption growth fill basic human needs, other needs and values centered on self-expression and self-actualization become prominent (Inglehart, 1997)—a shift that may result in ideational change.

Although previous research implicates each of these dimensions of social organization in the spread of ideas, not enough is known about the mechanisms linking any of these dimensions to the specific ideas that affect family change and variation. Therefore, investigation of each one remains a high priority for understanding how social forces shape the ideas that ultimately influence family systems and behaviors. Before turning to the competition among ideas we briefly review another potentially important source of new ideas—the family system itself.

Feedback Loops within Family Systems

Another potentially important source of ideational change may involve feedback loops within family systems (Thornton & Axinn, 1989). That is, changes in some family behaviors may promote new ideas about family behaviors in other domains. For example, a rising age at marriage, which leads to more average years of singlehood and a larger proportion of adults who never marry, may increase tolerance of premarital sex. Evidence from investigations of the attitude–behavior links in the United States is consistent with the conclusion that these types of feedback loops may exist (see chap. 5).

The increased prevalence of divorce in the United States provides a key example. The rapid rise in divorce during the 1960s and 1970s in the United States was accompanied by extensive publicity, and knowledge of this family trend became widespread. A particularly important aspect of the publicity was information about the negative psychological, social, and economic consequences that can be associated with divorce. It is likely that this information led to some questioning of the institution of marriage and decreased confidence in marriage as a way of life (Thornton, 1988; Weitzman, 1985). This change likely had many implications for ideas about family life, including ideas about premarital sex, cohabitation, marriage, and childbearing.

An extensive body of research shows that children of divorced parents have more positive attitudes toward premarital sex and are more sexually experienced (Thornton & Camburn, 1987). Given this empirical relationship and plausible theoretical reasons for expecting that rising divorce rates would have contributed to the trend toward more approving attitudes about premarital sex, it also seems very likely that the growing concerns about the viability of marriage and the increased acceptability of premarital sex played a major role in the rapid increase in unmarried cohabitation. Children of divorced parents also have more positive attitudes toward cohabitation and more negative attitudes toward marriage than other children (Axinn & Thornton, 1996).

The rise in divorce has also been linked to declining rates of marriage and increased rates of cohabitation, which themselves also influence ideas about the family. Children of divorced parents have substantially higher cohabitation rates and lower marriage rates than children from continuously married families, indicating that growing up in a family with divorced parents could lead to substituting cohabitation for marriage (Thornton, 1988). Parental divorce has also been linked to a reduced desire to have children (Axinn & Thornton, 1996), as has cohabitation (Axinn & Barber, 1997). Thus, the increased prevalence of divorce may be part of the reason for declining desires to have children in the United States.

Investigations of family trends in the United States and the micro-level studies of relationships among family experiences are consistent with many different potential feedback loops within these systems (Thornton & Axinn, 1989). It seems likely these behavioral feedback loops are fueled at least in part by ideational change. Changes within a family system itself may promote change and variation in ideas related to the family. More research is needed in the United States to better understand how ideational mechanisms interact with these feedback loops, and new research is needed in other settings where virtually no feedback loop research has been conducted.

Competition among Ideas

Finally, as we indicated in the opening chapter of this book, a key question in the study of ideational change is how and why some ideas replace other ideas. Why are previously held ideas rejected and new ideas adopted? And why are some new ideas adopted over others? The theories and evidence sketched earlier provide clues, but a sustained program of research into these questions in the family arena is among the highest priorities for new research. Given the breadth of potential influences on ideas just identified, such research will most likely need to include multiple simultaneous approaches focusing on multiple interlinked dimensions of the process. These dimensions include individual psychology, social networks and interactions, changes in social organization, and variations in personal experiences that bring access to and adaptation of new ideas. Simultaneous integration of these multiple dimensions is likely to require mixed-method research designs that are both multilevel and longitudinal (Thornton et al., 2001). Such research is both complex and demanding, but likely is needed to answer these fundamental questions about change in ideas related to the family.

UNDER WHAT CONDITIONS DO IDEAS HAVE THE MOST INFLUENCE ON BEHAVIORAL CHOICES?

Economic conditions, changes in social organization, or even ideational change itself may alter macro-level conditions in ways that alter the micro-level associations between ideas and family behavior.

Contextual affluence affects behavioral options, with greater affluence usually producing more options. Economic conditions that increase the breadth of behavioral options are likely to strengthen the association between ideas and family behaviors. This is because individuals with many options have more opportunity to rely on their attitudes, values, beliefs, and preferences to make choices among alternatives.

Changes in social organization that produce more options may have the same effect. As an arranged marriage society begins to permit spouse choice, ideas may become a more important influence on young people's behavior because they now participate in an important selection process. Likewise, as a society that prohibits premarital sex becomes more tolerant of premarital cohabitation, ideas may again become a more important influence on behavior because individuals have more choices to make. Thus, changes in social organization may provide individuals with more choices, and these additional choices may increase the association between ideas and family behaviors.

Even ideational changes themselves may increase the association between ideas and behaviors. For example, ideational shifts in the United States that began in the early 1960s spread new family ideas favoring individual freedoms and a norm of tolerance—changes that may have stabilized, but have not reversed (Thornton, 1989; Thornton & Young-DeMarco, 2001). Not only did those changes probably fuel changes in family behaviors, but they may also have strengthened the association between ideas and family behaviors. As societal-level values become more varied and a broader range of family behaviors is considered acceptable, individuals are likely to be increasingly free to act on their own attitudes and preferences in making behavioral decisions (Barber et al., 2002; Bellah, Madsen, Sullivan, Swidler, & Tipton, 1985; Bumpass, 1990; Lesthaeghe & Surkyn, 1988; Preston, 1987; Thornton, 1989; Veroff, Douvan, & Kulka, 1981). This change increases the likelihood that ideas will be an important force in shaping family behavior.

Although we have strong reason to believe that each of these dimensions of the economic, social, and cultural context can shape the association between ideas and family behavior, little research has been conducted on this topic. We need new research to investigate these possibilities—to compare the consequences of different dimensions of the social context and document how these contextual variations shape ideational influences on family behavior. This research is a particularly high priority because contextual factors that shape the nature of the association between ideas and family behaviors may explain other observed variations in which attitudes are influential or in which family behaviors appear to be influenced strongly by ideas.

WHICH APPROACHES ARE BEST SUITED
TO INVESTIGATION OF THESE QUESTIONS?

The complex and reciprocal relationships between ideas and behavior demand longitudinal research approaches that document changes in both ideas and behaviors over time to investigate these associations. Alternative study designs often provide evidence of strong associations between ideas and behavior, but they usually provide no empirical means to adjudicate between strong effects of behavioral experiences on ideational change versus consequences of ideational change for family behavior. Longitudinal measurement is not the perfect means to adjudicate these reciprocal forces, but it is a much stronger approach than most of the available alternatives.

Ultimately, because it is not usually feasible to randomly assign ideas to individuals, no research design can fully eliminate the possibility that the observed associations between ideas and subsequent behaviors may be the product of other, causally prior, unobserved factors. To address this concern, the rare opportunities to conduct experimental research featuring the random assignment of subjects to treatments remain a high-priority approach in the field of ideational influences on family behaviors. Sometimes this approach is possible under laboratory conditions, as in experimental psychology. Concerns regarding the external validity of laboratory conditions, however, leave the need to experiment in general populations (Moffit, 2005). Sometime such experimentation is feasible—for example, in the introduction of new programs or the evaluations of alternative media campaigns. Scientists interested in advancing our understanding of the ways ideas influence family change and variation should seek out opportunities to employ such experimental approaches and exploit them.

New research in this area should also feature innovative approaches to the measurement of ideas. As described earlier, more widespread measurements of general ideational constructs such as individualism, autonomy, and developmental idealism are an extremely high priority. To juxtapose these various ideational constructs, more innovative methods of measurement are also needed—such as rankings or other forced-choice measurement tools—that go beyond simple single-item rating. Particularly important are strategies designed to have respondents compare two or more alternatives for alignment with their opinion. Also likely to prove fruitful are vignette approaches to the measurement of ideas and content analysis to code ideational measures from text, media, or recorded sources. Given the dearth of ideational measures in most social studies around the world, the opportunity is great to develop more and better measures that would provide critical insight to this important set of influences on behavior.

Just as measurement of ideas is important, so is measurement of the factors that shape ideas and the factors that may shape the relationships between ideas and behaviors. The factors that shape ideas include parents, social networks, social organizations, and family experiences. The factors that shape the relationship between ideas and behavior include the economic, organizational, and cultural contexts of individuals. Individual personality may also be important, particularly characteristics related to openness to new ideas. Such personality factors may influence both the spread of ideas and the individual-level relationship between ideas and behaviors.

Finally, the choice of subjects to study also looms as an important element of approaches to the advancement of research on these topics. We believe that adolescents are a key group to study, as change and variation in their ideas may shape closely interrelated family behaviors for years to come. As discussed in several places in this chapter, more international research on ideational influences, featuring longitudinal measurement of ideas and family behaviors across many different settings, is a particularly high priority for advancing studies of ideational influences on the family. Of course, given their strong role in socializing the next generation, studies of parents' ideas are also a high priority. Such measures are likely to prove particularly fruitful when embedded in intergenerational study designs that directly link the ideas of parents to the ideas and behaviors of their children. Such intergenerational designs are an example of a general design that might link the ideas of key others to the ideas and behaviors of individuals. Research designs linking together such social networks are likely to prove a fundamental tool in the study of the spread and consequences of ideas.

CONCLUSION

Based on evidence described in this book, we argue that ideational forces are an important component of the factors shaping family change and variation. We also argue that because of increased affluence, tolerance, and behavioral choice, the recent changes in attitudes and values in many different settings around the world are likely to continue to shape family behaviors for some time to come. Thus, although the majority of social science research on family change continues to focus primarily on the role of social and economic structures in promoting family change and variation, we argue that research should also attend to the ideational influences on family behaviors. We cite many high-priority research needs in this area—needs that we hope will prompt new and innovative research studies.

REFERENCES

Ajzen, I. (1988). *Attitudes, personality, and behavior.* Chicago: Dorsey.

Alwin, D. F. (1984). Trends in parental socialization values: Detroit 1958–1983. *American Journal of Sociology, 90*(2), 359–382.

Alwin, D. F. (1988). From obedience to autonomy: Changes in traits desired in children, 1924–1978. *Public Opinion Quarterly, 52*(1), 33–52.

Alwin, D. F. (2001). Parental values, beliefs, and behavior: A review and pro- mulga for research into the next century. In T. Owens & S. Hofferth (Eds.), *Children at the millennium: Where have we come from, where are we going?* (pp.). New York: Elsevier Science.

Alwin, D. F., Cohen, R. L., & Newcomb, T. H. (1991). *Political attitudes over the life span: The Bennington women after fifty years.* Madison: University of Wisconsin Press.

Anderson, B. A. (1986). Regional and cultural factors in the decline of marital fertility. In A. Coale & S. Watkins (Eds.), *The decline of fertility in Europe* (pp.). Princeton, NJ: Princeton University Press.

Axinn, W. G., & Barber, J. S. (1997). Living arrangements and family formation attitudes in early adulthood. *Journal of Marriage and the Family, 59*(3), 595–611.

Axinn, W. G., & Barber, J. S. (2001). Mass education and fertility transition. *American Sociological Review, 66*(4), 481–505.

Axinn, W. G., & Pearce, L. D. (2006). *Mixed method data collection.* Cambridge: Cambridge University Press.

Axinn, W. G., & Thornton, A. (1996). The influence of parents' marital dissolutions on children's attitudes toward family formation. *Demography, 33*(1), 66–81.

Axinn, W. G., & Yabiku, S. T. (2001). Social change, the social organization of fami- lies, and fertility limitation. *American Journal of Sociology, 106*(5), 1219–1261.

Barber, J. S. (2000). Intergenerational influences on the entry into parenthood: Mothers' preferences for family and nonfamily behavior. *Social Forces, 79*(1), 319–348.

Barber, J. S. (2001). Ideational influences on the transition period to parenthood: Attitudes toward childbearing and competing alternatives. *Social Psychology Quarterly, 64,* 101–127.

Barber, J. S., & Axinn, W. G. (2004). New ideas and fertility limitation: The role of mass media. *Journal of Marriage and the Family, 66*(5), 1180–1200.

Barber, J. S., Pearce, L. D., Chaudhury, I., & Gurung, S. (2002). Voluntary associ- ations and fertility limitation. *Social Forces, 80*(4), 1369–1401.

Becker, G. S. (1996). *Accounting for tastes.* Cambridge, MA: Harvard University Press.

Bellah, R. N., Madsen, R., Sullivan, W. M., Swidler, A., & Tipton, S. M. (1985). *Habits of the heart: Individualism and commitment in American life.* Berkeley: University of California Press.

Bongaarts, J., & Watkins, S. C. (1996). Social interactions and contemporary fertility transitions. *Population and Development Review, 22*(4), 639–682.

Bumpass, L. L. (1990). What's happening to the family? Interactions between demographic and institutional change. *Demography, 27*(4), 483–498.

Caldwell, J. C. (1982). *Theory of fertility decline.* New York: Academic Press.

Coleman, J. S. (1990). *Foundations of social theory.* Cambridge, MA: Harvard University Press.

Casterline, J. B. Lee., R. D., & Foote, K. A. (Eds.). (1996). *Fertility in the United States: New patterns, new theories.* New York: The Population Council.

Fishbein, M., & Ajzen, I. (1975). *Belief, attitude, intention, and behavior: An introduction to theory and research.* Reading, MA: Addison-Wesley.

Freedman, R. (1979). Theories of fertility decline: A reappraisal. *Social Forces, 58*(1), 1–17.

Geertz, C. (1973). *The interpretation of cultures.* New York: Basic Books.

Goffman, E. (1982). On face-work: An analysis of ritual elements in social interaction. In *Interaction ritual: Essays on face-to-face behavior.* New York: Pantheon Books.

Inglehart, R. (1997). *Modernization and postmodernization: Cultural, economic, and political change in 43 societies.* Princeton, NJ: Princeton University Press.

Lesthaeghe, R. (1983). A century of demographic and cultural change in Western Europe: An exploration of underlying dimensions. *Population Development and Review, 9*(3), 411–435.

Lesthaeghe, R., & Neels, K. (2002). From the first to the second demographic transition: An interpretation of the spatial continuity of demographic innovation in France, Belgium and Switzerland. *European Journal of Population, 18*(4), 325–360.

Lesthaeghe, R., & Neidert, L. (2005). *The second demographic transition in the US: Spatial patterns and correlates.* Unpublished. Population Studies Center, University of Michigan, Ann Arbor.

Lesthaeghe, R., & Wilson, C. (1986). Modes of production, secularization and the pace of fertility decline in Western Europe, 1870–1930. In A. Coale & S. Watkins (Eds.), *The decline of fertility in Europe.* Princeton, NJ: Princeton University Press.

Lesthaeghe, R., & Surkyn, J. (1988). Cultural dynamics and economic theories of fertility change. *Population and Development Review, 14*(1), 1–45.

Mead, G. H. (1934). *Mind, self and society: From the standpoint of a social behaviorist.* Chicago: University of Chicago Press

Moffitt, R. (2005). Remarks on the analysis of causal relationships in population research. *Demography, 42*(1), 91–108.

Montgomery, M. R., & Casterline, J. B. (1993). The diffusion of control in Taiwan: Evidence from pooled cross-section time-series models. *Population Studies, 47*, 457–79.

Newcomb, T. M. (1943). *Personality and social change: Attitude formation in a student community.* New York: Dryden Press.

Preston, S. H. (1987). The social sciences and the population problem. *Sociological Forum, 2*(4), 619–44.

Rosenbaum, P. R. (2001). Replicating effects and biases. *The American Statistician, 55*(3), 223–227.

Schwartz, S. H. (2001). Extending the cross-cultural validity of the theory of basic human values with a different method of measurement. *Journal of Cross-Cultural Psychology, 32*(5), 519–42.

Schwartz, S. H., & Bilsky, W. (1987). Toward a universal psychological structure of human values. *Journal of Personality and Social Psychology, 53*(3), 878–91.

Schwartz, S. H., & Bilsky, W. (1990). Toward a theory of the universal content and structure of values: Extensions and cross-cultural replications. *Journal of Personality and Social Psychology, 58*(5), 878–91.

Thornton, A. (1988). Cohabitation and marriage in the 1980s. *Demography, 25*(4), 497–508.

Thornton, A. (1989). Changing attitudes toward family issues in the United States. *Journal of Marriage and the Family, 51*(4), 873–893.

Thornton, A. (2005). *Reading history sideways: The fallacy and enduring impact of the developmental paradigm on family life.* Chicago: University of Chicago Press.

Thornton, A., & Axinn, W. G. (1989). Changing patterns of marital formation an dissolution in the United States: Demographic implications. *International Union for the Scientific Study of Population 3*, 149–161.

Thornton, A., Axinn, W. G., Fricke, T., & Alwin, D. R. (2001). Values and beliefs in the lives of children and families. In A. Thornton (Ed.), *The well-being of children and families: Research and data needs* (pp. 215–243). Ann Arbor: University of Michigan.

Thornton, A., & Camburn, D. (1987). The influence of the family on premarital sexual attitudes and behavior. *Demography 24*(3), 323–340.

Thornton, A., & Fricke, T. (1987). Social change and the family: Comparative perspectives from the West, China, and South Asia. *Sociological Forum 2*(4), 746–779.

Thornton, A., & Lin, H. (1994). *Social change and the family in Taiwan.* Chicago: University of Chicago Press.

Thornton, A., & Young-Demarco, L. (2001). Trends in attitudes toward family issues in the United States: Late 1980s and early 1990s. *Journal of Marriage and the Family 63*(4), 1009–1037.

Veroff, J., Douvan, E., & Kulka, R. A. (1981). *The inner American: A self-portrait from 1957 to 1976.* New York: Basic Books.

Weitzman, L. J. (1985). *The divorce revolution: The unexpected social and economic consequences for women and children in America.* New York: Free Press.

Index

Abadan-Unat, N., 288
Abbasi-Shavazi, M.J., 186, 192
Abdollahyan, H., 185
Abu-Lughod, L., 10
Acharya, M., 264, 270
Adjamagbo, A., 47
Adjamagbo-Johnson, K., 68
African families, 45–80
  AIDS, 65
  birth spacing, 58
  city dwellers, age increase at first
    union, 49–52
  cohesive couples, emergence of, 73
  dependents, management of, 63–64
  education, 66–67
  elders, control over young, 46–47
  extended households, 58–59
  female heads of households, 62–63
  fertility, decline in, 54–58
  first union
    age difference between genders, 53
    women, median age, 51
  future developments, 64–75
  gender roles, 74–75
  imported models, 66–68
  impoverishment, effects of, 70
  independence of young, increase
    in, 72–73
  intergenerational solidarity, 47–48,
    71–72
  limitations on births, 58
  male domination, 47
  migration, 65–66
  mortality decline, 65
  new models, 70–75
  nuclear family, 59–62
  nuptiality, 49–54
  past heritage, 46–48
  polygyny, 52–54

production modes, 65–66
religions, influence of, 68–70
residence, 58–64
shifts in family structures, 48–64
urbanization, 65–66
weakening of old models, causes for,
  64–70
Aghahanian, A., 189
Ahearn, L.M., 10
Ahmad, F., 285
AIDS, Africa, 65
Ajzen, I., 132, 256, 317
Allman, J., 200
Alwin, D.F., 126, 131, 260, 267, 273,
  318, 322
Amani, M., 192
Anderson
  B.A., 255, 274–275, 320
  M., 283
Anderton, D.L., 124
Andro, A., 73–74
Antoine, P., 49, 52
Arat, Z.F., 287–288
Argentina, 151–176
  cohabitation, 157–159
  composition of households, 163–165
  demographics, 153
  development, family change concepts,
    19–44
  dissolution of marriage, 159–160
  education/development reports, 32
  family legislation, 154–155
  family values, 167–169
  fertility, 160–163
  gender roles, 165–167
  historical context, 151–154
  marital status, 158
  marriage, 155–157
  religious values, 167–169